December
2018

MISSION THEOLOGY:

1948-1975 Years of Worldwide Creative Tension
Ecumenical, Evangelical, and Roman Catholic

RODGER C. BASSHAM

Wipf and Stock Publishers
EUGENE, OREGON

Wipf and Stock Publishers
199 West 8th Avenue, Suite 3
Eugene, Oregon 97401

Mission Theology: 1948-1975 Years of Worldwide Creative Tension
Ecumenical, Evangelical and Roman Catholic
By Bassham, Rodger C.
©1979 Bassham, Rodger C.
ISBN: 1-59244-026-6
Publication date: August, 2002
Previously published by William Carey Library, 1979.

To Marlene

for sharing so much.

Contents

Abbreviations

AACC	All Africa Conference of Churches
ACCC	American Council of Christian Churches
AEAM	Association of Evangelicals of Africa and Madagascar
AMA	Asian Missions Association
CCA	Christian Conference of Asia
CCC	Canadian Council of Churches
CCIA	Commission of the Churches on International Affairs
CEC	Conference of European Churches
CELAM	Latin American Episcopal Conference
CGB	*Church Growth Bulletin*
CLADE	Latin American Congress on Evangelism
CSI	Church of South India
CLS	Christian Literature Society (Madras)
CT	*Christianity Today*
CWME	Commission on World Mission and Evangelism
DOM	Division of Overseas Ministries of NCCC
EACC	East Asia Christian Conference
EFMA	Evangelical Foreign Missions Association
EMQ	*Evangelical Missions Quarterly*
ER	*Ecumenical Review*
F&O	Faith and Order
FMC	Foreign Mission Conference of North America
ICCC	International Council of Christian Churches
IFMA	Interdenominational Missionary Council
IMC	International Missionary Council
IRM	*International Review of Mission*
LAM	Latin America Mission
NAE	National Association of Evangelicals
NCCC	National Council of Churches of Christ in the USA

NLFA	New Life For All
PACLA	Pan African Christian Leadership Assembly
PCR	Programme to Combat Racism
SCM	Student Christian Movement
SODEPAX	Committee on Society, Development and Peace
SVM	Student Volunteer Movement
UNELAM	Committee on Christian Unity in Latin America
WCC	World Council of Churches
WCL	William Carey Library
WEF	World Evangelical Fellowship
WMC	World Missionary Conference
WSCF	World's Student Christian Federation
YMCA	Young Men's Christian Association

Foreword

At long last the Christian Church has become a worldwide
phenomenon. There is virtually no nation without a Christian pres
ence in its midst. Increasingly, the Gospel is being taken to our
generation's hidden peoples and smaller ethnic groupings previousl
neglected in earlier decades of missionary advance and church exte
sion. Indeed, never has there been so much deliberate activity,
both formal and informal, to make Christ known, loved and served
throughout the world. Despite the darkness and confusion one
confronts on every side today, this reality of worldwide Christian
witness is one of the most hopeful signs of God's continuing grace
to the human race.

And yet, never has there been such intense debate and radical
difference of opinion within the Church over the nature of her
mission. Some argue her task is to concentrate on the work of
planting churches in those areas and among those peoples where non
now exist. Others contend that the central task is to do what is
needed to make Christians far more authentic than they now are.
They should be *the* serving and reconciling presence of Jesus Chris
in the midst of the world's acute material and social need. Still
others contend that the church should be in the vanguard of all
movements struggling for justice, for human rights and for the
equitable redistribution of the world's resources. During the
last 30 years this debate has engaged the leadership of large
segments of the Church. And this book has been written to acquain
us with its complexity.

The Protestant Ecumenical movement had its 20th century begin
nings in a worldwide missionary movement. That was largely biblic

xiii

pietistic, evangelical and conservative (Neill). In the closing
decades of the 19th century, missionaries of a great variety of
traditions experienced little difficulty working alongside one
another despite their confessional differences. They found that
cooperative efforts inevitably brought personal enrichment, largely
because of the openness they increasingly shared with one another.
This openness meant that particular confessional loyalties came to
be regarded as neither irrelevant nor restrictive, but rather as
the means whereby each separate churchly tradition was able to
contribute to the wholeness of the emerging Christian Movement
overseas.

It was only in the post-World War I era that serious tensions
long building up in the homelands began to influence missionaries
overseas. Self-styled "conservatives" and "liberals" were so
divided over the nature and authority of Scripture that great di-
vergencies in theological perspective were exported overseas and
eventually polarized the missionary community. Among conservative
missionaries the thesis rapidly gained widespread acceptance that
the Scriptures clearly taught the obligation to separate from those
with whom one disagreed. Although not all conservative scholars
subscribed to this easy thesis they were at first largely unable to
convince "separatist" church leaders of the absurdity of contending
for the doctrinal wholeness and spiritual renewal of the Church by
withdrawing from its fellowship. In response the separatists could
all too often point to devout Christians within mainline denominations who were excoriated for their alleged naivete, their simplis-
tic bibliolatry and their anti-intellectualism. The '20s and '30s
saw the Church troubled by much suspicion, by charge and counter-
charge, and by break-away movements that brought impoverishment to
many who participated in them.

However, with the founding of the World Council of Churches
in 1948, the call was sounded to grapple seriously with the biblical
mandate to become involved in the process of working for the visible
demonstration of the unity of the Church so that the world might
believe (Jn 17:21). At first, this call was only faintly heard in
conservative circles. Those who regarded themselves as "the
faithful church" and who were outside the growing conciliar movement, put forth little effort to take seriously this mandate. Their
energies were largely devoted to evangelism, to discipleship training and to church planting. They tended to ignore those evangelicals within the WCC who shared their evangelistic concerns but
whose understanding of the nature of the Church made them unwilling
to adopt the separatist position. Indeed, those non-conciliar
evangelicals who sought to establish lines of communication with
the World Council of Churches were all too frequently castigated for
betraying "The Cause." And when a few began to discern signs of
renewal within the Roman Catholic Church, particularly after the
enthronement of Pope John XXII, they were bluntly reminded that

Rome represents an unchanging monolith of resistance to the apostolic faith. One must not challenge the perspectives and actions of the Reformers of the 16th century!

However, over the years from 1948 to 1975, significant changes have begun to take place. This book records the details. By now it has become apparent that the World Council of Churches is here to stay. And the Roman Catholic Church is increasingly showing itself to be a complex dynamic movement, reflecting a pluralism of theological perspective not unlike that found in Protestant Churches. Many evangelicals who formerly capitulated to the pressure to maintain a united front against the World Council have begun to have deep misgivings about their deliberate isolation from major segments of the Church. Did Scripture actually endorse the popular thesis that it was right to separate from Christians with whom one seriously disagreed? Was it ever right to avoid personal communication with them? Should not any particular understanding of truth be taken into the midst of the arena of public debate? Is it not God's intention that what one segment of the Church regards as truth should be the common enriching possession of all?

The conviction surfaces in the '60s and gathered widespread acceptance in the '70s that responsible discipleship demanded theological confrontation. Catholics, conciliar Protestants, evangelicals and charismatics - all increasingly recognize that this confrontation must take place precisely on those points where differences are most clearly perceived and where one's deepest convictions may be sorely tested. And this, regardless of the pain involved. Christians here and there found no alternative but to bear courageous and humble witness to their understanding of Scriptural truth. And they sensed anew the obligation to regard with profound respect those who with equal courage were willing to challenge them. Nowhere has this theological debate been more intense and unrelenting that when it concerned the nature of the mission of the Church. Extreme positions have been taken by all sides which in turn have provoked vigorous reactions. The burning focus of this debate is the nature of the actual message the church has been sent by God to the nations to proclaim. Many questions have been raised related to 1) the nature of truth found in non-Christian religions; 2) the nature of the activity of God beyond the limits of the church; 3) the nature of the mission of the Church in those parts of the earth where people cry out for justice and 4) the nature of the Church in contrast to the non-Christian world around it.

Christians in our day are becoming increasingly aware of their incompleteness. The most enlightened confess that they only "know in part," seeing even the most central truths "through a glass

darkly." No one has the audacity to profess that he possesses all
the truth in perfect balance. No one's life embodies the fulness
of understanding he claims to possess. And none are so arrogant
as to believe they cannot learn from others.

It is in the light of this changing situation that we approach with profound gratitude this book by Rodger Bassham. This
devout servant of the Church has mastered a wide and complex literature. This enabled him to trace for us the multi-faceted debate on the theology of the Christian Mission that has taken place
within major segments of the Church during the past 30 years. We
are all in his debt, for reasons that quickly appear when one
evaluates his work in the light of recent similar studies. For,
not only has he a comprehensive grasp of all relevant sources, he
has deliberately eschewed the role of the polemicist. He wants us
to feel the full force of the varied positions taken by those who
have been most prominent in this debate. Furthermore, he wants us
to realize that all these men have been influenced in one way or
other by their peers. Non-conciliar evangelicals have obviously
studied the writings of their opposite numbers in the World Council
of Churches. Roman Catholic theologizing cannot be explained
apart from the influence of continental Protestant theologians.
And the worldwide charismatic movement in one way or other has pen-
etrated all segments of the worldwide Church.

Not all will agree with Bassham's final evaluation of the developments and tensions he has correctly identified in the debate
on mission from 1948-1975. But all will be grateful for the many
issues which he faithfully raised, and which demand the attention
of responsible missiologists in our day. Bassham hopefully traces
an emerging convergence - would God it were so! - although he
rightly underscores the serious tensions that persist, largely because of the Church's long-standing unresolved issue of religious
authority.

As you read and ponder this volume you will come to appreciate
the unique contribution Bassham has made to Christian knowledge in
our day. He is a worthly disciple of his distinguished mentor and
historian, W. Richey Hogg. Moreover, you will seek in your own
ministry to emulate his good example being "swift to hear and slow
to speak." Indeed, Bassham helps us to face more honestly and explore more deeply the central ecumenical problem of our day: "What
shall I do with the perspectives on mission of those whose profession of Christ I must take seriously, when I discover that I
seriously disagree with them?"

Arthur F. Glasser, Dean
School of World Mission
Fuller Theological Seminary

Preface

My main purpose in pursuing this study has been to clarify by way of historical and theological analysis some of the major issues confronting those concerned with the mission of the church, in order to foster an informed and constructive debate between representatives of various positions and traditions.

The Bridwell Library at Perkins School of Theology; the WCC Library at Geneva; the Mosher Library at the Dallas Theological Seminary; the Missionary Research Library in New York; and officers of the Christian Conference of Asia, the All Africa Conference of Churches, the Evangelical Foreign Missions Association, and the Interdenominational Foreign Missions Association were helpful in providing assistance. Individuals, including Gerald H. Anderson, Mortimer Arias, J. William Matthews, Wanda Smith, Helen and Brian Phillips, Tommy and Ruth Fowler, Miss Mary Klem, and Kay Springer, each contributed to the project.

I deeply appreciate the opportunity provided by the Graduate Program in Religion of the Southern Methodist University, Dallas, Texas, to enable me to undertake this work. W. Richey Hogg, my faculty adviser, has given generous and valuable encouragement, advice and counsel during the years it has taken to complete this book.

Without the active support of my wife, Marlene, this task could not have begun, continued or been completed. Her dedicated and skillful contribution in editing and typing the several drafts of this manuscript make it a joint effort in which she has shared completely.

Rodger C. Bassham

Rarongo Theological College
Papua New Guinea
Easter, 1979

Introduction

The Christian mission in and to the world is in process of massive change. Much of that change is mirrored in and much results from the creativity--and the inevitably resulting tension--evident in recent mission theology. Examining the components of that creative tension constitutes the purpose and focus of this book.

The introduction that follows offers the reader a glimpse into the historical setting for this change and also into the pattern and process of the study itself.

THE HISTORICAL CONTEXT OF MISSION

The present ferment in the contemporary understanding of the theology of mission involves all branches of the church--Protestant, Catholic, and Orthodox.

Within Protestantism, both the ecumenically related churches and groups, as well as the conservative evangelical denominations and agencies, are involved in a process of evaluating past experiences, debating present priorities, and planning future strategy in the face of an historical context which demands a radical reexamination of policy and practice by all involved in mission.

The Roman Catholic Church is going through a similar experience. Since Vatican II the diversity of views on the issue of mission has evoked considerable attention and action, including that of the Synod of Bishops on Justice and Evangelization, the development of a liberation theology in Latin America, and a theology of encounter in Asia.

The Orthodox contribution to this discussion has become one of full and open participation, especially since the entry of the majority of the Orthodox churches into the World Council of Churches (WCC).

What are the reasons for this present ferment about the mission of the church? In the context of the recent debate, the year 1910 can be taken as a watershed for understanding the development of modern mission theology. From that date, the year of the World Missionary Conference (WMC) held at Edinburgh, a growing and, especially since 1948, lively theological discussion about the nature, basis and meaning of mission has been responsible for generating new insights and developments within churches and the ecumenical movement. But, of even greater importance, the external context in which the missionary enterprise exists has changed strikingly. Historical factors have created a radically different environment for mission, and generated new developments in mission theology, even as the internal life of churches has developed through theological reflection and response to changing historical circumstances.

1. Western Culture and Christianity

The close association of the expansion of the church through its missionary outreach with the growth of Western influence throughout the world from the fifteenth century to the present created a relationship in which religion and culture were closely intertwined. During this era, when the military, economic and technological superiority of the West was either accepted or imposed, traditional cultures disintegrated rapidly as people were forced to accept Western domination. One element in that Western influence was the Christian religion.

The close relationship between Western culture and the Christian religion was implicit in the assumptions which many Europeans held. They sincerely believed that European culture and civilization represented the highest expression of the Christian gospel. This underlay the papal mandate given to Ferdinand and Isabella of Spain in May, 1493, when Pope Alexander VI set out the instructions under which the New World was to be divided and developed. Besides granting "full, free and integral power, authority and jurisdiction" to the Christian rulers, he required them also to evangelize the people of these regions by sending to them "honest and God-fearing men, learned, skilled and experienced, to instruct the natives and inhabitants in Christian faith and to imbue them with good morals."[1]

William Carey espoused the same close relationship when he argued,

> Can we hear that they [non-Christians] are without the gospel, without government, without laws, and without arts and sciences; and not exert ourselves to introduce amongst them the sentiments of men, and of Christians? Would not the spread of the gospel be the most effectual means of their civilization? Would not that make them useful members of society?[2]

However, it was not until the massive European expansion in the nineteenth century that Christianity can really be said to have been established as a world religion. Despite the Iberian conquests in the New World, and the planting of Roman Catholic churches in the Philippines, India, China and elsewhere, Christianity was largely confined to Europe and to Europeans who occupied the trading centers of Africa and Asia. "In 1800 it was still by no means certain that Christianity would be successful in turning itself into a universal religion."[3]

2. The Nineteenth Century

During the nineteenth century--aptly called the Great Century by Latourette[4]--an unparalleled growth and expansion of Christianity, especially of Protestantism, occurred. As in the previous three centuries, the spread of the Christian religion was frequently linked with the development of imperialism; but this pattern was also broken as missionaries worked in territories where their governments had no colonial interests.

Several new features emerged in the external conditions relating to mission. The establishment of the British Empire in India, parts of Africa, and in some islands of the Pacific, forged closer links between the West and Christianity in these territories. New scientific discoveries related to communications and industrial technology made for more rapid transmission of news and travel on sea and land, and laid the foundation for the industrial revolution which fostered capital growth for further expansion of Western imperialism.

Parallel with this expansion, evangelical Protestantism experienced a revival which revitalized the missionary thrust and gave birth to a large number of missionary organizations dedicated to evangelizing the world, the result of which was to make Christianity a universal religion. This internal regeneration of the churches enabled them to grasp the opportunities offered by the favorable external conditions.

Among Protestants, the founding of new societies proceeded rapidly and began in England with the Baptist Missionary Society in 1792, the London Missionary Society in 1795, the Church Missionary Society (Anglican) in 1799, and the Wesleyan Methodist Missionary Society, in an official way, in 1819. In America, the American Board of Commissioners for Foreign Missions began in 1810, the American Baptist Missionary Board in 1814, and many others followed. In Germany, the Berlin Society founded in 1824 and the Rhenish Missionary Society in 1828 marked the beginning of societies there.

The second half of the nineteenth century saw fresh signs of vitality. The United States emerged as a considerable influence and force in the missionary movement with the large-scale development of the Young Men's Christian Association (YMCA) and the Student Volunteer Movement for Foreign Missions (SVM), each giving high priority to the missionary enterprise. Another mark of the growing strength of the missionary enterprise was the formation of nondenominational agencies, such as the illustrious China Inland Mission, organized by Hudson Taylor in 1865.

A similar surge of life in the Roman Catholic Church found expression in new orders and congregations, such as the Picpus Fathers, the Marists and Salesians, and the renewal of old orders, for example, the Society of Jesus, which once more came into full legal existence in 1814. Contributing the most to Roman Catholic missions in the nineteenth century, France replaced Spain and Portugal as the main source of missionary manpower and finance.

3. The Twentieth Century.

The close alliance of Western civilization and Christianity, forged in an era of expanding Western influence around the world, has now been irrevocably shattered by the historical events of the twentieth century. The catastrophic upheaval caused by two world wars; the emergence of nationalism as a powerful influence in many nations previously under Western hegemony; the advent of Communism in Russia, Eastern Europe and China and the widespread influence of Marxist ideology; and the newly gained political independence of many former colonies created an entirely different environment for mission. Each of these factors has had a part to play in the present resistance to, or rejection of, Western culture and Christian influence throughout much of Asia, Africa, and Latin America.

Other forces have had an influence on the religious climate in many nations. The resurgence of non-Christian religions--Islam, Hinduism, and Buddhism in particular--has had a

marked impact on the reception of Christianity. In the West,
the decline of Christianity as a vital religious force claiming
the allegiance of the majority of the population in Europe
especially, together with an acceptance of the secularization
of society, has weakened the influence of Christianity.

The cumulative impact of these events has created a new
context and situation in which the mission of the church must
now be accomplished. The contrast in both the external and
internal circumstances affecting mission between the nineteenth
and twentieth centuries is enormous.

The WMC of 1910 held at Edinburgh can be conveniently used
to mark the transition between the two centuries. In much of
its work, mood and outlook, it summarized the essential features of the nineteenth century. Under the chairmanship of
John R. Mott, it reviewed a century in which Protestant missions
had shown a continually rising curve of missionary endeavor, and
it enthusiastically embraced the hope that the curve might continue to rise. Such was the aspiration and challenge of the SVM
watchword, "The evangelization of the world in this generation."

The 1200 Western delegates at Edinburgh viewed this goal as
a very real possibility based on the achievements of the past
century. Those present reached a fundamental agreement on the
continued and urgent challenge of missions and on the responsibility of the whole church to take the gospel to all non-
Christian peoples.

Yet a quick succession of events in the ensuing years
shattered that confidence: The Great War caused enormous disruption of the missionary enterprise and helped to foster a
growing resentment against the Western powers in the hearts and
minds of many in Africa and Asia. The alleged moral superiority
of the West collapsed with Christian country fighting against
Christian country. The emergence of a growing sense of nationalism and reaction to the racist attitudes of white Europeans
can be noted with greater frequency in the early part of the
twentieth century. A considerable xenophobia had long existed
in China and flared into open attack in the Boxer rebellion in
1900. The Indian National Congress began to press for more
power. Amongst the African States a variety of groups protested
against Western domination. The doctrine of "self-determination"
in the Charter of the League of Nations was widely acclaimed by
African and Asian leaders.[5]

In 1917 the Russian Revolution forced a new awareness of
the powerful influence which Marxist ideology could wield. The
success of the revolution with its militant atheism caused considerable alarm when Christianity was confronted with an ideol-

ogy and philosophy which attacked both Western colonialism and Christianity head-on. "There is no doubt that the nationalist movements in all Asian countries gained moral strength by the mere existence of a Revolutionary Russia."[6] The influence of Marxist thought on later generations of leaders in Africa, Asia, and Latin America has been considerable, and has certainly been a factor in the erosion of Western culture and religious domination.

Anti-Western feeling deepened in 1929-32 with the world-wide suffering and hardship caused by the Depression which began in the West and then rapidly engulfed all nations. The failure of the League of Nations, founded on Western assurances of commitment and support, to act in the Italian intervention in Ethiopia and the Japanese invasion of Manchuria further undermined confidence in the integrity of the West. Such actions hastened the resolve of the subject peoples to seek their independence as rapidly as possible. The years following World War II completed a process which had been gaining strength for a century, and the achievement of autonomous nationhood, beginning with the independence of the Philippines in 1946 and of India in 1947, marked a decisive stage in the evolution of conditions which exist in the contemporary world.

A significant element in the rise of nationalism and the search for independence has been the resurgence of traditional religions. In India this process began as early as the 1820s with Ram Mohan Roy, continued with Swamis Dayananda and Vive-kananda into the twentieth century, and culminated with Gandhi, who finally led the independence movement as a Hindu reformer. In Africa the strength of traditional religion has been one of the main factors in the considerable growth of independent African churches. Many African Christians were also involved in traditional African religion.[7]

This religious resurgence was closely linked with the renaissance of indigenous cultures. Because religion is at the heart of traditional culture, and culture is a primary means of national identity, the close alliance of traditional culture and religion against the imposition of the foreign Western religion and cultural forces was an important expression of nationalistic sentiment and part of the revolt against Western influence.

The widespread acceptance of Western culture through the expansion of Western imperialism created an environment in which church growth became possible in the nineteenth century. Chris-tianity expanded among a small handful of people and gained broader influence in association with the dominating empires which covered much of the earth. The dissatisfaction of many persons with their own traditional society, culture and reli-

gion, and the genuine desire to share in the benefits of Western
civilization, technology and education led some to the Christian
faith. Missions profited by that situation, especially as they
often supplied the educational institutions by which such benefits could be acquired.

But with the changes in historical circumstances and events
of the twentieth century, that external situation no longer
exists. Now Christianity has to make its own way, often with
the stigma of being a "foreign religion," rejected because of
its close association with the Western powers so long responsible for colonial domination and exploitation. The close relationship between anti-imperialism, anti-colonialism, and moral
indignation against racism, linked with the renewal and renaissance of traditional cultural and religious loyalties has led
to widespread rejection of Christianity as an integral part of
Western cultural and religious imperialism. These historical
changes which have altered the external context for the
missionary enterprise, have been partly responsible for the
profound theological changes which have occurred within Christianity and which have also demanded a reassessment of the
theology of mission.

The process of interaction between the church and its
external environment, and the internal context of mission at
work within the church through theological reflection, organic
development, worship, witness, and service, create the dynamic
situation in which mission theology and practice develop, frequently in tension with both the external and internal contexts.
It is the shape and form and direction of the development of
mission theology which this study will trace, analyze, and
reflect upon.

STRUCTURE AND THEMES

1. Definition of Theology of Mission

The term "theology of mission" in this book refers to those
theological presuppositions, statements, and principles which
critically reflect upon and explicate God's purpose for the
church in relation to the world.

2. Chronological Framework

The historical dimension of this work--to trace and analyze
the development of mission theology between 1948 and 1975--can
best be undertaken by way of a chronological framework. This
provides a clear way of presenting a vast amount of material in
its sequential development.

Such a presentation is demanded because there is no comprehensive study of the theology of mission of either the ecumenical or conservative evangelical positions covering this
period.

A chronological framework will give clear scope for comparison of data. It will allow for comment on the external
historical forces which have helped shape the development of
mission theology.

3. Theological Analysis

Five key issues, each of which contains a cluster of questions and ideas, provide an analytical tool through which theological developments can be studied and compared. Each issue
provides a focal point in studying the reports of meetings,
published works, and individual contributions to the development of mission theology.

These broad issues are:

a. Theological Basis. What are the theological bases
which inform a particular understanding of mission? These
have included such ideas as obedience to the Great Commis-
wion, church planting, church growth, participating in
God's work in history, and seeking the humanization of the
world. A trinitarian motif associated with *Missio Dei* is
now widely accepted.

b. Church-Mission Relations. What theological principles
determine the relationship between church and mission? A
large number of questions have emerged relating to this
broad area of concern. Some have argued for a complete
separation of church and mission, while others claim that
the church is mission. How can an indigenous church and
leadership best be developed; what constitutes a mature
relationship between a mission board and a church overseas?

c. Evangelism and Social Action. What is the relationship
between evangelism and social action in the mission of the
church? The ecumenical answer has generally been that both
constitute essential elements in mission; evangelicals have
argued for several different positions. The emergence of
liberation theology in Latin America has raised the whole
question in an acute way.

d. Christianity and Other Faiths. How should Christians
evaluate other faiths? The presuppositions, meaning,
purpose and validity of interfaith dialogue have emerged
as vital questions in mission theology.

e. *Mission and Unity*. The nature of the unity among churches, and the form of unity which they should seek together as part of mission have long constituted an important part of the agenda for mission theology. Answers have included cooperation in spiritual fellowship, organic unity, and conciliar fellowship. The debate is still in progress.

Obviously these issues are closely related to each other, and to some degree they will constitute an artificially imposed character on the analysis. But the benefits to be obtained from having a broad analytical tool for the purpose of investigation and comparison make it a worthwhile risk.

At any given time not every issue was equally important; some were emphasized more in one period, study or meeting than in another. But all have had an important place in mission discussions and still constitute basic continuing issues in the contemporary debate about mission. Even where there is a consensus about the importance of an issue (for example, evangelism, indigenous churches), tensions remain in the ways in which the particular question finds expression in the various groups.

It is only through a clear delineation of the way in which these issues have developed that an informed discussion can take place involving all segments of the church. The blending of the historical and theological dimensions of this work is an attempt to give a clear focus to present and future discussions on these issues.

4. Scope and Limitations

The primary focus of this study is on the two major streams of Protestant missionary thought represented by the ecumenical movement and conservative evangelicalism. Yet in view of the importance of the Roman Catholic contribution to, and participation in, wide-ranging ecumenical discussions, and parallel debate on similar issues in mission theology, a brief but important chapter will be included on the Roman Catholic Church.

a. *Ecumenical*. Attention will be devoted principally to the assemblies, meetings and study projects of the International Missionary Council (IMC) and the WCC into which the IMC was integrated in 1961. The contribution of particular individuals to the development of mission theology will be noted as a secondary concern.

The formation of regional ecumenical organizations concerned with similar problems of culture, outreach and

indigenization, has provided a new dimension to the
development of mission thought in specific areas.
Christians in Asia and Africa, especially, have worked
at creating new structures for communication and theological reflection. Thus one chapter will examine the
characteristics and importance of the development of
regional meetings.

b. Conservative Evangelical. In the post-World War II
period, the most significant and influential developments
within conservative evangelicalism have occurred in those
bodies and events which have their roots in the USA. For
this reason, this section will be devoted primarily to
developments in North America, especially toward two
missionary organizations: The Interdenominational Foreign
Mission Association (IFMA) and the Evangelical Foreign
Missions Association (EFMA). The leaders of these organizations have been among the principal figures in the
development of evangelical mission theology. The major
evangelical congresses at Wheaton, 1966, Berlin, 1966,
and Lausanne, 1974, will then be analyzed.

Evangelical developments in mission thought and practice in Latin America, Africa, and Asia will be the focus
of another chapter, which will provide a counterbalance
to the predominantly Western viewpoint of the earlier
analysis of evangelicalism.

c. Roman Catholic. This section will be devoted, first,
to the official documents of the papacy and of the Second
Vatican Council concerning mission; and, second, to
regional emphases, for example, liberation theology in
Latin America, and the process of encounter in India.
Recent links with Protestants will also be noted briefly.

The final section provides an interpretative essay on the
development of mission theology between 1948 and 1975. It will
attempt to show that a significant convergent development is
occurring in the ecumenical and evangelical positions. A
parallel movement can be discerned in the Roman Catholic Church.

Important points of tension still remain about the key
issues of mission, not only within each of the three positions
presented in this study, but also among them. This points to
the need for continuing analysis and discussion concerning the
practice and theology of mission by the whole church throughout
the world.

The writer has aimed at providing an overall perspective on
an enormous amount of material. He has not therefore sought to

provide a deep and probing analysis of individual persons, publications or events, but rather has emphasized the major features in the development of mission theology from 1948 to 1975 by means of a descriptive and analytical methodology.

NOTES

[1]Bull *Inter caetera Divinae* of Pope Alexander VI, 4 May 1493.

[2]William Carey, *An Enquiry into the Obligations of Christians to use means for the Conversion of the Heathens* (Leicester 1792; reprint ed., London: Baptist Missionary Society, 1934), p. 70.

[3]Stephen Neill, *A History of Christian Missions*. Pelican History of the Church, vol. 6 (Baltimore: Penguin Books, 1964), p. 243.

[4]Kenneth Scott Latourette, *A History of the Expansion of Christianity*, 7 vols. (New York: Harper and Row, 1937-45; reprinted ed. Grand Rapids: Zondervan, 1970). Vols. 4, 5, 6 cover the nineteenth century.

[5]K. M. Panikkar, *Asian and Western Dominance* (New York: John Day Book Company, n.d.), pp. 220, 251, 262-3, 265.

[6]Ibid., p. 251.

[7]*World Missionary Conference 1910*, 9 vols. (Edinburgh; Oliphant, Anderson and Ferrier/New York: Revell, 1910): vol. 1. *Carrying the Gospel to all the Non-Christian World*, pp. 14-21, 32-35, 229 noted the widespread resurgence of non-Christian religions, and the growing spirit of nationalism. Henceforth cited as *WMC, 1910*.

Part I

The Development of Ecumenical Mission Theology

1

Seeking a Theological Basis for Mission: 1910-1961

The fifty years embraced by this chapter are united by the delineation of a vision at the WMC of Edinburgh 1910 and its growth and outworking through the succeeding years until the integration of the IMC and the WCC at New Delhi in 1961.

A search to deepen the theological basis of the missionary enterprise marked the intervening years, especially in response to the challenges which buffeted the Christian community internally and externally. This process and struggle will be traced through the major missionary meetings of the IMC at Jerusalem 1928 and Tambaram, Madras 1938, and the post-World War II gatherings at Whitby 1947, Willingen 1952 and Ghana 1958. Similarly, it will be noted from the WCC's process of formation in 1938, to its First (and constituting) Assembly at Amsterdam 1948, and through subsequent Assemblies at Evanston 1954 and New Delhi 1961, how the WCC shared in the heritage of Edinburgh and with the IMC undertook the task of providing an adequate theological basis for mission in the contemporary world.

BACKGROUND

1. Uniting for Evangelism: Edinburgh, 1910

The WMC held at Edinburgh 1910 was essentially a meeting of the home base of missions, but the 1200 delegates (all Western, with the exception of 17 Asian Christians), from 159 missionary societies, outlined a theological vision from which has evolved the task and agenda of the ecumenical movement in the following years.

In the period of transition between the nineteenth and
twentieth centuries, the WMC summarized in a nine-volume report
the magnificent achievements of the nineteenth century Protestant missionary movement which had grown in strength from some
300 missionaries in 1815 to about 21,000 in 1910 and some 2 to
3,000,000 church members in Asia, Africa, and Latin America.[1]
Through a comprehensive survey of the state of the missionary
endeavor presented in the reports of the eight commissions,
Edinburgh raised the problems and potential of the future.[2]
The "Message From the Conference to the Church" challenged all
Christians:

> We have heard from many quarters of the awakening of
> great nations, of the opening of long-closed doors,
> and of movements which are placing all at once before
> the Church a new world to be won for Christ . . . .
> We need supremely a deeper sense of responsibility to
> Almighty God for the great trust which He has committed
> to us in the evangelization of the world.[3]

The primary understanding of mission as evangelism evident in
this statement pervaded the WMC presentations. In his Opening
Address, Lord Balfour spoke of the great hope shared by many
at Edinburgh:

> By common consent there is just now a great opportunity.
> Nations in the East are awakening. They are looking
> for two things: they are looking for enlightenment and
> for liberty. Christianity alone of all religions meets
> these demands in the highest degree.[4]

The urgent call to evangelism was forcefully present in
the Closing Address by John R. Mott. Having taken the watchword of the SVM, "The evangelization of the world in this
generation," as the guiding principle of his adult life, Mott
worked for world evangelism through the YMCA, the SVM, the
World Student Christian Federation (WSCF), and then as the
Chairman of the Edinburgh meeting. He closed that gathering
by speaking of the One who

> is summoning us to vaster, greater plans than we had in
> mind when we came here . . . . All of us who have been
> entrusted by God with large responsibility in the direc-
> tion of this missionary enterprise shall go quietly out
> of this hall to revise our plans, not in the light of
> our resources, but of His resources and wishes.[5]

How did Edinburgh envisage that this admittedly enormous
task of evangelism would be undertaken? It is from a consideration of the specific points made by the conference that the

major contribution of the WMC to the development of mission
theology may be assessed.

Edinburgh saw that mission is the task of the whole
church. The final message expressed this as clearly as possible when it declared that the responsibility for evangelism

> is committed to all and each within the Christian
> family; and it is incumbent on every member of the
> Church . . . . The missionary task demands from every
> Christian, and from every congregation, a change in
> the existing scale of missionary zeal and service.[6]

Dissatisfaction was also expressed with calling some
specific areas of the world "mission fields." The commission
on "The Church in the Mission Field" saw that "the whole world
is the mission field, and there is no Church that is not a
Church in the mission field."[7] Recent emphasis on "Witness in
Six Continents" has its roots in Edinburgh.

Concern for the indigenization of the church in particular
cultures as a prerequisite to effective communication of the
gospel and mature church-mission relations was also prefigured
at the WMC. In addressing Christians in non-Christian lands,
the conference stated:

> It is you alone who can ultimately finish this work:
> the word that under God convinces your own people must
> be your word; and the life which will win them for
> Christ must be the life of holiness and moral power,
> as set forth by you who are men of their own race. But
> we rejoice to be fellow-helpers with you in the work,
> and to know that you are being more and more empowered
> by God's grace to take the burden of it upon your own
> shoulders.[8]

Some delegates lamented that more had not been done to
foster and strengthen the growth of mature and independent
churches, especially because "too much real power has been
exercised by the Boards and Societies and by the Missions on
the foreign fields."[9] The fundamental problem of the dependence of some churches on outside resources was clearly recognized by some people sixty years before the moratorium debate
of the 1970s.

Specific action was taken in the years following Edinburgh
to strengthen the churches of Asia, where over half the total
missionary force was deployed. As chairman of the Continuation
Committee authorized by the WMC, John R. Mott toured through
Asia where he brought the Protestant missionary community in

touch with the spirit and aims of Edinburgh, using its major
agenda items as the focus for discussion. "Between November 11,
1912, and April 11, 1913, Mott convened twenty-one conferences
from Columbo to Tokyo."[10] From these gatherings emerged
National Continuation Committees which later became National
Christian Councils in the IMC, which was officially formed in
1921. Through the IMC, leaders of these councils met with
their Western counterparts on the basis of full equality. Mott
later commented that, "My first and my greatest contribution to
the International Missionary Council was to bring about the
formation of the National Christian Councils."[11] The theological vision of Edinburgh, which pointed to *one* church engaged
in mission, produced important practical results through this
work undertaken by Mott.

An Indian Christian leader, V. S. Azariah, spoke to those
gathered at the Edinburgh Conference on the question of race
relations in the Indian Church and in this way drew attention
to the close relationship between Christianity and social problems. Candidly, he portrayed the problem in this way:

> Race relations is one of the most serious problems con-
> fronting the Church today. The bridging of the gulf
> between the East and West, and the attainment of a
> greater unity and common ground in Christ as the great
> Unifier of mankind, is one of the deepest needs of our
> time . . . . In India, the relationship too often is
> not what it ought to be, and things must change, and
> change speedily, if there is to be a large measure of
> hearty co-operation between the foreign missionary and
> the Indian worker . . . . The official relationship
> generally prevalent at present between the missionary
> and the Indian worker is that between a master and
> servant . . . .
>
> There can never be real progress unless the aspira-
> tions of the native Christians to self-government and
> independence are accepted, encouraged, and acted upon.[12]

This question was not discussed further at the WMC in an
official way, but it raised an issue with which the church is
still struggling, both within its own life and in the broader
sphere of relations between races and nations. Again, a voice
raised at Edinburgh proved prophetic for later developments.

"The Missionary Message in Relation to Non-Christian Religions" was the subject of the fourth commission. In discussing
the relation of Christianity to other faiths, two major points
were developed. The first was how other faiths should be evaluated by Christians. The commission concluded that it was

> practically universal testimony that the true attitude
> of the Christian missionary to the non-Christian reli-
> gions should be one of true understanding and, as far
> as possible, sympathy . . . . In fact all these reli-
> gions without exception disclose elemental needs of the
> human soul which Christianity alone can satisfy, and
> that in their higher forms they plainly manifest the
> working of the Spirit of God.[13]

The second conviction related to Christianity. The commission
was fully persuaded of the "universal and emphatic witness to
the absoluteness of the Christian faith" offered by Christian
missionaries.[14]

The reiteration of these points has often occurred in
later ecumenical discussions of this matter, and certainly is
evident in much recent discussion of dialogue with people of
other faiths.[15]

A deep desire for closer unity among Christians was
evident in the work of Edinburgh. In addition to its emphasis
on one universal church, Edinburgh surveyed cooperation and
unitive efforts overseas and encouraged their continuation.
Indeed, the essential relationship between mission and unity
was clearly outlined by the commission on "Cooperation and the
Promotion of Unity" when it stated that

> for the achievement of the ultimate and highest end of
> all missionary work--the establishment in these non-
> Christian lands of Christ's one Church--real unity
> must be attained . . . . The Holy Spirit seems to be
> impressing men everywhere with deeper convictions of
> the claims of our Lord Jesus Christ to our undivided
> loyalty, of the sin and weakness of schism, and of the
> necessity for union to enable the Church to fulfil her
> mission, and do her work both at home and abroad.[16]

The supreme need in the move towards unity in mission was
seen to be "apostles of unity"--men who have seen, and could
lead others to see, the vision of unity.[17]

Edinburgh was directly responsible for enabling two
"apostles of unity" to begin their work through its authoriza-
tion of the Continuation Committee which became the IMC in
1921. Mott became chairman and his early endeavor to promote
mission and unity in Asia has already been noted. J. H. Oldham,
who organized the WMC, became the secretary of the Continuation
Committee and then of the IMC. His continuing efforts promoting mission and unity through the IMC, his incisive contributions to the ecumenical movement through his editing of the

International Review of Missions (IRM), and his organization of
the Oxford Conference on Church, Community and State (1937),
made him a unique apostle of unity.

The direct influence of the WMC vision of unity on one
delegate, Charles H. Brent, has important consequences. Brent
described himself as having been made there an "apostle of
Church unity," which led him through the Protestant Episcopal
Church in the USA to seek a world conference on faith and
order. He became president of the First World Conference on
Faith and Order (F&O) in Lausanne in 1927.

The WMC at Edinburgh laid the foundations for the evolution of the ecumenical movement in the twentieth century,
understood as "that growing consciousness in all churches of
the church universal conceived as a missionary community."[18]
The vision of unity and mission experienced and presented
there set out the theological agenda and began the process of
forming organizational structures which have contributed enormously to the development of mission thought and practice.

2. Relating Christ to the Whole of Life: Jerusalem, 1928

The Jerusalem meeting of the IMC in 1928 faced a world
which had changed significantly since the 1910 WMC. Its "Message" recognized that "throughout the world there is a sense
of insecurity and instability."[19] To meet this challenge, the
meeting directed its attention to the content of the Christian
message and its implications for the whole of life, in a world
where secularism was a major challenge to Christianity.

This understanding of the external context of mission
shaped the response which Jerusalem proposed in its final
statement on "The Christian Message." It was at heart a
christological affirmation, because the delegates believed
such an affirmation best expressed the central core of the
Church's message to the world. The statement read:

> Our message is Jesus Christ. He is the revelation of
> what God is and of what man through Him may become .
> . . . The message of the Church to the world is and
> must always remain the Gospel of Jesus Christ . . . .
> We cannot live without Christ and we cannot bear to
> think of men living without Him. We cannot be content
> to live in a world that is un-Christ-like . . . .
> Christ is our motive and Christ our end. We must give
> nothing less, and we can give nothing more.[20]

Whereas the primary thrust of Edinburgh had been on seeking
the best ways to accomplish the task of evangelism, Jerusalem

felt it necessary to concentrate its attention on the central
content of the faith, Jesus Christ.

Church-mission relations changed significantly between
1910 and 1928 as the vision of Edinburgh found practical
expression in the development of National Christian Councils
(NCCs) in which Christian leaders could meet together on the
basis of full equality of status. As Edinburgh had hoped, the
number of NCCs grew notably from only two in 1910 to twenty-six
in 1925, creating "a solidarity of aim and purpose among all
who are working for the extension of the Kingdom of God."[21]
Thus, at Jerusalem, out of a total of 231 delegates, 52 represented "younger churches." "The presence of a large representative group of spokesmen from the younger churches provided
the most readily apparent difference between Jerusalem and
Edinburgh."[22] This was deliberately planned; as Mott reminded
the delegates in his opening speech,

> here representatives of the older and younger churches
> meet on a fifty-fifty basis, that is on a parity as to
> numbers, status, participation, and interests to be
> served.[23]

Equality of status and the right of full participation by all
present at missionary conferences now became a basic assumption
in ecumenical thought and practice. Mott believed Jerusalem
would help institute

> the new and true conception of the Christian missionary
> undertaking as a shared enterprise. Then all churches
> will be regarded as sending churches; and all churches
> will be regarded as receiving churches.[24]

The indigenization of churches was a priority concern at
Jerusalem. In a brief but basic and notable programmatic
statement, the areas to be included in a policy of indigenization were noted.[25] It was the hope of delegates that "the
indigenous church will become the center from which the whole
missionary enterprise of the area will be directed," thus
subordinating the mission (composed of foreign missionaries)
to a true partnership working "with, through, or in" the
church in a particular locality.[26]

Jerusalem paid particular attention to the relationship
between evangelism and social action. Mott hoped that the
meeting would strive for "a synthesis in which the individual-
istic and social conceptions of the gospel of Christ are
regarded as integral, mutually supporting, and indispensable
aspects of Christ's all-inclusive mission."[27] The search for
wholeness in mission was evident in "The Christian Message"

when it spoke of the goal of mission as

> nothing less than the production of Christ-like
> character in individuals and societies and nations
> through faith in and fellowship with Christ the
> living Saviour, and through corporate sharing of
> life in a divine society.[28]

For the first time in the life of the IMC, Jerusalem provided an opportunity for an extensive study of social problems in relation to missionary work, and brought in noted experts to help in several fields, namely, racism, rural problems, and industrialization. Strong expressions of concern were recorded. The council's statement on racial relationships declared:

> Any discrimination against human beings on the ground
> of race or color, any selfish exploitation, and any
> oppression of man by man is, therefore, a denial of
> the teaching of Jesus.[29]

This was the first considered statement on race relations from an international ecumenical conference.[30] J. H. Oldham's role in these studies, and his continuing interest in social issues led to his being chosen in 1934 as the chairman of research for the Oxford Conference on Church, Community and State in 1937.

A sharp debate followed the production of preliminary papers on Christianity and other faiths, and on secularism, before Jerusalem. Many European delegates were concerned at the hint of syncretism and of the social gospel thought to be present in some papers. These, they believed, blunted the essential thrust of the Christian religion. The skillful work of William Temple produced a balanced statement in "The Christian Message," acceptable to all groups, which spoke appreciatively of "the noble quality in non-Christian persons or systems as further proof that the Father, who sent His Son into the world, has nowhere left Himself without witness," yet which also addressed all people of other faiths with an invitation "to share with us the pardon and the life we have found in Christ."[31] Two leading spokesmen in the discussion were W. E. Hocking of Harvard University and the Dutch missionary, Hendrik Kraemer. In the 1930s each would be responsible for contributions to the debate concerning Christianity and other religions, which generated enormous discussion.

Many delegates at the IMC meeting at Jerusalem expressed a longing for unity among Christians. They saw the NCCs as a necessary means of cooperation based on the belief that

> the spiritual implications of the Gospel demand

> unity . . . . Unity has been attained through
> united service in a common task for the evangel-
> ization of the world.[32]

Jerusalem's planners ruled out discussion of "theological
issues" relating to faith and order. Yet, despite the intent
to avoid theologically divisive matters, the conference could
not avoid theological issues. Thus delegates strongly affirmed
the true value of united Christian witness in the NCCs by declaring that such councils would "be judged not so much by the
efficiency of the machine as by the spiritual fellowship they
create."[33]

The external context of world affairs, and the challenge
of secularism, forced Jerusalem to turn its attention to the
basic content of the Christian message. In "The Christian Message" delegates drew attention to the new demands which the
gospel raised for mission, namely, the need for indigenous
churches bound together in the unity of Christian fellowship,
the urgency of evangelism, and the social implications of
Christianity for racism and the problems of society. The
potentially divisive issue concerning Christianity and other
faiths was temporarily held over, to re-emerge later in the
1930s.

3. The Church--God's Agent for Mission: Madras, 1938

The IMC meeting held at Tambaram, Madras, in December,
1938, gathered at a time of unprecedented international tension
in Europe and Asia. It drew together 471 people from 69 countries and was to that time the most widely representative
assembly of Christians ever gathered.

The central theme of Madras focused on "The World Mission
of the Church," including "the upbuilding of the younger
churches as part of the historic universal Christian community."
This involved a consideration of

> the Church itself, the faith by which it lives, the
> nature of its witness, the conditions of its life and
> extension, the relation it must hold to its environment,
> and the increase of co-operation and unity within it.[34]

The "witness-bearing" character of the church was crucial
to Madras' understanding of mission. The functional need for
the mission--understood as the pioneering evangelism done by
foreign missionaries--was accepted as the first stage in a
movement towards the goal of an indigenous church, a development which should proceed as rapidly as possible. Evangelism
was the function of the church for

> it is the Church and the Church alone which can carry
> the responsibility of transmitting the Gospel from one
> generation to another, of preserving its purity, and
> of proclaiming it to all creatures . . . . The place
> where this task is centered is the local Church or
> congregation.[35]

Madras viewed evangelism as an "unfinished task," with
Europe and the Americas, as well as Asia and Africa, included
in the mission field. The seed for "Witness in Six Continents," which was planted at Edinburgh, grew at Madras and
flowered twenty-five years later in Mexico City. The responsibility for evangelism was the task "of the whole Church for the
whole world."[36]

As Jerusalem had done a decade before, Madras emphasized
the close relationship between evangelism and social involvement in a holistic understanding of the gospel. The gospel
"carries with it the vision and hope of social transformation
and of the realization of such ends as justice, freedom and
peace." Therefore, no church can escape the responsibility of
making "active efforts to serve the community," Madras asserted,
for "social programs grow out of the Gospel."[37]

More clearly than any previous IMC meeting, Madras saw
that individuals and society both need to be changed if the
gospel is to have its full impact.

> It is not enough to say that if we change the individual
> we will necessarily change the social order . . . . It
> is also a half truth to say that social change will ne-
> cessarily produce individual change.[38]

The transformation of both individuals and society was necessary.

The issue of Christianity and other faiths was charged
with tension at Madras. Since Jerusalem 1928, the American
Report of the Commission of Appraisal of the Laymen's Foreign
Mission Enquiry, edited by William Ernest Hocking, had been
published. Besides gathering a vast amount of valuable data
about mission, the report suggested that in place of the
original objective of "the conversion of the world by Christianity," a new aim would now be more appropriate:

> The Christian will therefore regard himself as a co-
> worker with the forces which are making for righteous-
> ness within every religious system . . . . He will look
> forward, not to the destruction of these religions, but
> to their continued co-existence with Christianity, each

stimulating the other in growth toward the ultimate
goal, unity in the completest religious truth.[39]

This statement, viewing Christianity as one religion sharing
with all other religions a common search for truth, was
denounced by almost all mission leaders particularly because
it denied the uniqueness of Christianity and the absoluteness
of the revelation given in Christ. But it did raise the
question of the appropriate attitude of Christianity toward
other faiths.

Accordingly, in 1936 the IMC commissioned Hendrik Kraemer
to prepare a theological and biblical study for the next IMC
conference, dealing with evangelism in the modern world and the
attitude to be taken by Christians toward other faiths.[40]
Kraemer was strongly influenced by Barthian theology,[41] and by
the struggle of the Confessing Church in Germany against
Hitler's National Socialism which proclaimed its own revelatory
nature and sought to use the church as an instrument of political policy. Arguing for a biblical realism which focused on
the Christian revelation as the record of God's self-disclosure
in Jesus Christ, Kraemer pressed for an awareness of the discontinuity between Christianity and other religions.

While appreciative of his powerful contribution, most
delegates at Madras did not endorse Kraemer's views and
affirmed a position, similar to that adopted at Jerusalem, of
sympathy for the best in other faiths, coupled with a determination to witness for Christ to all people.[42]

In considering church unity, Madras affirmed that "the
spirit of God is guiding the various branches of His Church to
seek for the realization of a visible and organic union,"
especially in Asia and Africa.[43] The Church of South India
negotiations were commended to other churches for deep study.
The proposed formation of the WCC was welcomed. Concern was
expressed by Asian and African leaders over the difficulty
caused by the clash of loyalty to mother churches and to union
schemes. In the final recommendation, the Madras delegates
expressed their strong feelings about union, declaring that

> in view of the evident leading of God and the supreme
> urgency of the call for organic union on the part of
> the younger churches, the older churches take this to
> heart with the utmost seriousness, in the fields of
> prayer, thought and action.[44]

Those at Madras profoundly sensed and experienced the
meaning of belonging to a universal Christian fellowship.
Madras expressed that reality and that spirit permeated its

report. World War II severely tested the world Christian fellowship, but proved its growing strength. One vivid and concrete expression of that strength appeared in the commitment of
IMC members to mutual support through the Orphaned Missions
program of the IMC. First German, and then the whole of the
continental missionary work was affected. About five million
dollars were contributed over six years in which "the majority
of the orphaned missions were sustained by Christians from
countries at war with the lands of those who normally supported
them."[45]

4. Partners in Obedience: Whitby, 1947

Whitby provided the first real postwar reunion of the
worldwide Protestant community, and 112 delegates from 40
nations were present. The committee defined the primary function of the IMC as "the active encouragement of an expectant
evangelism," because it recognized that "above all earthly
circumstances stands unchanged the command of Christ to preach
the Gospel to every creature. This command has not yet been
fulfilled by the Church."[46]

Following previous IMC gatherings, Whitby also focused
attention on the universal Christian fellowship called to be
"Partners in Obedience" for the task of evangelism. The statement lamented the continued use of the terms "older" and
"younger" churches, for "the distinction is largely obsolete,
and that for the most part the tasks which face the churches in
all parts of the world are the same."[47] The report called for
complete partnership in personnel, finance, policy making, and
administration, in which the churches in Asia and Africa would
"put away once for all every thwarting sense of dependence on
the older churches," and stand firmly on the ground of "absolute spiritual equality" in their witness in the world.[48]

The need for both evangelism and an active social involvement was taken very seriously by the delegates at Whitby. Conscious of the enormous needs throughout the world which the
church must meet in its mission, the declaration on "Christian
Witness in a Revolutionary World" declared:

> As Christians, we are pledged to the service of all
> those who are hungry or destitute or in need; we are
> pledged to the support of every movement for the
> removal of injustice and oppression. But we do not
> conceive these things, good in themselves, to be the
> whole of evangelism, since we are convinced that the
> source of the world's sorrow is spiritual, and that
> its healing must be spiritual, through the entry of
> the risen Christ into every part of the life of the
> world.[49]

One of the most striking realities evident at Whitby was the sense of oneness and unity which the delegates experienced. The major report began, "Though separated from one another through six years of war, Christians have known by faith and in experience the reality of the universal Church." It continued, "Under the stress of trial, Christians have been driven to realize as never before the oneness that underlies their divisions."[50]

On the basis of a common loyalty to Christ uniting Christians together, and in the face of the divisions in the world which had been so evident during the war, Whitby sought to emphasize the "supranationality of missions" in which

more and more the Church may be seen as an ecumenical fellowship within which great differences are brought together--racial, national, cultural and economic-- but which by its very existence is token of a Kingdom in which these differences have been overcome.[51]

The precise nature of the unity to be sought was not explored at Whitby, but to meet the challenge of evangelism the delegates declared that Christ's command required "all the forces of all the churches, older and younger alike, [be] gathered in a common loyalty, inspired by a common task and mobilized in a common service."[52] The vitality of the experience of fellowship, and the desire to accomplish the task of mission, gave fresh assurance and hope that all churches could be partners in obedience.

To assist the members of the IMC to understand more fully the basic principles of the missionary enterprise, Whitby asked the Research Committee to

give immediate consideration to the need for a careful study of the problems of missionary advocacy, including the nature of the missionary claim upon the Church and the methods by which it is presented.[53]

This study was envisaged to be undertaken in cooperation with the WCC and proved one of the most important decisions Whitby made for initiating discussion on mission theology.

THE CHURCH AS GOD'S WITNESS
IN THE WORLD: AMSTERDAM, 1948

When the WCC met for its first assembly at Amsterdam in August, 1948, it officially established what had in fact been

in existence for ten years "in process of formation."[54] From
the time when the Faith and Order and Life and Work movements
came together at Utrecht in 1938 as the WCC, the IMC maintained
close relations with the new body, a relationship which was
strengthened in 1947 by the Joint Commission's proposal that
they should recognize themselves as being "in association" with
each other. This important step was suggested to make clear
"their identity of purpose and concern for the evangelization
of the world." They pledged to "co-operate in every possible
way" and "draw progressively closer together in all their under-
takings for Christian fellowship, witness and service."[55]

When the First Assembly met in 1948 to discuss the theme
"Man's Disorder and God's Design," 351 delegates from 147
churches in 44 countries were present. The majority belonged
to the Protestant tradition; a relatively small group represented the Orthodox churches; no Roman Catholics were present
officially since the invited observers were forbidden to
attend.

W. A. Visser 't Hooft was the first General Secretary of
the WCC, a position he held from 1938 until 1966. His previous
experience in ecumenical work through the YMCA and later as
General Secretary of the WSCF had placed him in close contact
with the leaders and functioning of the Life and Work and the
Faith and Order movements. In an appendix to his doctoral
dissertation (presented in 1928) Visser 't Hooft had argued
that a synthesis was necessary between the practical and
ethical and the doctrinal and church order aspects of the
church. Only when he was convinced that such a possibility
could occur in the newly proposed WCC did Visser 't Hooft
accept the invitation to become General Secretary.[56] During
the war years, he conducted a remarkable work from Geneva. His
concern for refugees, constant effort to arouse public and pri-
vate opinion concerning the war, and planning for reconstruction, while acting as a liaison across many borders and
barriers, made the WCC through Visser 't Hooft a valuable
organization. Instead of being a time of disruption for the
fledgling WCC, "the war proved a time of deepening and intensi-
fying ecumenical fellowship" with the General Secretary at
Geneva the center for a constant stream of visitors, messages
and assistance to people in need.[57]

When the WCC was officially inaugurated in 1948, Visser
't Hooft considered that finally

the Churches themselves accepted the responsibility
for the ecumenical movement and, conversely, that the
ecumenical movement received a firm foundation in the
continuous life of the Churches.[58]

The WCC could now provide a permanent means and method by which member churches could explore a variety of concerns and theological issues together, especially concerning the nature, mission, and unity of the church.

Amsterdam did not contribute a great deal of new material to the process of reflection on mission. Rather, as the assembly drew together the strands of Life and Work and Faith and Order into one body organizationally, it created a new context in which discussion of mutual concerns could occur. The resultant material gathered on mission used several motifs from past ecumenical meetings and also launched a new era of theological reflection by providing the means through which interaction could occur between these motifs.

Amsterdam's thematic study, "Man's Disorder and God's Design," was an attempt to explore the divine purpose for the world and for the church in the turbulent post-World War II years. Under four sections: The Universal Church in God's Design; The Church's Witness to God's Design; The Church and the Disorder of Society; and The Church and the International Disorder, the study covered the major areas of concern embraced by the ecumenical movement: Faith and Order, Mission and Evangelism, Life and Work, and the Commission of the Churches on International Affairs.[59]

The basic task of the church was summarized in a report from Section II on "Missionary and Evangelistic Strategy": "The evident demand of God in this situation is that the whole Church should set itself to the total task of winning the whole world for Christ."[60]

Amsterdam's deliberations centered on the church as the agency through which God would accomplish His purpose. Conscious of its new identity as a Council of Churches, the assembly dealt primarily with the limitations and the possibilities which the church has for mission. Whitby had called for "an expectant evangelism" to renew the missionary zeal of its members; Amsterdam challenged all Christians to "commit themselves to the Lord of the Church in a new effort to seek together, where they live, to be His witnesses and servants among their neighbours."[61]

Amsterdam emphasized the crucial place of the laity in the witness of the whole church and that became more pronounced in future WCC discussions. Highlighting the responsibility of the laity for witness at home, in daily work, and through special ministries, became a major contribution to mission theology.

In considering the disorder within the world to which the

church must witness, the First Assembly broke new ground. It
introduced the idea of "The Responsible Society" as a goal
toward which churches should work in whatever economic or political situation they existed.[62] The concept began with the
understanding that people are to be free beings, responsible to
God and others. At the corporate level this meant

> A responsible society is one where freedom is the
> freedom of men who acknowledge responsibility to
> justice and public order, and where those who hold
> political authority or economic power are responsible
> for its exercise to God and the people whose welfare
> is affected by it.[63]

On a closely related subject, religious liberty, the WCC
adopted a strong declaration calling for individual and
corporate freedom to give free expression to religious convictions as a right which ought to be given to all people.[64]
The implications of this declaration for evangelism were
evident: wherever limits are placed on the right to teach,
preach and persuade other people, there the missionary outreach of the church is limited.

Clearly recognized at Amsterdam was the need for unity
among the churches for the sake of witness. The statements
conveying this belief were similar to those made at all of the
major meetings since 1910. But with the inauguration of the
WCC, the delegates pledged anew to overcome their various divisions, saying, "We intend to stay together."[65]

Delegates to Amsterdam realized that the process of determining the nature and form of unity had really only just begun,
but willingly committed themselves to that task. They acknowledged that God was

> powerfully at work amongst us to lead us further to
> goals which we but dimly discern . . . . The World
> Council of Churches has come into existence because
> we already recognize a responsibility to one another's
> churches in Our Lord Jesus Christ. There is but one
> Lord and one Body. Therefore we cannot rest content
> with our present divisions.[66]

The WMC at Edinburgh 1910 had felt a similar divine discontent.
Now the WCC existed as a permanent way of searching for unity
together, among member churches from around the world, thus
fulfilling Oldham's prophetic prediction that some kind of
"world league of churches" would become essential. With the
organizational structure established, the work of seeking unity
could now enter a new stage.

THE CALLING OF THE CHURCH
TO MISSION AND UNITY: ROLLE, 1951

The decision of the Whitby meeting of the IMC to work with
the WCC in seeking a thorough survey of mission theology led to
the formulation of a study project, "The Missionary Obligation
of the Church." As part of this work the Central Committee of
the WCC, meeting at Rolle, Switzerland in August, 1951, reviewed
a paper on "The Missionary and Ecumenical Calling of the
Church."

An important observation was made by both Norman Goodall
and John A. Mackay that the title of the paper was a misnomer
since missionary and ecumenical both belong together as complementary terms, rather than two separate vocations. Mackay
argued for a comprehensive understanding of the word "ecumenical" and offered a classical definition:

> Ecumenics is the science of the Church universal,
> conceived as a world missionary community, which
> deals with the interconfessional relations and
> strategy of that community. I suggest we reserve
> the term "ecumenical" as the generic term includ-
> ing work for missions and for unity.[67]

The Central Committee accepted Mackay's basic argument,
and incorporated his insight into the statement "The Calling of
the Church to Mission and to Unity," which was commended for
study and comment by the churches.[68]

This important document drew together a number of theological insights which had long been accepted in the ecumenical
movement, but had never before been stated so clearly and
explicitly. The statement recognized that there had been a
problem in relating "church" and "mission" in an adequate way,
which had become even more acute with the existence of two
organizations--the IMC and the WCC. Rejecting immediately the
suggestion that "the IMC represents the calling of the Church
to evangelism, and the WCC its calling to unity,"[69] the statement noted that both had always been closely related.

> On the one hand the missionary movement has been from
> the beginning imbued with a deep sense of the calling
> to unity . . . . On the other hand, the movement to-
> wards unity has from the beginning concerned itself
> with the Church's witness in the world. Unity has
> been sought out of a deep conviction that only to-
> gether can Christians give true witness and effective
> service to the world.

The Central Committee wished to show the true interdependence
of the obligation to unity and the missionary obligation of the
church. It urged that the word "ecumenical" can be used

> to describe everything that relates to the whole task
> of the whole Church to bring the Gospel to the whole
> world. It therefore covers equally the missionary
> movement and the movement towards unity . . . . Both
> the IMC and the WCC are thus properly to be described
> as organs of the Ecumenical Movement.[70]

The theological basis undergirding the whole statement was
christological. It argued

> the obligation to take the Gospel to the whole world,
> and the obligation to draw all Christ's people together
> both rest upon Christ's whole work, and are indissol-
> ubly connected.

The widespread acceptance of the indissoluble connection of the
missionary movement and the movement towards unity became basic
to the direction which the whole ecumenical movement took in
the next decade.

Obviously it had implications for the future relationships
of the IMC and the WCC. Rolle noted that their being "in association with" one another expressed "the inseparability of the
unity and the mission of the Church." The question was raised
whether "association" should not yield to a much closer relationship and the Joint Committee was urged to explore thoroughly
this possibility.

Echoing the IMC meeting at Whitby, the Central Committee
called for "a fresh study of missionary principles and practice," to be conducted with the help of the IMC as a means of
awakening interest in "the vast unfinished mission of the
Church to all men and all nations."

In "The Calling of the Church to Mission and Unity," Rolle
made explicit certain principles which became widely influential in shaping the future of the whole ecumenical movement for
a decade. Missionary obligation and the movement towards unity,
it declared, are "indissolubly connected." Each derives from
obedience to God's work in Christ, and each intimately relates
to the other. A united church could give the best and clearest
evangelical witness to the world, because mission and unity together comprise the meaning of "ecumenical." The implications
of this insight for the IMC and the WCC suggested their very
close cooperation in study and practical endeavors, with the
possibility of integration at some time in the future.

SEEKING A DEEPER THEOLOGICAL
BASIS FOR MISSION: WILLINGEN, 1952

Whitby's directive to reassess the fundamentals of missionary theology resulted in a major study on "The Missionary
Obligation of the Church." Important preparatory contributions
came from Johannes C. Hoekendijk,[71] Walter Freytag,[72] M. A. C.
Warren[73] and others, and by especially constituted study groups
in Holland[74] and North America.[75]

These papers raised important issues for the ensuing discussion. Hoekendijk opened a sharp attack on the "church-
centric" view of mission, which he considered prevailed in the
"three-self" program outlined by Henry Venn and Rufus Anderson,
the German idea of the *Volkskirche*, and the notion of the
"world-wide Church" associated with the ecumenical movement.
His basic criticism was that "church-centric missionary thinking is bound to go astray because it revolves around an illegitimate centre."[76] The church constitutes an illegitimate
center, he held, because its prominence in recent mission
theology obscures the fact that the world is the scene for the
proclamation of the gospel.

Against this view, Hoekendijk argued that the church is
"an instrument of God's redemptive action in this world . . .
a means in God's hands to establish *shalom* in this world."[77]
This *shalom*, he argued, must be proclaimed, lived and demonstrated in an integrated evangelism. The eschatological character of mission received a strong emphasis in Hoekendijk's
work. Hoekendijk challenged others to look at what the church
was actually doing in a world separated from God, in the name
of evangelism.

The Dutch report stressed the eschatological aspect of
missionary activity, which has two dimensions: the fulfillment
of God's promises in Christ, and the expectation of the coming
of God's kingdom. Each involves the presence of the Holy
Spirit as the church seeks to work through a comprehensive
approach in meeting the physical and spiritual needs of people.
The aim was for "a reconstruction of human life in every
respect."

One of the most important insights of the comprehensive
North American study was the suggestion that the direction of
mission theology was moving "from vigorous Christo-centricity
to thoroughgoing trinitarianism." A consequence of this was to
see that a missionary obligation "grounded in the reconciling
action of the triune God," involved "the sensitive and total
response of the Church to what the triune God has done and is
doing in the world."[78] This focus on the world as the locus of

God's activity, rather than the church, was to become a dominant theme of much ecumenical thinking in the 1960s, although
it was not widely accepted at Willingen.

The process of theological reformulation undertaken before
Willingen was not complete by the time the 190 delegates and
consultants arrived for the conference in July, 1952. Rather,

> Willingen was envisaged, from the outset, not as the
> end of the process but as a time of stock-taking--a
> special opportunity for corporate reflection and dis-
> cussion on this two-fold task of theological enquiry
> and policy re-formulation.[79]

Certainly the theological question about the basis and nature
of mission raised in the preparatory documents embroiled the
meeting in sharp debate. The interim report, "The Theological
Basis of the Missionary Obligation," was received but not
adopted.[80] In its place, a small committee consisting of
Lesslie Newbigin, Paul Lehmann, Russell Chandran and Karl
Hartenstein produced another document, "A Statement on the
Missionary Calling of the Church," which was adopted.[81] While
covering the same basic material as the interim report, the
problems relating to the relationship of God to the church and
the world and eschatology were virtually removed, with the
major emphasis being given to God's mission through the church.

A number of significant developments may be noted in the
Willingen documents. For example, Willingen affirmed an explicitly trinitarian basis for mission:

> The missionary movement of which we are a part has
> its source in the Triune God Himself. Out of the
> depths of His love for us, the Father has sent forth
> His own beloved Son to reconcile all things to Himself,
> that we and all men might, through the Spirit, be made
> one in Him with the Father, in that perfect love which
> is the very nature of God.[82]

Drawing on the suggestion contained in the North American
Report relating mission to the signs of God's activity in the
world, a section on "Solidarity with the World" affirmed that
"the Church is in the world, and as the Lord of the Church
identified Himself wholly with mankind, so must the Church also
do."[83] As God's people in the world, Christians must there
"discern in it the sure signs of God's sovereign rule."[84] This
notion of the church taking part in God's plan for the salvation of the world received the hearty endorsement of the German
theologian Karl Hartenstein. He stated that "mission reveals
the deepest meaning of the Church being sent by God . . . . The

Church exists in its mission."[85]

The eschatological nature of mission, emphasized in the work of Hoekendijk, Warren, and the Dutch report, found a place in several statements at Willingen. Christians were urged to engage in "preparing the whole earth for the day of His Coming."[86] Within the cosmic reach of God's redemptive activity

the Christian mission to the ends of the earth is a necessary activity of the Church in preaching the Gospel to all the nations in the time between the resurrection and God's ultimate fulfilment of His purpose for mankind.[87]

Eschatology continued to be an important theme in ecumenical thinking in the 1950s and became the major emphasis of the Evanston Assembly of the WCC in 1954.

Hoekendijk had raised the question of the relationship between church and mission by stating that "the nature of the Church can be sufficiently defined by its *function*, i.e., its participation in Christ's apostolic ministry."[88] Willingen recognized at least part of Hoekendijk's proposition when it affirmed the church as "committed to full participation in His redeeming mission. There is no participation in Christ without participation in His mission to the world."[89] But it was not until the study on "The Missionary Structure of the Congregation" in the 1960s that the radical thrust of Hoekendijk's argument was thoroughly debated.

As with previous ecumenical meetings, Willingen strove to discover ways to implement mission as the common task of the whole church. A number of suggestions were made, including a call for international, interracial and interdenominational teams of missionaries; a plea to make better use of laypeople working abroad; a proposal to encourage joint action for missions between societies and churches in a given area; and a move to establish regional study centers on mission and church growth.[90]

Recognizing the radical changes--political, economic and social--which were taking place throughout the world in 1952, the delegates related the mission of the church to this external situation in a report, "Reshaping the Pattern of Missionary Activity." They endorsed a comprehensive notion of mission, including evangelism and social action. The report concluded:

Faced with the task of Christian witness in such a world, we are called to hear anew and accept once more our Lord's commission, 'Go ye therefore'; to realize

the Church as the instrument in God's hand; to face
the problems of Communism and secularism; to raise a
prophetic voice against social, economic and racial
injustice.[91]

A concern for unity for the sake of mission ran through
much of the discussion at Willingen. In "A Statement on the
Calling of the Church to Mission and Unity"[92] (similar to the
WCC Rolle Central Committee report), the meeting affirmed that
"the calling of the Church to mission and unity issues from the
nature of God Himself." Consequently, "division in the Church
distorts its witness, frustrates its mission, and contradicts
its own nature." Willingen called for closer cooperation between the various ecumenical agencies to move towards the unity
essential to fulfilling the church's mission.

This IMC meeting marked a milestone in the development of
mission theology within the ecumenical movement. Although its
members could not agree on the basic theological issues raised
in the interim report, several of Willingen's themes represented new developments which became important points for subsequent reflection. In a perceptive comment on the theological
problems Willingen faced, the German scholar, Wilhelm Andersen
noted that

> The principal source of perplexity was the form in
> which the main theme of Willingen had been stated:
> a theological redefinition of the basis of the
> Christian missionary enterprise cannot be worked out
> within the limits of the phrase "the missionary obli-
> gation of the Church."[93]

As Andersen observed, the church cannot be the starting point
of a theology of mission: the origin of mission is found in
the triune God, from whom the church receives the impulse and
power to engage in mission.

Drawing on the preparatory work, Willingen began to formulate new directions. It pointed to the triune God as the
source of the missionary enterprise; it spoke of mission belonging to the nature of the church as it witnesses in the
world; it outlined the eschatological function of mission--
these were important suggestions for future study, reflection,
and development.

UNITY AND MISSION:
LUND--FAITH AND ORDER, 1952

Many delegates went directly from Willingen to Lund,
Sweden, to participate in the Third World Conference on Faith

and Order. A public meeting was held on the relation of Faith
and Order to the mission of the church. The chairman, Henry
Smith Leiper, succinctly summarized the case for linking unity
and mission when he said,

> As truly as a world mission without an urge to unity
> is unthinkable, a Christian Church without a con-
> sciousness of world mission ought to be also unthink-
> able . . . . A Church without a world mission is not
> a Christian Church.[94]

The section report on "Continuity and Unity" related both unity
and mission to the will of Christ as reflected in the New Testament. It stated:

> In the New Testament the mission of the Church and
> the unity of the Church are deeply related. Christ
> called His apostles that they might be one and that He
> might send them forth to accomplish His mission in the
> world. He prayed for their unity that the world might
> believe. It was in obedience to this missionary task,
> including the willingness to suffer for Christ, that
> the Church experienced the dynamic power of its unity.[95]

The need to relate the mission and unity of the church,
because both flow from the purpose of Christ, was clearly
recognized at Lund. The process of incorporating that insight
into the life of the churches still had to be accomplished.
Movement towards that goal seemed imperative. Yet little had
been accomplished. Offering a challenge designed to move the
churches forward, Lund asked "whether they [the churches] should
not act together in all matters except those in which deep differences of conviction compel them to act separately."[96] The
aim was to move beyond "comparative ecclesiology" to action
together in obedience to God. This was similar to the suggestion made at Willingen that missionary societies and
churches should work for joint action in specific areas to
foster effective mission through united work.

Lund saw the need to relate mission and unity. How that
could be accomplished and what that might mean specifically for
churches still had to be investigated.

PARTICIPATING IN CHRIST'S
MISSION TO THE WORLD: EVANSTON, 1954

Eschatology became a dominant concern of the Second Assembly of the WCC meeting at Evanston, Illinois, June 15-31, 1954.
The main theme, "Christ--The Hope of the World," aroused considerable attention. A preparatory volume, *The Christian Hope*

and The Task of the Church,[97] raised issues which related
eschatology to the destiny of the church, individuals and the
human race, as the section headings show. The six sections
were:

> Faith and Order--Our Oneness in Christ and our Disunity
>   as Churches
> Evangelism--The Mission of the Church to Those Outside
>   Her Life
> Social Questions--The Responsible Society in a World
>   Perspective
> International Affairs--Christians in the Struggle for
>   World Community
> Intergroup Relations--The Church Amid Racial and
>   Ethnic Tensions
> The Laity--The Christian in His Vocation[98]

There were 1,298 official participants, of whom 502 were official delegates, from 132 member churches in 42 countries.[99]
Roman Catholics were again unable to participate in any formal
way, even as unofficial observers.[100]

The theological foundations of mission developed at Evanston centered on christology in a manner reminiscent of the
Jerusalem Message. No doubt following the christological theme
of the assembly Section II on evangelism began by pointing to
Christ's work:

> Jesus Christ is the gospel we proclaim. He is
> also Himself the Evangelist. He is the Apostle of
> God (Heb. 3:1) sent to the world to redeem it. As
> the Father sent Him so He sends us. He calls us and
> we must obey. He sends us and we must go.[101]

Evanston used the term "evangelism" to describe much more
than the verbal proclamation of the gospel. In fact, evangelism
and mission were used as synonyms. The three goals of evangelism were described as the transformation of society to conform
to the divine intention; the incorporation of people into the
full life of the church; and of primary importance, "the bringing of persons to Christ as Saviour and Lord . . . . There must
be personal encounter with Christ."[102]

The role of laypeople received particular emphasis for
"they are the missionaries of Christ in every secular
sphere."[103] The final section outlined the great privilege
and responsibility of the laity who

> draw together work and worship; it is they who bridge
> the gulf between the Church and the world, and it is

they who manifest in word and action the Lordship of
Christ over that world which claims so much of their
time and energy and labour . . . . Every member of
the Church, and therefore every layman, is called by
God to witness to the reality of this new creation,
that is to the redemptive work of Christ, in all his
work and words and life; this is the meaning of Christian vocation in secular affairs.[104]

The pressing social issues of the 1950s and the international tensions of the Cold War were of great concern to the
Second Assembly. The quest for "the Responsible Society" was
developed as "a criterion by which we judge all existing social
orders."[105]

Race relations was the subject of a whole section. Evanston outlined the calling of Christians to witness to "the Kingship of Christ and the unity of all mankind, and to strive
through social and political action to secure justice, freedom
and peace for all, as a foretaste of the Kingdom into which all
the faithful shall be gathered."[106] A basic principle was
stated: "any form of segregation based on race, color, or
ethnic origin is contrary to the Gospel."[107] The evangelical
and eschatological dimensions of the task of the church were
evident in this holistic conception of mission.

The discussion of unity at Evanston took place in the light
of the Central Committee statement from Toronto 1950 on "The
Church, the Churches and the World Council of Churches."[108]
This statement emphatically denied that the World Council is a
"Super-Church," or would ever seek to become such, for "it cannot legislate or act for its member Churches." Indeed, "the authority of the Council consists only 'in the weight which it carries with the Churches by its own wisdom' (William Temple)."[109]
Rather, the council was envisaged as a forum for discussion to
bring the churches into living contact with each other and thus
promote study and discussion of issues relating to unity.

The Evanston Assembly reaffirmed an Amsterdam declaration
and carried it further: "To stay together is not enough. We
must go forward. As we know more of our unity in Christ, it
becomes the more intolerable that we should be divided."[110]
Yet Evanston made little progress in defining the nature of the
unity which the churches were seeking. That would come at the
next assembly at New Delhi.

The problems to be faced in these discussions became even
more apparent when an Orthodox statement on unity declared that
on the basis of the section report "the whole approach to the
problem of reunion is entirely unacceptable from the standpoint

of the Orthodox Church." It was the Orthodox conviction that
"the Holy Orthodox Church alone has preserved in full and intact
'the faith once delivered unto the saints.'"[111]

   The six years from 1948 to 1954 saw the beginning of the
interaction between the major strands of the ecumenical movement concerned with the unity, mission and service of the church
in the world. Important steps were taken to deepen the theological basis of the ecumenical movement, including the thrust
towards bringing mission into the center of the life of the WCC.

INTEGRATING THE IMC AND THE WCC

   Relations between the IMC and the WCC were always close.
Both organizations shared common concerns and many people were
intimately related to each body. Indeed, Madras 1938 allowed
William Paton to become a secretary of the WCC even while continuing in his position with the IMC,[112] while Mott played an
important part in the Provisional Committee.

   Following World War II, the two organizations officially
established a Joint Committee to regulate matters of mutual
interest and the constitutional link of being "in association
with" each other was instituted.[113] From a structural viewpoint, the differences between the IMC and the WCC were practical in nature rather than theological; the IMC being an
organization of national *councils* and the WCC being a council
of *churches*.

   A number of joint ventures clearly demonstrated their
determination to work together. The Commission of Churches on
International Affairs (CCIA) for study and witness in international relations was established in 1946.[114] In 1947, following representation from the NCCs in India and China, an East
Asia Commission was begun under the auspices of both organizations which led to the East Asia Conference of 1949 in Bangkok.
Rajah B. Manikam of India was appointed as the East Asia Secretary of the IMC and the WCC.[115]

   Moves to reassess relations between the IMC and the WCC
were frequently suggested. The Rolle statement of the Central
Committee on "The Calling of the Church to Mission and Unity"
(1951), raised the question of an even closer relationship. An
East Asia study conference held in Lucknow in 1952 called for
integration of the IMC and the WCC study programs, a move which
was accomplished in 1954. In 1953 an agreement was reached
whereby the WCC Department of Inter-Church Aid and Service to
Refugees represented both the IMC and the WCC in matters of aid
and relief. The Joint Committee meeting prior to Evanston specifically addressed the question of integration, but decided

that, in view of the divergent views expressed, the matter
should be left aside for a time. However, at Evanston, the
committee was given a mandate to assess the advantages, dis-
advantages and implications of full integration.[116]

The Joint Committee was reconstituted in 1954 and began a
vigorous new phase of existence under Norman Goodall as full-
time secretary, with H. P. Van Dusen as chairman. The Joint
Committee meeting of July, 1955, decided not to press for
closer links. By 1956, however, a new mood was evident. The
Joint Committee at Herrenalb decided

> to recommend to the parent bodies that in the opinion
> of the Joint Committee the time has come when consider-
> ation should be given to the possibility of full inte-
> gration between the W.C.C. and the I.M.C., subject to
> an adequate safeguarding in any plan of integration of
> the distinctive expression of the Mission of the Church
> as this has been embodied in the I.M.C.[117]

A draft Plan of Integration was prepared at a meeting at Lam-
beth Palace in April, 1957, to be submitted to the WCC Central
Committee in 1957 and the Ghana meeting of the IMC in 1958.

Payne and Moses wrote a small booklet, *Why Integration?*,
to review past IMC-WCC relations and to indicate some of the
reasons for and against integration. The basic reason offered
for integration was that

> A basic and long-forgotten truth is being rediscovered
> in our time, which might be stated thus: the *unity* of
> the Church and the *mission* of the Church both belong,
> in equal degree, to the *essence* of the Church . . . .
> They exist to help the churches to witness to the
> wholeness of the Gospel and must, therefore, seek to
> express that wholeness in their own life.[118]

This was the fundamental point expressed in the Rolle statement,
"The Calling of the Church to Mission and Unity." The suggestion about the implications of this insight for the future of
the WCC and the IMC raised at that time now became embodied in
a specific proposal for integration. Mission and unity belong
together as essential aspects of the church's life.

Practical considerations also played a part. The intensified cooperation relating to inter-church aid and study programs, and the need to increase the efficiency of the daily
work of the two councils, especially with regard to the churches
in Asia and Africa, all seemed to suggest that integration was
desirable. Since the IMC and the WCC each face such issues as

evangelism, religious liberty, and social issues, they "have
clearly become converging rather than parallel bodies."[119]

The strong support of Walter Freytag of Germany, speaking
for integration from a context in which missionary bodies are
independent of the churches, was of great importance. He argued
that if mission is the heart of the church, the heart cannot be
separated from the rest of the church's life.[120]

Yet opposition to the Plan of Integration came from
several quarters. The Orthodox Churches were concerned to
avoid certain kinds of missionary activity which amounted to
proselytism of the Orthodox membership, and wished to avoid
bringing support for that kind of mission into the WCC. They
also wished to safeguard the ecclesiological interest of the
ecumenical movement. But with these reservations adequately
answered, the Orthodox were in favor of integration as a technical matter.[121]

Several regional bodies were opposed to integration. For
example, IMC members in Latin America and the Congo (Zaire),
were anxious to avoid integration because the "Christian Councils have long included in their membership societies which have
shown themselves unwilling to be associated with the WCC."[122]

Max Warren of the Church Missionary Society based his opposition to integration on the point that organs of coordina-
tion (WCC) and organs of voluntary action (IMC) have separate
functions and should not be constitutionally united, lest the
WCC dull the evangelical thrust of the churches. Finally, however, he cast a vote for integration because he felt the
leadership of the IMC were committed to that position.[123]

Consideration of the Plan of Integration claimed the major
attention of some 200 people who gathered at Accra for the
Ghana Assembly of the IMC held from 28 December, 1957, to
7 January, 1958. The theme of the meeting was "The Christian
Mission at This Hour."[124]

Orchard summarized the debate on integration under five
headings: The process of convergence seemed to point to integration as the next logical step. The theological insight that
mission and unity belong together was persuasive for many; but
opponents argued that, even if valid, it implied nothing for
integration between the WCC (which is not a church) and the IMC
(which is not a mission). To the argument that integration
would put mission at the heart of the ecumenical movement,
opponents countered that it might well result in a loss of
evangelical zeal.[125] Many people, from Asia and Africa especially, felt that the continued existence of two world bodies

was quite unnecessary; but others feared the creation of a mammoth organization. Finally, the draft plan allowed for present IMC member councils to retain links with the Commission on World Mission and Evangelism within the WCC. This was too close an association with the WCC for some people.[126]

At the end of the debate, by 58 affirmative votes to 7 against, delegates accepted in principle the integration of the two councils and recommended that further steps be taken towards that goal. The draft was sent to member councils for study and comment before the final vote in 1961.[127]

An urgent search for new foundations pervaded much of the discussion at Ghana. John A. Mackay and Walter Freytag both affirmed that the sense of dedication to God's mission remained, but that the most appropriate form and pattern for mission was still not clearly discernible. Freytag summed up his impression of the situation in a contrast with Jerusalem 1928: "Then missions had problems, but they were not a problem themselves." The issue was one of obedience in a radically changed situation:

> it is no question at all that there is no Christian life, no living with Christ without a missionary task. But the question is whether our present patterns of carrying out that task and the conceptions behind such patterns are the right expression of obedience God wants from us today.[128]

In order to facilitate discussion of the theological issues involved in new patterns of mission, the assembly recommended a study program on "Theology of Mission" to be undertaken in conjunction with the WCC, the WSCF, and other IMC projects. The central focus was on the question, "What does it mean in theological terms and in practice in this ecumenical era, for the Church to discharge its mission to the world?" The study was to include: 1) the biblical and theological basis and goal of mission, and 2) a theological evaluation of the existing structures, expressing the missionary responsibility of the churches and of those which are emerging.[129]

Another joint IMC-WCC study on "The Word of God and the Living Faiths of Men," was also approved at Ghana. The importance of this study became clear in the 1960s as regional study centers came to grips with the renascent faiths in Africa and Asia.

A practical project of great importance, the establishment of a Theological Education Fund, funded by a grant of two million dollars from the Sealantic Fund of the John D. Rockefeller, Jr. Foundation and an equal amount from USA mission boards, was

endorsed by the assembly. The principal aim was to strengthen
theological seminaries in Africa, Asia, Latin America, and the
Pacific.

The major decisions of Ghana concerning the integration of
the IMC and the WCC, and the study projects, each gave direction to the development of mission theology within the ecumenical movement. However, the task of interpreting this movement
for Christians within the worldwide church still required attention, and a valuable booklet by Lesslie Newbigin, *One Body,
One Gospel, One World*, undertook to explain the reasons why new
patterns of mission were necessary.[130]

Newbigin was uniquely qualified to write on mission.
Through his missionary work in South India beginning in 1936,
he became thoroughly involved in the evangelical outreach of
the church. Intimately concerned with the ecumenical significance of the Church of South India (CSI), he wrote a defense of
that body, *The Reunion of the Church*.[131] The CSI elected Newbigin a bishop of the diocese of Madurai and Ramnad. His complete immersion in the ecumenical movement through the CSI gave
him special insight for interpreting developments within mission theology.

Offering a brief description of mission as "the whole
Church, with one Gospel of reconciliation for the whole
world,"[132] Newbigin argued that the political changes in Africa
and Asia, and the rise of "younger churches," made many earlier
conceptions of mission, particularly those associated with geographic location, outmoded. Rather, he emphasized, there is
one church throughout the world involved in mission through the
work of the Holy Spirit; the body of Christ is the place where
people are being saved, and the agent of God's saving purpose
for all.[133] Missionary activity "lies in the crossing of the
frontier between faith in Christ as Lord and unbelief," with
the whole life of the church having a missionary dimension and,
in some aspects, a specific missionary intention. The unity of
the church is an important sign of reconciliation through the
gospel, locally, regionally, and globally.

Because he believed the integration of the IMC and the WCC
would help give organizational expression to some of these insights, Newbigin accepted the invitation of the IMC to become
its General Secretary in 1959, and then the Secretary of the
Commission of World Mission and Evangelism (CWME) in the WCC
when integration took place in 1961.

In November, 1961, at New Delhi, the last official steps
towards integration were taken when the final IMC Assembly
voted in favor and the Third Assembly of the WCC ratified the

proposal. Newbigin spoke of the changes involved for both parties. For the IMC, it meant new relationships in the wider
fellowship of the WCC, while for the WCC, it meant acknowledgement that the missionary task must be central to the life of
the church.[134] By this formal measure, many hoped that the WCC
would take "the missionary task into the very heart of its
life, and also that the missionary agencies of the churches
[would] place their work in an ecumenical perspective."[135]

This integration gathered together the three strands of
the ecumenical movement which had emerged from the 1910 WMC at
Edinburgh. The vision of mission and unity in service to the
world, which had arisen there, had borne rich fruit in the IMC
and the movements of Life and Work and Faith and Order. Now
the branches had come together to mutually interpenetrate one
another in the life of the churches.

STUDENTS IN THE LIFE AND MISSION OF THE
CHURCH: WORLD'S STUDENT CHRISTIAN FEDERATION

Many leaders in the ecumenical movement had first discovered the vision and experience of the worldwide church
through the WSCF. To this body--often viewed as the student
movement of the WCC--we must now turn to learn how it had developed mission theology since World War II. Across the years
its leaders had taken forward positions and developed creative
theological insights. Free from ecclesiastical restrictions,
the students explored ideas and insights which frequently became important in later ecumenical movement and WCC discussions.

The evangelical movement in the second half of the nineteenth century had a profound influence on the missionary movement and one of the most powerful results was the emergence of
a number of organizations for youth. The YMCA and the Young
Women's Christian Association (YWCA) were strongly evangelical
from their inception. Their international conferences were of
great importance in the development of an interdenominational
and ecumenical outlook.

Student work received a new thrust with the formation of
the SVM at Mt. Hermon, Massachusetts in 1886 where, under the
evangelist Dwight L. Moody, 100 volunteers, including John R.
Mott, pledged themselves to missionary activity. The SVM
spread rapidly throughout North America, Britain and on the
Continent. At the heart of the SVM was the personal challenge
of the declaration: "It is my purpose, if God permits, to become a foreign missionary." The larger purpose of the SVM was
expressed in the watchword: "The evangelization of the world
in this generation," which was used to describe the responsibility of Christians in each generation to proclaim the gospel

to the whole world in that generation. The response of students, during the first thirty years especially, was enormous and "to 1945, at the most conservative estimate, at least 20,500 students from so-called Christian lands who had signed the S.V. Declaration had reached the mission field."[136]

National SVMs developed within the wider framework of the Student Christian Movement (SCM) in each country and, through the vision of Mott, five SCMS--North America, Britain, Germany, Scandinavia, and "Mission Lands"--formed the WSCF at Vadstena Castle in Sweden in 1895.[137] Built upon independent national organizations, the WSCF was the first worldwide, representative, Non-Roman Catholic Christian agency, with the three-fold aim of leading students to become disciples of Jesus Christ, deepening the spiritual life of students, and enlisting students for missionary activity.

The WSCF and the national SCMs have made a profound and long-lasting impact on the ecumenical movement. These student organizations gave ecumenical training to several generations of Christian leaders. Mott and Oldham, the chief architects of the WMC at Edinburgh, both experienced the fellowship of Christians from various traditions in a common cause through the WSCF. Visser 't Hooft began his ecumenical career in Geneva as a WSCF secretary. The national and international student conferences provided valuable training for leaders and exposed students from many countries to ecumenical spokesmen and Christians from other cultural and denominational heritages. *Student World*, the journal of the WSCF, provided substantial theological reflection and material for students from 1908 to 1969 when it ceased publication.

During its first three decades, the WSCF gave a major thrust towards missionary service, but this gradually gave way to other concerns after World War I. The European Student Relief Fund collected over five hundred thousand pounds Sterling for relief work among students in nineteen countries.[138] Intensive study programs on biblical, ecumenical and political issues aroused new interest among students during the 1930s.[139] With the outbreak of World War II in 1939, WSCF activities diminished.

In 1948, Philippe Maury of France became General Secretary of the WSCF, with Robert Mackie, D. T. Niles, and Philip Potter as successive chairmen. The program of the WSCF had become more conservative, with renewed emphasis on Bible study, evangelical outreach within the university, and closer links with the churches than in the prewar period.[140] But as within the IMC, there was a good deal of hesitation and indecision about the direction and patterns of future activity.

The WSCF General Committee meeting at Tutzing, Germany, in August, 1956, made two important proposals to clarify the position of the WSCF regarding mission. A constitutional revision added the phrase, "within the life and mission of the Church," to the objective relating to discipleship. This was understood to be a part of the double discovery of the WSCF, namely, ecumenism and the Church.[141] The second proposal, introduced by Niles and Maury, suggested a study of the church's mission.[142]

Conscious of the problems of undertaking a major study and teaching project on mission when many leaders in churches and the ecumenical movement were themselves struggling to find a consensus, WSCF leaders felt nonetheless that much could be done

> to train large numbers of students to participate in an effective way in the present task of the Church, in accordance with the demands of its situation in today's world.[143]

The study was to last for five years, between 1958-1963, and included thorough preparatory material, a major teaching conference in 1960, and several regional follow-up meetings. Some twenty-eight writers contributed to the basic preparatory documentation covering the major historical and contemporary background of the missionary enterprise.[144]

The WSCF Teaching Conference at Strasbourg 1960 was built on an understanding of mission which emphasized that mission is entrusted to the church and the church as such is the bearer of the mission--such was the implication of the phrase added to the WSCF constitution in 1956.

Yet at the conference, leaders such as Niles, Newbigin, Visser 't Hooft and Karl Barth did not seem able to speak to or for the students. Hans Hoekendijk was received with more enthusiasm than any other speaker when he called for "full identification with man in the modern world," which required the church to move out of ecclesiastical structures to open, mobile groups; to "desacralize" the church; and to "dereligionize" Christianity.[145]

Strasbourg was a harbinger of things to come. No longer would the church be in the center of the picture as the bearer of salvation. Rather, the focus would be the world.[146] This decisive change of focus helped to point the way for the emerging theology of mission which would dominate ecumenical thinking in the 1960s.

The most important contribution of the WSCF to mission theology in the 1960s related to the concept of Christian pres-

ence.   The WSCF itself, however, struggled through a period of
internal debate leading to the "regionalization" of the Federation in 1968.   The regional groups act independently of each
other. With the cessation of *Student World* in 1969, the weakness of the organization at the worldwide level seems likely to
continue.

SUMMARY

When the WMC met at Edinburgh in 1910, "the Great Century"
of missionary activity was about to close. The mood of Edinburgh was expectant that the world could be evangelized in that
generation. Yet the very success of the missionary movement in
the nineteenth century had brought into being churches in many
countries outside the West, and those present at Edinburgh
realized that many changes would have to take place in the pattern of the missionary enterprise to take into account the
existence of a worldwide fellowship of Christians. The change
from a geographical notion of mission, undertaken by a small
group of people in response to the Great Commission, to a new
theological conception of the whole church involved in mission,
crossing frontiers of unbelief, took fifty years to evolve.
The integration of the IMC into the WCC provided an organizational symbol of that development.

Edinburgh gave a two-fold legacy to the ecumenical movement: *evangelism* must be a constant imperative for all Christians; and the search for *unity* among Christians for the sake
of effective evangelism must continue. The ecumenical movement
has been shaped by its response in seeking to be true to that
legacy in the midst of changing external circumstances.

The Jerusalem meeting of the IMC in 1928 turned to a consideration of the missionary message itself. This task was
necessary in order to communicate effectively with a world far
more hostile and difficult than Edinburgh envisaged. Acute
social problems faced Christians in many places. What did the
gospel have to say to people in these situations? Secularism
had emerged as a powerful force. What could Christians offer as
an answer? The response was clear: "Our message is Jesus
Christ," and in the gospel Christians find the motive and resources for social regeneration. The recognition that the
social implications of the gospel constitute an essential part
of the Christian message was now a basic part of ecumenical
thinking about mission.

At Madras in 1938, the church universal as the bearer of
the gospel message became the predominant emphasis of the IMC
Assembly. Against the relativism of W. E. Hocking's *Laymen's
Enquiry*, Madras spoke of God's "full revelation in Jesus Christ"

as the basis of the unfinished evangelistic task to which the
whole church is called. The indigenization of church life was
understood to be an important element in achieving effective
communication of the gospel in particular situations.

After World War II the strands of Christian fellowship
were renewed once more for IMC members at Whitby 1947. Here
delegates spoke of an "expectant evangelism," which they felt
challenged the church throughout the world.

A new venture in the history of the church took place in
1948 with the official inauguration of the WCC at Amsterdam.
This created a forum for discussion for churches throughout the
world and committed them to a search for unity together and to
the task of evangelism in which "the whole Church should set
itself to the total task of winning the whole world for Christ."

Recognizing the need for deeper theological study of mission in the ecumenical movement, the WCC at the Central Committee meeting at Rolle 1951 contributed an important paper on
"The Calling of the Church to Mission and Unity," which solidly
affirmed that mission and unity are "indissolubly united"
within the ecumenical movement and in the life of the church.

The IMC study on "The Missionary Obligation of the Church"
produced widespread discussion on the theological basis of mission, and at Willingen in 1952 the assembly pointed to the
trinitarian basis of mission in the whole church. However,
there was not clear agreement on what pattern of mission would
best serve the church in the present situation.

Closer cooperation between the IMC and the WCC, authorized
by the WCC Assembly at Evanston in 1954, led to moves to inte-
grate both organizations as a way of bringing together the missionary vocation and the call of the church to unity. After
intensive discussion at the IMC Assembly at Ghana in 1958 and
afterwards, this was achieved in New Delhi in 1961, thus signi-
fying that the WCC

takes the missionary task into the very heart of its
life, and also the missionary agencies of the churches
place their work in an ecumenical perspective.[147]

New Delhi fulfilled the vision of Edinburgh to involve the
whole church in mission, while drawing the churches together in
closer unity.

Yet the theological understanding of mission in which the
church occupied a central place as the bearer of salvation,
which had dominated ecumenical mission theology during most of

the previous sixty years, was about to be challenged by a new
perspective. In this new understanding, the emphasis began to
move to the world as the place where God is at work and where
the church must go to find him and cooperate with him. On this
move, the WSCF study program Teaching Conference at Strasbourg
in 1960 was a sign. We must now explore how this new emphasis
emerged and developed.

NOTES

[1]Harlan P. Beach and Charles H. Fahs, eds., *World Missionary Atlas* (New York: Institute of Social and Religious Research, 1925), p. 76.

[2]*WMC, 1910*, 9 vols.

[3]*WMC, 1910*, vol. IX: *The History and Records of the Conference*, pp. 108-109.

[4]Ibid., p. 145.

[5]Ibid., pp. 346, 348. Even the German delegate, Dr. Mirbt, who expressed dislike for the watchword was glad to acknowledge that "the great religious energy of the men who devised this watchword has, in a remarkable way, quickened the interest for missions," ibid., p. 217.

[6]Ibid., p. 109.

[7]*WMC, 1910*, vol. II: *The Church in the Mission Field*, p. 4.

[8]Ibid., vol. IX, p. 110; also vol. II, p. 2.

[9]Ibid., vol. II, p. 345, Arthur J. Brown, "The Church in the Mission Field."

[10]William Richey Hogg, *Ecumenical Foundations. A History of the International Missionary Council and Its Nineteenth-Century Background* (New York: Harper and Brothers, 1952), p. 156; also William Richey Hogg, "Edinburgh, 1910--Ecumenical Keystone," *Religion in Life* 29.3 (Summer 1960): 346.

[11]Quoted in Hogg, *Ecumenical Foundations*, p. 156.

[12]*WMC, 1910*, vol. IX, pp. 306, 311, 312.

[13]Ibid., vol. IV: *The Missionary Message in Relation to Non-Christian Religions*, p. 267.

[14]Ibid., p. 268.

[15]See, for example, the Preamble to Section III of the 5th WCC Assembly Report in David M. Paton, ed., *Breaking Barriers. Nairobi 1975. The Official Report of the Fifth Assembly of the World Council of Churches, Nairobi, 23 Nov.- 10 Dec., 1975* (London: SPCK/Grand Rapids: Eerdmans, 1976), pp. 73-74. Hereafter cited as *Nairobi, 1975.*

[16]*WMC, 1910,* vol. VIII, pp. 5, 8.

[17]Ibid., p. 142; cf. p. 138 where mission and unity are described as issues which concern "the whole Church of Christ."

[18]Hogg, *Ecumenical Foundations*, p. 141.

[19]*The Jerusalem Meeting of the International Missionary Council, March 24-April 8, 1928,* 8 vols. (London: IMC, 1928), vol. 1: *The Christian Life and Message in Relation to Non-Christian Systems of Thought and Life*, p. 401. Hereafter cited as *Jerusalem, 1928.* Rufus Jones was the main figure in identifying secularism as the major rival to Christianity in the changing world.

[20]Ibid., pp. 402, 403, 406, 407. Part of the above quotation was taken from the statement of the World Conference on F&O, Lausanne, 1927, which was included in the Jerusalem Message. William Temple prepared the final draft of the text accepted by the delegates.

[21]Ibid., vol. VII: *International Missionary Co-operation*, p. 51.

[22]Hogg, *Ecumenical Foundations*, p. 245.

[23]*Jerusalem, 1928,* vol. VIII: *Addresses on General Subjects*, p. 12.

[24]Ibid., p. 13.

[25]Ibid., vol. III: *The Relation between the Younger and Older Churches*, pp. 165-172.

[26]Ibid., pp. 166, 167.

[27]Ibid., vol. VIII, p. 16

[28]Ibid., vol. I, p. 407.

[29]Ibid., vol. IV: *The Christian Mission in the Light of*

Race Conflict, p. 195; cf. the statement on "Intergroup Rela-
tions: The Churches Amid Racial and Ethnic Tensions" in *The
Evanston Report: The Second Assembly of the WCC, 1954*, ed.,
W. A. Visser 't Hooft (London: SCM, 1955), pp. 131-160.

[30]Cf. W. A. Visser 't Hooft, *The Ecumenical Movement and
the Racial Problem* (Paris: UNESCO, 1954), p. 46.

[31]*Jerusalem, 1928*, vol. I, pp. 410, 412; cf. William
Temple, *Readings in St. John's Gospel.* First and Second Series
(London: Macmillan, 1955), pp. 10-11, where he links what is
good and true in other religions to God's Word, and specifically points to the *Jerusalem, 1928* "Message."

[32]*Jerusalem, 1928*, vol. VII, p. 52.

[33]Ibid., pp. 55-56. As early as 1920, J. H. Oldham prophetically saw that any group concerned with missionary cooperation, such as the IMC, would eventually discover it had
ecclesiological implications. He said
    . . . it is becoming less and less possible to dis-
    cuss missionary matters without representatives of the
    churches in the mission field, and any organization that
    may be created will probably have before very long to
    give way to something that may represent the beginnings
    of a world league of churches.
J. H. Oldham, *International Missionary Organization. For the
Crans Meeting 22-28 June, 1920* (London: printed privately,
n.d.), p. 8.

[34]*The World Mission of the Church. Findings and Recommendations of the IMC. Tambaram, Madras, India, December 12-29,
1938* (London: IMC, 1939), pp. 6-7, 22. Hereafter cited as
Madras, 1938, Findings. This theme was closely related to the
themes of the Edinburgh 1937 F&O meeting, and the Oxford 1937
Life and Work conference.

[35]Ibid., pp. 24, 26.

[36]Ibid., p. 31.

[37]Ibid., p. 36.

[38]Ibid., p. 107.

[39]William Ernest Hocking, chairman, *Re-Thinking Missions.
A Laymen's Inquiry After One Hundred Years* (New York: Harper
and Brothers, 1932), pp. 40, 44.

[40]Hendrik Kraemer, *The Christian Message in a Non-Christian*

World (New York: Harper and Brothers, 1938).

[41]Ibid., pp. 29-30, 131-132.

[42]*Madras, 1938, Findings*, pp. 20-21, 44, 46-47. See also the summary of the Madras debate by H. P. Van Dusen quoted in Gerald Harry Anderson, "The Theology of Missions: 1928-1958" (Ph.D. dissertation, Boston University Graduate School, 1960/ Ann Arbor, Michigan: University Microfilms, 1960), pp. 163, 165.

[43]*Madras, 1938, Findings*, p. 130.

[44]Ibid., p. 131.

[45]Hogg, *Ecumenical Foundations*, pp. 315-316.

[46]C. W. Ranson, ed., *Renewal and Advance. Christian Witness in a Revolutionary World* (London: Edinburgh House Press, 1947), pp. 174, 222. Hereafter cited as *Whitby, 1947*.

[47]Ibid., p. 174.

[48]Ibid., pp. 173-184. This IMC statement evolved from separate documents formulated by "older" and "younger" church groups--each stated the same basic points and a version combining both was adopted. See also Kenneth Scott Latourette and William Richey Hogg, *Tomorrow is Here: The Mission and Work of the Church as seen from the Meeting of the IMC at Whitby, Ontario, July 5-24, 1947* (New York: Friendship Press, 1948), pp. 68-69.

[49]*Whitby, 1947*, p. 215.

[50]Ibid., pp. 206-207.

[51]Ibid., p. 220.

[52]Ibid., p. 174.

[53]*Minutes of the enlarged meeting of the International Missionary Council and of the Committee of the Council, Whitby, Ontario, Canada July 5-24, 1947*, p. 63.

[54]See *The Ten Formative Years, 1938-1948. Report on the Activities of the WCC during its period of Formation* (Geneva: Wcc, 1948); also Willem Adolf Visser 't Hooft, "The Genesis of the World Council of Churches" in Ruth Rouse and Stephen Charles Neill, *A History of the Ecumenical Movement 1517-1948*, 2nd ed. (Philadelphia: Westminster, 1967), pp. 697-724; and Hogg, *Ecumenical Foundations*, pp. 343, 353.

55Visser 't Hooft in Rouse and Neill, *Ecumenical Movement*, pp. 717-718. The IMC and WCC together established the Commission of the Churches on International Affairs (CCIA) and an East Asia Commission, as concrete examples of such cooperation.

56W. A. Visser 't Hooft, *Memoirs* (London: SCM/Philadelphia: Westminster, 1973), pp. 76, 80-81.

57*The Ten Formative Years*, p. 14 and passim.

58Rouse and Neill, *Ecumenical Movement*, p. 721.

59*Man's Disorder and God's Design. The Amsterdam Assembly Series* (New York: Harper and Brothers, n.d. [1948]). A one-volume edition covering the four sections. Hereafter cited as *Amsterdam, 1948.*

60Ibid., vol. II, p. 216; cf. the Rolle definition of "ecumenical" in "The Calling of the Church to Mission and Unity," *The First Six Years 1948-1954* (Geneva: WCC, 1954), p. 126.

61*Amsterdam, 1948*, "Message."

62Visser 't Hooft, *Memoirs*, p. 205, reports that J. H. Oldham was the person who first suggested the phrase which served as a key concept in ecumenical thinking about social problems for about twenty years.

63*Amsterdam, 1948*, vol. III, p. 192.

64Ibid., vol. IV, pp. 225-228.

65Ibid., "Message."

66Ibid., vol. I, p. 209.

67*WCC Central Committee Minutes, Rolle, 1951*, p. 13; John A. Mackay, *Ecumenics: The Science of a Church Universal* (Englewood Cliffs, N.J.: Prentice-Hall, 1964), p. 27.

68*WCC Central Committee Minutes, Rolle, 1951*, pp. 63-68. The next three quotations are from this statement.

69The 1948 Constitution of the WCC stated that one of its functions was "To support the churches in their task of evangelism" (III, vii).

70Cf. Hogg's definition of the ecumenical movement as "that growing consciousness in all churches of the church universal conceived as a missionary community," *Ecumenical Founda-tions*, p. 141; and Visser 't Hooft's definition of the modern meaning of "ecumenical" as "that which concerns the unity and the world-wide mission of the church of Jesus Christ," in "The Word 'Ecumenical'--Its History and Use," Rouse and Neill, *Ecumenical Movement*, p. 735.

71"The Call to Evangelism," *International Review of Mis-sion* (IRM) 39.154 (1950): 162-175; "The Church in Missionary Thinking," IRM 41.163 (1952): 324-336. Hoekendijk, previously Secretary of the Netherlands Missionary Society, was writing as the Secretary for Evangelism in the WCC.

72"The Meaning and Purpose of the Christian Mission," IRM 39.154 (1950): 153-161. Freytag held the chair of Professor of Missions in the Universities of Hamburg and Kiel.

73"Eschatology and History," IRM 41.163 (1952): 337-350. Warren was General Secretary of the Church Missionary Society.

74An English translation in mimeographed form of the docu-ment produced by the Nederlandsche Zendingsraad was circulated at Willingen unter the title, "The Biblical Foundations of Foreign Missions."

75*Preparatory Studies for the Missionary Obligation of the Church, Why Missions?*, prepared by the Committee on Research in Foreign Missions of the Division of Foreign Missions and the Central Department of Research and Survey, The National Council of the Churches of Christ in the USA (NCCC), (mimeographed, February, 1952).

76"The Church in Missionary Thinking," p. 332.

77The Call to Evangelism," p. 170.

78Report of Commission I on the Biblical and Theological Basis of Missions: *Why Missions?*, p. 6.

79Norman Goodall, ed., *Missions Under the Cross. Addresses delivered at the Enlarged Meeting of the Committee of the International Missionary Council at Willingen, in Germany, 1952; with Statements issued by the Meeting* (London: IMC, 1953), p. 13. Hereafter cited as *Willingen, 1952.*

80Ibid., pp. 238-245. One reason for its rejection ap-pears to have been its emphasis on God's work outside the church, e.g., in personal life, political and social life, and scientific discoveries. This conception of God's mission was to emerge once more in the 1960s, as we shall see.

81Ibid., pp. 188-192.

82Ibid., p. 189.

83Ibid., p. 191.

84Ibid., p. 192.

85W. Freytag, K. Hartenstein, A. Lehmann, et al., *Mission Zwischen Gestern und Morgen* (Stuttgart: Evangelischer Missionsverlag, 1952), p. 63.

86*Willingen, 1952*, p. 192.

87Ibid., p. 209.

88"The Church in Missionary Thinking," p. 334.

89*Willingen, 1952*, p. 190.

90Ibid., pp. 205-206; 211, 220.

91Ibid., p. 216.

92Ibid., pp. 193-194.

93Wilhelm Andersen, *Towards a Theology of Mission. A Study of the Encounter between the Missionary Enterprise and the Church and its Theology.* IMC Research Pamphlet No. 2 (London: SCM, 1955), p. 10.

94Oliver S. Tomkins, ed., *The Third World Conference of Faith and Order. Held at Lund August 15th to 28th, 1952* (London: SCM, 1953), p. 205.

95Ibid., p. 24.

96Ibid., p. 16.

97*The Christian Hope and The Task of the Church: Six Ecumenical Surveys and the Report of the Assembly prepared by the Advisory Commission on the Main Theme, 1954* (New York: Harper and Brothers, 1954).

98Ibid., p. vi.

99*The Evanston Report*, p. 336. WCC membership had grown to 160 churches by 1954.

100Ibid., p. 27.

[101]Ibid., p. 98.

[102]Ibid., p. 101.

[103]Ibid., p. 103.

[104]Ibid., pp. 161, 165; cf. Vatican II, *Lumen Gentium*, Chapter 4, "The Laity."

[105]Ibid., p. 113.

[106]Ibid., p. 153.

[107]Ibid., p. 158.

[108]See *The First Six Years*, pp. 113-119.

[109]Ibid., pp. 114-115.

[110]*The Evanston Report*, p. 2.

[111]Ibid., "The Declaration of the Orthodox Delegates Concerning Faith and Order," pp. 92-95.

[112]Hogg, *Ecumenical Foundations*, pp. 285-286.

[113]*The Ten Formative Years*, pp. 73-74.

[114]Ibid., pp. 57-59; and Rouse and Neill, *Ecumenical Movement*, p. 716.

[115]*The Ten Formative Years*, p. 73; Rouse and Neill, *Ecumenical Movement*, p. 718; and Hogg, *Ecumenical Foundations*, pp. 346-347.

[116]*The Evanston Report*, pp. 322-324; *IMC Assembly Minutes, Ghana, 1958*, pp. 113-114.

[117]Quoted in Ernest A. Payne and David G. Moses, *Why Integration? An explanation of the proposal before the WCC and the IMC* (London: Edinburgh House Press for the Joint Committee of the WCC and IMC, 1957), p. 31.

[118]Ibid., p. 29.

[119]Ibid., pp. 16-17. Note how a similar convergence of interests brought together the WCC members and Roman Catholics in such organizations as the Committee on Society, Development and Peace (SODEPAX), and Faith and Order.

[120]Walter Freytag, "Integration," *Reden und Aufsätze,* Part II, *Theologische Bücherei* 13.1 (München: Chr. Kaiser, 1961), pp. 110-111, and Lesslie Newbigin, "Mission to Six Continents: in Harold E. Fey, ed., *The Ecumenical Advance: A History of the Ecumenical Movement;* vol. 2: *1948-1968* (Philadelphia: Westminster Press, 1970), p. 183.

[121]*IMC Assembly Minutes, Ghana, 1958,* pp. 139-140.

[122]Payne and Moses, *Why Integration?,* p. 26.

[123]Max Warren, *Crowded Canvas: Some Experiences of a Life-Time* (London: Hodder and Stoughton, 1974), pp. 156-160. S. C. Neill had a similar objection to integration. See Neill, *A History of Christian Missions,* pp. 557-8.

[124]Ronald K. Orchard, ed., *The Ghana Assembly of the International Missionary Council. 28th December, 1957 to 8th January, 1958. Selected Papers, with an Essay on the Role of the I.M.C.* (London: Edinburgh House Press, 1958). Hereafter cited as *Ghana, 1958.*

[125]The evangelical Arthur F. Glasser later argued that integration had proven a failure at this point. See "What Has Been the Evangelical Stance, New Delhi to Uppsala?," *Evangelical Missions Quarterly* (EMQ) 5.3 (1969): 130-131.

[126]*Ghana, 1958,* pp. 156-64.

[127]Margaret Sinclair, "The Christian Mission at This Hour," IRM 47.186 (1958): 141.

[128]*Ghana, 1958,* p. 139.

[129]*IMC Assembly Minutes, Ghana, 1958,* pp. 46-47. Anderson, "Theology of Missions," pp. 330-333, noted how this study arose out of a suggestion at Willingen 1952 that the IMC should pursue studies in the theology of mission. The Ghana recommendations gave direction to a decision of the WCC Central Committee at Galyatetö, 1956 to undertake a study in the Theology of Mission. From 1954 the IMC and WCC Department of Missionary Studies was a joint venture, thus accounting for the close relationship between the various proposals.

[130]Lesslie Newbigin, *One Body, One Gospel, One World: The Christian Mission Today* (London: IMC, 1958).

[131]J. E. Lesslie Newbigin, *The Reunion of the Church: A Defence of the South India Scheme* (London: SCM, 1948; 2nd rev. ed., 1960).

132*One Body, One Gospel, One World*, p. 12.

133Ibid., p. 26.

134W. A. Visser 't Hooft, ed., *The New Delhi Report: The Third Assembly of the World Council of Churches, 1961* (New York: Association Press, 1962), p. 4.

135Ibid., p. 250, from the "Report of the Committee of the Assembly on the Commission and Division of World Mission and Evangelism."

136Ruth Rouse, *The World's Student Christian Federation*, (London: SCM, 1948), pp. 93-94. The watchword declined in importance from the 1920s, following the British SVM Union's deletion of it in 1922.

137See Basil Mathews, *John R. Mott: World Citizen* (New York: Harper and Brothers, 1934), Chapter VI: "Foundation-Laying Abroad."

138Rouse and Neill, *Ecumenical Movement*, p. 604.

139*Federation News* 3.1960: 4, "65 Years of Tradition."

140*Witnessing in the University Communities: A Report on the Life of the WSCF and Related National SCMs during the years 1949-1952* (Geneva: WSCF, mimeographed), pp. 12, 24, 33.

141*Witnessing to Jesus Christ the Reconciler: A Report on the Life of the WSCF and Related National SCMs during the Years 1953-1956* (Geneva: WSCF, mimeographed), p. 48.

142Ibid., pp. 111-114.

143"The Life and Mission of the Church," (WSCF: mimeographed, 0763.VI.57), p. 4.

144Published as *History's Lessons For Tomorrow's Mission* (Geneva: WSCF, [1960]).

145Hans Hoekendijk, "Christ and the World in the Modern Age," *Student World* 54.1-2 (1961): 81-82.

146See Visser 't Hooft, *Memoirs*, p. 366; Fey, *Ecumenical Advance*, p. 400; "Strasbourg 1960," *Federation News* (Nov. 1960): 94, 96; and Lesslie Newbigin, "Mission and Missions," *Expository Times* 88.9 (1977): 260-261.

147*The New Delhi Report*, p. 250.

2

Mission in the World: 1961-1975

Mission theology in the ecumenical movement took a decisive turn in the 1960s in a trend which has continued until the present moment. The world emerged as the crucial locus for mission.

This change in perspective affected the whole range of concerns covered by the various sections of the ecumenical movement. The CWME emphasized the world of six continents, and began to seek ways to encourage effective witness throughout the whole world. The study project, "The Missionary Structure of the Congregation," emphasized the work of God in the world as the starting point for mission. The Conference on Church and Society in Geneva (1966) analyzed and explored the revolutionary nature of the world as the context for mission and involvement by Christians. All of this deeply influenced the Fourth WCC Assembly at Uppsala which concentrated its attention on the world as the arena for mission.

New dimensions appeared in Faith and Order studies, too, as work developed in the "Unity of the Church--Unity of Mankind" theme. The need to relate Christianity to other faiths in the world produced new efforts in the field of dialogue, which has emerged as an issue of very great importance.

The desire to understand the Christian faith more deeply in relation to the context of the world resulted in the CWME Conference on "Salvation Today" in Bangkok (1973). The comprehensive understanding of mission in the world which evolved there showed the direction of ecumenical thinking when the Fifth Assembly of the WCC gathered at Nairobi (1975). While maintaining that the world must be the context of the church's mission, Nairobi strengthened the theological basis of that mission.

INTEGRATING WITNESS, SERVICE
AND UNITY: NEW DELHI, 1961

When the Third Assembly of the WCC met at New Delhi in 1961, it marked an important point in the history of the ecumenical movement. The integration of the IMC and the WCC was finally accomplished. A large group of Orthodox churches, 11 African churches, and 2 Pentecostal churches from Latin America were admitted into the WCC, making a total of 199 member churches. An expanded trinitarian basis was adopted in the constitution of the WCC. Five official observers from the Roman Catholic Church were present among the 1,006 participants, of whom 577 were delegates. For the first time, an Assembly was held outside the Western matrix in which the WCC began.

As Edinburgh had done half a century earlier, New Delhi also summarized developments from previous decades and outlined new directions of thought, study and action. The integration of the IMC and the WCC brought together the two streams which had flowed from the WMC at Edinburgh. As Oldham had foreseen in 1921, discussion of mission would eventually lead to an organization embracing churches from all parts of the world. The WCC developed into a body in which Christians could meet together on the basis of equality. Meeting on Asian soil, the WCC received new member churches from Europe, Africa, and Latin America.

New directions became evident in the study projects authorized by the Assembly, undertaken to find new ways to implement the insights acknowledged by the WCC: that the whole church is involved in mission and that the mission of the church must be closely related to the world which it seeks to penetrate.[1]

The WCC from its founding had been implicitly trinitarian, but the trinitarian basis of the constitution of the WCC, adopted at New Delhi, made this more explicit and set out the theological grounds on which member churches gathered. The basis gave an indication of what the churches hoped to achieve together:

The World Council of Churches is a fellowship of Churches which confess the Lord Jesus Christ as God and Saviour according to the Scriptures and therefore seek to fulfil together their common calling to the glory of one God, Father, Son and Holy Spirit.[2]

The imperatives of the ecumenical movement include both unity and mission: Christians seek unity that the world may believe. New Delhi expanded the vision of the ecumenical movement in its famous description of the nature of the common goal to be sought by God's people when it stated:

> We believe that the unity which is both God's will and his gift to his Church is being made visible as all in each place who are baptized into Jesus Christ and confess him as Lord and Saviour are brought by the Holy Spirit into one fully committed fellowship, holding the one apostolic faith, preaching the one Gospel, breaking the one bread, joining in common prayer, and having a corporate life reaching out in witness and service to all and who at the same time are united with the whole Christian fellowship in all places and all ages in such wise that ministry and members are accepted by all, and that all can act and speak together as occasion requires for the tasks to which God calls his people.[3]

In this statement, the various aspects of the life of the church are brought into the closest possible framework. The unity of the church and its outreach in witness and service are all understood to belong to the essential nature of the church as a Christian fellowship which exists by the grace of, and for the service of, God.

The same closely woven interrelationship between mission, service, and unity appeared in the explanatory paragraph on the phrase, "a corporate life reaching out."

> Mission and service belong to the whole Church. God calls the Church to go out into the world to witness and serve in word and deed to the one Lord Jesus Christ, who loved the world and gave himself for the world. In the fulfilment of our missionary obedience the call to unity is seen to be imperative, the vision of one Church proclaiming one Gospel to the whole world becomes more vivid and the experience and expression of our given unity more real. There is an inescapable relationship between the fulfilment of the Church's missionary obligation and the recovery of her visible unity.[4]

At New Delhi the attempt to state the basic theological foundations for mission on a trinitarian basis, involving the interrelated aspects of the church's life of mission, service, and unity, received its most thorough formulation. The aim of integration, to bring the missionary task into the very heart of the WCC, certainly showed visible results in the Assembly report.

The widespread acceptance of the notion that the whole
church is responsible for mission had finally brought church
and mission together in ecumenical theology. But now discussions on church and mission began to take a new shape. A different question was posed: How do present structures of the
church affect mission? Implicit in that was a second question:
How should mission shape the structures of the church?

This gave rise to two proposals. A call was made to
examine the conventional structures of the church to see whether
they assist or hinder outreach. The study program to probe
this question was called "The Missionary Structure of the Congregation." It became one of the most influential sources for
the development of mission theology in the 1960s.[5]

In an attempt to get separate churches and related missionary bodies in a given location to work together, the CWME
report suggested a method called "Joint Action for Mission,"
in which all involved in a specific area would survey both their
needs and talents, and then attempt to relate the two, using
all available personnel and physical resources. It was hoped
this would help local congregations to see themselves as involved in the mission of the church, while overcoming divisions
within the Christian fellowship.[6]

The local congregation figured prominently in much of the
New Delhi material. The implication of the assertion that "the
Christian mission has a world-wide base" was clearly drawn:

> Every Christian congregation is part of that mission,
> with a responsibility to bear witness to Christ in
> its own neighbourhood and to share in the bearing of
> that witness to the ends of the earth.[7]

The conclusion was firmly enunciated: "We are concerned not
with three continents but with six."[8]

Evangelism was a prime concern at the Third Assembly.
This resulted in part from the integration of the IMC and the
WCC and the new constitution of the CWME which declared the aim
of the Commission to be "to further the proclamation to the
whole world of the Gospel of Jesus Christ, to the end that all
men may believe in him and be saved."[9] The report on Witness
affirmed

> the command to witness to Christ is given to every
> member of his Church. It is a commission given to
> the whole Church to take the whole Gospel to the
> whole world.[10]

Yet evangelism was always seen as an aspect of the total
mission of the church, and New Delhi consistently developed the
interrelated nature of evangelism and social action. For that
reason, witness to the gospel might also mean engagement in the
struggle for social justice and for peace as a form of practical ministry in the midst of the needs of the people Christians
seek to serve.[11]

The question of the relationship of Christianity to other
faiths came to the Assembly through a progress report on a
study, "The Word of God and the Living Faiths of Men." A summary of work done to that date indicated there was a need for
greater understanding and clarification of the issues involved,
especially with the active participation by the directors of
the centers for the study of other faiths.[12] This study was to
emerge as one of the most important undertaken by the WCC in
the 1960s.

The comprehensive statement on the common goal to be sought
by the churches introduced a new stage in the discussion of
unity and mission. More firmly than had ever before been
stated, the inescapable relationship between the call to unity
and the church's missionary obligation was emphasized. The
report on unity stated the theological basis for both vocations
when it declared: "the love of the Father and Son in the unity
of the Holy Spirit is the source and goal of the unity which
the Triune God wills for all men and creation."[13]

New Delhi marked an important step in the development of
ecumenical mission theology. Through the integration of the
IMC and the WCC, organizational reality was given to the point
frequently made earlier, that mission was meant to be an integral part of the life of the whole church. The Assembly firmly
established the trinitarian basis of mission theology in the
ecumenical movement. The interrelated nature of mission,
service and unity found clear expression in its reports.

However, the study proposals on "The Missionary Structure
of the Congregation" and "The Word of God and the Living Faiths
of Men" were signs of change which would lead to an emphasis on
the world as the locus of mission.

WITNESS IN SIX
CONTINENTS: MEXICO CITY, 1963

Some two hundred participants gathered in Mexico City from
8-19 December, 1963, for the first meeting of the newly constituted CWME. The theme, "God's Mission and Our Task," was
divided into four sections:

The Witness of

1. Christians to Men of Other Faiths
2. Christians to Men in the Secular World
3. the Congregation in its Neighbourhood
4. the Christian Church across National and
    Confessional Boundaries.

Mexico City began to wrestle with a new theological understanding of mission. Beginning with the affirmation that "God
is Lord not only of creation but also of history," the participants encountered serious difficulty in understanding the
nature of God's activity outside the church in relation to the
action to which he calls the church.

> Debate returned again and again to the relationship
> between God's action in and through the Church and
> everything God is doing in the world apparently
> independently of the Christian community. Can a
> distinction be drawn between God's providential action
> and God's redeeming action? If the restoration and
> reconciliation of human life is being achieved by the
> action of God through secular agencies, what is the
> place and significance of faith? If the Church is to
> be wholly involved in the world and its history, what
> is the true nature of its separateness.[14]

No direct answer was given to the problems raised; however,
several significant points were made. The most important was a
shift away from the preoccupation with the church which had
dominated ecumenical mission theology since Madras (1938), to
the idea that mission must take place within the world. The
Message affirmed, Christians must "discover a shape of Christian
obedience being written for them by what God is already actively
doing in the structures of the city's life outside the Church."[15]

Mission came to be seen in terms of six continents. There
could be only one mission throughout the whole world because
"every Christian congregation in all the world is called to show
the love of God in Christ, in witness and service to the world
at its doors."[16] The new missionary frontier, which runs
around the world, became the line between belief and unbelief
in every country.

The goal and aim of the missionary movement was still defined in the same general terms. "It must be a common witness
of the whole Church, bringing the whole Gospel to the whole
world."[17]

Taking up a question first posed at the Third Assembly at New Delhi, the CWME at Mexico City affirmed that with the changing character of many aspects of modern life, changes in the present forms of congregational life were required. It therefore endorsed the study project, "The Missionary Structure of the Congregation," as a way of "discovering the forms of missionary obedience to which Christ is now calling us."[18]

The place of the laity in mission received particular attention. The laity were described as the people of God who live and work in the world. Two frontiers were recognized. First, the growing numbers of Christians going abroad in commerce and industry who could contribute significantly to the Christian witness. Second, Christians involved in the secular world of the office, factory, school, and farm, and in the struggles for peace and justice in society. The laity were to be encouraged to "seek the power of the Holy Spirit to bear witness, by word and by life, to the reality of the living God, in whatever ways are open to them."[19]

Much discussion centered around the question, "What is the form and content of the salvation which Christ offers men in the secular world?"[20] While not exploring the issue at depth, participants stated that mission must be one of encounter with the real needs of people and work for the restoration of man's total relationship with God and other people.

"The Witness of Christians to Men of Other Faiths" reflected the struggle to understand how Christians could relate positively to people of other faiths, while avoiding the dangers of relativism and syncretism. The strongest part of the report related to the section on dialogue which presented a clear understanding of the need for honest encounter and its aims, yet recognized the difficulties involved in the process:

> True dialogue with a man of another faith requires a concern both for the Gospel and for the other man. Without the first, dialogue becomes a pleasant conversation. Without the second, it becomes irrelevant, unconvincing or arrogant . . . .
> Whatever the circumstances may be, our intention in every human dialogue should be to be involved in the dialogue of God with men, and to move our partner and oneself to listen to what God in Christ reveals to us, and to answer him.[21]

This discussion of dialogue highlighted an important issue which was becoming of growing concern in the search for an ecumenical mission theology. The crucial nature of this issue for Christians in Asia and Africa became increasingly clear as they contributed to this project.

Unity for the sake of mission was a challenge affirmed at
Mexico City.

> We believe that the time has now come when we must move
> onwards to common planning and joint action. The fact
> that Christ is not divided must be made unmistakably
> plain in the very structure of missionary work.[22]

However, the participants also recognized that "the most intractable frontier is that of structure, ecclesiastical and
missionary."[23] Delegates endorsed the proposal for Joint
Action in Mission as an interim step in the search for unity
into "a sacramentally united fellowship, which will make visible
that we are one family in Christ."[24] Clearly the close relationship between unity and mission was realized.

The Mexico City CWME gathering took a significant step
toward seeing the world as the primary locus for mission. This
was most explicit in the study, "The Missionary Structure of
the Congregation," which we must now analyze.

THE CHURCH FOR OTHERS: THE
MISSIONARY STRUCTURE OF THE CONGREGATION

"The Missionary Structure of the Congregation" study,
authorized by the Third Assembly of the WCC in 1961, grew out
of an attempt to define what forms or patterns of life would
best serve the missionary task of the church. The project had
access to a number of studies: the WCC Department of Evangelism
production, "A Theological Reflection on the Work of Evangelism;"
Hans J. Margull's book on evangelism was available; Johannes
Blauw's and D. T. Niles' works, together with a further WCC
research report based on them, were all but completed.[25]

A number of regional groups immediately began work on the
study with published materials appearing in North America,
Western Europe, and Asia. A final report, *The Church for Others*,
summarized the European and North American groups' findings.[26]

The basic theological idea presupposed or reflected in
much of this study was *missio Dei*. Long used in Roman Catholic
theology,[27] the phrase was first mentioned in Protestant mission
theology discussion about Willingen (1952) with the intention
of defining mission as an activity of God himself which he began with the sending of Jesus Christ and still continues today.
In a report on Willingen Karl Hartenstein summarized mission as
"participation in the sending of the Son, in the *missio Dei*,
with an inclusive aim of establishing the lordship of Christ

over the whole redeemed creation."[28]

But Willingen offered different interpretations of what
this implied for mission. One interpretation, following an
idea developed in the North American report "Why Missions?",
pointed to God's action in the world, independent of the
church, as a major part of God's mission. This view was
strongly evident in the interim report, "The Theological Basis
of the Missionary Obligation," which was not adopted at Willingen. Another understanding of the phrase linked God's mission
primarily with his evangelizing action through the church.
Willingen endorsed this interpretation[29] and it became widely
known through Georg Vicedom's book, *The Mission of God.*[30]

However, the primary meaning of *missio Dei* underlying "The
Missionary Structure of the Congregation" study was the one
which Willingen set aside, namely, the notion of participation
in God's action and presence in the world and in history.

The contribution of Johannes Hoekendijk was determinative
at this point. He argued,

> it is essential to recognize history as the decisive
> context of the Mission . . . . In no respect can the
> Church regard itself either as the subject of the
> Mission or as its sole (and exclusive) institution-
> alized form.[31]

Both the North American and Western European working groups
accepted completely that the main task of mission is to discern
God's presence in the world.[32]

The aim and goal of mission was described as *shalom* by the
European group and as humanization by the North Americans. Both
words indicated the same kind of reality, namely, fullness of
human life in its God-given potential.[33] However, the way in
which this fullness of life could be achieved was never described and the relationship between God's action and secular
events never explored.

A basic methodological difficulty was identified in this
way of approaching mission theology by a group who chose to
leave the North American study. To the critics, the notion of
"participating in God's mission in the world"

> ran too much risk of breaking away from the necessary
> controls (theological, liturgical, canonical) that
> the Church has painfully developed in the course of
> its history . . . . The method of searching for God's
> presence in contemporary situations runs the danger

of assuming a "second source of revelation" (in "the
world") uncontrolled by the theological criteria
provided by the given revelation in Christ.[34]

This new understanding of mission radically changed the traditional view of God and his relationship to the world. No longer
was mission accomplished primarily through the church: the new
emphasis stressed that God's primary relationship is to the
world and it is the world, and not the church, that is the focus
of God's plan. The value of this insight, as stated and developed, tended to overlook completely the meaning and importance
of God's covenant with his people and the call to "the obedience
of faith for the sake of his name among all the nations." (Rom. 1:5).

The old pattern of God-church-world was now changed to
God-world-church. The importance of this shift was summarized
by Williams in this way:

> Knowing that God's purpose enfolds the whole world,
> and that the Church is a segment of the world which
> exists for the world, it also knows that God is at
> work in the rest of the world outside the Church;
> that he speaks to the world also through pagan wit-
> nesses, and that the Church must therefore watch for
> the signs of God's presence in the world, ready to
> reach out to work with God at the points where he is
> at work and to be open to "humble dialogue with
> pagans."[35]

"The Missionary Structure of the Congregation" began as a
study to help evaluate the function of present church structures
for mission, of which the local congregation was an important
part. But, as the project developed, it became clear that congregations and parishes were not the main interest of the study
group participants. Indeed, the existing forms of congregational life were severely criticized for their "morphological
fundamentalism," particularly in regard to the parish system.[36]

What was proposed instead was a number of flexible structures closely related to the sociological realities of society.
Using the phrase "the world provides the agenda," it was suggested that the forms of church life must evolve around specific
needs of people in the world. By being open to human need, the
church would create "go-structures" through which the missionary
character of a congregation could respond to help victims of
injustice, racial hatred, loneliness and other personal crises.[37]

The laity were clearly understood to be the bearers and
main agents of mission in the world today. Only the laity have
the specialized knowledge through study or practical involve-

ment to share the Christian message in a dialogue with the whole
world. Heavy stress was given to the point that the laity,
through their secular occupations, their involvement in community affairs and politics, are the bearers of mission in these
contexts. Through sharing and participating in the world,
Christians are

> to discern the reality of the justifying and recon-
> ciling action of God in Christ in the context of
> particular situations which are shared by Christians
> and non-Christians.[38]

Evangelism has always been important in ecumenical mission
theology. In *Hope in Action*, H. J. Margull described evangelism
as "participation in God's mission to the world . . . . It
means, in terms of the eschatological context of evangelism,
kerygma and *diakonia* and *koinonia*."[39] Margull's formal definition of evangelism attempted to draw together the important
strands of the ecumenical discussion concerning evangelism,
particularly those relating to eschatology, proclamation, and
unity. He stated:

> Evangelism is the churches' participation in the
> messianic work of Jesus Christ. It is eschatologi-
> cal ministry to all men who have not as yet heard
> the gospel's call to repentance. In evangelism the
> churches live out their hope that Jesus Christ,
> with a view to his future, gathers men throughout
> the whole world for his congregation. More briefly:
> *Evangelism is hope in action.*[40]

Almost all of this understanding of evangelism as a call
to repentance and gathering into congregations was lost in *The
Church For Others*. Indeed, it was suggested that any attempt
to incorporate those who have accepted the faith into the
church was an indication of proselytism, the very opposite of
mission.[41] In place of a traditional understanding of evangelism which, for many, had focused on conversion as a turning
away from the world, the North American report stated that "the
issue of conversion arises not so much on the individual-
personal level, but on the corporate level in the form of
social change. But it is the same question."[42]

Consequently, mission was seen as participation in secular
programs for urban renewal, in the civil rights movement, and
in community development, understood as means of "humanization."
From this point of view, evangelism in any traditional sense
and the church as an instrument of mission have become peri-
pheral concerns.

The understanding of unity which emerged in *The Church For Others* had little interest in previous foci evident in ecumenical Faith and Order discussions. The whole denominational system was declared to be "irrelevant."[43] Unity occurs when people join together in participating in God's mission in the world, in many diverse ways, all of which are recognized as valid structures of mission.

No attempt was made in *The Church For Others* to relate this new understanding of unity with the consistent work undertaken through Faith and Order studies over the previous forty years. By sweeping aside any concern for local congregations and denominations this study, which had begun with the conviction that "the Church is the Mission," had come to the point where the church was practically eliminated from any discussion on mission.

The broad range of studies undertaken as part of "The Missionary Structure of the Congregation" and which finally resulted in *The Church For Others* emphasized several distinctive ideas about mission.[44] Beginning with *missio Dei*, understood not as God's mission to the world through the church but as God's activity in the world in which the church participates, the focus on the world as the context for mission gained wide acceptance in ecumenical literature.

As a corollary, the main agents of mission had to be the laity. Through their secular work and involvement in community and politics, the laity were to be the church in dialogue with the world, identifying and participating in God's action.

The congregation in mission was no longer the parish church, but those flexible structures and forms which evolve around specific needs of people in the world. As agents of social change, Christians become aware of their unity while participating with God in the world.

The shift in emphasis reflected in this study was strengthened by another idea which developed in the WSCF, the notion of "Christian Presence."

CHRISTIAN PRESENCE

In the 1960s a key phrase began to occur in ecumenical mission theology: "Christian presence." The term was used by a number of different people, including M. A. C. Warren, as the editor of the "Christian Presence Series," and then by the WSCF to describe a method of work in the university. Through its adoption in *The Church For Others*, the term became practically a slogan for ecumenical mission strategy and was obvious in the preparatory documentation for the Fourth Assembly at Uppsala.

The idea of "Christian presence" as a method for mission apparently began to have wide currency after the worker-priest movement in France, from 1944 to 1954, which attempted to reestablish contact with the working class by engaging in the life of the people as co-workers in the mines and in industry.

Influenced by the example and spirit of Charles de Foucauld, a French Roman Catholic who worked among Muslims in North Africa, Warren in 1959 began editing a series of books aimed at approaching other religions with deep sympathy in place of the "aggressive attack," which had frequently been the image of the Christian witness to other faiths.[45] The high quality of work produced by this series gained broad acceptance for the phrase.

"Presence" also appeared in Blauw's book *The Missionary Nature of the Church* where, in a survey of the missionary perspective in the Old Testament, it was affirmed that "the evangelization of the world is not a matter of words or of activity, but of presence: *the presence of the people of God in the midst of humanity, the presence of God among His people.*"[46] This idea became a central component in later ecumenical mission theology.

The WSCF began looking for a new ecumenical strategy for student work in 1960 and, after a series of consultations, in 1964 recommended a paper, "The Christian Community in the Academic World,"[47] as a stimulus for local groups to determine specific goals. The basic thrust centered around the theme "Christian presence."

Instead of the traditional words, such as witness, mission and evangelism, the WSCF report suggested "presence" as the most suitable word to describe the task of Christians. "Presence" was defined in this way:

> We use it to express both the centre of Christian faith and our response to it. As an expression of our faith, it points to the incarnation: God became man like us and lived among us . . . .
> We use the word "presence" (*présence, presencia*) to describe that way of life. It does not mean that we are simply there; it tries to describe the adventure of being there in the name of Christ, often anonymously, listening before we speak, hoping that men will recognize Jesus for what he is and stay where they are, involved in the fierce fight against all that dehumanizes, ready to act against demonic powers, to identify with the outcast, merciless in ridiculing modern idols and new myths. When we say "presence," we say that we have to get into the midst of things even when they frighten us. Once we are there, we may witness fearlessly to

>   Christ if the occasion is given; we may also have to
>   be silent. "Presence" for us means "engagement," in-
>   volvement in the concrete structures of our society.
>   It indicates a priority. First, we have to be there
>   before we can see our task clearly. In one sense of
>   the word, presence precedes witness. In another sense,
>   the very presence is witness. [48]

The word "presence" was used in a variety of ways but, as Colin
Williams stated, "the word 'presence' has become an indispen-
sable in-word in the contemporary discussion on mission." [49]
Why did its usage become so widespread?

In the midst of difficult or hostile situations which
Christianity faces in many places, presence points to a way of
establishing and maintaining open communication with people in
a way consistent with the spirit of Christianity. Charles de
Foucauld described a missionary as a person who is in the place
with a presence willed and determined as a witness to the love
of God in Christ. Christian presence maintained that spirit of
loving obedience.

Warren pointed to the idea of prevenient grace which "presence" includes. As God was in Christ reconciling all people
to himself, so Christ is universally present now in all of
humanity's search for truth and in judgment and correction.
Raymond Panikkar developed this idea when he said, "the Christian attitude is not ultimately one of bringing God *in*, but of
bringing him *forth*, of discovering Christ; not one of command
but of service." [50]

The identification of Christ with the human situation
pointed the way for the identification of Christians with the
people they wished to serve and witness to as an act of "presence" based on the principle of the incarnation. In this way
Christians could overcome the remoteness of the church from the
situations in which people live in the world, as the French
worker-priests had attempted to do.

Based on an active participation in specific situations,
the Christian could accurately assess the best way to work with
non-Christians to most appropriately meet their needs. Presence
in such a manner allows a personal encounter to occur, rather
than working with predetermined plans which may or may not suit
existing conditions. In such circumstances the possibility of
a genuine encounter of people in dialogue could also occur.

The basic intention of Christian presence in mission
theology--to get Christians into close personal contact with
people in the world, with an open, expectant attitude towards

other people, whatever their beliefs--has been widely accepted.
But, because the notion of presence has been used with many
different meanings, a number of objections have been raised.
When used as a justification for Christian involvement in movements for radical social reform, devoid of any Christian proclamation, it has not been accepted, especially by many conservative evangelicals.

For some people, particularly in the WSCF, it may have
been used to cover up confusion, hesitation or uncertainty
about the Christian faith itself when many students felt uneasy
about witness and mission as being "too big and too definite."[51]
This whole issue of presence occurred at a time when the question of "open" membership was being hotly debated within the
Federation.[52]

The phrase "Christian presence" is now used far less than
previously in ecumenical mission theology discussion. However,
the concerns which prompted its use--the need to identify with
people in an open way, the need for dialogue in the midst of
situations in the world--have been accepted as valid and have
been included in WCC statements. For example, from the Fourth
Assembly of the WCC, the Uppsala report, "Renewal in Mission,"
cited a variety of opportunities for mission, and clearly envisioned the church as becoming involved in these situations,
in the sense of being a "Christian presence."[53] The Fifth
Assembly at Nairobi had the spirit of Christian presence in
mind when, in a paragraph on methodology, it stated

> nothing can replace the living witness in words and
> deeds of Christian persons, groups, and congregations
> who participate in the sufferings and joys, in the
> struggles and celebrations, in the frustrations and
> hopes of the people with whom they want to share the
> gospel . . . . They should be directed by a humble
> spirit of sensitivity and participation.[54]

The widespread acceptance of presence theology, despite
the range of ways in which it was understood, contributed to
the focus on the world as the arena for mission, and thus to
the primary thrust of ecumenical mission theology in the 1960s.
This focus was even more evident in the Geneva Conference on
Church and Society in 1966, to which we must now turn.

CHURCH AND SOCIETY:
GENEVA, 1966

The ecumenical movement has always "sought to keep abreast
of social and theological developments through an intensive
study programme on social questions," declared the WCC Central

Committee in 1962. In keeping with that tradition, it recommended a "World Conference on Church and Society: Christians
in the Technical and Social Revolutions of our Time."[55] Four
major preparatory volumes were prepared, touching on the issues
of worldwide social change.[56]

To assure the freedom of participants to engage in creative
thinking, the WCC Central Committee at Enugu, Nigeria, in 1965
altered the nature of the conference

> from one speaking on behalf of the churches to one
> which would speak to the churches and advise them
> on the Christian response to the challenges of
> revolutionary changes in our time.[57]

Of the 338 official participants at the Geneva Conference, 180
were laymen; almost half were from Asia, Africa, and Latin
America.

The conference also provided an opportunity for Roman
Catholic and ecumenical theologians to work together on social
issues. Two preliminary consultations were held and eight
Roman Catholic observers made a significant contribution to the
work of the meeting. Following these contacts, Roman Catholic-
WCC cooperation has increased greatly in the study of matters
of common concern.[58]

The influence of the Geneva Conference on Church and
Society on ecumenical mission theology can be seen in three
particular areas. First, a strengthening of the thrust towards
the world as the locus for mission; second, by providing deeper
insights into the issues affecting the world, it helped determine the shape and form of the structures needed by the church
to respond to those issues; and, third, its attempt to develop
the theological undergirding for mission.

Initially criticism was directed to the whole idea of the
conference by some who argued that the most important thing
Christians have to do is proclaim the gospel in direct personal
evangelism. In his opening address, W. A. Visser 't Hooft
responded to this argument by stating

> Our conference is about the full meaning and implica-
> tions of a true turning to God, about the implications
> of conversion, about the fruits of repentance. . . .
> It is in our day to day decisions in our social life
> that the reality of our turning to God is constantly
> tested. We will never be able to convince the modern
> world of the truth of the Gospel unless we offer it
> in its fullness; that is with its radical critique of

our social attitudes and our social structures confirmed by our personal and corporate obedience.[59]

The Geneva Conference strengthened considerably the emphasis on the world as the arena for mission, which had become
the major thrust of ecumenical mission theology in the 1960s,
especially in "The Missionary Structure of the Congregation"
study which was drawing to a close at the same time. This
understanding of mission was evident in the section report,
"Man and Community in Changing Societies," when it stated:

> We start with the basic assumption that the triune God
> is the Lord of his world and at work within it, and
> that the Church's task is to point to his acts, to
> respond to his demands, and to call mankind to this
> faith and obedience. Christians would surely not dis-
> pute this. . . . In this document, "mission" and "mis-
> sionary" are used as shorthand for the responsibilities
> of the Church in the world, and include the prophetic,
> kerygmatic, and diaconic or serving functions.[60]

In language almost identical to that found in *The Church
For Others*, the principles for determining structures for mission were outlined. This understanding of mission was based
primarily on the work of the laity in secular functions and
situations, whose task it was to "encounter the structures of
society." The recommended principles were

a) The planning of the Church's mission should be
    determined by the concept of the "zone humaine."
b) Engagement in public life requires that the
    Church devise structures able to encounter the
    structures of society. Such structures should
    be capable of including and relating to those
    who are unable to make credal affirmations, but
    who can see the secular significance of what are
    in fact theological truths.
c) The devising of structures will require great flex-
    ibility, and development of indigenous patterns.
d) High priority must be given to selective training,
    spiritual equipment and deployment of the laity.
e) The training and retraining of the clergy must
    equip them to exercise a relevant ministry in a
    Church structured for mission.
f) Competent full-time professionals in such fields
    as social work, community organization, education,
    etc., should be employed by the Church as an
    integral part of its essential staff.
g) In structuring themselves for mission, the churches
    should use as consultants churchmen from the social

sciences and related fields.[61]

In seeking to determine what issues are of vital importance for Christians engaged in mission, Visser 't Hooft suggested that the concept of "the responsible society" now needed to be expanded to the international level to include the notion of "a responsible world society in which each nation feels responsible for the welfare of all other nations."[62] This idea was evident in the report on "Economic Development in a World Perspective," which appealed for international economic justice when it said:

> Economic growth in the relatively few richer nations
> of the world makes it incumbent on them to assist in
> the enormous task of helping the developing countries
> to move along the road to self-sustaining development.
> This is the biggest issue in the world today, and it
> will be with us for generations to come.[63]

The mission of the church in relation to the issue of development was considered to be a prophetic one, in which education would play an important part. This was envisaged to include theological education on the moral aspects of development, economic education to encourage understanding of world economic structures in developed and developing countries, political education to produce the political will for a world order compatible with Christian conscience, and social education to help society accept the cost of world economic development.[64]

Revolution was an issue of first importance at the conference. Delegates held different attitudes towards various methods of social change. The urgent and necessary need for fundamental change in political and social structures was widely agreed upon; concerning the best way to work for such transformation there was no such consensus. The "Message of the Conference" affirmed that while some Christian thought change should be brought by working in and through established institutions, other Christians were committed to radical revolution as a responsible Christian position.[65]

Part of the original intention of the Geneva meeting was "to develop a body of theological and ethical insights which will assist the churches in their witness in contemporary history."[66] But as the official report recognized, "this conference was not able to discuss adequately its theological orientation."[67]

In a sharp criticism of both procedural and substantive aspects of the theological work done at Geneva, Paul Ramsey argued that too little time was allowed to achieve any respon-

sible theological reflection. He felt the whole approach of
the conference contributed to the problem because

> the conference began with "man's disorder" (or man's
> revolutionary prospects) rather than with "God's
> design" (as Barth said of Amsterdam); and of neces-
> sity one cannot go very far in "prolonging" that into
> theological ethics even if he is accustomed to dis-
> ciplined reflection.[68]

The discussion on revolution exhibited the weakness of the
theological analysis. An evening plenary session was devoted
to the subject "The Relevance of Theology to the Social Revolutions of our Time." Three speakers opened the debate, and each
called for a much more active participation by Christians in
revolutions in solidarity with other people in their political
and social struggles against injustice, as part of a struggle
to humanize the secular orders.[69]

The participants who followed each alluded to the same
basic point: How can Christians distinguish authentic revolution, understood as the will of God, from all the revolutionary
events and ideologies in history? The question was not answered
by the conference. A contributing factor to the problem of
finding adequate theological criteria for assessing the term
"revolution" was the vagueness and systematically ambiguous way
in which it was used.

The main point of the mission theology developed during
the 1960s was based on a participation in God's action in the
world. Thus the need to understand precisely where God was at
work was of crucial significance. But the theological reflection necessary to produce such insight was not accomplished at
Geneva. Consequently, the whole method and direction of ecumenical mission theology underlying the conference was seriously
weakened.

By focusing on the world and identifying the major social
issues confronting Christians, the Conference on Church and
Society confirmed the direction in which ecumenical theology
was moving. It directed attention to the need for Christians
to be involved in movements for social change. Prominent in
the discussions were issues of revolution and economic development. Christians were challenged to strive for justice and
peace. The influence which the conference had on the WCC was
significant for "the theological and intellectual ferment thus
created very substantially influenced the thinking of the
Fourth Assembly of the World Council."[70] It is to the Uppsala
Assembly that we must now turn.

RENEWAL IN MISSION:
UPPSALA, 1968

In a time marked by "the excitement of new scientific discoveries, the protest of student revolts, the shock of assassi-
nations, the clash of wars,"71 the Fourth Assembly of the WCC
met at Uppsala, Sweden, between 4-19 July, 1968. One of the
most notable characteristics of the Assembly was its concern
for the world. The 704 delegates, from 235 WCC member
churches,72 met to discuss the theme, "Behold, I make all things
new." The strong Roman Catholic contingent to the Assembly included fifteen delegated observers, indicating the vitality of
the new relationship between the WCC and the Roman Catholic Church.

The work of the Assembly revolved around the six sections:
"The Holy Spirit and the Catholicity of the Church," "Renewal
in Mission," "World Economic and Social Development," "Towards
Justice and Peace in International Affairs," "Worship," and
"Towards New Styles of Living."

Debate about mission theology began with the publication
of the preparatory documentation for the Assembly, especially
Drafts for Sections.73 The objective of mission envisaged in
the draft document "Renewal in Mission" was "the new humanity."
Points of tension in human existence--religious, social and
political--were designated as the places of opportunity for
mission which would probably require the development of "new
instruments of mission."74 These proposals were heavily in-
debted to the study report *The Church For Others* and the Geneva
Conference on Church and Society as the commentary acknowledged.75

Donald McGavran, of the Fuller Theological Seminary in
California, led an attack on the whole tone and thrust of the
proposals. The *Church Growth Bulletin* ran a special "Uppsala
Issue."76 McGavran answered the rhetorical question in the
lead article, "Will Uppsala Betray the Two Billion?" with a
resounding "yes," arguing that the document said nothing about
the necessity of faith, nothing about the two billion who have
never heard of Jesus, and nothing about sending missionaries.
In a later comment, Arthur Glasser noted that conservative
evangelicals reacted strongly to "Renewal in Mission" because
it "appalled them with its secularized gospel and reduction of
the mission of the Church to social and political activism."77

Visser 't Hooft was one of those sensitive to the need for
a balanced and holistic understanding of mission and he challenged the Assembly to produce an adequate presentation of the
Christian gospel by setting out his own thoughts in this way:

I believe that, with regard to the great tension

between the vertical interpretation of the Gospel as
essentially concerned with God's saving action in the
life of individuals, and the horizontal interpretation
of it as mainly concerned with human relationships in
the world, we must get out of that rather primitive
oscillating movement of going from one extreme to the
other, which is not worthy of a movement which by its
nature seeks to embrace the truth of the Gospel in its
fulness. A Christianity which has lost its vertical
dimension has lost its salt and is not only insipid in
itself, but useless for the world. But a Christianity
which would use the vertical preoccupation as a means
to escape from its responsibility for and in the common
life of man is a denial of the incarnation, of God's
love for the world manifested in Christ.[78]

The Section II Report, "Renewal in Mission," has three parts.
The first, "A Mandate for Mission," provides a theological introduction; the second, "Opportunities for Mission," outlines
some crucial situations for mission, and some criteria for determining priorities; and the third, "Freedom for Mission,"
addresses the need for new missionary structures in the church.[79]

The dominant theological motif in "A Mandate for Mission"
concentrated on the idea of "a new humanity" in Jesus Christ:

There is a burning relevance today in describing the
mission of God, in which we participate, as the gift
of a new creation which is a radical renewal of the
old and the invitation to men to grow up into their
full humanity in the new man, Jesus Christ.[80]

The christological focus of the new humanity is firmly established in the succeeding paragraphs, which point to the significance of the life and death of Christ in overcoming alienation
from God. Through the response of faith, the new life had an
effect on all relations for "there is no turning to God which
does not at the same time bring a man face to face with his
fellow men in a new way."[81]

Uppsala clearly acknowledged the human context for mission,
for Christians belong to a humanity that "cries passionately
and articulately for a fully human life." In the community of
the new life, people break through racial, national, and religious barriers that divide humanity.

The theme of dialogue received special attention. As
Christians meet people of other faiths or no faith, sharing a
common humanity "each meets and challenges the other; witnessing
from the depths of his existence to the ultimate concerns that

come to expression in word and deed."[82]   Christ speaks in such
dialogue.

The relationship of church to mission found expression in
two different ways in "Renewal in Mission." The influence of
the church growth school associated with Donald McGavran and
some conservative evangelicals was evident in the first part
which affirmed that new life will find results in church growth.

> Mission bears fruit as people find their true life in
> the Body of Christ, in the Church's life of Word and
> Sacrament, fellowship in the Spirit and existence for
> others. There the signs of the new humanity are ex-
> perienced and the People of God reach out in solidarity
> with the whole of mankind in service and witness. The
> growth of the Church, therefore, both inward and outward,
> is of urgent importance.[83]

In the later parts of Section II another line of reasoning,
associated with *The Church For Others*, was developed. This
pointed to the Church itself as part of the arena for mission,
together with centers of power, revolutionary movements, universities, and urban areas. Uppsala offered the following
criteria for evaluating mission priorities:

> -do they place the church alongside the poor, the
> defenceless, the abused, the forgotten, the bored?
> -do they allow Christians to enter the concerns of
> others to accept their issues and their structures
> as vehicles of involvement?
> -are they the best situations for discerning with
> other men the signs of the times, and for moving
> with history towards the coming of the new humanity?[84]

The emphasis evident here was on creating flexible structures
using the laity in their secular occupations as the major
thrust in mission outreach. Theological education for clergy
and laity would be necessary to enable small groups to fulfill
a missionary vocation.

Joint Action for Mission, an idea first suggested at
Willingen (1952), was strongly advocated as a way of imple-
menting the insight that there is only one mission in six continents. Only through multilateral relations and decision
making, Uppsala suggested, could "the resources of the whole
Church in terms of men, money and expertise [be] available for
the use of the whole Church."[85]

Evangelism was linked with the theme of a new humanity,
because, while the Holy Spirit provides the gift of a living,

converting word, Christians share in the process by "bringing about the occasions for Men's response to Jesus Christ."[86] This turning towards God and others was likened to a new birth.

Uppsala stressed social engagement as a sign of the new humanity. It was claimed that people must see achievements of greater justice, freedom and dignity as a part of the restoration of true humanity in Christ. The priority situations described in "Opportunities for Mission" emphasized participation in dynamic social movements as a major part of the Church's mission.

Other sections of the Uppsala report outlined specific areas in which Christians could make contributions to the global community. The process of "World Economic and Social Development" explored in Section III, and the search for "Justice and Peace in International Affairs" (Section IV) were subjects of special concern. The final section, "Towards New Styles of Living," tried to indicate some of the dimensions of Christian commitment in the 1960s and what it meant for Christians to be "signs of *agape*, that is to say, examples of that love for one another by which men recognize disciples of Christ."[87]

The discussion of unity and mission in terms of catholicity marked a distinctive contribution of the Uppsala Assembly. Understanding catholicity to be both a gift and a task given by God to the Church, it could also describe the goal of the Church's mission

> to bring people of all times, of all races, of all
> places, of all conditions, into an organic and
> living unity in Christ by the Holy Spirit under the
> universal fatherhood of God.[88]

Indeed, by its catholicity, the church could speak of itself as "the sign of the coming unity of mankind" because in Christ the church was constituted as a new community of new creatures.

This discussion of catholicity closely paralleled the idea of "the new humanity" expressed in "Renewal in Mission." The catholicity of the church seeks to judge and repudiate the tragic distortions of humanity (for example, racism), because by overcoming such divisions, the church could demonstrate the fullness of redeemed humanity in Christ. The goal of making visible the bonds which unite Christians in a universal fellowship was something the assembly saw as an urgent imperative to fulfill the purpose of creation in which sinful people are reconciled in the one divine sonship of which Christ is both author and finisher.

The Uppsala Report, "Renewal in Mission," has been described as

> a hotchpotch, a compromise document, a variegated
> patchwork quilt sewn together out of bits and pieces
> contributed by delegates and advisers whose convic-
> tions were in fundamental disagreement.[89]

Advocates both of conservative evangelicalism and of a radical
mission theology could point to sentences in the text which
could be used to support their position.

Uppsala reflected a diversity of viewpoints within the
member churches themselves concerning mission theology. On the
one hand, the trends evident in *The Church For Others* and the
Geneva Conference on Church and Society exerted a strong influence on the Assembly. The goal of "the new humanity," the
stress on participating in dialogue with the secular movements
for change in the world, and the emphasis on flexible structures for mission involving the laity, all confirmed this basic
trend. But on the other hand, resistance to this understanding
of mission from people who felt that insufficient emphasis had
been retained on the traditional elements of mission, such as
proclamation and witness by the church as the agent of God's
mission, resulted in the reaffirmation of these aspects of
mission as well.

The concerned effort of some conservative evangelicals,
like John R. W. Stott and David Hubbard, to influence the
Uppsala discussions marked the entry of the evangelicals into
the contemporary debate on mission within the ecumenical movement. The voice of evangelicalism gained new strength in the
1960s, especially after the Berlin World Congress on Evangelism
and the Wheaton Congress on the Church's Worldwide Mission,
both held in 1966. Anglican evangelicals made their own decision to enter fully into the ecumenical dialogue at a meeting
at Keele in 1967, when they declared, "we are no longer content
to stand apart from those with whom we disagree."[90]

The lack of common understanding evident at Uppsala was
due in no small part to the interaction between two major positions: the evangelical advocates of proclamation for conversion and church growth, and the advocates of a greater involvement by Christians in the world. The debate centered on the
question of the substance and nature of the gospel itself. No
consensus was reached, but various opinions were presented and
highlighted. This was a valuable contribution even if at the
time agreement was impossible. We will see how the debate continued in the meetings which followed, especially the CWME
meeting at Bangkok and the WCC Assembly at Nairobi.

DIALOGUE WITH PEOPLE OF OTHER FAITHS

How Christians relate to people of other faiths has been an important subject at all of the major missionary conferences held this century.

The 1910 WMC at Edinburgh asserted that the true attitude of the Christian to non-Christian religions should be one of understanding and sympathy, even while proclaiming the absoluteness of Christianity.[91] The Jerusalem meeting of the IMC in 1928 appealed to Christians to undertake mission in a spirit of humility and penitence and love. The Message also called for cooperation with non-Christians in matters of common concern, but carefully pointed to Jesus Christ as the fulfillment of all the good evident in other religions.[92]

The report *Re-Thinking Missions* constituted an important part of the background for the debate at Madras in 1938. Hocking had called on Christians to join with people of other religions in a common search for truth, a position which many missionary leaders judged to be an implicit denial of the ultimacy of the gospel and thus a relativizing of the Christian faith. Kraemer's book, *The Christian Message in a Non-Christian World*, profoundly influenced the IMC gathering, and through its stress on the discontinuity between the biblical revelation and all religions, tended to make the relationship of Christianity to other faiths a secondary matter.[93]

It was not until the 1950s that the relationship of Christianity to other faiths again became a vital concern. A theologian from Asia, D. T. Niles, raised the issue at the Evanston Assembly in 1954. The Report on Evangelism spoke of the renascent non-Christian religions which "necessitate a new approach in our evangelizing task."[94] This led to a long-term study on "The Word of God and the Living Faiths of Men,"[95] endorsed by both the Central Committee of the WCC in 1956 and the Ghana Assembly of the IMC in 1958. A meeting in Nagpur, India in 1961 evaluated the work done in a number of consultations, and indicated points of agreement and those requiring further discussion. These included the realization that religions are living faiths; an awareness of human solidarity in a common humanity; the need for a re-evaluation of the relationship of the gospel to other religions; and the need for a fresh approach to the task of Christian witness.[96] The New Delhi Assembly of the WCC in 1961 voted to continue the study, "The Word of God and the Living Faiths of Men," through work at local study centers. It also encouraged dialogue in order to witness effectively.[97]

"The Witness of Christians to Men of Other Faiths" report

at the CWME meeting at Mexico City in 1963 declared that

> the Christian attitude towards men of other faiths
> is basically one of love for all men, respect for
> sincerity wherever found, and patience to search
> for ways to bear effective witness.[98]

In an important statement on dialogue with people of other
faiths, the nature of dialogue was explored.

> True dialogue with a man of another faith requires
> a concern both for the Gospel and for the other man.
> Without the first, dialogue becomes a pleasant conver-
> sation. Without the second, it becomes irrelevant,
> unconvincing and arrogant . . . . Our intention in
> every human dialogue should be to be involved with
> the dialogue of God with men, and to move our partner
> and oneself to listen to what God in Christ reveals
> to us, and to answer him.[99]

The Mexico City statement affirmed that dialogue is a serious
endeavor. Through dialogue Christians must seek to be open to
hearing the other partner, yet without denying the finality of
the Christian revelation since both partners are open to the
dialogue of God with humanity.

The Second East Asia Christian Conference Assembly at
Bangkok in 1964 strongly recommended contacts with people of
other living faiths in the report "Christian Encounter with Men
of Other Beliefs."[100] The divine presence and mission operative in dialogue was emphasized by this report which stated:

> The dialogical situation within which the Christian
> encounter takes place is characterized, therefore, by
> the Universality of the Gospel as it encompasses all
> men, the Mutuality that is promised when dialogue takes
> place in honest and loving openness, and the Finality
> of Christ Himself who alone is Lord.[101]

Amid the plurality of religions in Asia, the necessity for dialogue with people of other faiths was constantly present. The
Asian concern at this point stimulated the development of this
issue within the whole ecumenical movement.[102]

A major gathering, involving Protestants, the Orthodox and
Roman Catholics, was held at Kandy, Ceylon in 1967. The chief
action of the meeting was an invitation to dialogue with people
of other faiths: "We Christians would express our sincere
desire to enter into dialogue, admitting our past failures in
both charity and understanding."[103]

The Kandy Statement outlined a three-fold basis for meeting
with people of different religious convictions. It affirmed
that Christians are aware of a human solidarity with all other
people; all mankind is caught up in a universal history; the
Christian recognizes that all people are created in the image
of God and Christ died for every person.[104] The essence of
dialogue was described as the

> genuine readiness to listen to the man with whom we
> wish to communicate. . . . Dialogue means a positive
> effort to attain a deeper understanding of the truth
> through mutual awareness of one another's convictions
> and witness. . . . Dialogical existence naturally
> starts with living in openness of heart and spirit.[105]

A distinction was made between dialogue and proclamation.
Proclamation means "the sharing of the Good News about God's
action in history through Jesus Christ." Yet, it affirmed,
"dialogue may include proclamation, since it must always be
undertaken in the spirit of those who have good news to share."[106]

The Fourth Assembly of the WCC at Uppsala did not address
the issue of the relationship of Christianity and other faiths,
but did emphasize that dialogue was an indispensible part of
the approach of Christians to others. It declared:

> A Christian's dialogue with another implies neither a
> denial of the uniqueness of Christ, nor any loss of his
> own commitment to Christ, but rather that a genuinely
> Christian approach to others must be human, personal,
> relevant and humble. In dialogue we share our common
> humanity, its dignity and fallenness, and express our
> common concern for that humanity. It opens the possi-
> bility of sharing in new forms of community and common
> service. Each meets and challenges the other; witness-
> ing from the depths of his existence to the ultimate
> concerns that come to expression in word and action. As
> Christians we believe that Christ speaks in this dia-
> logue, revealing himself to those who do not know him
> and [correcting] the limited and distorted knowledge of
> those who do. Dialogue and proclamation are not the
> same. The one complements the other in a total witness.[107]

This comprehensive statement reflected the understanding
of dialogue which had developed in the ecumenical movement.
Dialogue concerns the attitude of Christians towards others; it
is a serious encounter between people who share a common humanity
and may lead to common service. Christ is present in dialogue.

Major developments took place in the ecumenical approach

to dialogue in the following months. In August, 1968, Stanley
J. Samartha became the director of the WCC's dialogue program.
As a minister in the Church of South India and a professor of
the history of religions at Bangalore and later at Serampore
College, he was one with firsthand experience of interfaith
dialogue and well qualified to give new direction to the
"Living Faiths" study in the WCC. Then in 1969, the Central
Committee of the WCC approved plans for a WCC-sponsored conference in which representatives of different faiths would meet
together. This signaled a shift from discussion about dialogue
to actual dialogue itself.

The Ajaltoun Conference of March, 1970, drew together four
Buddhists, twenty-eight Christians, three Hindus, and three
Muslims for ten days of conversation "to see what could be
learned for future relations between people of living faiths.[108]
From the report of the meeting, it is clear that participants
felt dialogue to be quite consistent with a complete commitment
to a particular faith. They affirmed that dialogue was a method
of communication undertaken in an attitude of openness, through
which opinions could be clarified, and perhaps in some instances
lead to common action on issues of mutual concern.[109]

A consultation of twenty-three theologians met at Zurich
in May, 1970, to evaluate the theological dimensions of the
Ajaltoun meeting. It produced an *Aide-mémoire* published as
"Christians in Dialogue with Men of Other Faiths."[110] Dialogue
was acknowledged to be an invaluable and urgent means of communication based on openness to and respect for others in which
Christians may participate in the full confidence that Christ
is already at work in the lives of all people. The report considered dialogue a part of the church's calling to work for the
unity of all humanity.

A basic question needing further clarification was identified:

> What is the relation of God's economy of salvation
> in Jesus Christ to the economy of his presence and
> activity in the whole world, and in particular in the
> lives and traditions of men of other living faiths?[111]

This remains one of the important questions relating to dialogue
and, indeed, to the whole question of mission in the world.

Further developments concerning the significance of dialogue in the ecumenical movement occurred at the Central Committee of the WCC meeting at Addis Ababa in January, 1971,
which explored dialogue as a major theme and took two important
actions. First, it received "An Interim Policy Statement and

Guidelines"[112] concerning dialogue, and adopted Part III of
that statement covering recommendations for further study and
involvement of Christians in meetings with people of other
faiths. Second, within the WCC's structural reorganization, a
new sub-unit on "Dialogue with People of Living Faiths and
Ideologies" was authorized. This gave a new status to the
whole inquiry in relation to the other three elements of
Mission and Evangelism, Faith and Order, and Church and Society
in Unit I, entitled "Faith and Witness."

Now dialogue was recognized as a concern of the whole ecumenical movement. This represented a significant expansion of
ecumenical concern and involvement in a world having a variety
of faiths, cultures and ideologies. In acknowledgement of the
practical importance of dialogue in a world filled with tension
and hostility (partly as a result of religious differences),
dialogue now constitutes a permanent part of the WCC agenda.[113]

Basic theological work still needed to be done on the issue
of dialogue, as the Addis Ababa statement recognized. The diverse views present in the WCC made agreement difficult and
three questions seemed of special significance. What are the
fundamental implications of dialogue? What is the relationship
between dialogue, witness and mission? How is dialogue to be
understood and practiced in the context of indigenization?[114]

A short statement, "On Dialogue with People of Living
Faiths,"[115] was produced at the CWME meeting in Bangkok (1973).
The theological basis for dialogue in the statement pointed to
God's movement towards people as Creator and Saviour, bringing
them to wholeness and leading them into a wider community.
Christians were invited to discover God's activity among people
of other faiths. Because they shared common human aspirations
and responsibility for others, Christians ought to engage in
dialogue with those also concerned about ultimate questions.

In discussing the relationship between dialogue and evangelism, Bangkok affirmed that Christians must be "faithful to
our Lord's command to mission and witness, which is part of our
title deed," and noted that "mission is being carried on in
this spirit of dialogue without the subsequent decrease in the
sense of urgency in evangelism."[116]

Noting the increasing interdependence between people and
nations in the world community, Bangkok stressed another important object of dialogue which was the need to work together in
meeting human necessities, relieve human suffering, establish
social justice, and share in the struggle for peace.

Bangkok reaffirmed dialogue as an essential ecumenical

concern in which people of various faiths meet together in an open manner, in full obedience to their respective religious obligations. The primary goals were stated to be: the reduction of misunderstanding; the honest presentation of deeply-held convictions; and the hope of achieving common action in response to human need.

Dialogue again became the subject of a major discussion within the ecumenical movement during the Fifth Assembly of the WCC at Nairobi (1975). As invited guests, representatives of other living faiths contributed to the work of Section III on "Seeking Community: The Common Search of People of Various Faiths, Cultures and Ideologies." The report proved to be controversial but was finally approved after a preamble was added to clarify the intention of the discussion.[117]

The preamble includes three fundamental points to allay the apprehensions of critics. First, the Great Commission, it was stated, "should not be abandoned or betrayed, disobeyed or compromised." Second, syncretism, understood as the attempt "to create a new religion composed of elements taken from different religions," was rejected.[118] Third, dialogue was defined as "a matter of hearing and understanding the faith of others, and also of witnessing to the gospel of Jesus Christ."[119]

From its inception as a program concerned with the relation of Christians to people of other living faiths, the discussion of dialogue in the ecumenical movement had now expanded to include cross-cultural communication and discussions with people of different ideologies.

As with previous meetings, the theological implications of dialogue were disputed. No single conclusion could be reached concerning the basis on which dialogue is to be conducted. A diversity of opinion was evident, too, in responses to the question of how God works among people of other faiths. The main point of consensus was on the importance of continuing dialogue to secure the cooperation of all people in order to establish a just and peaceful society.

The superiority of Western culture as a manifestation of Christianity, so long assumed by many, was implicitly set aside by Nairobi's affirmation that "no culture is closer to Jesus Christ than any other culture . . . . The church is called to relate itself to any culture critically, creatively, redemptively."[120] The catholicity of the church contributes to the search for world community, the report declared.

The dialogue of Christians and Marxists, especially in Eastern Europe, pointed to the problems and prospects related

to dialogue.[121] The main thrust of this section was to declare
that "we accept the responsibility to judge critically and
openly the ways in which our Christian faith may interact with
various cultures and ideologies."[122]

Nairobi broadened the scope of dialogue so that Christians
could see the possibilities of communicating with all people
throughout the world, even those who proclaim no religious
faith.[123] However, the theological presuppositions of dialogue
remain to be clarified. But few would deny that the interaction
of people together in an open, constructive way should be encouraged.

In summary, dialogue by Christians with those of other
faiths is now an important part of the program of the WCC. It
arose as a way of promoting positive communication with people
outside of the life of the church, especially with people of
other faiths. It has since grown into a more inclusive endeavor,
seeking honest, open, and deep relations with all people.

Although it has proven difficult to develop a theological
basis for dialogue, a number of ideas have been advocated: our
common humanity, the presence of God at work in and for all
people, the need to create a world community and act jointly to
meet common need; but no one argument has been universally
accepted.

The process of dialogue has been recognized as a means of
communicating with others on the basis of openness and honesty,
with the challenge of sharing basic convictions. Understood in
this way, it is not a substitute for the proclamation of the
gospel in Christian mission; rather, it is an important way of
clearing away hindrances to effective communication so that the
interchange of fundamental beliefs can occur. Dialogue does
not and need not involve syncretism; it is a means of clarifying basic issues, and then learning what differences and points
of agreement exist.

Two main kinds of situations call for dialogue, indeed,
demand it: First, dialogue offers a helpful method of discovering how Christians and other people can work together to
promote justice and peace, and the alleviation of human suffering and hardship. Such dialogue concerns itself with the
search for a world community.[124] Second, dialogue also functions to achieve a deeper level of communication. Visser 't
Hooft had this situation in mind when he wrote:

> The Gospel is proclaimed by people to people. There
> must be a real encounter between those people. And
> that is impossible when one party considers the other

simply as an object or as a victim. Both parties must
be able to listen. And he who has come to say what he
has discovered in and through the Gospel must give the
example. He may only begin to speak after he has lis-
tened so carefully that he begins to understand how he
can tell the story of Jesus to these people with whom
he has come into contact, in such a way that it becomes
relevant to their lives and can be understood in their
situation.[125]

The need for this kind of dialogue is quite obvious, as
Christians seek to serve their neighbors and witness to the
gospel in this pluralistic world. Principles laid down at
Edinburgh 1910, of sympathetic understanding of another's position, and of firm conviction regarding the truth of the Christian witness of faith, still seem basic today, even though the
extent of their application has become far greater in scope in
the modern world.

UNITY OF THE CHURCH--UNITY OF MANKIND:
FAITH AND ORDER

Faith and Order studies in the 1960s began to broaden in a
move related to what was happening in the whole of the ecumenical movement. The discussion of church unity became related to
the discussion of the unity of all people, a theme with deep
implications for mission theology.

From the "promising chaos" of the Conference on Faith and
Order at Montreal (1963),[126] in which the Orthodox churches and
Roman Catholics became intensively involved in discussion,
emerged the suggestion that Faith and Order studies should be
set within a broader theological framework than the fairly narrow ecclesiastical limits within which they had previously occurred. Thus, as the other sections of the ecumenical movement
had come to take the world with far greater seriousness, Faith
and Order began a study on "Creation, new creation and Church
unity" in which God's work in universal history was discussed.
From this, it became clear that the churches face the challenge
of a humanity which needs the united witness and services of
the church as a sign of the Lordship of Christ.[127]

At the Bristol Faith and Order meeting in 1967, the question was raised: "what . . . is the relation of the churches'
quest for unity among themselves to the hope for the unity of
mankind?"[128] The answer came in the study on the catholicity
of the church undertaken for the Uppsala Assembly, that "the
Church is bold to speak of itself as the sign of the coming
unity of mankind."[129] From this arose the Faith and Order
study, "The Unity of the Church and the Unity of Mankind,"

which was the central focus of the Louvain Faith and Order meeting in 1971.

Louvain related church unity to five secular contexts: political struggle, racism, cultural differences, interreligious dialogue, and the handicapped.[130] The fruit of this effort is reflected in the Nairobi report on "What Unity Requires."

The Fifth Assembly report on unity grew out of new discussions on what "the unity of the Church" means. The concept of "conciliar fellowship" has been developed to describe in a fresh way the unity which the church seeks.[131] Not intended to replace the goal of full organic unity described at New Delhi, conciliar fellowship attempts to point to the reality of "unity in diversity" as an aspect and quality of the life of the church at all levels. The meaning of this understanding of unity for mission clearly relates to what Nairobi said about "confessing Christ"--it must be done in a specific way in each particular cultural setting, yet be part of the confession of the whole church. As the Faith and Order study at Accra in 1974 on "Giving Account of the Hope That is Within Us,"[132] demonstrated, different churches give very different expressions of the hope they experience in the one Christ.

The different human contexts in which unity must be achieved also found a place in the Nairobi report, reflecting the influence of the Louvain discussions. The handicapped, the relationship of men and women, the tension often felt between personal freedom and organizational unity, political struggle and the church, and differences in cultural identity, all received brief attention as part of the context in which unity must take place. The importance of this for mission was revealed in this sentence: "It is as a community which is itself being healed that the Church can be God's instrument for the healing of the nations."[133]

IN SEARCH OF A COMPREHENSIVE
UNDERSTANDING OF SALVATION: BANGKOK, 1973

The Bangkok Conference on "Salvation Today" drew together some 330 participants from 69 countries.[134] The theme emerged from the 1963 Mexico City CWME meeting in the question: "What is the form and content of the salvation which Christ offers men in the secular world."[135] In 1968, the CWME chose "Salvation Today" as the topic of the next Assembly and initiated the preparatory study process.[136]

The specific preparatory material for Bangkok, as well as the conference itself, planned to concentrate on the experience

of salvation. The booklet sent to participants, "Tell Out,
Tell Out My Glory," drew together a large number of texts on
the general theme of salvation.[137] At the conference a series
of small groups met for study and reflection on the meaning of
salvation as experienced by the participants. Later, the format for the section meetings followed an "action-reflection"
model, in which reports from specific areas (for example, the
White Fathers withdrawal from Mozambique; X minus Y group in
Holland; project among Tondo squatters in Manila) were presented
and written reports compiled, taking this detailed material
into account.

One consequence of this experience-centered approach was
that serious theological reflection was difficult to achieve at
the conference. Although the aim of relating salvation to concrete situations was laudable, the method reduced the amount of
probing theological analysis which could be undertaken. This
was a serious deficiency. Thomas Wieser, the CWME staff member
responsible for the study on "Salvation Today," noted at the
beginning of the conference that, while God's saving work
transcends the walls of the church, serious study was still
needed to evaluate precisely where God was at work.

Obviously, this does not mean a blanket endorsement
of any political movement or ideological trend. The
task of identifying God's saving purpose in the midst
of historical events requires solid theological criteria on the basis of which critical judgements can be
made. Here an important task remains to be undertaken
in order to ensure that the Church's credibility will
not again be lost in a dash for a short-lived relevance.[138]

Bangkok was the poorer because the demanding theological
task confronting the participants (and the ecumenical movement)
was not adequately handled.[139]

What were the main thrusts of the conference for ecumenical mission theology?

No consensus was sought, or achieved, on the main theme of
salvation. Rather, a variety of responses, meditations, and
affirmations were included in the conference report to indicate
the richness and diversity of salvation to which the participants testified. "An Affirmation on Salvation Today"[140] sought
to embrace what the whole conference was striving for--a comprehensive notion of salvation which integrated the personal and
corporate, individual and social, ecclesiastical and secular
dimensions of salvation.

At least two different descriptions of salvation were offered in the Bangkok report. The first, from Section II, "Salvation and Social Justice," pointed to the comprehensive significance of salvation, bringing wholeness to all life.

> The salvation which Christ brought, and in which we
> participate, offers a comprehensive wholeness in this
> divided life. We understand salvation as newness of
> life--the unfolding of true humanity in the fulness
> of God (Col. 2:9). It is salvation of the soul and
> the body, of the individual and society, mankind and
> "the groaning creation" (Rom. 8:19). As evil works
> both in personal life and in exploitative social
> structures which humiliate humankind, so God's justice
> manifests itself both in the justification of the sin-
> ner and in social and political justice.[141]

Specifically relating salvation to various liberation movements at work in the world, it was affirmed that: "we see the struggles for economic justice, political freedom and cultural renewal as elements in the total liberation of the world through the mission of God."[142]

Clearly the WCC concern for social justice and development, expressed at the Geneva Conference on Church and Society and at Uppsala, informed this understanding of mission. But the problem inherent in this statement is precisely that pointed out by Weiser: It seems to give "a blanket endorsement of any political movement" without adequately identifying criteria for judging whether it truly belongs to the mission of God.

The second description of salvation came in Section III, "Churches Renewal in Mission," which linked salvation with Christ's working in freeing people from sin.

> Salvation is Jesus Christ's liberation of individuals
> from sin and all its consequences. It is also a task
> which Jesus Christ accomplishes through His church to
> free the world from all forms of oppression.[143]

In this statement, the cultural-socio-economic dimensions of oppression are implied to be the consequences of sin. The church is regarded as the primary agent in God's mission for removing oppression, rather than the secular liberation movements to which the previous passage alluded.

An ambivalence runs through the Bangkok report which has its roots in the two different understandings of *missio Dei* which appeared as early as the debate at Willingen in 1952, came into open tension at Uppsala, and continued to remain unsolved at Bangkok. Should mission primarily be understood as

God's work in the world in which the church participates; or
should mission be viewed as something which God accomplishes
through the church in the world?

These contrasting views are evident behind Section II and
Section III, respectively. Section II suggests that the
churches themselves are in need of liberation:

> Without the salvation of the churches from their cap-
> tivity in the interests of dominating classes, races
> and nations, there can be no saving church. Without
> liberation of the churches and Christians from their
> complicity with structural injustice and violence,
> there can be no liberating church for mankind.[144]

This statement related closely to that part of the Uppsala
report which dealt with "the churches as an arena for mission."
The hope which was expressed that a church freed from "compli-
city with structural injustice and violence" could then become
"the catalyst of God's saving work in the world."

Yet Section III describes the church as the bearer of
God's mission in the world:

> It is our mission
> -to call men to God's salvation in Jesus Christ
> -to help them to grow in faith and in their know-
> ledge of Christ in whom God reveals and restores
> to us our true humanity, our identity as men and
> women created in his image
> -to invite them to let themselves be constantly
> re-created in this image, in an eschatological
> community which is committed to man's struggle
> for liberation, unity, justice, peace and the
> fulness of life.[145]

A significant new emphasis on church growth was added through
the influence of conservative evangelicals involved in Section
III.[146] A comprehensive understanding of growth developed
through the assertion that growth means

> at the same time the numerical growth of the church
> and the development of a new man in every person, the
> rooting of Christians' faith in local realities and
> their commitment to society.[147]

While the church is still central to this view of mission, it
does reflect the influence of other concerns, for example, "new
man" from the new humanity theme of Uppsala, and "commitment to
society" as a necessary implication and expression of faith.

Thus, Section III developed "a pro-church concept of evangelism
and salvation together with a pro-world concept of the church.[148]

Conversion, or the human phenomenon of change in a person's
or group's thinking and perspective on reality, was described
as the process through which in Christian conversion people are
related to God in Christ and are gathered into "the worshipping
community, the teaching community, and the community of service
to all men."[149]   The report "On Conversion and Cultural Change"
noted that conversion is closely related to the cultural context in which it occurs, even as salvation is experienced in a
specific cultural milieu.

The search for a comprehensive way of describing salvation
developed as an attempt to overcome the polarization of two
aspects of mission: evangelism and social action. Both were
considered essential to a balanced and comprehensive understanding of salvation.

> Our concentration upon the social, economic and poli-
> tical implications of the gospel does not in any way
> deny the personal and eternal dimensions of salvation.
> Rather, we would emphasize that the personal, social,
> individual and corporate aspects of salvation are so
> inter-related that they are inseparable.[150]

This attempt at formulating an adequate description of
salvation in which the personal and social, the individual and
corporate dimensions of life each find expression was the most
significant result of the Bangkok deliberations. John V. Taylor
judged that "to a remarkable extent Bangkok released us from
the old polarization between personal and social salvation."[151]
He attributed this in part to the pressure of the many participants from Africa, Asia, and Latin America.

However, at this point the conservative evangelicals, at
least one Roman Catholic and part of the Orthodox community
felt Bangkok was seriously deficient. If proclamation and service were "inseparable," why was so little said about evangelism?   Arthur Glasser had "deep feelings of ambivalence" about
the meeting because so much was said about the church's social
responsibilities and so little about evangelism.[152] Father
Jerome Haber of the Vatican was reported to have said he was
appalled that "I haven't heard anyone speak on justification by
faith. I've heard no one speak of everlasting life. What
about God's righteous wrath against sin?"[153] The Orthodox criticism spoke of the "essential shortcomings" of the documents
in which "nothing is said about the ultimate goal of salvation,
in other words, about eternal life in God."[154]

The strongest emphasis at Bangkok related to the analysis of the various aspects of the social dimensions of salvation. The conference listed four affirmations:

a. Salvation works in the struggle for economic jus-
    tice against the exploitation of people by people.
b. Salvation works in the struggle for human dignity
    against political oppression of human beings by
    their fellow men.
c. Salvation works in the struggle for solidarity
    against the alienation of person from person.
d. Salvation works in the struggle of hope against
    despair in personal life.[155]

These affirmations were offered as specific examples in which Christians could give evidence of the wholeness of life in sal-vation. Implications of this for mission became clear in the forthright appeal for involvement in the pressing social, poli-tical, and economic aspects of human need as the practical evi-dence of Christian commitment contained in the urgent pleas of the "Letter to the Churches from the Bangkok Assembly."[156]

Many participants at Bangkok expressed the need for diver-sity within the church. Section I on "Culture and Identity" noted that in the place of any one form of Christianity there should be "a rich diversity" in the way Christianity responds to different cultural situations. Black theology was cited as an example of an indigenous emphasis which had grown out of a special context.[157]

The issue of moratorium arose at Bangkok from the need felt by some churches to discover new patterns of mission. The report concluded that in order to allow "the receiving church to find its identity, set its own priorities and discover with-in its own fellowship the resources to carry out its authentic mission,"[158] a moratorium, involving the cessation of either funds and/or personnel for a period, may be advisable in some circumstances. Moratorium was never proposed as a policy for every situation, but as a possibility for some areas to enable churches to become mature, free from dependent relationships. By using the policy of moratorium, it was hoped that an authen-tic diversity in mission method might emerge.

The relationship between unity and diversity was identi-fied in this formulation:

Unity must be expressed; this is the essence of mission.
Diversity in structural expression and objectives is
    essential to our renewal and growth.
We accept this *diversity* in *unity* which we have in Christ.[159]

Bangkok marked an important stage in the development of mission theology in the ecumenical movement. By concentrating attention on the meaning of salvation, it sought to make explicit the heart of the gospel as it relates to mission in the world. The search for a comprehensive understanding of salvation, drawing together all the essential elements contained in God's gift of newness of life in Christ, was the hope and goal of the meeting.

The action-reflection methodology attempted to give concrete emphasis to both the content and the diversity of salvation as it was actually experienced by people from many contemporary situations. The diverse nature of the Bangkok report, which included some meditations, prayers, and litanies, reflected the broad range of contributions from participants elicited by this method. But the aim of producing a comprehensive understanding of salvation involving the personal and corporate, religious and social elements of salvation was not really achieved.

In comparison with the heavy stress on participation in movements for social and political liberation, salvation, understood as the renewal of the relationship between God and individuals through Jesus Christ, received slight emphasis. For this reason, the conference did not fulfill the hope expressed in the stated aim of the CWME: "to further the proclamation to the whole world of the Gospel of Jesus Christ to the end that all men may believe in him and be saved."[160]

Yet the search for a comprehensive understanding of mission within the ecumenical movement continued, and further fruit of this struggle may be seen in the Fifth Assembly of the WCC held at Nairobi in 1975.

HOLISTIC MISSION:
NAIROBI, 1975

More than two thousand people gathered in Nairobi, Kenya, in November, 1975 for the Fifth Assembly of the WCC to discuss the theme "Jesus Christ Frees and Unites." The 676 delegates from 286 member churches[161] shared together in study groups, hearings to evaluate the WCC's past program and performance, and in six sections to study the current concerns of the WCC. The sections were:

I. Confessing Christ Today
II. What Unity Requires
III. Seeking Community: The Common Search of People of Various Faiths, Cultures and Ideologies
IV. Education for Liberation and Community

    V.   Structures of Injustice and Struggles for
          Liberation
   VI.   Human Development: The Ambiguities of Power,
           Technology and Quality of Life[162]

Nairobi may best be described as a consolidating Assembly,
"firm on keeping and working out the programmes of the previous
period, anxious to make explicit the dimension of faith which
inspired them."[163] The thrust of Uppsala--to put Christians,
the Church and the ecumenical movement in the world rather than
over against it--was certainly sustained at Nairobi. Yet the
strong interest in evangelism, and the definite attempt to give
a theological rationale for the work of the church in the world
were efforts to make clear that such an involvement was in
response to the call of God, and a sign of the church's obedience to its divine vocation.

The most distinctive phrase used at Nairobi to outline the
mission of the church was the description of it as the whole
church bringing the whole gospel to the whole person in the
whole world.[164] The four elements of this phrase provide a
framework for understanding much of what Nairobi affirmed concerning mission in Section I, "Confessing Christ Today."

"The whole gospel" clarified both the content and the norm
for understanding the good news of God in Jesus Christ. It was
summarized in this way:

> The gospel always includes: the announcement of God's
> Kingdom and love through Jesus Christ, the offer of
> grace and forgiveness of sins, the invitation to repen-
> tance and faith in him, the summons to fellowship in
> God's Church, the command to witness to God's saving
> words and deeds, the responsibility to participate in
> the struggle for justice and human dignity, the obliga-
> tion to denounce all that hinders human wholeness, and
> a commitment to risk life itself.[165]

This summary outlined the full scope of the gift and task which
God offers his people through Jesus Christ. It expressed in a
comprehensive way the wholeness and newness of life which God
wishes his people to discover. What Bangkok had tried to do in
terms of a comprehensive understanding of salvation found its
explication here. The influence of Mortimer Arias and the
widespread appreciation of his address on evangelism were significant factors in the development of this thorough summary.

A norm for the presentation of the gospel in any particular
context was clearly stated: "we must remain faithful to the
historical apostolic witness as we find it in holy Scriptures

and tradition as it is centered in Jesus Christ." Only with
this kind of safeguard can Christians hope to prevent an accom-
modation "to our own desires and interests."[166]

The paragraph on "the whole person"[167] showed how the gospel addresses "all human needs." Forgiveness brings reconciliation with God, satisfying the hope of eternal life. Union
with God's people answers the need for community and fellowship.
The revelation of God's love for all persons puts Christians
into society as responsible, critical, and creative people who,
through the resurrection, can live with hope and courage as they
work towards the fulfillment of God's righteous purpose in
history.

God's love for "the whole world" was given as the basic
motive for the church's concern for all people. Those who have
heard of Christ and those who have not remain part of the all-
embracing mission described in this way:

> Our obedience to God and our solidarity with the human
> family demand that we obey God's command to proclaim
> and demonstrate God's love to every person of every
> class and race, on every continent, in every culture,
> in every setting and historical context.[168]

Several key ecumenical themes were compressed within this sentence. The reference to the Great Commission, the implied
reference to witness on six continents, and the inclusion of
culture as a specific concern, were each significant points
long discussed in ecumenical mission meetings.

The idea of "the whole church" being the responsible agent
for evangelism was one of the strong emphases in "Confessing
Christ Today."[169] While gifted individuals and specialized
agencies may share in evangelism, the entire church, beginning
with each local congregation, however imperfect, must actively
seek to fulfill the commission to carry the gospel to the whole
world, allowing it to permeate all areas of human life.

One sign of the commitment of the whole church to evangel-
ism was the number of conferences held within a two-year period
dealing with this vocation of the church. These were: the CWME
Bangkok Conference (1973) on "Salvation Today"; the Faith and
Order Conference at Accra (1974) on "Giving an Account of the
Hope that is Within Us"; the International Congress on World
Evangelization at Lausanne (1974); the 1974 Synod of Bishops of
the Roman Catholic Church on "Evangelization in the Modern
World."[170] This widespread interest in evangelism by all
branches of the church continued at Nairobi.

The relationship between the church and its mission
received considerable attention in both Sections I and II at
Nairobi. Identified as a crucial element in the church's proclamation of Christ was the personal nature of Christian witness by individuals and the community of faith, for

> nothing can replace the living witness in words and
> deeds of Christian persons, groups and congregations
> who participate in the sufferings and joys, in the
> struggles and celebrations, in the frustrations and
> hopes of the people with whom they want to share the
> gospel.[171]

Nairobi acknowledged that the search for cultural identity
will shape the way in which Christ is confessed in a particular
setting.[172] Yet the diversity of the church's witness in various cultural settings finds a unity in that each proclaims
Christ as God and Saviour according to the Scriptures.

The participation of the church in oppressive and dehu-
manizing structures (for example, forms of racism, sexism, economic structures, and some forms of nationalism), could obscure
the witness of Christ which the church seeks to give. Nairobi
called on Christians to address public issues in the name of
Christ and to adopt a life style appropriate to discipleship.[173]

Once more, the church became the focal point of ecumenical
mission theology at Nairobi. The disregard of the local congregation evident in *The Church For Others* was overcome. But the
point that the church must be responsive to the context of the
world in which it is situated was reaffirmed, and may be seen
as a deepening of a concern for an indigenous church, evident
in mission discussions throughout the whole of this century.

Evangelism and social action were affirmed as having an
integral relationship. The confession of Christ in word and
deed, in a holistic approach to mission, was one of the strongest emphases at Nairobi. The task of mission, committed by
Christ to His disciples, was described in this way:

> Christians are called to engage in both evangelism and
> social action. We are commissioned to proclaim the
> gospel of Christ to the ends of the earth. Simulta-
> neously, we are commanded to struggle to realize God's
> will for peace, justice, and freedom throughout society. [174]

Clearly the Fifth Assembly affirmed that evangelism and social
action cannot be separated from one another without distorting
the confession of Christ. In content, the gospel addresses the
whole person; in form, the gospel is communicated through word

and deed.

Considerable attention was given to the nature of the
church's involvement in social action. Philip Potter challenged delegates to realize that

> if, then, the issues of our time . . . are global in
> character and need global perspectives for action,
> there is urgent need for mobilizing world Christian
> forces to meet them.[175]

One of the most controversial of the WCC's initiatives has
been the Programme to Combat Racism (PCR). Begun in 1969, the
educational and practical aspects of this program have raised
the issue of racism before churches and countries.[176]

The last three section reports of the Nairobi Assembly
discussed and analyzed the staggering dimensions of the task to
be undertaken in education, human rights, sexism, racism, and
human development. Recognizing that the primary responsibility
for all these elements in the total developmental process will
be exercised by secular bodies, the basic task of Christians
and the churches will be "to assist in the definition, valida-
tion, and articulation of just political, economic and social
objectives and in translating them into action."[177]

A "sustainable global society"[178] was fundamental to a
criterion for working out these objectives. Only such a
society, noted Charles Birch, the Australian biologist, could
meet the threats posed to human survival by the population explosion, food scarcity, the limited availability of nonrenew-
able resources, environmental deterioration, and war.[179]

Here one can see the ideal of a responsible society transposed into a larger framework of the global society, and taking
into account the problems of energy resources and ecology,
which have emerged in recent years, as well as the long recognized dilemmas of war and hunger.

The description of unity adopted at Nairobi spoke in terms
of a "conciliar fellowship," in which

> each local church possesses, in communion with the
> others, the fullness of catholicity, witnesses to the
> same apostolic faith, and therefore recognizes the
> others as belonging to the same Church of Christ and
> guided by the same Spirit.[180]

This concept was chosen because

it enabled a clearer understanding of the universality
of the Church. Each local church lives in fellowship
with the others, each depending on the others, each
responsible for the others. Though each retains its
individuality, they together form one body throughout
the world.[181]

Conciliar fellowship relates closely to mission because it
recognizes the diversity of forms which the church must take
in order to become truly part of the cultural context in which
it must live and witness. Yet it also affirms that all churches
are "one in their common commitment to confess the Gospel of
Christ by proclamation and service to the world."[182] The notion
of conciliar fellowship encourages a legitimate diversity-in-
unity for the sake of mission.

The amended Constitution of the WCC as adopted at Nairobi
underlined the close relationship of mission and unity. Under
"Functions and Purposes" the first clause reads:

to call the churches to the goal of visible unity in
one faith and in one eucharistic fellowship expressed
in worship and in common life in Christ, and to advance
towards that unity in order that the world may believe.[183]

The purpose of seeking "visible unity," characterized by a
fellowship based on faith, the eucharist, and a common life in
Christ, was "in order that the world may believe." Unity must
be sought for the sake of mission.

The Fifth Assembly of the WCC at Nairobi was an important
meeting for the development of ecumenical mission theology. The
mission theology espoused at Nairobi commits the WCC to a
forthright confession of the Christian faith by word and deed,
and to a serious engagement with the world in which that confession must be made.

The recovery of a strong emphasis on evangelism (understood as a comprehensive act including the proclamation and
service of the whole church in obedience to Christ's example
and commission), indicated an appreciation of and a commitment
to the fact that the ecumenical movement was born out of a
desire to promote the proclamation of the gospel.

Yet there was no drawing back from involvement in the
world, either. Uppsala had taken the needs of the world seriously, with racism, development and the struggle for justice
and peace being recognized as real issues which must be addressed
by the Christian message. Nairobi accepted that emphasis and
strengthened the Christian witness which must take place in a

faithful confession of Christ. Lesslie Newbigin has rightly
commented:

> as compared with Uppsala, Nairobi was much more truly
> centered in the Gospel but it did not for that reason
> lose any of the sharpness of Uppsala's call for action
> in the world.[184]

SUMMARY

With the integration of the IMC and the WCC at the Third
Assembly of the WCC at New Delhi (1961), a theological vision
that mission and unity belong together in the church found
structural expression in the WCC. This completed a process
which began with the WMC in 1910, branched into the three
streams of the IMC, Life and Work, and Faith and Order, and
drew together again at New Delhi.

"Witness in Six Continents," the title of the CWME report
from Mexico City (1963), pointed to the understanding of mission as the responsibility of the universal Church involved in
crossing the frontiers of unbelief wherever they are encountered
throughout the world. New emphasis was placed on reaching out
through dialogue to people struggling for liberation: mission
must take place in the world as the common witness of the whole
church, bringing the whole gospel to the whole world.

These theological movements which were evident at Mexico
City developed rapidly and changed the focus of ecumenical
mission theology in the 1960s. The WSCF Strassbourg Conference
on "The Life and Mission of the Church" in 1960 pointed the
way. Students wanted to see the church active in the world in
a mission freed from ecclesiastical structures. Christian presence in the world became the new mode of mission in which
Christians participate in an open dialogue with the world,
seeking to discover where God is at work, bringing people
towards their full humanity.

The study on "The Missionary Structure of the Congregation"
in North America and Europe became a demand for a profound re-
orientation of the Christian mission. Emphasis shifted to participation in God's mission in the world to achieve *shalom* or
humanization. The local congregation seemed no longer to have
had any function in mission. Instead, the laity, involved in
secular vocations within the world, became the spearhead of the
missionary enterprise. Structures for mission would evolve
around the points of human need discovered in the dialogue with
the world.

Another major WCC project, the Geneva Conference on Church

and Society (1966), further developed this approach to mission.
The world context of mission was now understood to embrace the
search for economic, political, and social development throughout the continents of Africa, Asia, and Latin America, where
revolutionary movements were active. Mission pointed to the
need to share in the transformation of society toward justice
and peace.

At the Uppsala Assembly of the WCC (1968), mission became
a controversial matter when conservative evangelicals particularly attacked what they saw as the reduction of mission to
social and political activism. The report "Renewal in Mission"
was hammered out: It bears the marks of a compromise document,
reflecting a deep concern for mission in the world, and a call
for church growth to reach out to those who have never heard of
Christ.

After 1968, the center of the debate shifted to the content
of the gospel and the method of its communication to the world.
Growing interest in dialogue with people of other faiths and
ideologies developed as Christians in Asia and Africa struggled
to share openly and honestly the deep issues of religious faith
and of practical concern to meet human need.

The search for a comprehensive understanding of salvation
dominated the 1973 CWME Conference at Bangkok. While the
report of the conference reflected a variety of theological
opinions, the aim of striving for an integral approach to mission, embracing evangelism and social action, was accepted by
most within the ecumenical movement. Yet it failed to provide
a comprehensive description of salvation in its attempt to take
seriously the social involvement of Christianity. The dimension of mission dealing with repentance and faith received
insufficient attention.

Other issues surfaced: The need for diversity in expressing the faith in various cultural settings was affirmed at
Bangkok and at the Faith and Order meeting at Accra (1974). The
call for a moratorium on personnel and finance, to enable the
development of new identies and allow the establishment of new
relationships, aroused some spirited debate.

Much of the work over the previous years was consolidated
at the Fifth Assembly of the WCC at Nairobi (1975). Few disputed that the world and its problems and possibilities must be
the arena for mission. However, there was a renewed emphasis
on evangelism, and the church as God's agent for mission. The
church, by proclamation and social action in word and deed,
must reach out to all people to confess Christ. Nairobi
affirmed the whole church must be in the whole world, bearing

witness through dialogue, proclamation, and service to the whole gospel which God gives to meet the needs of the whole person.

Nairobi pointed to a convergence of theological viewpoints: it confirmed the emphasis on the world as the locus for mission and highlighted the concern for evangelism expressed at the International Congress on World Evangelization in Lausanne (1974), the Synod of Bishops meeting on evangelism, and the Orthodox contribution on "Confessing Jesus Christ Today." In drawing together these strands, it strove to present a comprehensive understanding of salvation and of the mission of God's people in the world.

NOTES

[1] These two points were developed in books published as part of the ecumenical study projects on the mission of the church. See Johannes Blauw's *The Missionary Nature of the Church: A Survey of the Biblical Theology of Mission* (New York: McGraw-Hill, 1962) and D. T. Niles, *Upon the Earth: The Mission of God and the Missionary Enterprise of the Churches* (New York: McGraw-Hill, 1962).

[2] *The New Delhi Report*, p. 426, "The Constitution and Rules of the World Council of Churches."

[3] Ibid., p. 116. For insight into, and background on, the development of this statement see Albert C. Outler, *That the World May Believe: A Study of Christian Unity* (New York: Joint Commission on Education and Cultivation, Board of Missions of the Methodist Church, 1966), pp. 50-52. Outler also noted the importance of the North American Conference on Faith and Order, Oberlin (1957) for furthering study on "the nature of the unity we seek." See Paul S. Minear, ed., *The Nature of the Unity We Seek: Official Report of the North American Conference on Faith and Order 3-10 September 1957, Oberlin, Ohio* (St. Louis: Bethany, 1958).

[4] *The New Delhi Report*, p. 121. Notice how "witness" and "mission" are used as synonyms in these last two quotations. In the report on Witness (ibid., pp. 85-86, par. 28) "witness" and "evangelistic task" are used interchangeably. This is a clear example of a comment made by Philip Potter that "ecumenical literature since Amsterdam has used 'mission,' 'witness' and 'evangelism' interchangeably." See Philip Potter, "Evangelism and the World Council of Churches," *Ecumenical Review* (ER) 20.2 (1968): 176.

[5] *The New Delhi Report*, pp. 88-89, 189-190.

[6]Ibid., pp. 251-252. This proposal drew heavily on an essay by R. K. Orchard, *Out of Every Nation.* IMC Research Pamphlet No. 7 (London: SCM, 1959), especially pp. 75-77.

[7]*The New Delhi Report*, p. 249.

[8]Ibid., p. 250. This was probably the seed which grew into the phrase "Witness in Six Continents" in Mexico City two years later.

[9]Ibid., p. 421.

[10]Ibid., p. 85

[11]Ibid., p. 86.

[12]Ibid., p. 193.

[13]Ibid., p. 116.

[14]Ronald K. Orchard, ed., *Witness in Six Continents: Records of the Meeting of the Commission on World Mission and Evangelism of the World Council of Churches held in Mexico City 8-19 December 1963* (London: Edinburgh House Press, 1964), p. 157. Hereafter cited as *Mexico City, 1963.* Cf. Robert O. Latham, *God For All Men* (London: Edinburgh House Press, 1964), p. 19.

[15]*Mexico City, 1963*, p. 174.

[16]Ibid., p. 175.

[17]Ibid., p. 158.

[18]Ibid., p. 158.

[19]Ibid., p. 175.

[20]Ibid., p. 153. This important question became the focal point for the next CWME meeting in Bangkok (1973) when the theme was "Salvation Today."

[21]Ibid., pp. 146-147. M. M. Thomas, the Director of the Christian Institute for the Study of Religion and Society at Bangalore, India, argued persuasively concerning the need for dialogue with modern secularism and the renascent religions because "for the first time they are in a situation in which Christianity can participate because the questions which they are asking about human existence and salvation are those for which the Gospel has the answer," ibid., p. 19.

22Ibid., p. 174.

23Ibid., p. 164.

24Ibid., p. 165.

25Johannes Blauw, *The Missionary Nature of the Church*; Hans J. Margull, *Hope in Action: The Church's Task in the World*, trans. by Eugene Peters (Philadelphia: Muhlenberg Press, 1962); D. T. Niles, *Upon the Earth*; "A Theological Reflection on the Work of Evangelism," *WCC Division of Studies Bulletin* 5.1 and 2 (1959)--Hoekendijk called this the "first ecumenical consensus on evangelism" in *Horizons of Hope* (Nashville: Tidings, 1970), p. 13; "Theological Reflections on the Missionary Task of the Church," *WCC Division of Studies Bulletin* 7.2 (1961): 1-17.

26For North American contributions see: Colin W. Williams, *Where in the World? Changing Forms of the Church's Witness* (New York: National Council of Churches, 1963) and *What in the World?* (New York: National Council of Churches, 1964); Eugene L. Stockwell, *Claimed by God for Mission: The Congregation Seeks New Forms* (New York: World Outlook Press, 1965); Thomas Wieser, ed., *Planning for Mission: Working Papers on the New Quest for Missionary Communities* (New York: U. S. Conference for the WCC, 1966); European contribution: J. G. Davies, *Worship and Mission* (London: SCM, 1966); Asian contribution: John Fleming and Kenyon Wright, *Structures for a Missionary Congregation: The Shape of The Christian Community in Asia Today* (Singapore: EACC, 1964); and *The Church For Others and The Church For the World: A Quest for Missionary Structures for Missionary Congregations. Final Report of the Western European Working Group and North American Working Group of the Department on Studies in Evangelism* (Geneva: WCC, 1968).

27See Georg F. Vicedom, *The Mission of God*, trans. by Gilbert A. Thiele and Dennis Hilgendorf (St. Louis: Concordia, 1965), p. 7.

28Freytag, Hartenstein, and Lehmann, *Mission zwischen Gestern und Morgen*, p. 54.

29See H. H. Rosin, *Missio Dei* (Leiden: Inter-university Institute for Missiological Research, n.d.) and the review of this book by Karsten Nissen in IRM 62.248 (1973): 495-497; also Johannes Aagaard, "Some Main Trends in Modern Protestant Missiology," *Studia Theologica* (1965): 244-245 and "Trends in Missiological Thinking During the Sixties," IRM 62.245 (1973): 11-15.

[30]Vicedom, *The Mission of God*, esp. pp. 5-6, 92-96.

[31]J. C. Hoekendijk, "Notes on the Meaning of Mission (-ary)," in Wieser, *Planning for Mission*, pp. 42-44.

[32]*The Church For Others*, pp. 14, 62, 75.

[33]Ibid., pp. 14, 77-78. Hoekendijk was also responsible for describing *shalom* as the goal of mission in a number of articles, for example, "The Call to Evangelism," "The Church in Missionary Thinking," and in Wieser, *Planning for Mission*, "Notes on the Meaning of Mission (-ary)."

[34]*The Church For Others*, pp. 63-64. Colin W. Williams had also noted this problem in *What in the World?*, pp. 41-42. The same question arose at the Geneva Conference on Church and Society in 1966.

[35]*Where in the World*, pp. 48-49.

[36]A phrase used by Hoekendijk in "Morphological Fundamentalism," Wieser, *Planning for Mission*, p. 134. However, the Asian study group deemed it highly important to focus on the local congregation as a minority amid a population adhering to other religions, and thus changed the title to *Structures For a Missionary Congregation* to reflect this. The Western group's thinking probably was shaped by the rejection of the patterns of old Christendom, while the Asians faced quite a different situation.

[37]*The Church For Others*, pp. 19-23, 70-71.

[38]Ibid., pp. 24-25; also pp. 80-81.

[39]Margull, *Hope in Action*, p. 279.

[40]Ibid., p. 280.   .

[41]*The Church For Others*, p. 75.

[42]Ibid., pp. 75-76.

[43]Ibid., p. 35; see also pp. 90-91. Cf. Hoekendijk in "Notes on the Meaning of Mission (-ary)," p. 48, where he stated, "In any missionary structure the existing confessional denominational differences are completely irrelevant." Other background work on unity and mission was not mentioned, for example, Margull, *Hope in Action*, pp. 224-246; Williams, *Where in the World?*, pp. 50-57.

[44]Hans Hoekendijk has called this study "the second ecumenical consensus on the work of evangelism"--see *Horizons of Hope*, p. 15.

[45]This widely recognized series included: Kenneth Cragg, *Sandals at the Mosque: Christian Presence amid Islam* (New York: Oxford University Press, 1961); Raymond Hammer, *Japan's Religious Ferment: Christian Presence amid Faiths Old and New* (New York: Oxford University Press, 1962); and John V. Taylor, *The Primal Vision: Christian Presence amid African Religion* (New York: Oxford University Press, 1963).

[46]Blauw, *The Missionary Nature of the Church*, p. 43. Blauw was quoting from R. Martin-Achard's work, *Israel et les Nations*.

[47]"The Christian Community in the Academic World," *Student World* 57.4 (1964): 357-377.

[48]Ibid., pp. 362-63.

[49]Colin Williams, *Faith in a Secular Age* (New York: Harper and Row, 1966), p. 12. For other discussions of "presence" see *Student World* 58.3 (1965) on "Christian Presence"; three articles in Donald McGavran, ed., *The Conciliar-Evangelical Debate: The Crucial Documents 1964-1976* (South Pasadena: William Carey Library, 1977), pp. 187-230; A. R. Tippett, *Verdict Theology in Missionary Theory*, 2nd ed. (South Pasadena: William Carey Library, 1973), pp. 49-63; and *The Church For Others*, pp. 29-35, 67, 78.

[50]Raymond Panikkar, *The Unknown Christ of Hinduism* (London: Darton, Longman and Todd, 1964), p. 45.

[51]Philip Potter, "Christian Presence," *Student World* 58.3 (1965): 211.

[52]"Openness," *Federation News* 5 (December 1964): 9-10; cf. John Arthur, "Critical Questions about Christian Presence," *Student World* 58.3 (1965): 236-239.

[53]Norman Goodall, ed., *The Uppsala Report 1968: Official Report of the Fourth Assembly of the WCC, Uppsala July 4-20, 1968* (Geneva: WCC, 1968), p. 31.

[54]*Nairobi, 1975*, p. 54.

[55]*World Conference on Church and Society: Christians in the Technical and Social Revolutions of our Time. Geneva, July 12-26, 1966. The Official Report with a Description of the Conference by M. M. Thomas and Paul Abrecht* (Geneva: WCC,

1967), p. 8. Hereafter cited as *Geneva, 1966.*

[56]These were:

John C. Bennett, ed., *Christian Social Ethics in a Changing
    World: An Ecumenical Inquiry* (New York: Association
    Press/London: SCM, 1966).
Z. K. Matthews, ed., *Responsible Government in a Revolutionary
    Age* (New York: Associan Press/London: SCM, 1966).
Denys Munby, ed., *Economic Growth in World Perspective* (New
    York: Association Press/London: SCM, 1966).
Egbert de Vries, ed., *Man in Community: Christian Concern for
    the Human in Changing Society* (New York: Association
    Press/London: SCM, 1966).

[57]*Geneva, 1966,* p. 9.

[58]In 1968 a major joint conference on development was held
in Beirut. See *World Development: Challenge to the Churches.
The Official Report and Papers of the Conference on Society,
Development and Peace (SODEPAX) held at Beirut, Lebanon, 21-27
April 1968 under the joint auspices of the Vatican Commission
on Peace and Freedom and the WCC,* ed. by Denys Munby (Washington, D.C.: Corpus Books, 1969).

[59]W. A. Visser 't Hooft, "World Conference on Church and
Society," ER 18.4 (1966): 418.

[60]*Geneva, 1966,* pp. 179-180.

[61]Ibid., pp. 180-181; see also p. 110.

[62]"World Conference on Church and Society," p. 421.

[63]*Geneva, 1966,* p. 53.

[64]Ibid., pp. 88-89.

[65]Ibid., p. 49.

[66]Ibid., p. 8.

[67]Ibid., p. 205. A consultation held at Zagorsk in 1968
considered some of the theological issues raised at the Geneva
Conferece. See "Theological Issues of Church and Society,"
Study Encounter 4.2 (1968): 70-81.

[68]Paul Ramsey, *Who Speaks for the Church? A Critique of
the 1966 Geneva Conference on Church and Society* (Nashville:
Abingdon Press, 1967), p. 75.

69For a summary of these addresses by H. D. Wendland of Germany, Richard Shaull of the USA, and Vitali Borovoy of the USSR, see *Geneva, 1966*, pp. 23-27.

70Paul Abrecht, "The Development of Ecumenical Social Thought and Action" in Fey, *Ecumenical Advance*, p. 252.

71From "A Message From the Fourth Assembly of the WCC" in *The Uppsala Report, 1966*, p. 5.

72Ibid., p. xv.

73*Drafts for Sections prepared for the Fourth Assembly of the WCC, Uppsala, Sweden 1968* (Geneva: WCC, n.d.).

74Ibid., Section II, "Renewal in Mission," pp. 28-32.

75Ibid., "Commentary," pp. 32-51.

76*Church Growth Bulletin* (CGB) 4.5 (May 1968). This is reproduced in McGavran, *The Conciliar-Evangelical Debate*, pp. 233-248.

77Arthur Glasser, "Salvation Today and the Kingdom" in Donald A. McGavran, ed., *Crucial Issues in Missions Tomorrow* (Chicago: Moody Press, 1972), p. 33. See also, Glasser, "What Has Been the Evangelical Stance, New Delhi to Uppsala?": 143-49.

78*Uppsala Report, 1968*, pp. 317-18, W. A. Visser 't Hooft, "The Mandate of the Ecumenical Movement." See also the report of Eugene Carson Blake, the General Secretary of the WCC, when he addressed this issue, ibid., pp. 286-89; and the speech by John V. Taylor, calling for a "passion for Christ" and a "passion for mankind," ibid., p. 24. Taylor appears to have been the leader responsible for shaping the Section II Report drafted at Uppsala. See David Hubbard, CGB 5.2 (Nov. 1968): 331. This edition of the CGB is also reproduced in McGavran, *The Conciliar-Evangelical Debate*, pp. 259-79.

79The exact text of "Renewal in Mission" is not entirely clear. A note in ER 21.4 (1969): 362 partly clarifies the situation by warning that in the official volume, *The Uppsala Report, 1968*, a preliminary text of Section II was printed by mistake rather than the version which the Assembly adopted. [This preliminary text of Section II was also printed in the IRM 58.230 (1969): 143-47 and 58.231 (1969): 534-60.] The ER note then says, "This error was corrected in *Uppsala Speaks*." But, *Uppsala Speaks: Section Reports of the Fourth Assembly of the WCC, Uppsala 1968*, 2nd rev. ed. (Geneva: WCC/New York: Friendship Press, 1968) states on the page opposite the Table of Contents, "This is a special edition of the same pages of 'The Uppsala Report.'" *Uppsala Speaks* therefore still contains the preliminary draft. It seems then that the final version adopted by the Assembly is the one in ER 21.4 (1969). The text found in ER was printed in substantially the same form in the CGB 5.1 (Sept. 1968); and the exact ER text may be found in McGavran, *The Conciliar-Evangelical Debate*, pp. 249-58.

Apart from some editorial changes, six differences can be noted between the final ER text and the preliminary draft in *The Uppsala Report, 1968* and in *Uppsala Speaks*. The final text makes the following alterations to the preliminary drafts:
(1) In Part I, "A Mandate for Mission," par. 3, the words "by the forgiveness of God and" are deleted and a new sentence is added: "The unconditional love and mercy of God offers all men forgiveness from guilt and freedom for each other."
(2) In Part II, "Opportunities for Mission," par. 1, "for those who have not heard the Gospel and for those who have" is deleted and this sentence added: "It has an unchanging responsibility to make known the Gospel of the forgiveness of God in Christ to hundreds of millions who have not heard it." (The preliminary text had substantially the same content in par. 2 (g), which was transposed as above in the ER text.)
(3) Part II, par. 2 (e)--Suburbia, rural areas--deletes "wives trapped in the small world of their children and chores" and adds, "dwellers insulated from the challenging issues of the world around them."
(4) Part II, par. 3, deletes "priorities" and adds, "activities as to whether they bear witness to Jesus Christ in contemporary and persuasive terms."
(5) Part III, "Freedom for Mission"--The Church in the Local Situation, par. 2, adds, "If a congregation is engaged in mission, it needs biblical nurture; if it is opposed or persecuted, it needs biblical encouragement; if it fails in missionary calling, it needs biblical vision. A congregation can be a living letter of Christ only in so far as it is rooted in the Gospel."
(6) Part III--The Church in the Local Situation, par. 5, deletes "in society" and adds, "appropriate to the priorities of mission."

One other important change should be noted. In Part I, par. 6, the sentence, "As Christians we believe that Christ speaks in this dialogue, revealing himself to those who do not know him and connecting [should be 'correcting'] the limited and distorted knowledge of those who do."

It is a serious matter when the exact text of a major WCC statement is not available until more than a year after the Assembly, with no statement of clarification in the IRM in which the document was first incorrectly printed.

None of the changes noted above substantially alter the thrust of the document, but for some who struggled at Uppsala over "Renewal in Mission," the inclusion of the phrases about those who have not heard the gospel, witness to Jesus Christ, and the biblical character of mission, does strengthen the total impact of the section on mission.

[80]*The Uppsala Report, 1968*, p. 28.

[81] Ibid.

[82] Ibid., p. 29.

[83] Ibid.

[84] Ibid., p. 32.

[85] Ibid., p. 35.

[86] Ibid., p. 28.

[87] Ibid., p. 88.

[88] Ibid., p. 13.

[89] David Allan Hubbard, "The Theology of Section Two," CGB 5.2 (Nov. 1968): 331. Hubbard, President of Fuller Theological Seminary, is an evangelical who has actively participated in ecumenical gatherings. Other contributors to the same CGB substantiated his opinion. Eugene L. Smith, the Executive Director of the WCC in New York, described Section II as "a committee document possessing the ambiguities and unevenness of such authorship." Philip Potter, Secretary of the CWME, noted "the document shows traces of debate and disagreement on some important issues." John R. Stott, Rector of All Souls Church, London, pointed to some "inner contradictions" in his assessment of the document.

[90] See Philip Crowe, ed., *Keele 1967: The National Evangelical Anglican Congress Statement* (London: Church Pastoral Aid Society, 1967).

[91]*WMC, 1910*, 4: 267-268.

[92]*Jerusalem, 1928*, 1: 407, 410-412. This was a mediating position between the main thrust of the preliminary papers which had stressed that values are to be found in non-Christian religions, although fulfilled in Christ; and the conservative

position held by many Continental delegates which accentuated
the fundamental difference between Christianity and the non-
Christian religions.

[93]See *Madras, 1938, Findings,* pp. 40-47; Carl F. Hallen-
creutz, *New Approaches to Men of Other Faiths: 1938-1968. A
Theological Discussion.* Research Pamphlet No. 18 (Geneva: WCC,
1970), pp. 30-38; and Carl F. Hallencreutz, "A Longstanding
Concern: Dialogue in Ecumenical History 1910-1971" in S. J.
Samartha, ed., *Living Faiths and the Ecumenical Movement* (Geneva:
WCC, 1971), pp. 59-60. Hereafter cited as *Living Faiths.*

[94]*The Evanston Report,* p. 106.

[95]For a thorough analysis of this study, see Gerard Vallee,
*Mouvement Oecumenique et Religions Non Chretiennes: un Debate
Oecumenique sur la Recontre Interreligieuse de Tambaram a
Uppsala (1938-1968)* (Tournai/Declee and Montreal: Bellarmin,
1975), pp. 83-215.

[96]See the summary by Gerard Vallee in *Living Faiths,* p. 172.

[97]*New Delhi Report,* pp. 81-84, 193.

[98]*Mexico City, 1963,* p. 144.

[99]Ibid., pp. 146-47.

[100]*The Christian Community within the Human Community.
Containing Statements from the Bangkok Assembly of the EACC
Feb.-March, 1964. Minutes--Part 2* (Bangalore: EACC, n.d.),
pp. 9-16. This statement was also adopted by the EACC Faith
and Order Consultation in 1966.

[101]Ibid., p. 16.

[102]Cf., Carl F. Hallencreutz, *Dialogue and Community: Ecumenical Issues in Inter-religious Relationships* (Uppsala: Swedish Institute of Missionary Research/Geneva: WCC, 1977), p. 29.

[103]"Christians in Dialogue with Men of Other Faiths," IRM
56.233 (1967): 338. See also "Dialogue with Men of Other
Faiths," *Study Encounter* 3.2 (1967): 51-83.

[104]"Christians in Dialogue with Men of Other Faiths," p. 339.

[105]Ibid., pp. 339-340. Note how closely this parallels
what E. Stanley Jones described in *Christ at the Round Table,*
(New York: Grosset and Dunlap, 1928), for example, pp. 11,
21, 189.

[106]"Christians in Dialogue with Men of Other Faiths,"
p. 342. The importance, and confusion, of issues in the
understanding of the relationship between mission and dialogue
in the WCC and the Roman Catholic Church have been explored in
a dissertation by Anton Paul Stadler, "Mission-Dialogue. A
Digest and Evaluation of the Discussion in the Roman Catholic
Church and within the World Council of Churches 1965-1975"
(Ph.D., New York: Union Theological Seminary, 1977).

[107]*The Uppsala Report, 1968*, p. 29.

[108]"The Ajaltoun Memorandum" in S. J. Samartha, ed.,
*Dialogue between Men of Living Faiths: Papers presented at a
Consultation held at Ajaltoun, Lebanon, March 1970* (Geneva:
WCC, 1971), p. 107.

[109]Ibid., p. 108.

[110]Samartha, *Living Faiths*, pp. 33-43 reproduces the full
text. Also found in IRM 59.236 (1970): 382-91.

[111]Samartha, *Living Faiths*, pp. 36-37.

[112]Ibid., pp. 47-54. This document has three parts: Part
I, "Preamble," is a brief introduction to the place of dialogue
in the WCC; Part II, "Points to be noted and issues to be
studied," assesses the significance of the work on dialogue for
Christians; Part III, "Recommendations," outlines future possibilities for Christians involved in dialogue.

[113]Cf. Hallencreutz, *Dialogue and Community*, pp. 32, 34.
Informal meetings on dialogue were held with Study Center
directors in 1971. A Christian-Muslim dialogue took place at
Broumana in 1972. See S. J. Samartha and J. B. Taylor, eds.,
*Christian-Muslim Dialogue: Papers Presented at the Broumana
Consultation, 12-18 July 1972* (Geneva: WCC, 1973). For a
listing of publications on dialogue since Uppsala 1968 see S. J.
Samartha, ed., *Towards World Community: The Colombo Papers*
(Geneva: WCC, 1975), pp. 164f. The strategic importance of
the study centers--of which there were 21 in 1970--for Christianity was outlined in S. J. Samartha, "Christian Study Cen-
ters and Asian Churches," IRM 59.234 (1970): 173-179.

[114]Samartha, *Living Faiths*, pp. 51-52. For a brief dis-
cussion of these questions, see Anton P. Stadler, "Dialogue:
Does it Complement, Modify or Replace Mission?" *Occasional
Bulletin of Missionary Research* 1.3 (1977): 2-9.

[115]*Bangkok Assembly 1973: Minutes and Report of the Assembly of the CWME of the WCC, December 31, 1972 and January 9-12,*

1973 (Geneva: WCC, 1973), pp. 78-80. The IRM 62.246 (1973) report on Bangkok has only one part-paragraph from the eleven paragraph section on dialogue.

[116]Ibid., p. 79.

[117]*Nairobi, 1975*, pp. 73-74.

[118]This cursory answer does not adequately address the problem of syncretism. See, for example, W. A. Visser 't Hooft, *No Other Name: The Choice Between Syncretism and Universalism* (Philadelphia: Westminster, 1963), and "Accommodation--True and False," *South East Asia Journal of Theology* 8.3 (1967): 5-18.

[119]For a specific example of Christian-Muslim dialogue, see "Christian Mission and Islamic Da'Wah," IRM 65.260 (1976).

[120]*Nairobi, 1975*, p. 79. While appreciating the aim of affirming the validity of cultural diversity, the question of the relationship between Christianity and culture has not been adequately dealt with in this context--the depth and the perspective of H. Richard Niebuhr's *Christ and Culture* is sorely needed at this point.

[121]For an earlier discussion of this Christian-Marxist dialogue, see "Dialogue Between Christians and Marxists," *Study Encounter* 4.1 (1968).

[122]*Nairobi, 1975*, p. 82.

[123]Cf., Vatican II, *Gaudium et Spes*, chapters 1 and 2.

[124]See, for example, Samartha, *Towards World Community*.

[125]W. A. Visser 't Hooft, *Has the Ecumenical Movement a Future?* (Belfast: Christian Journals, 1974), p. 66.

[126]P. C. Rodger and Lukas Vischer, eds., *The Fourth World Conference on Faith and Order, Montreal 1963* (New York: Association Press, 1964), Foreword by Oliver Tomkins.

[127]One part of the study on creation was the paper on "God in Nature and History," *New Directions in Faith and Order: Bristol 1967. Reports--Minutes--Documents*. Faith and Order Paper No. 50 (Geneva: WCC, 1968), p. 25. Cf., Conrad Simonson, *The Christology of the Faith and Order Movement* (Leiden: E. J. Brill, 1972), pp. 157-162.

[128]*New Directions in Faith and Order*, p. 132.

[129]*The Uppsala Report, 1968*, p. 17.

[130]*Faith and Order: Louvain 1971. Study Reports and Documents. Faith and Order Paper* No. 59 (Geneva: WCC, 1971), pp. 190-93.

[131]*Nairobi, 1975*, pp. 59-60. The concept of "conciliar fellowship" was recommended by a Faith and Order consultation at Salamanca in 1973.

[132]*Uniting in Hope: Accra 1974. Reports and Documents from the meeting of the Faith and Order Commission, 12 July --5 August, 1974.* Paper No. 72 (Geneva: WCC, 1975).

[133]*Nairobi, 1975*, p. 64.

[134]The Assembly of the CWME, meeting in conjunction with the conference on "Salvation Today," met on 31 December, 1972, and 9-12 January, 1973, and had 107 voting members. A majority of the conference participants (52%) were from Asia, Africa, and Latin America.

[135]*Mexico City, 1963*, p. 153.

[136]See especially IRM 57.228 (1968); IRM 60.237 (1971); Thomas Wieser, "The Experience of Salvation," IRM 60.239 (1971); IRM 61.241 (1972); and the abbreviated report of the Bangkok Conference in IRM 62.246 (1973); also ER 25.2 (1973) which has several essays on the meaning of salvation in various religious traditions.

[137]*Risk* 9.3 (1973). The selections vary considerably in style and content. Some seem to have only the most tenuous relationship to salvation.

[138]Thomas Wieser, "Report on the Salvation Study," IRM 62.246 (1973): 177.

[139]Conservative evangelical participants were particularly concerned at this point. See Ralph Winter, ed., *The Evangelical Response to Bangkok* (South Pasadena: William Carey Library, 1973), especially C. Peter Wagner, pp. 79-80; Peter Beyerhaus, pp. 113, 116; and Arthur F. Glasser, p. 148; also Orlando G. Costas, *Theology of the Crossroads in Contemporary Latin America: Missiology in Mainline Protestantism: 1969-1974* (Amsterdam: Rudopi, 1976), p. 319.

[140]*Bangkok Assembly, 1973*, p. 43.

[141]Ibid., p. 88.

[142]Ibid., p. 89.

[143]Ibid., p. 102.

[144]Ibid., p. 89.

[145]Ibid., pp. 102-103.

[146]Winter, *Evangelical Response*, pp. 81, 149-153.

[147]*Bangkok Assembly, 1973*, p. 101

[148]Orlando E. Costas, *The Church and Its Mission: A Shattering Critique from the Third World* (Wheaton: Tyndale House Publishers, 1974), p. 280.

[149]*Bangkok Assembly, 1973*, p. 76.

[150]Ibid., p. 87.

[151]John V. Taylor, "Bangkok and After," *CMS Newsletter* 370 (April 1973). He also reports the story of a conservative evangelical who said, "These Asians really do hold the two truths together. For them salvation means something completely revolutionary in their society and yet, for the sake of that revolution, they call men to conversion and personal faith in Christ."

[152]Winter, *Evangelical Response*, pp. 99-102; cf. Costas, *The Church and Its Mission*, p. 286.

[153]Quoted in Winter, *Evangelical Response*, p. 92.

[154]Patriarch Pimen to M. M. Thomas, IRM 63.249 (1974): 127.

[155]*Bangkok Assembly, 1973*, p. 89.

[156]Ibid., pp. 1-2.

[157]Ibid., pp. 73-74.

[158]Ibid., p. 106.

[159]Ibid., p. 102. Compare the same development in Faith and Order discussions inherent in the term "conciliar fellowship." The Faith and Order meeting in Accra (1974) also laid heavy emphasis on the diversity of the various confessions of faith in Christ.

[160]Ibid., p. 114, from the Constitution of the CWME.

161*Nairobi, 1975*, p. 4.

162Preparatory papers on each of these sections were published in six dossiers under the title, *Jesus Christ Frees and
Unites* (Geneva: WCC, 1974).

163A. H. van den Heuval, "The Fifth Assembly at Nairobi,"
ER 28.1 (1976): 97.

164The essence of the phrase was included in the plenary
address of M. M. Thomas, Moderator of the Central Committee,
and Philip Potter, General Secretary of WCC. Mortimer Arias
also used it in his plenary address, "That the World May
Believe," IRM 65.257 (1976): 17.

165*Nairobi, 1975*, p. 52.

166Ibid., p. 53.

167Ibid.

168Ibid.

169Ibid., pp. 53-54; see also, ibid., pp. 44, par. 11;
48, pars. 32-33; 49, par. 43; 51, par. 49.

170One can note also the Orthodox meetings held in preparation for the Fifth Assembly. The report of their consultations
was published as *Orthodox Contributions to Nairobi* (Geneva:
WCC, 1975) and included a substantial paper on "Confessing
Jesus Christ Today."

171*Nairobi, 1975*, p. 54.

172Ibid., pp. 45-46, pars. 21-24; cf. p. 64, par. 12 in
Section II.

173Ibid., pp. 47-48.

174Ibid., p. 43, par. 3.

175Ibid., p. 249.

176For a brief description of the history and activity of
the PCR, see David Enderton Johnson, gen. ed., *Uppsala to
Nairobi 1968-1975. Report of the Central Committee to the
Fifth Assembly of the World Council of Churches* (New York:
Friendship Press/London: SPCK, 1975), pp. 152-162; and ER 25.4
(1973): 513-519 and ER 26.4 (1974): 672-675.

[177]*Nairobi, 1975*, p. 123.

[178]Ibid., p. 125.

[179]Charles Birch, "Creation, Technology and Human Survival: Called to Replenish the Earth," ER 28.1 (1976): 66-79.

[180]*Nairobi, 1975*, p. 60.

[181]Johnson, *Uppsala to Nairobi*, p. 79.

[182]*Nairobi, 1975*, p. 60.

[183]Ibid., p. 317-318

[184]Lesslie Newbigin, "Nairobi 1975: A Personal Report," *National Christian Council Review* (India) 96.6-7 (June-July 1976): 348.

3

The Search for Regional Mission Structures

A regional consciousness has developed rapidly in Asia, Africa, Latin America, and the Pacific since World War II. Throughout these areas countries have discovered that common problems and geographical proximity make mutual discussion and support beneficial.

The churches associated with the ecumenical movement in Asia were the first to seek a closer association which could strengthen both the quality of church life and the work of the ecumenical movement and therefore pressed for a regional organization. This led to the formation of the East Asia Christian Conference (EACC), which in 1973 became the Christian Conference of Asia (CCA). A similar desire in Africa resulted in the All Africa Conference of Churches (AACC). Other regional associations have been formed in Latin America, the Middle East, Europe, the Pacific, and the Caribbean.

The growth and development of these regional organizations will form the substance of this chapter.[1] In a brief concluding segment, North American ecumenical agencies will be noted.

These developments are important in seeking an understanding of contemporary mission theology for two reasons. First, Christians from Asia, Africa, and Latin America have exerted a growing influence on the ecumenical movement through the leadership they have given to the WCC and its related bodies. Second, some of the concerns discussed at the regional level have become significant WCC priorities for study and action. One may note three matters of prominence in regional discussions: Joint

Action for Mission; the study of conditions concerning social,
economic, and political development; and the issue of dialogue
with people of other faiths. The urgent consideration of these
matters at the WCC has frequently been prompted by the importance attached to them at the regional level.

The relative importance of Christianity in Africa, Asia,
and Latin America is increasing as the number of Christians in
these continents grows. Certainly within the next two decades
there will be more Christians in Latin America, Africa, and
Asia than in the Western countries of the world. The most
rapid church growth is occurring in Africa and Asia. It
behooves Christians in other places to try to understand the
concerns and theological influences which have developed in
these regions.

The basic thrust of regionalism in the ecumenical movement
is not that the church should be more African or Asian than
Christian. Christians in these regions want to maintain the
universality of Christ's Church, but contribute to that universality in a way which is authentically African or Asian or
Latin American. Only such an indigenous Christianity can
counterbalance the strong Western character of much existing
church life. A strong regionalism, which brings Christians
into fellowship with each other and the church universal, can
help achieve that goal.

Many of the conferences held by regional organizations
include a large number of subjects on the agenda, but only that
material which is distinctive to the region or is important for
the influence which it has exerted on the wider ecumenical
movement can be included in this study.

CONFESSING THE FAITH IN ASIA: THE EMERGENCE OF THE CHRISTIAN CONFERENCE OF ASIA

The development of regional cooperation in Asia represents
a continuing development from 1949, with prewar roots. Indeed,
when Asian Christians met together at Bangkok in 1949 for the
First EACC, that gathering fulfilled a hope which had been expressed in Asia for more than a decade that "representatives of
churches and Christian councils in this area could meet and
strengthen their fellowship with one another, and make joint
plans to participate more fully in the life of the ecumenical
Church."[2] The idea had been discussed at the IMC meeting in
Madras (1938) but was dropped when war intervened.

1. Proclaiming the Gospel in East Asia: Bangkok, 1949

Evangelism constituted the central concern of the whole

conference at Bangkok.3 In "A Message to the Churches of
Asia," the ninety-three participants declared:

> Constrained by [Christ's] love and directed by his
> plain command, we declare again that the gospel is
> the saving truth for this and every generation, and
> we urge upon the churches of Eastern Asia the duty
> of making the gospel known to every creature.4

Conscious that Asian Christians must bear the primary obligation for evangelism, those present called for "the early
completion of the process by which the responsibility for the
missionary task in every place is transferred to the church in
that place," while at the same time acknowledging that "both
younger and older churches are bound together in a partnership
of obedience"5 in this task. The conference assumed that the
entire church membership would be involved in evangelism.

Participants were constantly reminded of the Asian context
within which they were discussing evangelism. The region was
in the midst of a gigantic revolution in which five colonial
empires had collapsed (British, American, French, Dutch, and
Japanese), and civil wars were still being fought in China and
Burma. Within a total population of 1,160 million in Asia in
1949, the church of 50 million, of whom only 16 million were
Protestant, was a small minority in every country (with the
exception of the Philippines) among a vast number of people of
other faiths.

Bangkok participants became firmly convinced that the task
of evangelism must be undertaken with a serious regard for the
cultural situation in which it is proclaimed. Many saw the
indigenization of the church as an essential prerequisite for
the effective communication of the gospel.

In view of the social and political turmoil throughout
Asia, the conference declared: "it is the will of God that the
Church should witness to his redeeming love through an active
concern for human freedom and justice."6 The widespread influence of communism challenged the participants.7 In an
instructive comment, Visser 't Hooft called attention to the
distinction between a social revolution, which seeks justice,
and the totalitarian ideology which is used to support communism. M. M. Thomas pointed to the concern which Christians
must have for social justice as the motive for involvement in
any revolution.8

A strong plea was made for religious freedom within Asia.
This fundamental freedom, which guarantees the right of the
church to proclaim the gospel, had important consequences for

evangelism, as the conference recognized.

The first regional conference in East Asia marked an important stage in the development of an Asian self-consciousness when it declared that Asians must bear primary responsibility for evangelism among Asians, actively pursue religious freedom for the sake of evangelism, and become involved in the social revolution transforming Asian society.

To the Christians in Asia, the EACC became an important symbol of sharing in a regional and worldwide fellowship.[9] In order to strengthen the churches in their evangelistic task and to establish closer contact between Asian Christians and the worldwide ecumenical movement, the conference decided to appoint an Asian "ambassadorial representative."[10] One year later, Rajah B. Manikam of India began to fulfill this function on behalf of the IMC and the WCC in Asia.

2. Christ--the Hope of Asia: Lucknow, 1952

As part of the preparatory process for the Second Assembly of the WCC, sixty Christians gathered at Lucknow, India, to discuss the subject: "Christ--the Hope of Asia."

Succinctly capturing the major thrust of the WCC "Rolle" statement on mission and unity, and the Willingen Assembly's proposals on the subject, D. G. Moses summarized the discussion in this way:

> It is quite clear that the mission and unity of the church, the apostolicity and the catholicity of the church, are two aspects of the one single entity, like two sides of a coin . . . . It is no longer a question of mission *and* unity but of "mission *in* unity."[11]

The strong desire to join together mission and unity, evident in Moses' statement, was shared by many at Lucknow.

This deep concern found expression in a recommendation to the Joint Committee of the IMC/WCC that the integration of the IMC and the WCC should proceed as rapidly as possible. As a first step, the Asians suggested that the study departments of the WCC and the IMC be integrated,[12] an event which occurred following the Evanston Assembly in 1954.

Two other proposals from Lucknow marked significant points of departure for future study programs. The report recommended that the Madras debate of 1938 on the mission of the church in relation to renascent religions should be revived, and study

schools for research into Hinduism and Buddhism be established
to complement the Islamic study center.[13] The WCC study, "The
Word of God and the Living Faiths of Men," authorized by the
Central Committee in 1956, may be seen as a response to this
request.

The Lucknow Conference suggested an intensive study of the
social conditions in Asia to enable the church to focus on the
major issues and opportunities in that region. Five areas of
concern were identified: land, population growth, industrial
development, international relations, and the church's role in
Asian society. Christians were urged to strive for the imple-
mentation of a Responsible Society in the Asian setting.[14]

The concern for the social implications of the gospel evident in these recommendations opened the door to a larger vision
of the Christian responsibility in society. Western perspectives had dominated the WCC thinking to this time--now Asian
voices added a new dimension to the ecumenical discussion.[15]

3. Asia Council on Ecumenical Mission

Some Presbyterian and United Church mission boards and
their churches in East Asia came together in July, 1955, to
form the Asia Council on Ecumenical Mission. This council,
while small in size, planned to take concrete steps for united
action in Christian mission, by allocating funds on the basis
of need rather than the source from which they came, and to
foster the exchange of personnel between churches in Asia. It
also hoped to initiate study projects on a number of subjects
of regional significance, for example, mission, stewardship,
theological education, and the use of mass media.

The theological justification for the new organization was
set out in the statement of principle.[16] It declared that the
whole body of Christ is charged with the responsibility for
mission: each church must therefore give and receive in the
sharing of personnel and resources, according to ability.

4. The Common Evangelistic Task: Prapat, 1957

The creation of the Asia Council stimulated churches that
were soon to create the EACC to consider establishing a more
permanent body on a representative basis. The members of the
Asian Council on Ecumenical Missions joined the EACC. The
Prapat Conference convened to consider this proposal drew 107
participants, including 44 delegates from 11 Asian countries.

Two convictions became evident at Prapat: first, the
Asian churches had become more aware that they were responsible

for evangelism in Asia and needed to share this obligation
together. Second, the unity the churches experienced in Jesus
Christ has to be manifested in some external way.

The Prapat Preparatory Assembly adopted a "Plan of Future
Action," which stated that:

> we have come more fully to realize that the churches in
> Asia are eager and ready to share in the world-wide task
> of Christian mission, particularly in the evangelistic
> task so insistently needed in our contemporary situation,
> and to engage in these tasks unitedly convinced that *"we
> can do together what we cannot do separately."*[17]

The meeting resolved that the EACC be formed,[18] with a
permanent secretariat of D. T. Niles of Ceylon as Secretary,
U Kyaw Than of Burma as Assistant Secretary, and Alan A. Brash
of New Zealand as Secretary for Inter-Church Aid.

D. T. Niles brought exceptional skills to the task of
Secretary. As a Methodist minister in Ceylon he lived in close
contact with the realities of Asian life. Yet his long association with the global ecumenical movement through the YMCA,
WSCF, and WCC, and as a preacher in every continent, enabled
him to develop the EACC as an instrument of fellowship and
cooperation between Asian churches, and ensure a more effective
contribution from Asia in the ecumenical movement throughout
the world. At the time of his death in 1970 he was both a
President of the WCC and the Chairman of the EACC.

Prapat signified the end of the old conception of mission
for the Asian churches.

> The distinction between sending churches and receiv-
> ing churches was found to be no longer tenable. There
> is but one world, one Church, one mission, one Gospel
> . . . . The era of the Church in East Asia has begun.[19]

5. Witness Together: Kuala Lumpur, 1959

At the Inaugural Assembly at Kuala Lumpur, the EACC was
formally constituted "as an organ of continuing cooperation
among the churches and the National Christian Councils in East
Asia, within the framework of the wider ecumenical movement."[20]
With 176 participants, including 99 official representatives
from 48 churches and NCCs in 14 nations, the EACC clearly
demonstrated a comprehensive membership.

The plenary addresses and commission reports challenged
the church in Asia to become a full participant in the dynamic

changes occurring in the economic, political, and social dimensions of Asian life.[21] The world now became the locus for mission. The EACC pointed to a movement in mission theology which
was to become widespread throughout the ecumenical movement in
the 1960s.

The Assembly addressed itself to the historic fact that
had long dominated the Asian scene by recognizing that many
churches in Asia related primarily to the denominational body
responsible for their birth and development rather than to
sister churches in the region. The weakness of this pattern of
relationship, which the EACC hoped to correct, concerned the
fact that

> the Churches in Asia have all suffered from isolation,
> from one another and from the universal fellowship of
> the Churches, because their relationships have so often
> been confined to one direct line with their parent
> Church. The WCC and the EACC bring the Asian Churches
> into new and wider relationships . . . .[22]

An important expression of the new Asian identity expressed
in the EACC was the recognition that many churches were now
involved in sending personnel and money to other lands as well
as receiving them. The "Message" from the Assembly declared
that "Asian churches are having to live in this pattern of
common sharing, and we believe that our meeting here will
strengthen these bonds and open up new ways of mutual helpful-
ness."[23] The Assembly report included a short survey of
mission work being undertaken by Asian churches.[24]

Unity for the sake of mission had long been stressed by
Asian Christians. At Kuala Lumpur the Chairman of the EACC,
Bishop Enrique C. Sobrepena of the Philippines, reminded delegates that many in Asia believed "the mission which the Church
and her people would undertake for Christ was inextricably
bound up with unity among God's instruments for mission." It
was his conviction that:

> Unity for its own sake is certainly desirable; unity
> for the task of mission which Christian disciples are
> summoned to undertake is urgent; and unity among all
> who call him Lord and would be partakers of his glori-
> ous and perfect kingdom is an indispensable requisite
> (John 17:21-22).[25]

In a notable lecture, D. T. Niles spoke on "A Church and
its 'Selfhood,'" pointing to a new consciousness among Asian
Christians of their selfhood expressed through the EACC.

> The selfhood of the church is its selfhood as a worship-
> ping community. It is its selfhood as the church in
> and for a place. It is its selfhood in the width of its
> secular engagement. This selfhood grows in relationship
> with other selves . . . . The EACC is one more expression
> of this growth of the churches in Asia into selfhood. It
> is the instrument of our resolve to be churches together
> here in Asia. It is the means by which we enter into a
> meaningful participation in the missionary task of the
> church.[26]

The EACC brought the churches of Asia into conversation with
each other, giving them a sense of belonging together, through
a visible organization which was a symbol of their unity. The
vehicle through which Asian churches could share in mission had
now become a reality.

Other results flowed from the evolution of this Asian
identity. The *South East Asian Journal of Theology* commenced
publication in 1959 to foster scholarship and contributions
from theological educators throughout the region, especially
those related to the newly formed Association of Theological
Schools in South East Asia, to which more than twenty institutions in eight countries belonged.

Busy years followed for members of the EACC. A series of
"situation" conferences, convened in India, Japan, and Singapore, discussed what practical steps could be taken to
strengthen the missionary outreach of the Asian churches. Serious attention was given to the idea of Joint Action for Mission. The aim of this work was "to keep probing each situation
until new vision is embodied in fresh obedience."[27]

An Asian contribution to the study of "The Missionary
Structure of the Congregation" drew together material from many
sources throughout the region relating to renewal for mission.[28]
These data proved useful at the 1964 Bangkok Assembly of the EACC.

6. The Christian Community Within the Human Community:
   Bangkok, 1964

The range of work undertaken by the EACC found a clear
reflection in the conferences it convened. Immediately prior
to the Third EACC Assembly a series of meetings discussed three
important issues--Responsible Parenthood, Asian Missions, and
Confessional Families and the Churches in Asia. Statements
summarizing the work of these gatherings were received by the
EACC Assembly and printed as part of the Minutes, so that they
could receive the widest possible distribution.[29]

Four important developments may be noted at the Third
Assembly held at Bangkok in 1964. The "Asian Missions" report
endorsed strongly the conviction that Asian churches must be
engaged in mission. Investigations had shown that over two
hundred men and women were serving as missionaries from Asian
churches, but some serious problems had also been revealed
because many were not being adequately supported.[30] The practical problems of responsible support, remuneration, training
and EACC sponsorship of missionaries were explored.

The relationship of Christianity to other faiths had long
been of vital interest to Christians in Asia. The report of a
Bangkok commission on "The Christian Encounter with those of
Other Beliefs" attempted to break new ground on this subject.
Several steps aimed at producing a deeper encounter between
Christians and others were recommended: The first priority
related to understanding the present beliefs and practices of
those with whom Christians would converse; second, Christians
should seek common ground on questions raised by all people;
and third, friendships should be established with others in the
common affairs of community life.[31]

The theological basis for encounter with people of other
faiths was grounded in Christ, for

He makes possible an unveiled and honest openness
between men when they seek to converse concerning
Him or concerning the world within which He has
wrought the new creation. He is open to men and
to the world: and in Him is the only true way for
the Christian to be open both to the secular and
religious man in truly Christian encounter.[32]

It was the firm conviction of the Assembly, expressed in the
report, that the Lordship of Christ makes such an encounter
possible and necessary as part of the mission of the church.
By the authority of Christ "the Christian community seeks to
bring all forms of human community to an acceptance of Christ's
Lordship." The final sentence of the report on encounter
summarized the hope and faith on which encounter is based:

The dialogical situation within which the Christian
encounter takes place is characterized, therefore, by
the Universality of the Gospel as it encompasses all
men, the Mutuality that is promised when the dialogue
takes place in honest and loving openness, and the
Finality of Christ Himself who alone is Lord.[33]

In a wholly new development, the EACC began fraternal
relations with Roman Catholics. Noting the vast changes in

attitude since Vatican II had begun, the report on "Relations with Roman Catholics"[34] rejoiced that Roman Catholics were now eager for fellowship with other Christians. While recognizing that serious doctrinal differences still remained, the report looked forward to EACC members and Roman Catholics sharing together in study, fellowship, service, and prayer.

Anticipating future developments within the EACC, the Assembly stressed that the laity would have to play the most important part in the church's witness to Christ. As mission theology in Europe and North America had come to focus on the role of the laity, so, too, Asians saw that in the discipleship of laypersons the presence of Christ would be made real and effective in the world.[35]

The participants at Bangkok decided that the time had come to hold a Faith and Order Conference in Asia. Two years later, after much preparatory work,[36] the Consultation gathered in Hong Kong.

7. Confessing the Faith in Asia Today: Hong Kong, 1966

The Faith and Order Consultation in Hong Kong undertook to produce a statement which would express their unity in Jesus Christ and to do it in such a way that it would be understandable in contemporary Asia. The missionary impulse behind the meeting was clearly recognized: the issues arose in the struggle to discover what Christians must confess together before the world.[37]

From the outset participants aimed at a confessing, in contrast to a confessional, theology. A confessional theology was held to concentrate on the things which divide Christians, and thereby become a source of division, while a confessing theology grows from confessing churches that are "committed in the totality of their lives to the Christian confession of faith in God through Jesus Christ by the Holy Spirit."[38] The confessing life of the church signified for the consultation "a whole life in which, in the depth of our being, we turn to the world in love, service and witness."[39]

The desire to confess the faith in Asia led to a double commitment: a commitment to the Christian faith centered in Jesus Christ; and a commitment to Asian society and culture in an attitude of participation with discernment. This two-fold responsibility determined the shape of the whole report.

The obligation to be faithful to God in Christ involved a discussion of several issues: What are the criteria of confession? The report noted several points. Is the confession of

the church grounded in Scripture, making plain the deeds of God
in history and leading others to commitment to Christ, and
establishing the household of God? The church must acknowledge
Jesus Christ and all that God has accomplished in him for the
whole creation. How can confession lead to a more complete
unity, considering the common life which the churches share
together?

At Hong Kong, confessing Christ in the world meant dealing
with the realities of Asian life. The religious pluralism of
Asia necessitated a consideration of dialogue. Political and
social ferment raised the question of the church's role in
facing these issues. Injustice, and the absolute claims made
by some governments, highlighted the difficulty of the task for
Christians who are in the world but not of the world. The
Faith and Order Consultation showed the determination of Asian
Christians to deepen their awareness of and commitment to a
genuine confession of Christ.[40]

While cognizant of the fact that to be alive to its missionary vocation the church must confess Christ concretely in
Asia, the participants were also aware that this confession
must happen in full communion with the Church universal. By
taking that two-fold responsibility seriously, the EACC sought
to fulfill its ecumenical mandate. By placing the Faith and
Order discussions within the wider context of the task of the
church in the world, the EACC consultation prefigured a movement which characterized the WCC Faith and Order discussions
from Bristol in 1967 onwards.

8. In Christ All Things Hold Together: Bangkok, 1968

When the Fourth Assembly of the EACC gathered in Bangkok
in early 1968, the war in Vietnam was escalating sharply. Thus
the first section of the agenda, "A Divided Church in a Broken
World," has a special urgency to relate Christianity to the
context from which some one hundred Asian delegates came.

The major task confronting the Assembly concerned devising
strategies and programs to "make the Christian presence effective" in the midst of traditional societies which were becoming
modernized and secularized.[41] A central problem identified at
Bangkok was how to achieve the "peaceful, voluntary, and at the
same time, fundamental transformation involving the masses" in
order to secure a truly just society, which must involve
"revolutionary change in power structures."[42] Specific areas
of concern included: human rights, urbanization, rural and
agricultural development, and the Vietnam war.

D. T. Niles, the retiring General Secretary, reported in

his summary of the first ten years of the EACC that its main contribution had been "to inject into situations ideas which we felt right at this time, to get key individuals in every country committed to these ideas, and then to put pressure behind these ideas so as to make costly any attempt to disregard them."[43] The most effective means of communication used by the EACC was the considerable number of consultations convened, from which had come recommendations endorsed by Asian Christians to which they themselves were committed.

Aspects of Christian mission developed by the Fourth Assembly included dialogue with Muslims, conversations to improve relations with Roman Catholics and conservative evangelicals, and practical aid to Vietnam through Asian Christian Service. Each of these matters arose out of the cultural context in which the church in Asia lived.

The specific question of Christian-Muslim encounter had not previously appeared on the EACC agenda. But, in view of the size of the Muslim population in Asia and the tensions encountered by Christians in Malaysia and elsewhere when dealing with Muslims, the report included a "Call to Dialogue." "Ignorance and fear make the Church introverted," Christians were reminded, while "it is to openness, with its attendant risks, that the followers [of] Jesus Christ are called" to live out in their lives.[44]

Members of the EACC undertook to improve relations with other Christians, particularly conservative evangelicals and Roman Catholics. The objections of evangelicals to the ecumenical movement were noted and plans made to encourage better fraternal relations at the Asian and the worldwide levels.[45] The Fourth Assembly rejoiced at "the possibility of new adventures in cooperation" with Roman Catholics and aimed at appropriate joint study and work ventures.[46]

The Vietnam war found Asians divided on some issues (for example, whether Chinese expansionist policies or intervention by outside nations--notably the USA--posed the more serious threat to peace), but united in their desire to find a negotiated settlement to meet the needs of the Vietnamese people from both the south and the north. The importance of the aid provided through the Asian Christian Service in giving concrete expression to Christian compassion rated highly in the estimation of Asian Christians.[47]

The Fourth Assembly demonstrated the hopes and possibilities and also the difficulties of the EACC. It had much to build on from previous gatherings and actions; but so much remained to be done within all Asia. The meeting struggled to

bring to reality the vision outlined by such leaders as D. T.
Niles, that through the ferment of ideas might come acts of
Christian fellowship, obedience, and service by Christian congregations motivated to reach out into society as Christian
witnesses.

9. Christian Action in the Asian Struggle: Singapore, 1973

     When the Fifth Assembly of the EACC met in Singapore be-
tween 6-12 June, 1973, significant changes were evident to the
121 delegates from 93 constituent members in 16 countries.[48]
D. T. Niles had died in July, 1970 and his outstanding contribution to the organization was recognized in the Niles Memorial
Lectures given at the Assembly.[49] Proposals for a name change
and reorganization were adopted, and the EACC became the Christian Conference of Asia (CCA) to give recognition to the total
area now included in its membership. In a structural organization three working units on Message and Communication, Justice
and Service, and Life and Action identified the program areas
of the CCA's activities.

     M. M. Thomas, the main speaker, noted that Christian
action in the Asian struggle was not a new theme for him or for
the CCA, as his summary of past EACC statements confirmed. Declaring that the transformation of all spheres of Asian life
had always been the goal of the Christian involvement in Asia,
Thomas pointed to the struggle for social justice as the crucial element in the contemporary situation, by which he meant
"the transformation of existing structures of State, economic
order and society so that the poor and the oppressed may become
full participants in the total life of society."[50] He concluded
that the renewal of the church and the spiritual and theological education of the laity must be accomplished if the churches
were really to become involved in that struggle.

     Much of what Thomas argued found its way into the section
reports of the Assembly. Affirming again that "the primary
agent of mission is the Asian church," the report on mission
stressed the need to "develop missionary congregations who are
reaching out in love, witness and service to the entire commu-
nity--and especially to the poor and oppressed."[51] The Life
and Action program spoke of the conscientization of the laity
in order to prepare Christians for effective witness "in liberating the people of the world from the traditional bondages of
social structures for the common good."[52] Strong emphasis was
placed on the vital need to reach rural youth. After listing
problems relating to health, education, racism, and citizenship
in Asia, the Justice and Service report declared that "conscious
people are beginning to be awakened to the fact that passive
expectation will not bring distributive justice and equal oppor-

tunity for all." Only constructive efforts would achieve these
goals "as Christians participate in the struggles of the peoples of
Asia for the total liberation and fullness of life promised by
God."[53]

Clearly liberation theology, most often associated with
Latin America, had deeply influenced Christians in Asia also.
Several major elements of liberation theology--the demand for
structural change in society, by and for the whole of society
(especially the oppressed), to achieve justice--can be found in
this Assembly's work. From involvement at the level of charitable service, the contribution sought of Christians in society
had now broadened to include action aimed at changing structures
of economic and social life. While this point had been raised
by Masao Takenaka at Kuala Lumpur in 1959,[54] the demand for
social change linked with charitable service had now become the
double thrust of the Asian emphasis on the role of the church
in society.[55]

In his report the retiring General Secretary of the EACC,
Kyaw Than, spoke of the aim of the organization "to develop a
vision of the corporate fellowship and mission of the church in
the world."[56] The work accomplished by the Fifth Assembly of
the CCA showed that Asians were taking seriously the fact that
"mission in Asia is now primarily the responsibility of Asian
churches."[57]

The CCA continues as an important ecumenical organization
providing a link between Asian churches and a voice for Asian
Christians in the wider ecumenical movement. The concerns evident in the EACC/CCA from 1949 onwards include a search for an
authentic Asian Christian self-expression, related both to the
Asian context and to the Christian faith--a confessing faith,
evident in mission and service in Asia. Consultations on a
wide range of subjects for the education of the total church
for informed ministry remains a vital part of the CCA's work.
The importance of interreligious dialogue for Asian Christians
is evident from the emphasis placed on this issue in CCA reports,
and in the leadership provided by people such as M. M. Thomas
and S. J. Samartha in the wider Christian fellowship. The
nature and aims of the involvement of Christians in society
constitutes one of the pressing issues for the CCA, which it
again addressed at the Sixth Assembly held at Penang, Malaysia
in June, 1977, when discussing the theme "Jesus Christ in Asian
Suffering and Hope."

THE AFRICAN STRUGGLE FOR SELF-RELIANCE

Africa's history in the nineteenth century saw the continent divided among the Western powers as they carved out

colonial empires. Missionaries came, too, and as they were
able to penetrate the interior of Africa, began the work of
evangelism, health care, education and industry. As in Asia,
the relations of African churches were principally confined
within the confessional family both in Africa and overseas.
The isolation of Africans from one another continued into the
twentieth century with tribal, political, cultural, linguistic,
and religious differences all barriers to contact between them.

The development of the All Africa Conference of Churches
(AACC) closely parallels the period of Africa's struggle for
independence from 1957, and still continuing in 1978 in Zimbabwe (Rhodesia), Namibia (South-West Africa), and South Africa.
The search for liberation and self-reliance in the newly independent countries provides the context in which the churches in
Africa have sought to relate themselves to African churches,
and to each other, in a growing self-reliance.

The first international conference on Christian mission in
Africa, planned by J. H. Oldham of the IMC, met at Le Zoute,
Belgium, in 1926. It focused attention on Africa's needs
relating to the church, race relations, evangelism, and education.[58] Three years later, the IMC created an International
Committee on Christian Literature for Africa to promote the
production and distribution of literature for use by missionaries throughout Africa.

However, it was not until the African delegation traveled
together to the IMC Assembly at Madras in 1938 that African
Christian leaders came together on a continent-wide basis. The
experience at Madras made a profound impact on the Africans who
attended. Mina T. Soga wrote, "My journey out of Africa turned
me from a South African into an African. Madras made me a
world Christian."[59]

African participation in the ecumenical movement remained
meager at this time. The First WCC Assembly at Amsterdam had
only six African nationals present. Within Africa it was not
until the 1950s that African Christians really came together
from all parts of the continent for fellowship.

1. The Church in Changing Africa: Ibadan, 1958

Following the Ghana meeting of the IMC over New Year
1957-58 (the first world ecumenical body to meet in Africa),
96 African church leaders from 25 countries met together for an
AACC at the invitation of the Christian Council of Nigeria.
Dr. Akanu Ibiam, Chairman of the Provisional Committee of the
AACC, described the profound impression this gathering made on
the participants in this way:

The ten days in Ibadan were a period of real and warm Christian fellowship. For the first time in known history, the Churches of Africa had an opportunity "to discover and love one another, to speak to one another, and to learn something from one another." In that atmosphere, charged with vision and inspired by high ideals for Christian service, the Church in Africa woke up from its slumber, so to speak, and realized with great force and intensity the tremendous tasks and responsibilities which were here in the evangelization of the peoples of Africa.[60]

The major decision taken by the meeting related to the appointment of a Continuation Committee and/or Regional Secretary to implement the report of the conference. This action laid the foundation for what would soon become the AACC.

A wide range of subjects found a place on the agenda at Ibadan, showing the major concerns of the delegates. The sections were: The Church, Youth and Family; The Church and Culture; and The Growing Church.

The discussions sought to relate Christianity to the realities of African life, and were summarized in the Message with the hope that in the midst of change, the church would fulfill its responsibility as the champion, teacher, counselor, and shepherd of the people. Particular attention was given the place of family life in African society. The conference again examined the thorny issue of polygamy which had caused so many problems for church disciplinary practices in the past, and made a plea for sympathetic consideration of the question. Participants addressed other aspects of African traditional life relating to marriage customs, bride price, widows, and female circumcision.[61]

Recognizing the basic changes taking place in the political, economic and social life of many African countries, the conference affirmed that the churches have a prophetic, educational, and pastoral role to fulfill. The movement towards self-government and the liberation of African talent and potential received strong support. The Message pledged the churches "to work for the removal of all injustices based on racial discrimination which we believe to be contrary to the will of God."[62]

Conference delegates rejoiced in a sense of oneness in Christ which they experienced as they met together. Many were filled with "astonished joy" that the gospel had spread so widely in Africa; yet the knowledge that there were millions who had not heard the gospel raised the challenge of evangelism, which was gladly accepted.

In response to a concern to improve relations between
Christians and Muslims, a request was made for a study center
to be established to aid the church in its mission to Muslims.[63]
This led to the founding of the "Islam in Africa Project" as an
autonomous organization, with Pierre Benignus as Secretary. To
fulfill the educational and missionary aims adopted by the Project, a permanent Study Center for Islam and Christianity was
founded at Ibadan in 1965 to train students and encourage
research in the Arabic language and Islamic texts. This important enterprise demonstrated the value of witnessing to Christ
in love as the truest form of witness, instead of a hostile and
aggressive approach, or a silence which communicated nothing.[64]

Ibadan proved a valuable starting point in bringing African
church leaders together to discover their common fellowship in
the Christian faith, and to explore some of the problems and
prospects Christianity faced throughout Africa. What began
there in unifying people from many African nations was of great
significance in a continent where eighteen countries gained
independence between 1958 and 1961.

2. Freedom and Unity in Christ: Kampala, 1963

In 1963, when 32 African nations established the Organization of African Unity, the AACC held its inaugural Assembly at
Kampala with some 340 delegates from 100 churches and 43 countries in Africa.[65] Ibiam spoke for many when he said the
establishment of the AACC "opens a new chapter in the life and
history of the church in Africa."[66]

The Constitution adopted by the AACC, and the five Commissions established to study issues relating to it--the Life of
the Church; Social, National and International Responsibility
of the Church; Youth; Education; Literature and Mass-communication,
showed a close resemblance to the work being done in Asia by
the EACC. The concern of the Assembly for evangelism, the
desire to deepen fellowship among African churches and the
wider ecumenical movement, the encouragement of Christians to
participate in the development of African nations, and the need
to build up the Christian community in faith and life were similar to the major themes of the EACC. Yet, D. T. Niles noted
how large in numbers and influence the church in Africa seemed in
comparison with the position of the church in Asia.[67]

The main thrust of the Kampala Assembly concerned the
acceptance by the African churches of their selfhood. For the
Africans, this involved both autonomy from outside control and
the ability to determine their own goals.[68] The formation of
the AACC became a sign that the church in Africa now assumed
primary responsibility for evangelism and Christian outreach

in that continent.

Implications of this for various areas of the church's life formed the substance of the report of the First Assembly. Missionaries and mission organizations were challenged to channel their efforts through the African churches in order to give the churches a sharpened sense of their own responsibility for evangelism in Africa. New frontiers for evangelism which the Assembly identified were the challenge of Islam, the urban and industrial areas, and Africa's new intelligentsia.[69]

The Kampala report encouraged African Christians to identify with and share in the aspirations of the African nations: "we exhort the churches on this continent to participate wholeheartedly in the building of the African nation."[70] Aware of the power of nationalism, the assembly spoke of the church as a prophetic watchman, "witnessing to the Divine demands for truth, justice and peace, and against all forms of oppression, discrimination, injustice and oppression," throughout Africa as countries achieve liberation from colonialism.[71]

The AACC was constituted as "a fellowship of consultation and cooperation within the wider fellowship of the universal church."[72] One of its important functions in the future would be the overcoming of doctrinal and denominational divisions, many of which had been created by the importation of ecclesiastical differences by missionaries, and the "foreignness" of many churches which led to the formation of African independent churches.[73] The presence of Orthodox delegates at the Assembly, and of three Roman Catholic observers, affirmed the universality of the church evident to participants, who spoke with confidence that God would use the AACC "as an instrument of His purpose to quicken the life of His Church in Africa."[74]

The First Assembly of the AACC demonstrated the strength of, and the necessity for, an African witness to the Christian faith--a witness that would include all Christians in a deeper unity, related to the needs and aspirations of Africans striving for independence and maturity. Another regional Assembly now stood with the EACC to bring a new perspective and voice into the universal Christian fellowship of the ecumenical movement.

3. With Christ at Work in Africa: Abidjan, 1969

When the Second Assembly of the AACC met at Abidjan, Ivory Coast in 1969, with some 160 delegates representing more than 130 churches and Christian councils in 42 countries,[75] the agenda reflected the hard realities facing Christians in Africa --realities with which the AACC had had to struggle since the First Assembly in 1963. Delegates came from countries which

had now been independent for several years and were "learning
from reality what it really means to be the Church in the
situations created by the aftermath of independence."[76]

Reporting on the past six years, the Secretary-General
commented on the problems caused by inadequate finances, the
difficulties of broadening ecumenism to include all Christians
in Africa, and the halting efforts to create African study projects and programs of action.[77] In addition, the AACC had been
involved in negotiations between African groups fighting in the
Sudan, and was seeking to help in the Nigeria-Biafra conflict.
Refugees also needed assistance which the churches sought to
give, along with other groups.

As the theme declared, "With Christ at Work in Africa
Today," African Christians were convinced that in the turmoil
Christ continues to work and they must work with him in the
realities of African life. Three sections indicated the areas
of concern:

  1. Working with Christ in the Contemporary Social,
      Economic and Political Situation
  2. Working with Christ in the Cultural Revolution
  3. Working with Christ for the Renewal of the Church

Essentially practical in orientation, the Assembly highlighted a number of areas where Christians faced difficult
situations in the context of Africa. The theological vision
underlying the work of Christians in the political and economic
sphere was described thus:

  All men are created in the image of God, are equal before Him, and are entitled to a share of the world's
  wealth according to their needs, and are stewards of
  the same.[78]

In both rural and urban development projects, the Assembly
stated the church's concern related to making society truly
human. The most valuable contribution the church could make
in achieving this goal involved the training of local leadership for community development.

The crucial need to relate Christianity to African culture
motivated several AACC projects. One of the most important of
these was the consultation of African theologians in Ibadan
(1966).[79] Cultural adaptation in liturgical forms presented
another pressing issue for Christians seeking to transmit "the
call of God in Africa so as to lead Africans to the obedience
of the Christian faith."[80] Only by the intellectual and practical adaptation of Christianity in Africa could the church

fulfill its responsibility to communicate the gospel in Africa.

Church renewal received much attention at Abidjan, particularly in regard to relations with other Christian groups.
The presence and active participation by observers from some
African independent churches, the Roman Catholic Church, and
some conservative evangelicals, pointed to the active work of
the AACC in fostering such contacts.[81] The Assembly faced the
task of getting churches involved together in such joint mission activities as education, medical work and evangelism. An
appeal sent to missionary societies and overseas churches asked
them to cooperate with the local church efforts at joint action.
Yet, much depended on developing financial resources from the
African churches themselves. This involved a discussion of
stewardship. Abidjan outlined the dimensions of the task to be
faced in the renewal of the churches in Africa.

4. The Struggle Continues: Lusaka, 1974

The years following Abidjan saw the AACC taking specific
steps to fulfill its responsibilities. In 1971, Canon Burgess
Carr, an Anglican from Liberia, became the General Secretary of
the AACC, bringing to that position of leadership valuable
skills developed while Secretary for Africa in the WCC's
Division of Inter-Church Aid, and Executive Secretary of the
Churches' Commission on International Affairs. His forthright
declarations have challenged and stimulated discussion and action among many in Africa, and the wider ecumenical movement.

A major initiative concerning evangelism reached an important point with the completion of a comprehensive religious
affiliation survey covering all Africa by David Barrett and
others in 1972.[82] At a follow-up consultation, it was learned
that of the 860 tribes of Africa, 213 were Muslim, 411 could be
called evangelized, and 236 remained relatively open for evangelism.[83] Carr spoke of evangelism as being empowered by the
Holy Spirit "to work for wholeness, liberation, repentance and
renewal," to which the whole church in Africa is called, "that
we should EVANGELISE AFRICA IN OUR GENERATION."[84]

The Third Assembly of the AACC in Lusaka, Zambia, in 1974
made its most prominent thrust in calling for a moratorium on
missionaries and finance from overseas. This was not a completely new idea for as early as 1971 John Gatu, Vice-Chairman
of the General Committee of the AACC, had called for a withdrawal, for a period, of Western missionaries.[85]

Five hundred participants (including 215 African delegates
from 112 member bodies) heard Burgess Carr press the issue of
moratorium at Lusaka, saying:

The call for a moratorium is a demand to transfer the
massive expenditure on expatriate personnel in the
churches in Africa to programme activities manned by
Africans themselves . . . .

After a hundred years of missionary activity in
Africa, the churches are still not able to *stand on
their own feet*. We are still far too dependent!

The simple truth about the moratorium is that we,
African Christians, have no desire to be the channel
through which the continued domination of Africa is
assured. Therefore, we are determined to move speedily
towards achieving self-reliance for our Churches.[86]

Two issues emerged in the discussion at the Assembly: the need
for Africans to be freed from their dependence on foreign personnel and finance, and the urgent concern for renewal in African churches to achieve self-reliance in undertaking the essential mission of the church in Africa.[87] It is this latter emphasis on self-reliance which has become the continuing thrust
in current budget proposals in the AACC.[88]

The underlying motivation toward freedom in order to be a
force for liberation and renewal in African society influenced
the way the Assembly approached other concerns on the agenda.
Discussion of theological education, worship, family life, and
the churches' part in the struggle against racism, and for
liberation and development, each reflected the urge to relate
Christianity to African society with a new freedom on the part
of the churches.

When the AACC admitted the Kimbanguist Church, the Church
of the Lord Aladura, and the Presbyterian Church in Africa into
its membership in 1974 it officially recognized what may be one
of the most important developments in modern ecclesiology: the
emergence of a new form of indigenous African Christianit· in
the independent churches. The ecclesiological and theological
significance of these churches has not yet really been assessed.
Yet Burgess Carr commended the self-reliance of these bodies,
and noted their creative attempts to discover new insights for
a deeper and more profound expression and understanding of
Christian faith in terms of African traditional religion.[89]

Lusaka strongly supported Africans involved in the struggle
for independence from Portugal, and for liberation in South
Africa, declaring, "we affirm our solidarity with the Liberation Movements." The report called on all Christians to stop
supporting oppressive political, military, and economic structures which "hinder the fulfilment of God's plan for full free-

dom and justice for all mankind."[90]

Concern by the AACC for human rights throughout Africa led
to a consultation on "Structures of Injustice" in early 1975,
which recommended that churches become actively involved in
"promoting human rights in Africa through training, awareness-
building, protests, encouragement and support for those in
society whose human rights are abused."[91]

The AACC's basic thrust of support for African liberation
--understood to include economic justice, liberation from all
forms of oppression and exploitation, peace, and an authentic
response to Christ as Lord over the whole of life--received a
firm commitment from the General Committee of the AACC in "The
Confession of Alexandria" endorsed by the committee in February,
1976 when it pledged "to continue the struggle for the full
liberation of all men and women, and of their societies."[92]

The search for African Christian theologies, understood as
the quest "to translate the one Faith of Jesus Christ to suit
the tongue, style, genius, character and culture of African
peoples,"[93] has been aided by the AACC as it has faced the
practical issues of relating Christianity to African life. The
call for liberation and self-reliance has arisen from the need
to overcome the domination of Western finance and personnel;
the thrust towards unity has emerged from analyzing the evangelistic task which still remains to be completed in Africa;[94]
the search for new styles of worship and ministry has grown
from an awareness that the independent churches had grown by
relating to the spiritual, cultural and physical needs of Africans, while other churches had been unable to provide a place
for Africans "to feel at home." African theology has emerged
from facing practical tasks; the themes of liberation and unity
for the sake of Christ's mission have been raised "in order
that the church may be an agent of God's mission for liberation, justice and reconciliation among men and women."[95]

The African struggle for self-reliance through the AACC
has developed rapidly from a tentative beginning at Ibadan
(1958) when many African Christian leaders met for the first
time. The pledge to join together in the AACC "as a fellowship
of consultation and cooperation within the wider fellowship of
the universal church" led to a determined effort to seek African selfhood in the churches, and to an identification and participation in the African struggle for independence.

The implications of this struggle became clearer to the
AACC churches through continuing studies of their actual situation and that of the nations in which they exist. From these
studies emerged the emphasis on evangelism, development and

renewal, and, finally, liberation and self-reliance. Although
the AACC is a strong voice, with able leaders like Burgess Carr
and John Gatu, its membership represents only a small number of
the many churches throughout Africa. But it has raised the
Issues which African Christians must face in seeking to relate
Christianity to their life and culture in the new era of independence.

THE SEARCH FOR A REVOLUTIONARY
CHRISTIANITY IN LATIN AMERICA

Latin America has traditionally been regarded as a predominantly Roman Catholic region. Yet by its own admission,
Catholicism has been weak with reference to the deep allegiance
of the masses and anti-clericalism has been a recurrent factor
in the struggle for independence. Still, Protestantism in
Latin America has been characterized by its minority status,
with many continuing divisions. By the 1960s, Pentecostal
churches in Latin America accounted for nearly two-thirds
(sixty-three percent) of the total Protestant membership, while
mainline denominations comprised about twenty-five percent of
the total membership.[96] Only ten percent of the Protestants
belong to churches in membership with the WCC. Many of the
churches have strong anti-Catholic sentiments and work in complete isolation from one another.

Regional meetings of Protestants have not really been able
to overcome the fragmentation, and while some countries have
continuing bodies for discussion and limited cooperation, no
body equivalent to the Asian and African regional ecumenical
organizations has come into existence.

1. Panama, 1916

Several continent-wide meetings occurred in Latin America
prior to World War II. Following the 1910 WMC (which excluded
discussion of Latin American missionary activity), the Congress
on Christian Work in Latin America, arranged by the Committee
on Cooperation in Latin America of the Foreign Missions Conference of the USA, met in Panama from 10-19 February, 1916. It
was a near replica of the WMC, with Mott present to chair the
business sessions, and the same eight commissions used in preliminary studies. This congress of nearly five hundred nationals and missionaries from Latin America conducted a thorough
analysis and survey of mission work in the continent.[97] The
Committee on Cooperation in Latin America became the authorized
continuing organization. Subsequent national conferences met
in eight countries. A series of National Christian Councils
gradually came into existence.[98]

2. Montevideo, 1925

In 1925, the Second Congress of Christian Work in South
America met in Montevideo, Uruguay. Unlike the Panama Congress,
which had been heavily dependent on missionary leadership, the
Montevideo Congress was almost wholly conducted by nationals,
with Spanish the main language.[99] While many churches reported
significant growth in membership, the conference also revealed
the great diversity among South American countries and the
resultant difficulty in attempting to plan for overall cooperation. The Congress stressed the churches' social responsibility in Latin America, with education being a key tool in
missionary strategy.

3. Havana, 1929

An Hispanic American Evangelical Congress, organized and
led completely by Spanish speaking evangelicals, held in
Havana in 1929, gave further evidence of the growing maturity
of Protestantism in Mexico, Central America, and the Caribbean
area. At this Congress, the establishment of a Latin American
Evangelical Federation was recommended for the first time.[100]
But two decades passed before Latin American Christian leaders
pursued this matter.

4. Latin American Evangelical Conference:
   Buenos Aires, 1949

Prompted by a suggestion from the NCCs in Mexico and the
River Plate area, delegates at the Whitby meeting of the IMC
(1947) planned for a study conference called the First Latin
American Evangelical Conference (CELA I) which met in Buenos
Aires in July, 1949, with some one hundred delegates and visitors.[101] Under the leadership of the conference president,
Dr. S. U. Barbieri, a Methodist from Argentina, participants
considered the background of Protestantism in Latin America,
its message and mission, and the strategies and priorities for
the future. Particular emphasis was given to the Bible as the
foundation of the Christian message of salvation which trans-
forms individuals,[102] as well as the social and institutional
orders of life. The report linked evangelism, education, and
social action as the constituent elements of the Christian mission. While closer cooperation between denominations was recommended by the conference, nothing was done to assure this goal.

Other ecumenical agencies began work in Latin America in
the 1950s. The WSCF appointed Valdo Galland as traveling
secretary for the continent, and he expanded and intensified
work among students. The WCC's Church and Society study on
rapid social change held five consultations on the Christian

responsibility in society in Brazil and the River Plate area
and staff visited other countries.[103]

5. CELA II: Lima, 1961

When the Second Latin American Evangelical Conference met
in Lima, Peru from July 29-August 6, 1961, new emphases were
evident, in addition to a continued concern for evangelism and
Christian education.[104] The 220 delegates and visitors from 34
denominations, representing all of the Latin American countries
except Panama and Nicaragua, heard a report from a consultation
on Church and Society, which called for Christians to become
deeply involved in the struggle for social justice in Latin
America.[105] With new seriousness, the delegates faced the
basic problem of underdevelopment as evidenced by the low stan-
dard of living of most people in Latin America and by the un-
equal distribution of wealth and income. They pledged to discover how the gospel message could be applied to assist in the
process of social transformation, a concern expressed especially
by the laity in South America.[106] The conference basically
sought the development of society through educational reform,
widening the democratic process, and the reform of social
structures.[107] It also proposed a Continuation Committee to
maintain links between churches in Latin America.

Some Protestant leaders wanted a stronger regional organization, and in 1964 formed the Provisional Committee on Christian Unity in Latin America (UNELAM) with Emilio Castro, Uruguay's most widely known Methodist minister, as General Secretary. Created with the intention of becoming a "permanent
organism for consultations and encounters among the Protestant
churches of Latin America," UNELAM began officially in 1965 at
a constituent Assembly in Campinas, Brazil.[108] UNELAM sought
to be an autonomous and broadly representative organization,
but was widely viewed in Latin America as an agency of the WCC.

3. CELA III: Buenos Aires, 1969

A year after the landmark meeting of the Latin American
Roman Catholic bishops at Medellin, Protestants held the Third
CELA at Buenos Aires in July, 1969. UNELAM had helped to promote the gathering. With 43 churches, ecclesiastical bodies
and para-church organizations represented, and with conservative evangelicals and Pentecostals present, CELA III represented
a wider range of Protestants than had previously gathered in
Latin America.

In a reciprocal invitation for the Roman Catholics' recognition of two Protestant observers at the Medellin Conference
(1968), two official Roman Catholic observers were present at

Buenos Aires.[109] The influence of Vatican II in producing this change of attitude between Roman Catholics and Protestants was gratefully acknowledged, although it was also recognized that:

> there are still other great sectors of the Roman
> Catholic Church which in their attitude and actions
> reflect an almost complete lack of any influence of
> these new tendencies.[110]

The major impact of the Third CELA on Protestant mission theology in Latin America related to the new understanding of the context of mission which it revealed, and of the consequent changes in mission strategy which that understanding required. The Roman Catholic Conference at Medellin (1968) had pointed to the socio-political oppression of many people in Latin America, and urged the participation of Christians in the process of transforming political systems from structures of oppression to achieve the liberation and humanization of society. The CELA Conference also followed a similar line of thinking.[111]

The theological undergirding for this participation in society pointed to the incarnation of Christ as the model for Christian obedience, in which through identification and service, Christians witness to new life in Christ.[112] Explicit acknowledgment of the Holy Spirit as the dynamic power in the creation of a new humanity and in the renewal of the church came through the presence and impact of Pentecostals at CELA III.

The question of unity again proved a difficult one. A report recognized that a fundamental impediment to cooperative action involved the serious lack of communication between Protestant groups and churches. In a resolution addressed to UNELAM, the Third CELA commended UNELAM's work and asked that body to organize and coordinate future CELA meetings.[113]

Those who sought to strengthen UNELAM for a larger role restructured that organization in June, 1970, to broaden its constituency from NCCs alone to include also other associations, Protestant groups and unaffiliated churches.[114] However, while UNELAM sponsored several study projects, the organization suffered a severe crisis of leadership when Emilio Castro left to become Director of the WCC's CWME. It has never really been a strong regional ecumenical organization.[115]

Two other regional organizations have contributed to a greater understanding of the mission of the church in Latin America through the study of particular areas of concern. The Latin American Evangelical Council of Christian Education (CELADEC) and also the movement for Church and Society in Latin America (ISAL) began just prior to the Second CELA in 1961.

CELADEC attempted to stimulate and coordinate Protestant
involvement in Christian education and ISAL had promoted the
study of issues involving the Christian responsibility in and
to society.[116] Both became proponents of liberation theology
in the 1970s.

     Finding suitable ecumenical structures in and for Latin
America thus far has proven to be an intractable problem. In
his summary statement on recent attempts at ecumenical activity,
Costas concluded:

> none of the forms that the quest for an authentic ecu-
> menism has taken have been able to produce an effective
> solution to the urgent practical problems of organiza-
> tional competition, interecclesial and interecclesias-
> tical strife and missiological imperatives.[117]

While more frequent contacts between various Protestant churches
and groups have occurred, and substantial and enduring relations have been fostered between some Protestants and Roman
Catholics, the search for any broadly based organization to
stimulate, coordinate, and implement study and action concerning the mission of the church in Latin America remains a challenge which still has to be met.

OTHER REGIONAL ORGANIZATIONS

     Having traced the development of the major regional ecu-
menical bodies in Asia, Africa, and Latin America, the rather
more limited organizations which have emerged in the Middle
East, Europe, the Pacific, and the Caribbean will be dealt with
more briefly. Because they are so well known, the important
ecumenical agencies in North America can be covered concisely
in this survey.

1. The Middle East

     The Middle East is the cradle of Judaism, Christianity and
Islam. In the predominantly Muslim countries that spread in an
arc from Pakistan to Morocco, the small Christian minorities
have been deeply divided among various ancient Eastern churches,
the Roman Catholic Church, and numerous Protestant bodies.
Cooperation and ecumenical activity among churches has been
difficult.

     Following conferences on Christian work among Muslims in
1911 at Lucknow and a more extensive series of meetings in 1924
under the leadership of John R. Mott, committees for literature
promotion and cooperative activity were formed, which, in 1929,
became the Near East Christian Council (NECC), with Robert P.

Wilder as its first secretary. It remained an almost exclusively Protestant body.[118]

The Christian approach to Islam constituted a major concern of the NECC, and a study pamphlet series, *Operation Reach* (1957-1962) prepared Christians for their missionary encounter with Muslims. A study conference held in 1959 at Asmara, Eritrea, expressed a new spirit, a penitence, and hope for better relations with Muslims: "We wish to relate the Christian message constructively to Islamic thought and experience and to enter as fully as we may into areas of mutual practical concern."[119]

In recent years relations between Protestant and Orthodox Churches have improved for several reasons. The WSCF sponsored ecumenical work camps and regional activity, promoted by WSCF regional Secretary, Gabi Habib, produced fruitful contacts. The Orthodox participation in the WCC stimulated new contacts and reduced misunderstanding and complaints about proselytism, as well as creating a new interest by the Orthodox in evangelism.[120] The enormous numbers of refugees stranded after the Arab-Israeli wars brought Protestants and Orthodox together in relief work. In 1964 the NECC reconstituted itself as the Near East Council of Churches, becoming a more inclusive body. Fuller participation by the Orthodox led to another change in 1974 when the Middle East Council of Churches was formed; at the time all the historic Orthodox churches in the area, together with the Protestant churches, joined in an ecumenical fellowship.[121]

The most important factors in the development of ecumenical relations in the Middle East relate to a desire to witness effectively with the Muslim population; the urgent needs of the refugees, requiring joint action for the best possible assistance; and a desire for Christian fellowship.

2. Europe

National and ecclesiastical differences in Europe restricted the scope for ecumenical activities for the first half of the twentieth century, even though some Christian leaders, among them G. K. A. Bell, Nathan Söderblom, and W. A. Visser 't Hooft, maintained contacts with Christians throughout Europe. During and after World War II, the Inter-Church Aid and Service to Refugees Department of the WCC assisted in many European countries.

Not until January, 1959, at Nyborg, Denmark, did a substantial number of small Protestant--as well as Lutheran, Anglican and Orthodox--churches meet to begin the succession of "Nyborg" meetings. The fourth of these inaugurated the Conference of European Churches (CEC). Indeed, in October, 1964, it had to gather at sea on board the M.S. "Bornholm" to overcome visa difficulties for some participants from the German Democratic Republic.[122] By 1968, the CEC had appointed a full-time Secretary.

The CEC has found it difficult to become a strong regional body. Participants have mostly been limited to bishops, church presidents, and pastors, with little lay involvement. The linguistic, political and cultural divisions of the Continent itself hinder close cooperation. Also, the number of other organizations of a confessional and ecclesiastical character appear to prevent the CEC from being a truly effective voice for the ecumenical movement in Europe.[123]

3. The Pacific

Christianity's progress through the South Pacific islands marks one of the truly heroic missionary ventures of the nineteenth century. Yet not until 1961 did many of the churches and mission groups in the area first meet together.[124] Participants from an enormous area, bounded by New Guinea, New Zealand, Tahiti and Hawaii, assembled in Western Samoa to discuss evangelism, the ministry, young people and the church (nearly fifty percent of the island population was under twenty-one years of age), the Christian family, and the relationship of the gospel to the changing conditions in the Pacific.

The first conference formed a Continuation Committee to plan continuing study of these issues and to foster better relations between churches in the Pacific. Two significant events helped draw the predominantly Protestant Christian fellowship together again in 1966. In that year, with the inauguration of the Pacific Conference of Churches in May-June, 1966 at Lifou, New Caledonia, and with the establishment of the Pacific Theological College in Fiji, a new era of ecumenical endeavor began.[125] New work on Christian education and Christian communication began after the Second Assembly in 1971.[126] The Third Assembly broadened the membership of the conference greatly by inviting and receiving the Roman Catholic Church into membership in the Pacific Conference of Churches (PCC).[127] This numerically small but important regional organization has helped to develop strong relations among churches separated by distance, language, and tradition as they struggle to witness in the changing social and economic context of the Pacific.

4. The Caribbean

The most recent ecumenical regional organization to come into existence is the Caribbean Conference of Churches.[128] The

inauguration of this conference in November, 1973, demonstrated
how far ecumenical relations with the Roman Catholic Church had
developed in the previous decade, for the Catholic community
shared in the council as a founding member, and the Archbishop
of Jamaica, Samuel Carter, became its President. As with the
other regional conferences, its work has been to foster better
relations between churches and to seek more effective ways of
relating the gospel to contemporary society.

5. North America

      North of the Rio Grande, the North American continent
alone among the world's major regions lacks an all-embracing
ecumenical conference. Yet that observation must be qualified
by recognizing that the churches and agencies of this vast,
predominantly English-speaking area early initiated large cooperative endeavors. From 1893, for example, the Foreign Missions Conference of North America (FMC) linked American and
Canadian mission agencies in cooperative planning and action.129
Other ecumenical agencies emerged, especially in the USA, including the Federal Council of the Churches of Christ in America, from 1908.

      From conversations rooted in common and shared concerns in
the 1940s the Canadian Council of Churches (CCC) emerged in
1946, and in 1950, the National Council of Churches of Christ
in the USA (NCCC). The NCCC incorporated the work and functions
of eight earlier ecumenical bodies, including that of the Federal Council of Churches.130 The Canadian mission agencies,
once in the FMC, now make up the CCC's Commission on World
Concerns. Their American counterparts now constitute the
NCCC's Division of Overseas Ministries (DOM). The CCC and the
NCCC cover the continent in their cooperative work among member
churches.

      The DOM, for example, includes the whole range of mission
activities--evangelism, service, refugee assistance, education,
development, et cetera--on behalf of the member churches. The
North American ecumenical agencies have been active in other
projects also. Faith and Order studies throughout the ecumenical movement benefitted greatly from the work of the North
American Faith and Order Conference at Oberlin in 1957 on "The
Nature of the Unity We Seek."131

      Three stages may be discerned in the evolution of the
FMC-DOM. During the first period of its existence, the FMC was
essentially a consultative body in which administrators of member boards and organizations met to discuss matters of mutual
concern.

The second stage saw the development of a wide range of cooperative activities which drew together those interested in a particular issue, for example, medical missions, literacy and education, mass media. The FMC developed into a group of important substructures in which continuous studies and services were carried on.[132] Most of the work of the DOM continues at this level.

The third stage, most evident since the 1950s, points in the direction of united planning and action in conjunction with agencies and churches overseas. Such activity seeks to maximize the use of personnel and material resources and to further unity among Christians engaged in a common task.

This process closely parallels the stages of development evident in the regional councils of Asia and Africa, although in those areas the movement has taken place over a much shorter period of time than in the USA.

SUMMARY

Regional ecumenical bodies now exist on all continents and in Oceania. This striking new development of Christian conferences has appeared chiefly since the 1950s in Asia and Africa, the Middle East, Europe, and the Pacific, while Latin America evolved a number of bodies for continent-wide interconfessional communication.[133] The emergence of these organizations provides important evidence for the shift from what has been a predominantly Western base in the WCC toward a genuinely universal Christian fellowship in which Christians from all continents participate equally.

One participant at the WCC's Second Assembly (1954) referred to the WCC as a combination of German theology, American money, and Dutch bureaucracy.[134] Now Christians from all continents share leadership responsibilities in the WCC, and at the Fifth Assembly of the WCC in Nairobi, Kenya (1975) delegates from Asia, Africa, and Latin America composed fully one-third of the total number of participants. The total agenda of the WCC has been markedly shaped by concerns which first appeared in regional gatherings.

Ecumenical regionalism emerged (as did the ecumenical movement at large) from a sense of responsibility for evangelism, and a desire for unity among Christians. In an era of political independence and growing regional and cultural identity, the development of regional organizations signaled a new sense of responsibility in the churches paralleling massive external changes in Asia and Africa in particular.

For the churches in these areas, the growth of regional organizations marked the start of a new era in which the churches themselves began to accept full responsibility for the task of evangelism and Christian witness throughout that area. The statements on mission assumed the integration of the church and mission and called for external personnel and agencies to work in, with, and through indigenous churches, rather than continuing a separate life and identity as had frequently been the case in the past. Only in this way could a "form" of Christianity emerge, faithful to the gospel, yet related to the culture in which it was set. Effective evangelism demanded such an engagement.

As the regional conferences have grown, they have sought to become increasingly self-reliant, while maintaining and developing a sense of belonging and participation in the wider fellowship of the universal church. People such as D. T. Niles, M. M. Thomas, José Miguez-Bonino, and John Gatu have exemplified this double interest by providing leadership in both regional and worldwide ecumenical agencies.

Within the span of twenty-five years, the understanding in the regional gatherings of the involvement of the church in society has broadened and developed from concern for education, charity, and relief work to an increasing emphasis on conscientization and liberation of the people by means of structural changes in society to achieve justice and peace. These changes in theological understanding occurred as it became apparent that political independence and nationalism did not produce the kind of development which many in Africa, Asia and Latin America had desired. The political awareness of the implications of neo-colonialism, racism, and the continued dependence on others brought to many the recognition and conviction that only radical structural changes in society and the world economic and political systems would accomplish the desired goals of liberation with justice and freedom for all. The WCC study programs on rapid social change, the Geneva Conference on Church and Society, and the emergence of liberation theology in Latin America all contributed to this change of understanding of the church's role and relationship to the society in which it exists. The role of Christian leaders such as M. M. Thomas and José Miguez-Bonino in the WCC and regional studies has been especially important at this point.

The serious endeavor to relate Christianity and culture in regional discussions stimulated another development which has become important for the whole ecumenical movement: the dialogue of Christians with people of other faiths. First evident in Asia but soon seen also in Africa and the Middle East, this led to several emphases. Study centers became increasingly im-

portant in identifying data of significance for understanding
other faiths. Discussion on the meaning, purpose and goals of
dialogue received a high priority in the ecumenical movement.
The appointment of S. J. Samartha of India to the WCC gave new
direction to this work. John Mbiti's contribution to the study
of African traditional religion brought a fresh focus to this
question in Africa. Projects in Africa and the Middle East
encouraged deeper study of the approach of Christians to Mos-
lems. This concern for dialogue, first raised by Christians
from Asia, has now broadened to include relations between
Christians and people of other ideologies, as well as the difficult issue of cross-cultural communication.

        One of the most important developments to have occurred
through the regional ecumenical gatherings is the growing fellowship between Christians in a particular area. Prior to
World War II, churches were related primarily through confessional links; churches in a given region were frequently isolated from each other. The joy and amazement in discovering
deep Christian fellowship together in regional meetings produced initiatives for joint projects and, in some instances,
plans for church union.

        Relations between the Roman Catholic Church and other
Christian churches in regional organizations improved greatly
after Vatican II. In all areas, fraternal relations have
developed, while in the Caribbean Conference of Churches the
Roman Catholic Church was a founding member. This development
parallels the close bonds which now link Roman Catholics with
the ecumenical movement at every level.

        Despite the enormous gains achieved in the development of
regional ecumenical organizations, serious problems still face
them in the future. The vast gap between what happens at
assemblies and consultations and the understanding attitude and
involvement of Christians at the local level continues. Financial problems remain great, with most money for regional activities coming from Europe and North America. Ideas for improving Christian education for developmental projects are difficult to implement. In many places people prepared to work
for structural changes in society have faced hostile reactions
from government, economic, and middle class interests. Much
remains to be done before the regional ecumenical organizations
are able to achieve all their plans and hopes. Yet they do
provide a continuing means of fellowship, study and action for
all Christians, and for that reason will continue to play an
important role in the ecumenical movement at the regional and
worldwide level.

NOTES

[1]The great need for thorough histories of regional ecumenical organizations, especially the Asian and African Conferences, because of their size and influence, is obvious to
anyone who attempts to do research on these gatherings.

[2]Rajah B. Manikam, "The Task of the Bangkok Conference,"
in *The Christian Prospect in East Asia: Papers and Minutes of
the Eastern Asia Christian Conference, Bangkok, December 3-11,
1949* (New York: Friendship Press, 1950), pp. 1-2. See also
Hans-Reudi Weber, *Asia and the Ecumenical Movement 1895-1961*
(London: SCM, 1966), pp. 281-83.

[3]P. D. Devanandan, "The Bangkok Conference of East Asian
Leaders: An Impression," IRM 39.154 (1950): 147.

[4]*Christian Prospect*, p. 120.

[5]Ibid., pp. 119, 121. The phrase "partnership in obedience" came from the IMC meeting at Whitby (1947).

[6]Ibid., p. 114.

[7]Ibid., pp. 129-135 for the conference discussion on this
issue; cf. Visser 't Hooft, *Memoirs*, p. 233.

[8]This became the thrust of M. M. Thomas's contribution to
the WSCF the following year. See M. M. Thomas and J. D.
McCaughey, *The Christian in the World Struggle* (Geneva: WSCF,
1950), p. 14. There is a clear line between Thomas's concern
for social justice at this point and his chairmanship of the
Geneva Conference on Church and Society in 1966.

[9]W. A. Visser 't Hooft, "Asian Churches," ER 2.3 (1950): 239.

[10]*Christian Prospect*, p. 143.

[11]*Christ--The Hope of Asia: Papers and Minutes of the Ecumenical Study Conference for East Asia, Lucknow, India, December 27-30, 1952* (Madras: Christian Literature Society, 1953),
p. 9.

[12]Ibid., p. 36.

[13]Ibid., pp. 24, 26.

[14]Ibid., pp. 32, 98.

[15]P. D. Devanandan, "Comments on the First Report of the

Advisory Commission on the Theme of the Second Assembly,"
ER 4.2 (1952): 163.

[16]"Statement of the Asia Council on Ecumenical Mission,"
*The Common Evangelistic Task of the Churches in East Asia:
Papers and Minutes of the East Asia Christian Conference,
Prapat, Indonesia, March 17-26, 1957* (EACC: n.d.), pp. 158-160.

[17]Ibid., p. 103.

[18]The numbering of EACC Assemblies sometimes varies. The
following scheme will be herein followed:
    1957 Prapat--Preparatory Assembly
    1959 Kuala Lumpur--Inaugural Assembly
    1964 Bangkok--Third Assembly
    1968 Bangkok--Fourth Assembly
    1973 Singapore--Fifth Assembly: EACC becomes CCA
    1977 Penang--Sixth Assembly

[19]F. S. de Silva, "The Significance of Prapat," IRM 46.183
(1957): 308; cf. Visser 't Hooft, *Memoirs*, p. 239.

[20]"Constitution of the EACC" in U Kyaw Than, ed.,
*Witnesses Together: Being the official report of the Inaugural
Assembly of the EACC, held at Kuala Lumpur, Malaya, May 14-24,
1959* (Rangoon: EACC, 1959), p. 17.

[21]See ibid., pp. 33-51 for the addresses by M. Takenaka,
"A New Understanding of Theological Renewal," and M. M. Thomas,
"Some Notes on Christian Interpretation of Nationalism in Asia."

[22]Ibid., p. 102.

[23]Ibid., p. v, "A Message from the First Assembly of the
EACC to its Member Churches and Councils."

[24]Ibid., p. 162-166.

[25]Ibid., p. 5.

[26]*A Decisive Hour for the Christian Mission: The EACC
1959 and the John R. Mott Memorial Lectures* (London: SCM,
1960), p. 96.

[27]*Report of Situation Conferences: Convened by the EACC
February-March, 1963* (EACC: n.d.), p. 4; see also Frank Short,
"Situation Conferences on Joint Action for Mission," IRM 52.207
(1963): 323-324.

[28]John Fleming, ed., *Structures For a Missionary Congrega-*

tion (Singapore: EACC, 1964).

[29]The Bangkok Minutes were published in two parts:
*Assembly of the EACC held at Bangkok, Thailand from 25 Feb. to
March 1964: Minutes (Part One)* and *The Christian Community
within the Human Community. Containing Statements from the
Bangkok Assembly of the EACC Feb.-March, 1964: Minutes (Part
Two)* (Bangalore: CLS, 1964).

[30]G. C. Jackson, "Report from Bangkok," IRM 53.211 (1964):
309. The problem of different salary scales was vividly portrayed by the Reverend Mr. D. Pallilu, an Indonesian working in
Sarawak. He spoke of four missionary groups working in Asia--
elephants (Americans), buffaloes (British), goats (Asians), and
rabbits (local pastors), ibid., p. 313.

[31]*The Christian Community Within the Human Community,*
pp. 12-13.

[32]Ibid., p. 14.

[33]Ibid., p. 16.

[34]Ibid., pp. 81-84.

[35]Ibid., pp. 2-8.

[36]*The South East Asia Journal of Theology* 8.1 and 2
(July/October 1966) was devoted entirely to preparatory material. Addresses given at the Consultation appeared in the
following issue, 8.3 (January 1967).

[37]*Confessing the Faith in Asia Today: Statement issued by
the Consultation convened by the EACC and held in Hong Kong
October 25-November 3, 1966* (Redfern: Epworth, 1967), pp. 9, 11.

[38]Ibid., p. 7.

[39]Ibid., p. 32.

[40]For an evangelical assessment of the issues raised by
the Hong Kong Conference, see Bruce J. Nicholls, "Toward an
Asian Theology of Mission," EMQ 6.2 (1970): 67-78.

[41]*In Christ All Things Hold Together: Bangkok 1968.
Statements and Findings of the Fourth Assembly of the EACC*
(EACC: n.d.), p. 3. The Assembly met between 30 Jan. to
8 Feb. 1968.

[42]Ibid., p. 4. Some issues relating to the problems of

Asian society had been clarified by the conference on "Modernization of Asian Societies" held in Seoul, Korea, 1967, as a
regional response to the Geneva Church and Society Conference
of 1966.

[43]Reported in "Fourth Assembly of the EACC, Bangkok," ER
20.2 (1968): 184. Niles' report was "Ideas and Services: A
Report of the EACC 1957-67."

[44]*In Christ All Things Hold Together*, p. 13.

[45]Ibid., pp. 33-34.

[46]Ibid., pp. 32-33.

[47]Ibid., pp. 7-8, 39.

[48]*Christian Conference of Asia Fifth Assembly: 6-12 June
1973 Singapore* (Bangkok: CCA, 1973), p. 8.

[49]The lectures were published in *Christian Action in the
Asian Struggle* (Singapore: CCA, 1973). The keynote speaker,
M. M. Thomas, had long shared with Niles in active involvement
in the ecumenical movement and in the EACC since its inception.

[50]Ibid., p. 7. Thomas's commitment to social justice
remained unchanged from his earliest contributions to the then
EACC in 1949.

[51]*Fifth Assembly*, p. 38. The difficulty of achieving this
kind of transformation in local congregations was noted by Song
Choan-Seng in "Whither Protestantism in Asia Today?," *South East
Asia Journal of Theology* II (Spring 1970): 69-72.

[52]*Fifth Assembly*, p. 40.

[53]Ibid., pp. 51-52.

[54]*Witnesses Together*, pp. 39-40.

[55]*Christian Action in the Asian Struggle*, pp. 3, 9.

[56]Kyaw Than, *Joint Labourers in Hope: A Report of the
EACC 1968-1973* (Bangkok: CCA, 1973), p. 36.

[57]*Fifth Assembly*, p. 24.

[58]See Edwin W. Smith, *The Christian Mission in Africa. A
study based on the work of the International Conference at
Le Zoute, Belgium, 14-21 September 1926* (London: IMC, 1926)

and Hogg, *Ecumenical Foundations*, pp. 232-233.

[59]R. I. Seabury, *Daughter of Africa* (Boston: Pilgrim Press, 1945), p. 77. See also the similar comment of Albert Luthuli, *Let My People Go* (New York: Meridian Books, 1962), p. 79.

[60]Kyaw Than, *Witnesses Together*, p. 145. Ibiam was a fraternal delegate to the EACC meeting at Kuala Lumpur in 1959. The Ibadan meeting received an account of the establishment of the EACC at Prapat in 1957, a fact which may well have influenced the African delegates to consider the same proposal. See L. B. Greaves, "The All Africa Church Conference," IRM 47.187 (1958): 263; also Donald G. S. M'Timkulu, "All African Church Conference," IRM 51.201 (1962): 63-66.

[61]*The Church in Changing Africa: Report of the All-Africa Church Conference held at Ibadan, Nigeria, January 10-19, 1958* New York: IMC, n.d.), pp. 26-29.

[62]Ibid., p. 15.

[63]Ibid., p. 74.

[64]See John Crossley, "The Islam in Africa Project," IRM 41.242 (1972): 150-160.

[65]*Drumbeats from Kampala: Report of the First Assembly of AACC. Held at Kampala April 20 to April 30, 1963* (London: Lutterworth, 1963), p. 4.

[66]Ibid., p. 9; cf. the General Secretary of the AACC D. G. S. M'Timkulu's remark that "Kampala is undoubtably the most historic single event that has taken place within the life of the churches of Africa during this century," ibid., p. 4.

[67]D. T. Niles, "The All Africa Conference of Churches," IRM 52.208 (1963): 413. At that time Christians composed between 15-20% of the total population of Africa, compared to 1-2% in Asia. See *Drumbeats from Kampala*, p. 46.

[68]*Drumbeats from Kampala*, pp. 31-37.

[69]Ibid., pp. 41-43.

[70]Ibid., pp. 15-16; cf. 34-35.

[71]Ibid., pp. 61-62.

[72]Ibid., pp. 15, 63.

[73]Ibid., pp. 32-34; 40-41.

[74]Ibid., p. 15.

[75]*Engagement: The Second AACC Assembly, 'Abidjan 1969'* (Nairobi: AACC, 1969), p. 72.

[76]Ibid., p. 88, "Report of the Secretary-General," S. H. Amissah.

[77]Ibid., p. 86.

[78]Ibid., p. 107.

[79]The papers given at this meeting were published in Kwesi A. Dickson and Paul Ellingworth, eds., *Biblical Revelation and African Beliefs* (Maryknoll: Orbis, 1969).

[80]*Engagement*, p. 118.

[81]Ibid., pp. 78-79; 122-124. See also the cautious but thorough summary of Abidjan by the conservative evangelical Jacques Blocher, "All Africa Conference Put Under Evangelical Scrutiny," EMQ 6.3 (1970): 175-180.

[82]David Barrett, et al., "Frontier Situations for Evangelization in Africa" in R. Pierce Beaver, ed., *The Gospel and Frontier Peoples* (South Pasadena: William Carey Library, 1973). Barrett made some important predictions on the basis of this survey; see, "AD 2000: 350 Million Christians in Africa," IRM 59.233 (1970): 39-54. The hope and vision of Barrett's work gave inspiration to the Kinshasa Declaration of the AACC Executive Committee issued in 1971; see IRM 61.242 (1972): 115-16.

[83]*Evangelization of Frontier Situations in Africa: Report of a Consultation organized by the AACC, 15-19 December 1973, Nairobi, Kenya,* compiled and edited by George K. Mambo and Wanjiru Matenjwa (Nairobi: AACC, 1974): 3-4.

[84]Ibid., pp. 27-28.

[85]The "Moratorium Debate" developed from 1971 with contributions from Emerito Nacpil of the Philippines, the Ecumenical Sharing of Personnel Committee of the WCC, the CWME Bangkok 1973 Conference, the Lusaka AACC Assembly, and later at the Lausanne International Congress on World Evangelization 1974, with a few references at the Fifth Assembly of the WCC at Nairobi in 1975. For an introduction to the moratorium debate see: Emerito P. Nacpil, "Whom does the Missionary Serve and What does he do?" in *Missionary Service in Asia Today: A*

Report on a Consultation held by the Asia Methodist Advisory
Committee, February 18-23, 1971 (Hong Kong: Chinese Christian
Literature Council, 1971), pp. 76-80; *Bangkok Assembly, 1973*,
pp. 104-106; Alan R. Tippett, "The Suggested Moratorium on
Missionary Funds and Personnel," *Missiology* 1.3 (1973): 275-
280; IRM 62.248 (1974), "Mature Relationships: Structures for
Missions," especially the editorial by Emilio Castro; IRM 64.254
(1975), "Moratorium?," especially the article by C. Peter
Wagner, "Colour the Moratorium Grey," pp. 148-164; Gerald H.
Anderson, "A Moratorium on Missionaries?" *Christian Century*
(Jan. 16, 1974): 43-45; *The Struggle Continues: Official
Report of The Third Assembly of the AACC Lusaka-Zambia 12-24
May 1974* (Nairobi: AACC, 1975), pp. 53-54, and especially
Burgess Carr's address, pp. 76-77, 81 (hereafter cited as
Lusaka, 1974); J. D. Douglas, ed., *Let the Earth Hear His Voice:
International Congress on World Evangelization, Lausanne,
Switzerland: Official Reference Volume, Papers and Responses*
(Minneapolis: World Wide Publications, 1975), pp. 6, 251, 302
(hereafter cited as *Lausanne, 1974*); and *Nairobi, 1975*, pp. 18,
47, 57, 64, 251; and "The Moratorium Debate in Africa," ER 27.4
(1975): 409-411.

[86]*Lusaka, 1974*, pp. 76-77.

[87]Ibid., pp. 52-53.

[88]See *A Time for Self-Reliance: AACC 1975-78* (Nairobi:
AACC, 1975). The problem was highlighted in the financial
report--African member churches contributed only about 3% of
the AACC administrative budget. Even if all member organizations paid the new proposed scale of contributions, only about
20% of the budget would be covered. "The great portion of the
AACC income comes from overseas," *Lusaka, 1974*, pp. 60-61.

[89]*Lusaka, 1974*, p. 76. Barrett had already shown how the
independent churches developed an indigenous Christianity. See
David B. Barrett, *Schism and Renewal in Africa: An Analysis of
Six Thousand Contemporary Religious Movements* (Nairobi: Oxford
University Press, 1968), pp. 273-74 for a summary; cf. Marie-
Louise Martin, *Kimbangu: An African Prophet and His Church*,
trans. by D. M. Moore (Grand Rapids: Eerdmans, 1975), and
Victor E. W. Hayward, *African Independent Church Movements*
(London: Edinburgh House Press, 1963).

[90]*Lusaka, 1974*, p. 50. Note a similar emphasis on liberation in the CCA.

[91]*Structures of Injustice: A Report of a Consultation on
Violations of Human Rights, held in Khartoum, Sudan, 16-11 February, 1975* (AACC: mimeographed copy, n.d.), p. 20.

[92]"The Confession of Alexandria," *Mission Trends No. 3: Third World Theologies*, ed. by Gerald H. Anderson and Thomas F. Stransky (New York: Paulist/Grand Rapids: Eerdmans, 1976), pp. 132-134.

[93]E. W. Fashole-Luke, "The Quest for African Christian Theologies" in Anderson and Stransky, ibid., p. 141.

[94]See Burgess Carr, "The Relation of Union to Mission" in Anderson and Stransky, ibid., pp. 158-168.

[95]Burgess Carr in *Lusaka, 1974*, p. 77.

[96]William R. Reed, Victor M. Monterroso, and Harmon A. Johnson, *Latin American Church Growth* (Grand Rapids: Eerdmans, 1969), p. 58; cf. Victor Hayward, "Latin America--An Ecumenical Bird's Eye View," IRM 60.238 (1971): 167.

[97]See Harlan P. Beach, *Renascent Latin America: An Outline and Interpretation of the Congress on Christian Work in Latin America, held at Panama, 10-19 February 1916* (New York: Missionary Education Movement of the US and Canada, 1916); Hogg, *Ecumenical Foundations*, pp. 173-174; also Samuel McCrea Cavert, *Church Cooperation and Unity in America--A Historical Review: 1900-1970* (New York: Association Press, 1970).

[98]See Hans-Ruedi Weber, "Out of All Continents and Nations" in Fey, *Ecumenical Advance*, pp. 86-87.

[99]Robert E. Speer, Samuel G. Inman, and Frank K. Sanders, eds., *Christian Work in South America. Official Report of the Congress on Christian Work in South America, at Montevideo, Uruguay, April 1925*, 2 vols. (New York: Fleming H. Revell, 1925); and Hogg, *Ecumenical Foundations*, pp. 235-236.

[100]*Hacia la Renovacion Religiosa en Hispano-America. Report of the Congress Evangelico Hispano-Americano, Havana, 1929* (Medico: CUPSA, 1930) and Weber, "Out of All Continents and Nations," p. 86.

[101]*El Christianismo en la America Latin* (Buenos Aires: La Aurora, 1949); B. Foster Stockwell, "Latin American Evangelical Conference, Buenos Aires, 18-30 July 1949," IRM 39.153 (1950): 76-82; also the Messages from the First Evangelical Conference of Latin America in ER 2.2 (1950): 179-83.

[102]For examples of lay evangelism based on the Bible, see Alberto Rembao, "Protestant Latin America: Sight and Insight," IRM 46.181 (1957): 31-32.

103Weber, "Out of All Continents and Nations," pp. 87-88; also *Student World* 4, 1956.

104For an assessment of evangelism in Brazil, see Antonio de Campos Goncalves, "Evangelism in Brazil Today: Its Significance and Results," IRM 48.191 (1959): 302-308.

105*Christians and Social Change in Latin America: Findings on the First Latin American Evangelical Consultation on Church and Society, 23-27 July 1961, Huampani, Peru* (Montevideo: Latin American Commission on Church and Society/Geneva: WCC, n.d.).

106Howard W. Yoder, "The Second Latin American Evangelical Conference," IRM 51.201 (1962): 77.

107O. E. Costas, *Theology of the Crossroads in Contemporary Latin America: Missiology in Mainline Protestantism: 1969-1974* (Amsterdam: Rodopi, 1976), pp. 86-87 which quotes José Miguez-Bonino's description of CELA II as "basically developmentalistic." Cf. José Miguez-Bonino, *Doing Theology in a Revolutionary Situation* (Philadelphia: Fortress Press, 1973), p. 25, where he links "developmentist" thinking with John F. Kennedy's "Alliance for Progress" which began in 1961.

108Costas, *Theology of the Crossroads*, p. 114.

109Ibid., p. 91.

110Quoted in Hayward, "Latin America--An Ecumenical Bird's Eye View," p. 162. For a negative reaction to these new trends by a conservative evangelical, see Emilio Antonio Nuñez, "Perilous Ecumenical Overtures," EMQ 5.4 (1969): 193-201.

111Costas, *Theology of the Crossroads*, pp. 87-88; cf. pp. 110-111 for Miguez-Bonino's summary of the Third CELA. At least one commission produced a minority report, rejecting this liberation theology.

112Ibid., pp. 92-94.

113Ibid., p. 114.

114Ibid., p. 150.

115Ibid., p. 152; see pp. 149-175 for further details of UNELAM's problems and achievements.

116Ibid., Chapters VIII and IX provide an extended analysis of these organizations. CELADEC and ISAL represent attempts by some Protestants to face specific concerns on a continent-wide basis, functions which CELA and UNELAM have not been able to pursue.

[117]Ibid., p. 267.

[118]Hogg, *Ecumenical Foundations*, pp. 236-237; Weber, "Out of All Continents and Nations," p. 79.

[119]Quoted in R. Park Johnson, "Renewal of the Christian Mission to Islam: Reflections on the Asmara Conference," IRM 48.192 (1959): 440.

[120]See C. Samuel Calian, "Eastern Orthodoxy's Renewed Concern for Mission," IRM 52.205 (1962): 33-37.

[121]Johnson, *Uppsala to Nairobi*, p. 24.

[122]Weber, "Out of All Continents and Nations," p. 83.

[123]Ibid., pp. 84-85.

[124]*Beyond the Reef: Records of the Conference of Churches and Missions in the Pacific. Malua Theological College, Western Samoa, 22 April-4 May 1961* (London: IMC, 1961); and John A. Havea, "The Pacific Meets Beyond the Reefs," IRM 51.201 (1962): 72-74.

[125]The report of the 1966 Assembly is contained in *The Fourth World Meets: The Report of the Pacific Conference of Churches Assembly, Davuilevu, Fiji 1-14 May 1971* (Suva: PCC, 1972), pp. 111-140.

[126]*The Fourth World Meets*, pp. 83-92, and *Market Basket Media: The Report of the Evaluation Conference on Christian Communication in the Pacific, Suva, Fiji* (Honoria: Provincial Press, n.d.).

[127]*Report of the Third Assembly: The Pacific Conference of Churches* (Suva: PCC, 1976); also "Ecumenical Diary," ER 28.2 (1976): 213-214.

[128]Johnson, *Uppsala to Nairobi*, pp. 24-25.

[129]Hogg, *Ecumenical Foundations*, pp. 74-79, 248; Kenneth Scott Latourette, "Ecumenical Bearings of the Missionary Movement," and Ruth Rouse, "Other Aspects of the Ecumenical Movement in Rouse and Neill, *Ecumenical Movement*, pp. 374, 621-24; and Frank Short, "National Councils of Churches" in Fey, *Ecumenical Advance*, pp. 99-100.

[130]For a thorough description of the Federal Council of Churches and the NCCC, see Samuel McCrea Cavert, *The American Churches in the Ecumenical Movement* (New York: Association Press, 1968) and Cavert, *Church Cooperation and Unity in America.* In 1970 about 42 million Christians in the USA were related to the NCCC through its member churches.

[131]Minear, *The Nature of the Unity We Seek.*

[132]See successive *Foreign Mission Conference of North America: Annual Reports, 1893-1950;* and *Division of Foreign Missions. Annual Reports, 1951-1965;* and *Division of Overseas Ministries: Annual Reports, 1966-1975* for details of specific programs. Latourette, "Ecumenical Bearings," p. 374, listed 24 committees operative in 1948.

[133]Continent-wide gatherings of conservative evangelicals in the same period in some ways parallel this development.

[134]Visser 't Hooft, *Memoirs*, p. 252. The original "formula" was: "German brains, American money, and a Dutch autocrat."

Summary of Part I

    Two major historical stages are discernible in the development of mission theology in the ecumenical movement since 1948: The first stage, from 1948 to 1961, essentially focused on the church as the agent of God's mission in the world. The second, from 1961 to 1975, emphasized the world as the locus for God's mission in which the church participates by its witness in word and deed.

THE FIRST STAGE: 1948-1961

    These years were characterized by an internal struggle for self-understanding by those involved in the missionary enterprise. Through a process of debate and reflection, the ecumenical movement began to complete the vision of Edinburgh (1910), of the whole church involved in mission, with the churches drawing closer together in unity. The joining together of mission and unity as integral and inseparable parts of God's will for the church fulfilled the dream which the World Missionary Conference of 1910 bequeathed to future generations in the ecumenical movement.

    In the IMC, the Assemblies at Whitby (1947), Willingen (1952), and Ghana (1958) engaged in a process of theological reflection and organizational development. Both the theological and organizational thrusts emerged in an effort to shape the church's mission to the world. From an understanding of mission in which the church and especially Western missionary agencies were the prime agents of outreach, a new conception developed through the study "The Missionary Obligation of the

Church." From Willingen the notion of *missio dei* emerged to
express the conviction that, as God has sent his Son to the
world, so now he sends the church throughout the whole world
to share in his mission.

Links between the IMC and the WCC grew closer as people in
both organizations shared common study projects and recognized
the integral relationship between mission and unity. This led
to increased cooperation between the organizations. After considerable discussion, the Ghana Assembly of the IMC (1958)
approved the steps which finally led to the integration of the
IMC and the WCC in New Delhi (1961). The leadership of the
Secretary of the IMC, Charles W. Ranson, and people closely related to both bodies through the Joint Committee (especially
Norman Goodall and Henry P. Van Dusen), aided the move towards
integration.

From its official beginning in 1948, the WCC became subject to much misunderstanding about its aims and purposes. The
self-understanding of the WCC was clarified considerably
through the Toronto statement on "The Ecclesiological Significance of the WCC" (1950), and the Rolle statement on "The Calling of the Church to Mission and Unity" (1951). The WCC
existed to encourage fellowship between churches, and to help
them fulfill their common calling to mission and unity.

The WCC began to become a truly worldwide fellowship of
churches as more Christians from Asia, Africa and Latin America
became involved in various aspects of the ecumenical movement.
With the full-scale entry of the Orthodox Churches linked closely
with the Moscow Patriarchate into the WCC in 1961, together
with additional churches from Africa and several Pentecostal
churches, the WCC became more nearly a representatively worldwide council. It was committed to work for unity among churches,
to encourage universal mission, and to engage the churches in
the service of all people. Among the great church families,
only the Roman Catholic Church remains outside this fellowship
of churches, although it is officially a member of Faith and
Order, and many individual Roman Catholics show great interest
in the work of the WCC. Visser 't Hooft, as General Secretary of
the WCC, encouraged closer contacts wherever possible between
Roman Catholics and Protestants in this pre-Vatican II era.

THE SECOND STAGE: 1961-1975

The 1960s brought a new development in mission theology.
In the preceeding years, the major concentration had been on
the internal understanding and organization of mission in the
churches of the ecumenical movement. The new emphasis turned
to the world and its problems as the arena for mission.

Already in 1960, the new trend had become evident in the WSCF Conference, "The Life and Mission of the Church," when students called for closer contact with the world. The study on "The Missionary Structure of the Congregation," which Hans Hoekendijk so decisively influenced, developed a quite different understanding of the notion of *missio dei* in which God's action in the world became the focus of mission. Christians, especially the laity, were called to discern and participate in that mission, usually by sharing in secular movements for liberation and humanization.

The Geneva Conference on Church and Society in 1966 reflected a similar understanding of mission, and challenged Christians to become involved in movements to change society in order to achieve justice for all people. The Fourth Assembly of the WCC at Uppsala (1968) endorsed the notion of "the new humanity" in Jesus Christ, and directed its attention to the world and its needs.

Faith and Order studies, especially "The Unity of the Church and the Unity of Mankind," partly reflected this change in orientation by insisting that the work of the church must take into account the context of the world if the church is to fulfill its mission. It spoke of the church as a "sign" of what God is doing in the world.

Meanwhile, the Second Vatican Council (1962-1967) exerted a decisive influence on the whole Roman Catholic Church and encouraged its full entry into the world and its selective engagement in ecumenical endeavors. Participation by Roman Catholics in WCC meetings, regional ecumenical organizations, and local church gatherings widened the scope of ecumenical discussions at all levels. Leaders in the Roman Catholic Church, for example, Popes John XXIII and Paul VI, Cardinals Bea and Jan Willibrands, and Charles Moeller, have contributed significantly to the spirit of ecumenism among churches of all denominations. Joint WCC-Roman Catholic involvement in the ecumenical movement has been fruitful.

In the encounter with the world which characterized much of the ecumenical mission theology in the 1960s, the question of the place of the church in the world had to be reconceived. An emphasis on "Christian presence" in the world pointed to an engagement of world and church in a process of dialogue and witness. This became a particular thrust of the WSCF in the mid-1960s.

Dialogue also gained wide acceptance as a means of relating with people of other faiths. Prompted by Christians from Asia, and work done in the EACC, a series of studies and consultations concentrated on probing the relationship between Christianity

and other religions. The WCC took new initiatives under the
direction of S. J. Samartha in moving from talk about dialogue
to dialogue with people of other faiths.

The importance of dialogue as a means of fostering open,
honest, and deep conversations remains a valuable methodology
in all WCC discussions. No consensus has been reached in the
WCC about the theological basis and objectives of dialogue,
although there is general agreement on the need to remove misunderstanding and work for common action on matters of mutual
concern in meeting human need and striving for peace in the
world community.

Close attention has been devoted to the content of the
Christian faith in major meetings of the WCC. The CWME Bangkok
Conference on "Salvation Today" (1973) sought to describe a
comprehensive understanding of salvation. Yet many, among them
members of WCC churches, conservative evangelicals, Orthodox
and Roman Catholics, regarded its conclusions to be inadequate.
The choice of the subject--salvation--however, indicated a renewed interest within the WCC in the fundamental task of mission.

The Fifth Assembly of the WCC at Nairobi (1975) addressed
the theme "Confessing Christ Today." Nairobi seriously studied
both the world and the Christian faith. The context of the
world in which mission must be fulfilled remained a vital concern. The Assembly strove to remain faithful to the divine
mandate to witness to Christ in word and deed as the essential
task of the church in mission.

The influence of a wide range of viewpoints, including
those of the Orthodox, conservative evangelicals, and mainline
Protestants, can be traced in this attempt to discover the most
appropriate ways for the church to be faithful to God's mission
in the world today. Accordingly, the distinctive conservative
evangelical contribution to mission theology will be the subject of the next three chapters.

Part II

The Development of Conservative Evangelical Mission Theology

4

Evangelicals Seek
an Identity: 1917-1966

The emergence and development of conservative evangelical mission structures and theology will constitute the substance of this chapter.

Primary attention will be given to developments in the United States of America, because it is there that the main expansion and growth of the conservative evangelical missionary enterprise has taken place, especially since World War II. North American evangelicals, by the size of their contribution in terms of personnel and finance to the missionary movement, have decisively influenced the structure, shape, and direction of evangelism around the world.

Since the 1920s there has been a definite and decisive shift from Europe (particularly Britain) to North America as the major source of personnel and finance for mission activity.[1] Conservative evangelicals played an important part in that shift and have, since World War II, constituted a rapidly increasing proportion of the total number of missionaries sent from North America.[2] By 1968, the two largest evangelical organizations, the Interdenominational Foreign Mission Association (IFMA), and the Evangelical Foreign Missions Association (EFMA), between them had the majority of conservative evangelical missionaries related to them, and provided important leadership for non-WCC related groups.[3]

The term "conservative evangelical" is here used to describe those Christians and organizations primarily related to churches and bodies outside the WCC and the ecumenical move-

ment. Theologically, conservative evangelicals are characterized by a strong emphasis on personal Christian experience and
a strict adherence to a doctrinal position including usually
the verbal inspiration and inerrancy of scripture, the divinity
of Jesus Christ, the Virgin Birth, a substitutionary theory of
the Atonement, and the physical resurrection and bodily return
of Christ.[4] Some Christians closely related to the conservative evangelical movement do belong to churches which are members of the WCC (for example, John R. W. Stott of the Church of
England, and Donald A. McGavran of the Christian Church [Disci-
ples of Christ]), but their doctrinal position relates them to
evangelicalism primarily. The terms "conservative evangelical"
and "evangelical" will both be used to describe the position
espoused by these Christians and groups.[5]

As described by Harold Ockenga, pastor of the Park Street
Church, Boston, the term "evangelical" is used to differentiate
that position from Roman Catholicism, liberal or modern Christianity, and fundamentalism. While evangelicals and fundamentalists may share common doctrinal beliefs, the evangelicalism
which has emerged in the USA since World War II repudiated the
defensive and divisive attitude which characterized fundamentalism.[6]

This chapter will now trace and analyze the development of
evangelical mission thought and practice, first noting its
nineteenth century background, and then turning to focus on
developments in the twentieth century, especially in the USA.

BACKGROUND

Protestant Christianity in the nineteenth century developed
with an unprecedented vitality Evangelists such as Charles
Simeon in England, and Charles G. Finney and Dwight L. Moody on
both sides of the Atlantic, stimulated considerable interest in
the Christian faith and influenced many people to express a
personal commitment to Christ and then express that piety in
tangible ways.

Two means of demonstrating personal commitment were support of missionary activity and involvement in movements for
social reform. New missionary societies and groups for the
abolition of slavery grew out of this evangelical tradition.

Many evangelicals recognized the need for closer unity,
and their concern led to the formation of the Evangelical Alliance in England in 1846. The Alliance based its membership on
individual persons, who then joined together in national
branches to deepen brotherly affection, manifest the unity of
the disciples of Christ, and counteract infidelity and Romanism.[7]

Members subscribed to a doctrinal basis covering the authority
of scripture, the Trinity, the work of Christ, justification by
faith, the work of the Holy Spirit, and eschatology.[8] For some
fifty years it contributed valuable service to the causes of
mission, religious liberty, Christian education through a week
of prayer for Christian unity, international conferences, and
journals.[9]

    Certain independent missionary organizations, later called
"faith missions," established themselves in the latter part of
the nineteenth century. The best known of these, the China Inland Mission, began in 1865 with J. Hudson Taylor as its founder.
This interdenominational mission was not associated with any
church and never directly appealed for funds because Taylor believed that "God's work done in God's way will never lack sup-
plies." Other such groups emerged, including the Sudan Interior
Mission (1892), and the Africa Inland Mission (1895).[10]

    During the last half of the nineteenth century Protestant-
ism began to face a series of challenges which profoundly affected its shape and development. At least four issues aroused
considerable controversy. Modern historico-critical biblical
scholarship raised questions about the authority and inspiration of the Bible. The findings of scientific studies in geology,
botany, and physics (especially Darwinism), seemed to many to
cast doubt on the veracity of the Bible. The emergence of "the
social gospel" suggested to some that the Kingdom of God could
be established by social action rather than spiritual transformation of people. New scholarship in the fields of the comparative study of religion and psychology apparently refuted Christian claims regarding the truth and uniqueness of Christianity.

    Debate and tension generated by these issues polarized
Christians in many countries. This chapter, however, will
focus on the American scene because developments there, related
to these questions, provide the essential background for this
study of mission theology, especially in the post-World War II
period.

    In a series of Bible conferences, especially those held at
Niagara from 1883 to 1897, evangelicals came together to affirm
their understanding of the Christian faith. A fourteen-point
creed, formulated by James Hall Brookes in 1878, was officially
adopted at the Niagara Conference in 1890.[11] In later attempts
to set forth the fundamentals of the faith the Presbyterian
General Assembly adopted a five-point declaration in 1910, and
Amzi Dixon and Reuben Archer Torrey edited a series of volumes
entitled *The Fundamentals: A Testimony to the Truth*. Authors
from England and the USA contributed to these volumes which
appeared between 1910-1915, and people who subscribed to these

views became known as "fundamentalists."

Within many American churches, a theological polarization
took place between the fundamentalists and the liberals or
modernists. The most famous fundamentalist-modernist clash
occurred in the Scopes trial in Dayton, Tennessee in 1925.
William Jennings Bryan, a national fundamentalist leader, was
the prosecuting attorney against a teacher--John Scopes--accused
of teaching evolution. Clarence Darrow defended Scopes in a
trial which aroused the attention of the whole of America.
"Bryan officially 'won' the trial but lost the larger contest
for the hearts and minds of America . . . Fundamentalism was
henceforth associated in the popular mind with bigotry, ignorance and intolerance."[12]

The fundamentalists began to withdraw from the mainstream
of American society and church life, some forming their own
Bible schools, seminaries, and denominations.[13] This led to
what has been called "the great reversal," in which fundamentalists became inturned and opposed any involvement in movements
for social change and reform. Carl F. H. Henry lamented this
change in attitude when he described the stance of fundamentalists in this way:

> Whereas once the redemptive gospel was a world-changing
> message, now it was narrowed to a world-resisting mes-
> sage . . . . Fundamentalism in revolting against the
> Social Gospel seemed also to revolt against the Chris-
> tian social imperative . . . . It does not challenge
> the injustices of the totalitarianisms, the secularisms
> of modern education, the evils of racial hatred, the
> wrongs of current labor-management relations, the in-
> adequate bases of international dealings . . . . There
> is no room . . . for a gospel that is indifferent to
> the needs of the total man nor of the global man.[14]

Henry's analysis of the situation pointed to a change in
attitude evident among those who called themselves "evangelicals" following World War II. Many of these people were related to the IFMA, and the emerging National Association of
Evangelicals with its missionary agency, the EFMA. The next
section will trace and analyze the developments of these
bodies to discover how the evangelicals sought to regain a
positive identity and promote an effective missionary policy.

Because they are primarily service organizations for mission agencies, the IFMA and the EFMA themselves do not produce
detailed material outlining evangelical mission theology. Only
the broadest principles are evident from the official documents.
These will suffice to indicate the primary thrusts of evangeli-

cal mission theology. Yet these groups provide a matrix in
which evangelical leaders formulate policies, develop plans,
and promote theological studies among their constituencies.

SENDING THE GOSPEL TO THE ENDS OF THE EARTH:
THE INTERDENOMINATIONAL FOREIGN MISSION ASSOCIATION

Amid the theological controversies of the early twentieth
century, faith missions continued their activities. Among some
of these interdenominational mission groups there arose a spontaneous desire for some form of fellowship and mutual support.
As a result they met and formed the IFMA, which became an officially organized body at Princeton, New Jersey, on September 29,
1917 with seven founding member missions.

The IFMA adopted a statement of faith entirely in accord
with the fundamentalist position. From its inception, the
guiding principles which bound the members of this organization
together have been "strict adherence to the evangelical doctrines and standards of historical Christianity and the burden
to carry the Gospel to those regions where Christ has not been
named."[15] On the basis of its statement of faith, as some
official statements of the IFMA explicitly declare, any organizational association, cooperation or fellowship with the ecumenical movement is impossible.[16]

The IFMA has grown enormously, especially since 1940.
Prior to 1940, the annual meeting consisted of less than a
dozen mission executives who met for several hours. But with
post-World War II growth, an office was established in 1949.
J. O. Percy became full-time administrator in 1956, and served
until 1962 when Edwin L. (Jack) Frizen, Jr. became the executive director. In 1976, the IFMA served 47 member societies
with a total of 9,483 missionaries and staff.[17]

The IFMA sponsored the first meeting of conservative evangelicals which attempted to review the missionary enterprise
throughout the world. This was the Congress on World Missions
held at Chicago, 4-11 December, 1960. About 500 missionaries
were present, of whom 400 were from IFMA member missions.[18]
Only one EFMA-related missionary, Vincent Brushwyler of the
Conservative Baptist Missionary Society, contributed to the
formal presentations of the Congress. Relations between the
IFMA and the EFMA were not very close in 1960.[19]

Many of the presentations at the Congress made reference
to the revolutionary events and times facing the missionary
enterprise. Yet most of the major speeches were devotional,
exegetical or horatory in character, essentially reaffirming
the two major themes basic to IFMA mission theology, namely,

obedience to the Great Commission and concern for saving lost souls.[20]

The Congress made an effort to lift up anew the Student Volunteer Watchword: "The evangelization of the world in this generation." This may be seen as a sign of the conservative evangelicals' understanding of themselves as the inheritors of the tradition and impulse of the nineteenth century Protestant missionary movement and of the 1910 World Missionary Conference, to which reference was made several times.[21]

The implied goal of IFMA missionary policy is the establishment of indigenous churches of sound faith. Confronted by changing circumstances in many mission fields, several speakers underlined the importance of this goal by calling for the training of indigenous Christian leaders, able to communicate the Christian faith effectively in their own countries.[22] Yet the fact that only four speakers were present from Asia, Africa, and Latin America indicated that much still remained to be done in this area.[23]

The overwhelming emphasis of the Congress concerned evangelism as the major task of mission work. Several references to a survey of the needs of eighty-seven evangelical mission boards, taken just prior to 1960, indicated that an enormous expansion of the missionary force seemed essential. The needs listed included 18,247 missionaries, 20 radio stations, 100 Bible institutes, seminaries and colleges, 50 hospitals and medical training centers, 24 printing presses, and 200 bookstores.[24]

R. Kenneth Strachan's presentation suggested the only real change in strategy proposed at the Congress. In a statement outlining the principles which became the basis of the Evangelism in Depth movement, he declared that the key to evangelization must be

> the totality of the Christian believers. The only way we can reach Latin America or any other part of the world is by mobilizing the totality of the Christian believers in continuous evangelistic action . . . .
> The key person in the evangelism of tomorrow is the layman.[25]

This marked a fresh approach to evangelism which became very important among evangelicals around the world in the next decade.

The note sounded by G. Christian Weiss was also unusual. He argued that the slogan of faith missions, "not to educate, but to evangelize," represented an unrealistic and undesirable goal because only an adequately trained Christian leadership

could give effective direction to the policies of countries
becoming newly independent.[26]

The desire for unity among evangelicals found frequent
expression at the Chicago meeting. For example, Woodbridge
declared "the evangelical yearns for genuine spiritual unity"
founded in the Holy Spirit who "baptizes believers into a mystical unity. This is the type of unity which we seek to promote."[27]

It seems clear from pleas made at the Congress, however,
that even this kind of spiritual unity proved difficult for
many in the IFMA. In an appeal to delegates, Alan Redpath,
pastor of the Moody Church, Chicago, and the host for the
Congress, asked his listeners to consider these issues:

What about the tragic division in evangelical churches?
What about the failure to recognize the unity of the
Spirit because we are all one in Christ, and in place
of this demanding a unity in every point of doctrine
before we can even speak with each other?[28]

The need for greater cooperation and unity in practical matters
relating to the establishment of mission institutions (for
example, schools and seminaries) was also mentioned.[29]

Strong antipathy toward the views of other Protestants,
and toward Roman Catholicism in general, can be noted at
several points.[30] There seemed to be little indication that
other Christians should be considered part of the church in any way.

The IFMA-sponsored Congress on World Missions marked an
important stage in the development of an evangelical identity.
While virtually no EFMA participants shared in the meeting,
"for the first time it brought together numerous evangelical
missionaries and gave a hitherto disparate group a visible
sign of unity."[31]

. The major theological thrusts of the Congress reiterated
the basic themes of obedience to the Great Commission and the
saving of souls as the motives for mission. The importance of
founding indigenous churches with a trained leadership also
received emphasis. The SVM watchword, "The evangelization of
the world in this generation," was revived and included in the
Congress Resolution.

Other evangelical groups besides the IFMA had become
active in the post-World War II period and to these we must
now turn.

REGAINING AN EVANGELICAL HERITAGE:
THE NATIONAL ASSOCIATION OF EVANGELICALS AND
THE EVANGELICAL FOREIGN MISSIONS ASSOCIATION

One organization seeking evangelical cooperation in the
USA in the early part of this century was the New England
Fellowship (NEF), formed under the leadership of J. Elwin
Wright. The NEF developed an extensive range of activities,
including radio broadcasting, Christian education in schools,
bookstores, Bible conferences, and assemblies for the laity.
In the late 1930s and early 1940s the NEF determined to organize
a national evangelical fellowship.[32]

Wright began an intensive campaign to gather support for a
national evangelical body, leading up to a conference for interested persons in St. Louis on 7-9 April, 1942. Those present
recommended "that the time had come for setting up an organization for united action at the national level."[33] An executive
committee with Harold J. Ockenga as president was elected by
the conference. A Constitutional Assembly in Chicago in 1943
formally established the National Association of Evangelicals
(NAE), adopted a statement of faith closely resembling other
evangelical confessions, and detailed the future areas of concern for the NAE.[34] The NAE understood itself as a purely voluntary organization, with a constituency of denominations, organizations, and churches which wholeheartedly subscribed to
the doctrinal statement and the aims of the body.[35]

Three major reasons motived the founders of the NAE.
First, many evangelicals expressed dissatisfaction with existing organizations, and undoubtably those present at St. Louis
had the Federal Council of Churches of Christ in America in
mind when they declared:

Whereas we realize that in many areas of Christian
endeavor the organizations which now purport to be
the representatives of Protestant Christianity have
departed from the faith of Jesus Christ, we do now
reaffirm our unqualified loyalty to this Gospel as
herein set forth, declaring our unwillingness to be
represented by organizations which do not have such
loyalty to the Gospel of Christ; and we express our
unqualified opposition to all such apostasy.[36]

Second, many evangelicals expressed a desire for unity in
place of "the failures, divisions and controversies" which had
plagued fundamentalism.[37] The approach of Carl McIntire and
the American Council of Christian Churches (ACCC), characterized as polemical and negative by Murch, was not accepted as an
adequate way of expressing a positive evangelical witness.[38]

Third, cooperation among evangelicals seemed necessary in a number of fields to ensure adequate evangelical representation at the national level and to assist the presentation of a united voice in matters of mutual concern. Areas of particular importance included evangelism, Christian education, mission, and radio work.[39]

The primacy of evangelism in the self-understanding of the NAE received attention in the periodical, *United Evangelical Action*, which commented that

> evangelism quietly, but powerfully, flows through many channels of the National Association of Evangelicals' endeavor . . . . In their respective fields of service many of the agencies and commissions of the NAE further the cause of evangelism.[40]

To promote the NAE's interest in the field of mission, the EFMA was formally established on December 29, 1945, with Clyde W. Taylor as its chief officer. From its first year, with 20 member missions and 1,519 missionaries in 1946, the EFMA has now grown to be the largest North American missionary association with 72 affiliated agencies representing 7,012 North American and 1,095 non-North American missionaries for a total of 8,107.[41]

The Constitution outlined the purpose of the EFMA in this way:

> To provide a medium of voluntary united action among the evangelical foreign mission agencies without, however, exercise of executive or legislative council over the constituent members.

The specific fields of action in which the EFMA seeks to promote evangelical Christianity include united approaches to governments, cooperative arrangements for transportation and purchasing, the promotion of comity and cooperative arrangements, the encouragement of missionary vocations, and the establishing of coordinating offices overseas, where necessary.[42]

As may be expected, the EFMA emphasizes the importance of maintaining strict adherence to the evangelical Statement of Faith. One of the major reasons given by Murch for the formation of the EFMA related to the disaffection of many evangelicals with the Foreign Missions Conference of North America which, it was argued, had become increasingly controlled by liberal theological influences. (The validity of this judgment was confirmed for some evangelicals when the Foreign Missions Conference became the Division of Foreign Missions in the NCCC

in the USA in 1950. The Southern Baptist Foreign Mission Board
left the FMC at this time.)[43]

The Constitution of the EFMA explicitly affirms that evangelism in obedience to the Great Commission is the primary task
of Christians in the present time. The Preamble reads in part:

> The authoritative claim of Christ's command, "Go ye,"
> the dire need of mankind, and the lateness of the hour,
> present an urgent call to all evangelical foreign
> mission agencies to more effectively evangelize the
> unreached of our generation and thus contribute to the
> completing of the Church. This need and the rapidly
> developing world situation challenge us to present a
> united front in this God-given task.[44]

This statement assumes that Christians who are obedient to
Christ's command will share in the support of evangelism which
leads to the development of the church embracing all who accept
Jesus Christ.

The practical demands of missionary work provide another
sphere for EFMA activity. Comity agreements help to mitigate
friction between member bodies and with churches in a given
area. (This does not appear to apply to churches and groups
which are not related to evangelical organizations.) Service
and purchasing facilities are maintained by the EFMA for the
benefit of member agencies.

The constituency of the EFMA includes both denominational
and independent foreign mission agencies. Unlike the IFMA, it
also accepts Pentecostal churches into fellowship.

The development of the IFMA and the EFMA brought a new
sense of identity to their member organizations, re-establishing
their independence from mainline Protestant churches and
agencies like the NCCC. While not closely related to one another before 1966, the IFMA and the EFMA provided strong and
effective organizations, able to articulate and meet the concerns of evangelicals.

Both groups followed parallel courses in the 1950s and
early 1960s, gradually becoming committed to a partnership
which each accepted as beneficial.[45] This occurred as they
became involved in a series of ventures in which leaders of
both groups were involved, for example, Evangelical Literature
Overseas (1953), the Evangelical Committee on Latin America
(1957), the Committee on Evangelical Missionaries to Islam
(1958), and an Evangelical Committee for Africa (1960, which
led to an African Evangelical Office in Nairobi, Kenya (1962).

They jointly sponsored the *Evangelical Missions Quarterly*
(1965). A joint mission executives retreat for IFMA and EFMA
leaders, first held in 1963, has become an important regular
gathering for the discussion of matters of common importance.[46]

WORLD EVANGELICAL FELLOWSHIP

The resurgence of evangelicalism in the USA created a desire for a wider fellowship at the international level. In 1946
the NAE sent J. Elwin Wright to London to share in the centen-
nial anniversary of the Evangelical Alliance.[47] From this contact emerged efforts to foster interest in a world organization
for evangelicals which led to a constitutional convention at
Woudschoten, Holland, in August, 1951, to form the World Evangelical Fellowship (WEF). Seven national fellowships became
charter members.[48] Members subscribe to a statement of faith
covering the major points of similar conservative evangelical
confessions (for example, the infallibility of the Bible, the
Virgin Birth of Jesus Christ). The purposes for which the WEF
was formed include spiritual renewal of the churches, cooperation among evangelicals, and a constructive defense of the
Christian faith.

Meeting at Clarens, Switzerland in 1953, the WEF made
plans for future developments. Commissions on Evangelism,
Christian Action, Missionary Cooperation, and Literature were
proposed. A new central world headquarters with a permanent
secretariat was envisaged, but "the founders' ambitious dreams
for the future of WEF exceeded subsequent performance."[49] Lack
of financial support made such dreams impossible. The work of
the WEF has depended largely on people employed by other
agencies who also support the WEF.

FUNDAMENTALIST REPUDIATION OF FELLOWSHIP:
THE AMERICAN COUNCIL OF CHRISTIAN CHURCHES

At least one group of fundamentalists refuses fellowship
with any of these evangelical organizations, namely, the American Council of Christian Churches (ACCC), and its missionary
organization, The Associated Missions of the International
Council of Christian Churches (TAM-ICCC).

When J. Gresham Machen left the Presbyterian Church, USA,
because he refused to surrender his ties with the Independent
Board for Presbyterian Foreign Missions, one of his students,
Carl McIntire, shared his convictions and stood with him. As
the pastor of a church which withdrew from the Presbytery,
McIntire formed an independent church, the Bible Presbyterian
Church of Collingswood.[50]

On September 17, 1941, the ACCC was formed, drawing together a number of fundamentalist churches under the leadership of
McIntire.[51] McIntire held that "the issue here was just the
concept of a true, pure church, the question of separation from
apostasy,"[52] particularly in regard to relations with or attitudes toward the Federal Council of Churches of Christ in America and to all denominations associated with that organization.
On the issue of separation, or double separation--from apostasy
and from those who continue to associate with denominations
linked with the ecumenical movement--McIntire disagreed with
others of similar faith, including those who formed the NAE.[53]

An implacable opposition to the ecumenical movement at the
national and worldwide level appears to be the main motivation
behind McIntire's position. He asked, "Shall the Ecumenical
Movement lead us to slavery? I believe that that is where it is
taking the world."[54] McIntire argued that the International
Council of Christian Churches (ICCC), a body he had founded in
1948 to parallel the WCC,

> with its emphasis upon the infallibility of the Scrip-
> tures, is calling for a reformation. The Council is
> made up of sound churches which have separated and
> divided from others over the question of apostasy and
> modernism, especially in the United States of America.
> It is sin not to separate when fellowship with unbelief
> is the position of a church. It is sin not to establish
> a true church when a church body turns away to become a
> synagogue of Satan.[55]

The Constitution of the ICCC requires that only churches and
denominations *not* represented by or affiliated with the WCC or
any of its cooperating agencies may belong to the ICCC.

As an integral part of the ICCC a Missions Commission was
established "to seek by every proper means to facilitate the
missionary work of member bodies."[56] This led to the formation
of TAM-ICCC in 1952. Few details have been available regarding
its size and operation. In 1969 several of the agencies of
TAM-ICCC withdrew and formed a new association known as the
Fellowship of Missions.[57]

The organizations associated with McIntire have consistently been characterized by a divisive, vindictive, and sec-
tarian spirit, opposed to the conservative evangelicals represented in the NAE, and to the ecumenical movement. Internal
fragmentation continued, and in 1970 McIntire lost control of
the ACCC.[58]

This group of fundamentalists has contributed little to

mission theology. With that widely shared judgment made, we must now turn to one of the most creative segments within the evangelical movement--the students.

EVANGELICAL STUDENTS AND MISSION: INTER-VARSITY CHRISTIAN FELLOWSHIP AND THE URBANA CONVENTIONS

In the final decades of the nineteenth century the Student Volunteer Movement for Foreign Missions (SVM) emerged in the USA in 1886 with John R. Mott and Robert E. Speer as early leaders, and the Student Volunteer Missionary Union (SVMU) in Britain in 1892. Each proclaimed the same watchword: "The evangelization of the world in this generation."

The influence of these organizations in drawing students into the missionary movement was remarkable. The SVM reached its recruiting highpoint in 1920 when 2,783 volunteers enrolled;[59] but by 1930 its influence was already in sharp decline. By 1945 the SVM had recruited some 20,500 missionaries, almost three-quarters of them from North America.[60]

Other Christian organizations for students also existed. The best known British group was perhaps the Cambridge Inter-Collegiate Christian Union (CICCU), formed in 1877. In the theological debates of the early twentieth century, tension began to emerge between the SCM and the strictly evangelical Christian unions like the CICCU. However, interaction between them was still common in the 1920s and Max Warren reports that while in Cambridge in 1926 he was the last of a generation who could belong to both organizations. On that he reflected:

> In matters Christian it was the last in which it was possible to be at one and the same time college representative of the CICCU, as I was, and also Secretary of the SVMU, and also on the SCM Executive at the headquarters in London. A greater rigidity on the part of the CICCU set in which was to make such a combination in future impossible.[61]

In 1928 a number of British Christian unions banded together to form the Intervarsity Fellowship of Evangelical Unions (IVF). Howard Guinness, a leader of the IVF, traveled to Canada, Australia, and New Zealand to report on the new organization; evangelical student movements soon emerged in these countries.[62]

Evangelical student groups in Scandinavia and Europe met for a series of international conferences in the 1930s under the guidance of Ole Hallesby, Robert Wilder, and Howard Guinness. The International Conference of Evangelical Students, an essentially European body, was formed in 1935, but international tension and the war interrupted this fellowship and made further meetings impossible.

The initiative in evangelical student activity shifted to the USA in 1940 when, with the help of the Canadian IVF, the United States Inter-Varsity Christian Fellowship (IVCF) organized on a national basis. Later, C. Stacey Woods became the secretary of the growing American IVCF.[63]

Following World War II, international evangelical student conferences began again. In 1947 the International Fellowship of Evangelical Students (IFES) was inaugurated at Harvard University, Cambridge, Massachusetts, with C. Stacey Woods as General Secretary. The IFES adopted a basis of faith closely resembling other conservative evangelical doctrinal statements. The IFES Constitution described the central aim of the organization to be, "to awaken and deepen personal faith in the Lord Jesus Christ and to further evangelistic work among students throughout the world."[64]

As the WSCF conferences often heralded changes in ecumenical mission theology, so the IVCF conventions at Urbana, Illinois, have been important indicators of trends in the conservative evangelical understanding of mission. The first conference was held in Toronto in 1946, under the auspices of the Canadian and US Fellowships, but since 1948 the conventions have met at the University of Illinois in Urbana.

These conferences have attracted students from the USA and overseas, with speakers drawn from throughout the world, to share in plenary sessions, discussions, studies, and fellowship. Many evangelical missionary organizations also participate in the Urbana meetings. They have grown in size from some 575 participants in 1946, to a gathering of more than 15,000 students in 1976.[65]

Several aims are evident from the structure of the conventions. Biblical studies on mission and evangelism have always been a feature and, since 1964, John R. W. Stott has presented that section of the program. Christian leaders from around the world have brought students into contact with the thoughts and perspectives of Christians in other countries. The challenge of missionary work has been clearly presented to students, and crucial issues for mission theology have been raised in lectures, panels, and publications.

The early meetings were for the most part inspirational in nature. Leaders in the evangelical movement, like Harold J.

Ockenga and C. Stacey Woods, presented addresses on the need
for world evangelization, and on the failure of liberal Christianity adequately to promote mission and evangelism. Representatives from missionary societies provided information on
various forms of outreach and service.

New approaches may be noted from 1961. Prior to that convention a preparatory volume, *Missions in Crisis: Rethinking
Missionary Strategy*,66 raised many issues confronting the whole
missionary enterprise, including revolution, nationalism, communism, and the lessons to be learned from China. Several
leaders in 1961 focused attention on the SVM watchword. Billy
Graham amended it from "The evangelization of the world in this
generation," to "The World must be evangelized in one decade."67

The following conventions addressed the issues of racism,
development, and war as part of the context of mission. Speakers
such as Ruben Lores of Costa Rica and Samuel Escobar from Latin
America challenged North American evangelicals to recognize the
need to ensure social justice and political reform as part of
their responsibility as Christians.

The convention in 1970 confronted evangelical students
with a new awareness of the world. Black evangelist Tom Skinner
warned students of the danger of racism hindering the evangelical thrust. Samuel Escobar spoke passionately on the need to
relate social concerns and world evangelism. George J. Taylor
pointedly asked why there were not more black missionaries.
Myron S. Augsburger highlighted the relationship between revolution and world evangelism. The theme, "Christ the Liberator"
challenged IVCF members to seek a personal involvement in suffering and in society as an important dimension of relevant
evangelism. Richard Quebedeaux has referred to this meeting as
one of the signs of the revolution in orthodoxy which has
recently produced a much deeper understanding of the social
dimensions of the gospel.68

The single most impressive aspect of the evangelical student movement is its strength and vitality, especially in comparison with the weak and diffuse nature of ecumenical student
activity. The growth of the North American evangelical mission
agencies in comparison to the decline of DOM-NCCC groups is
surely not unrelated to the involvement of students in mission-
related studies and gatherings such as Urbana.69

During the 1960s, the range of concerns and issues involved
in the discussion of evangelical mission theology broadened
considerably. This trend became evident as early as 1961 at
Urbana, and certainly in comparison with the IFMA-sponsored
Congress on World Missions (1960), the issues raised at Urbana

showed significant progress in serious reflection on the implications of changing conditions in the world for mission. The
stimulus of bringing together evangelical leaders from around
the world to the Urbana conventions has been fruitful in pointing the way in which evangelical mission theology has developed.

CHURCH GROWTH: THE TEST OF MISSION

Donald Anderson McGavran has been the chief proponent of
Church Growth as the strategic methodology to be used in missionary outreach in the post-World War II period. His interest
in and involvement with the development of strategies for mission grew out of his long experience as a missionary in India
with the United Christian Missionary Society (The Christian
Church, Disciples of Christ). Influenced by J. Waskom Pickett's
Christian Mass Movements in India (1933), and the writings of
Roland Allen, McGavran began his own study of Christian mission
in India, particularly relating to group conversion. The in-
scription in the volume of essays by McGavran and others on
"people movements" reads:

> Dedicated to those men and women who labor for the
> growth of churches, discarding theories of church
> growth which do not work, and learning and practicing
> productive patterns which actually disciple the
> peoples and increase the Household of God.[70]

That dedication may also be taken as a summary of the work in
which McGavran himself has been engaged from that time onwards,
in India until 1954 and after that primarily in the USA, especially through the Institute of Church Growth, first established
in 1960 at the Northwest Christian College, Eugene, Oregon and
from 1965 at the Fuller Theological Seminary, Pasadena, California.

Since moving to the Fuller Theological Seminary, the
school has expanded and developed the basic thrusts of the
church growth movement first set out by McGavran. A number of
colleagues have been associated with McGavran in this enterprise. Alan R. Tippett, a missionary-anthropologist, joined
the Institute of Church Growth in 1962; Ralph D. Winter has
contributed to the historical and statistical insights of the
school; C. Peter Wagner brought his wide experience in Bolivia
and South America to focus on the Latin American contribution
to church growth theory and anthropology; and Arthur Glasser
has helped in developing the theological basis of the movement.
Each has contributed to the interdisciplinary character of
church growth research. Despite certain individual differences
in emphasis, these men all understand the church's task as
having to do primarily with outreach and evangelism leading to
church growth.

The practical result of evangelism in relation to church growth has been an important critical perspective emphasized by the church growth movement: this issue has challenged the missionary enterprise at both the theological and theoretical levels. While the influence of church growth thought is most evident in evangelical groups, it has been felt throughout the whole church.[71] The reports from the ecumenical meetings at Uppsala and Bangkok clearly show the influence of the church growth movement.

The continuing basis of church growth thought and study has been the authority of the Bible and of those passages which command discipling, particularly the Great Commission. For McGavran this has always meant church growth because "a chief and irreplaceable purpose of Christian mission is to proclaim Christ *and to persuade men to become His disciples and responsible members of His Church.*"[72] McGavran and his colleagues have devoted their attention to these goals: to lift up church growth as an irreplaceable goal of mission, to research and show what factors help or hinder that process, and to disseminate through various publications, educational instruments and teaching opportunities the fundamental principles of church growth.[73]

McGavran began to publish his views widely in 1955 with the book, *The Bridges of God*, and an article in the IRM, "New Methods for a New Age in Missions."[74] He argued that the Mission Station Approach which had been predominant for the past one hundred and fifty years, based on a highly institutionalized Christian mission compound of largely Western culture into which individual Christians were brought, was wholly inadequate for the present situation. Instead, he proposed a "People Movements to Christ" strategy in which groups of people become Christians and form indigenous churches, and are then encouraged to use their natural cultural links to bring other responsive people to Christ, with minimal missionary oversight and institutional life.

This latter pattern was biblically based and historically fruitful, McGavran argued. He also has consistently maintained that the primary focus of missionary activity should be on the

> hundreds of thousands, who can be discipled this year and every succeeding year for the forseeable future, only if resources are concentrated behind the growing churches which exist in the midst of these responsive myriads.[75]

While other difficult and resistant fields should not be neglected, he has insisted that growing churches should receive major attention.

McGavran believed strongly that in India the mission, instead of being the servant of the church, had in fact become its master, controlling leadership, financial resources, strategy, and development of the church. He proposed that a People Movement Church would correct that situation because,

> when the mission serves a great growing People Movement church it readily and correctly comes under its control. It then becomes explicitly what it is now implicitly, the servant of the church. Missionaries would then be seen not as parents doing things for immature children but as useful foreign servants of the self-directing and self-governing People Movement churches. Missionaries would then be put under the direction of the national church to extend the Gospel . . . . The relationship of the future is that of missionary assistants, probably from several lands, accepted by a fully independent national church for the extension of the faith.[76]

It seemed obvious to McGavran that future missionary policy should encourage the transfer of authority to the indigenous church and develop self-support wherever possible, including the systematic reduction of grants; all this prefigured arguments later used in the "moratorium debate." However necessary the indigenization of the church is, nevertheless, McGavran argued, this was merely secondary to the main task of the church--evangelism--for which the mission was to be the servant of the church.

> In the harvesting which lies ahead in all lands, problems of prestige, protocol and organization are secondary to winning the winnable now, and can be solved satisfactorily for all concerned as we concentrate on the main task.[77]

By holding a clear distinction in function between church and mission, McGavran believes the issue of their relationship can be solved. In his view:

> the missionary society is not the church . . . . The mission plants church after church which, when established, touches every aspect of life, including both propagating the gospel and changing the culture so that it conforms more to God's will.[78]

The narrow, concise definition of mission as essentially church planting helped McGavran achieve conceptual clarity at this point.

In the determination of missionary policy, which has always been the aim of McGavran's endeavors, he has seen that thorough research is essential to understand and then to promote an adequate conception of church growth.

The ways by which churches grow, or are hindered in growth, have been explored and investigated through research and analysis with people from various parts of the world at the Institute of Church Growth. Examples include Keith E. Hamilton (Bolivia), William R. Read (Brazil), J. C. Wold (Liberia), and R. E. Shearer (Korea). The theological, anthropological, cultural, and historical, and methodological dimensions of church growth have been delineated through this research. The task of fostering interest in church growth through lectures, seminars, teaching schools, and consultations continues apace.[79]

Church Growth, as the movement uses the term, describes a complex process. McGavran began with the terms "discipling" and "perfecting" to describe the growth of a church. Tippett has added to this a third notion of "organic" growth and has refined church growth theory into quantitative, qualitative, and organic growth. Quantitative growth refers mainly to numerical increase by conversion. Qualitative growth relates to the internal growth of the fellowship of Christians in sanctification and perfection. Organic growth points to the emergence of a church as "the church in a community, an indigenous body," in which organizational patterns reflect development in depth and outreach.[80]

In the statistical and analytic study of church growth another three-fold distinction has been made among biological, transfer, and conversion growth. Biological growth derives from those born into Christian families. Transfer growth refers to the increase of certain congregations at the expense of others, by change of location or denominational affiliation. Conversion growth,

> in which those outside the church come to rest their
> faith intelligently on Jesus Christ and are baptized
> . . . is the only kind of growth by which the Good News
> of salvation can spread to earth's remotest end.[81]

To critics who contend that this approach emphasizes quantity over quality, Ralph D. Winter responded that properly and carefully understood, quantity statistics are reliable indicators of qualities, because quantities and qualities are inseparable parts of the same reality.[82]

Evangelism is central to church growth theology and the heart of that evangelism is that people who are lost must be

found. In the midst of all the other activities in which the
church must be engaged this was, is, and remains a crucial
issue: "God-in-Christ desires beyond question that persons can
be found, be reconciled to Himself." This theology of *harvest*
has been the distinctive mark of the church growth movement.[83]

Firmly convinced of the above goal of mission or evangelism
(the two are virtually synonymous for McGavran) as "the purpose-
ful communication of the Good News of God's redeeming act,"[84]
the Institute of Church Growth organized a program of research
on responsive peoples, because McGavran believed "that never in
1900 years have there been as many winnable people in the world
as there are today."[85] The continual thrust of his statement
in the 1960s was that

> *Millions want to be told of the Saviour and persuaded
> to believe in Him.* The hyper-cautious strategy of
> the fifties, suited to "mission" in Europe, and assum-
> ing non-Christians always to be hostile to the Gospel,
> no longer applies in half of the world . . . . We
> face the most winnable populations which ever existed.[86]

The research program at the Institute of Church Growth
presented carefully documented case studies of responsive
peoples in many places--Bolivia, Korea, Mexico, New Guinea were
early studies--and these have extended to over 150 books,
theses, and papers by 1976. Both responsive and unresponsive
situations have been analyzed to discover what factors enhance
or hinder the growth of churches. This intensive focus on
research continues to be one of the most valuable features of
the whole church growth movement.

Research on evangelism, involving several academic disciplines, has been an important growing point in the church growth
school. One major focus has been the identification of *ta ethne*
in the Great Commission not as "all nations," but as "all
peoples." That particular exegetical point has then been linked
with a sociological and anthropological analysis of the world
as a cultural mosaic in which the population of the earth is
viewed as a vast mosaic of "peoples," consisting of homogeneous
units of people sharing common characteristics, especially a
common racial, linguistic, and class heritage.[87] McGavran has
argued that recognition of this enormous variety will mean that
methods and means of evangelism must constantly be shaped and
measured to see whether they further discipling in that particular piece of the mosaic.

The insight that the world consists of many cultural
groups has given rise to a notable development in the analysis
of different types of cross-cultural evangelism necessary to

complete the task of church planting among all peoples. Ralph
D. Winter described this in his distinctions between E-1, E-2,
and E-3 evangelism. He argued that:

> Most non-Christians in the world today are not cultur-
> ally near any neighbours of Christians, and that it
> will take a special kind of "cross-cultural" evangelism
> to reach them.[88]

From his analysis and research Winter has become convinced that
E-1 evangelism, involving persons of similar culture, can only
reach a small proportion of non-Christians; consequently, E-2
evangelism to a culturally related person, and E-3, evangelism
to a culturally unrelated person, remain of paramount importance.[89] Winter has also argued that specialized groups of
missionaries prepared for cross-cultural witness will be necessary to fulfill the mission of the church.[90]

McGavran's understanding of the primacy of evangelism has
consistently led him to stress that small Christian communities
are often unable effectively to fulfill the task of outreach
because of the size of the remaining task. While arguing for
local churches to be strong and free from outside domination,
he also maintains that cross-cultural missionaries are still
needed in large numbers.[91]

An important distinction in McGavran's thought is the difference between discipling and perfecting. The discipling
stage is marked by a transition from a non-Christian religion
to "putting Christ at the centre on the Throne." Only when
this necessary stage has been passed will the process of perfecting the people begin. Perfecting is the "bringing about of
an ethical change in the discipled group, an increasing achievement of a thoroughly Christian way of life for the community as
a whole."[92] While both these processes go together in a congregation, in dealing with non-Christian peoples, discipling
must precede perfecting growth. McGavran's writings are characterized by an apparently one-sided bias toward discipling.
His emphasis, however, has aimed at redressing a serious imbalance because "there is a constitutional bias toward perfecting. The churches gravitate toward caring for what they have.
Their inbuilt nature prefers perfecting."[93]

Yet the church growth movement has not neglected perfecting
and, in recent years especially, leadership training[94] has become an essential aspect of church planting, with the development of theological education by extension, an important feature of perfecting.

To understand the relationship between evangelism and

social action in the thought of the church growth movement, one
must consider the main thrust and emphasis towards discipling
which has just been noted. Nowhere does McGavran say that discipling is the *only* task which the church must accomplish.
Rather, he teaches, only when churches have been planted can
effective progress be made in the areas of education, medical
care, and agricultural improvement, that is, to "lift" people.
In one of his most balanced summaries, he stated:

> I thoroughly agree that the church must lift. One
> wants her to lift far more widely than she is now
> doing. One wants a congregation to exist in every
> section of every city and in every village and hamlet
> throughout the earth, for only then will the passion
> of God for righteousness and justice working through
> men dedicated to His will and feeding on His Word be
> applied to every community.[95]

McGavran clearly gave priority to discipling, and his consistent reiteration of this position has tended to create an impression of an imbalance in his writings which, while understandable, does not do justice to his best statements on the
relationship between evangelism and social action.

The influence of the church growth movement as a corrective
and stimulus to the mission theology debate has been valuable.
With a clear conception of mission as evangelism designed to
produce church growth, McGavran and his followers have developed
a thorough study of the various types of evangelism as they relate to the variety of cultural situations in which missionaries
must work. The church growth movement's research program has
explored a wide range of situations and can give deep insight
into factors which hinder or foster church growth. The term
church growth itself has evolved into a comprehensive notion
involving qualitative, quantitative, and organic growth factors.
New methods of leadership training have been developed, for
example, theological education by extension--widely used first
in Central America and now throughout the world--with materials
specifically created and disseminated for that purpose.

Yet church growth theology has some serious weaknesses
which should be probed and examined. All that can be done here
is to raise issues for discussion. The narrow conception of
mission as evangelism in obedience to the Great Commission has
given clarity to the church growth position, but any theology
of mission which does not seriously take into account the whole
task of mission runs the risk of being distorted and imbalanced.
At this point, the church growth movement appears to have neglected a substantial discussion which has taken place over the
past twenty-five years, in which the meaning of mission, evan-

gelism, witness, service, and salvation have been explored and developed.[96]

One specific example may be offered. The understanding of evangelism primarily as verbal proclamation, which is largely assumed by church growth proponents, does not do justice to either the biblical understanding of the communication of the gospel or the gospel itself, which seeks the total transformation of humanity. The incarnational nature of communication, exemplified by the Word becoming flesh and by the command of Christ to his disciples, "As the Father has sent me, even so I send you," points to a process of communication involving physical, spiritual, intellectual, and social dimensions by which concepts, attitudes, and experiences are shared with others. The good news of Jesus Christ relates to the kingdom of God, which involves the total life of people in their relations with God and each other. An understanding of evangelism primarily in terms of verbal proclamation limits that understanding of the nature and aim of God's good news for all people.

The strategy of evangelism evolved in church growth thought has attempted to involve several disciplines—theological, historical, and anthropological insights particularly. But the approach in the use of these disciplines has tended to be quite narrow, namely, to see how they can contribute to the understanding of evangelism. Thus, social change is considered as a valuable area of study because it helps mission strategists to see which groups are likely to be most responsive to the gospel. The larger questions relating to the forces involved in social change, the direction of change, and the ethical responsibility which Christians have towards those in all kinds of needs, are virtually ignored.[97]

The disjunction between discipling and perfecting seems artificial and unnecessary. The act of discipling must be seen in an ethical context and not merely in terms of a decision for Christ. While Christians may be going on to perfection the whole of their lives, the beginning of that process must include an awareness and acceptance of the implications of discipleship according to the teaching of Christ. Baptizing and teaching are equally part of "making disciples."

The ecclesiological implications of church growth theory need further probing. Hoekendijk's strictures about the church being an illegitimate center for missionary thinking have had no discernible effect on church growth thinking. Indeed, the major point which emerges is that the quantity of church growth has become the most important criterion for mission, with negligible emphasis on other aspects of qualitative or organic growth,[98] and little on the renewal of existing church life.

While church growth understands itself to be a corrective to the kinds of mission which have lost touch with the need to reach those outside the life of the church with the gospel of Christ, only churches which are themselves renewed can undertake that task. Church growth cannot therefore neglect church renewal and criteria for determining faithfulness to the gospel in existing churches if in fact it is the existing churches which must be involved in mission.

Virtually nothing appears in church growth thought concerning the unity of the church. In fact, the emphasis on ethnic churches would seem to suggest that church growth has little interest in unity. Such a theological omission in a theory of mission which concentrates so heavily on the church seems dangerous.[99]

The church growth movement shares with liberation theology a deep concern for praxis, which recognizes that theological formulations must be understood in relation to the forms of historical action which they encourage or support. The research accomplished by church growth proponents has clearly shown two things: first, that there are many people who are responsive to the gospel today; second, that most missionaries are concentrated among a relatively small proportion of the non-Christian population of the world.[100] As yet, little has been done to show how the present imbalance of missionary effort can be overcome. McGavran asked in 1968 "Will Uppsala Betray the Two Billion?" but neither he nor his colleagues have yet offered proposals for reaching the vast numbers of Chinese, Hindu, or Muslim persons who constitute the great proportion of that number. The Institute of Church Growth and the newly established United States Center for World Mission (of which Ralph Winter is president) confront a major challenge in providing a feasible plan to accomplish this task in the future.

When McGavran began the Institute of Church Growth in 1960, he stood virtually alone, struggling to have his views heard in both conservative evangelical and ecumenical circles. The influence of the church growth movement since then on all missionary agencies has made it one of the most creative and important forces to emerge in this study of Christian mission theology.

SUMMARY

The theological ferment which characterized the last decades of the nineteenth and early part of the twentieth centuries in Protestantism created a division between those who supported the attempt to relate Christianity to modern movements in historical, scientific, and theological developments, and those who opposed such an attempt because it seemed to deny the

truth, uniqueness, and validity of the Christian religion. In
the USA this became a struggle between "liberals" and the fundamentalists, the latter term describing those who adhered to the
doctrines expressed in a series of essays entitled *The Fundamentals*.

Fundamentalists became alienated from the mainstream of
Protestant denominations, preferring to establish independent
institutions and churches. Frequently the fundamentalists
repudiated all attempts to relate positively to movements seeking reform in society and cooperation between churches. In
denying these influences which characterized evangelicals in
the nineteenth century, fundamentalists suffered and fostered
"a great reversal" from their earlier heritage.

In the years since World War II, a resurgence of life,
vitality, and identity amongst evangelicals has emerged. Unhappy with the divisive, negative attitude of fundamentalists,
evangelicals (while holding similar doctrinal views), have
created structures for cooperation and organizations for arti-
culating and fostering shared interests in the fields of mission, outreach, and service.

The oldest evangelical missionary association, consisting
of affiliated independent missionary groups, is the IFMA. Begun
in 1917, it has grown rapidly since World War II and sponsored
the first evangelical Congress on World Missions in Chicago in
1960. That meeting basically reaffirmed evangelical mission
theology, centering on evangelism in obedience to the Great
Commission to those who are lost. At this time, the IFMA had
few contacts with other evangelicals and viewed other Protestants
and Roman Catholics with very great suspicion. The beginnings
of cooperative contacts with EFMA leaders in matters of common
concern can be noted from 1957 through the early 1960s.

Other American evangelicals supported the NAE and its missionary arm, the EFMA, when they became established in the 1940s.
Motivated by a desire to advance an evangelical viewpoint not
adequately expressed in the Foreign Missions Conference or the
Federal Council of the Churches of Christ in America, and by
the need to further evangelical cooperation and unity, the EFMA
has fostered missionary activity among evangelical denominations and groups, stressing evangelism and a firm doctrinal
commitment as central aspects of missionary policy.

Evangelicalism at the worldwide level found organizational
identity in the World Evangelical Fellowship established in
1951. This body has remained relatively weak but is one way
evangelicals from many national associations remain in contact
with each other.

Student activities in many countries have been encouraged through national inter-varsity groups. The strongest of these is the American Inter-Varsity Christian Fellowship which has sponsored missionary conventions since 1946. These triennial gatherings at Urbana have been valuable highpoints for promoting Christian mission, with evangelical leaders from around the world providing stimulus and challenge for student participants.

The most persuasive and extensive evangelical contribution to mission theology has come through the Church Growth movement with Donald McGavran as its chief spokesman, in the period following 1960. Based upon a belief that evangelism leading to church growth is an essential dimension of the Christian mission, McGavran and his colleagues have developed an extensive research and teaching facility in the Institute of Church Growth, located first at Northwest Christian College, Oregon and, since 1965, as part of the Fuller Theological Seminary. The interdisciplinary approach used in analyzing and assessing factors which hinder or assist church growth (understood primarily in quantitative terms, but with some concern for qualitative and organic development), has challenged both ecumenical and conservative evangelical agencies to consider this dimension of mission theology, especially through the study of what is actually happening at many specific points of engagement. The weakness of church growth theology in relation to a comprehensive understanding of mission and concerning ecclesiology cannot detract from the fruitful influence of this important movement.

In 1966 two major events involving evangelicals gave notice of the new surge of vitality which had been developing, especially in the USA, since World War II. The Berlin World Congress on Evangelism and the Wheaton Congress on the Church's Worldwide Mission mark the start of a new engagement by evangelicals with each other, the whole church, and the whole world. The next chapter will deal with these meetings.

NOTES

[1]W. Richey Hogg, "The Role of American Protestantism in World Mission" in R. Pierce Beaver, ed., *American Missions in Bicentennial Perspective* (Pasadena: William Carey Library, 1977), p. 369.

[2]Ibid., p. 387.

[3]For comparative figures see Edward R. Dayton, "Current Trends in North American Protestant Missions Overseas," *Occasional Bulletin of Missionary Research* 1.2 (1977): 6-7. This position had changed somewhat by 1976. Dayton noted that be-

tween 1968 and 1976 unaffiliated missionary groups, of which
the Wycliffe Bible Translators and the Southern Baptists are
the largest, had become the fastest growing and largest part
of the total missionary force from North America.

[4]See, for example, the IFMA "Confession of Faith"; the
"Statement of Faith," adopted by the National Association of
Evangelicals (NAE) and its missionary arm, the EFMA; and the
"Doctrinal Basis" of the International Fellowship of Evangeli-
cal Students.

[5]Both terms are used by the publication, *Christianity Today*
(CT), which was founded to promote the conservative evangelical
position; see Harold John Ockenga, "Resurgent Evangelical
Leadership," CT 5.1 (Oct. 10, 1960) and G. C. Berkouwer, "What
Conservative Evangelicals Can Learn from the Ecumenical Movement," CT 10.17 (May 27, 1966). Cf. Ralph D. Winter in *The
Evangelical Response to Bangkok*, pp. 2-5, where he argues
against evangelicals accepting the term "conservative." The
use of the word "evangelical" to describe the position developed
in the next three chapters does not deny that there are many
Christians in the ecumenical movement who rightfully describe
their own faith as "evangelical," namely, who are firmly committed to God's good news in Jesus Christ and are seriously and
actively involved in proclaiming and witnessing to that faith.

[6]Ockenga, "Resurgent Evangelical Leadership," pp. 11-13.

[7]Of the 800 Christian leaders present from at least 11
countries at the founding of the Alliance in 1846, some ten
percent came from America. However, the slavery issue proved
troublesome and it was not until 1867 that a branch of the
Alliance was organized in the USA through the work of William
E. Dodge. Philip Schaff and Josiah Strong provided strong
leadership in the Alliance in the USA until it withered around
1900; see Don Herbert Yoder, "Christian Unity in Nineteenth-
Century America" in Rouse and Neill, *Ecumenical Movement*,
pp. 254-56.

[8]John W. Ewing, *Goodly Fellowship* (London: Marshall,
Morgan and Scott, 1946), pp. 15-18.

[9]Ruth Rouse, "Voluntary Movements and the Changing Ecumenical Climate" in Rouse and Neill, *Ecumenical Movement*, pp. 320-22.

[10]J. Herbert Kane's *Faith, Mighty Faith* (New York: IFMA,
1956) briefly describes these and many other faith missions.

[11]Ernest R. Sandeen, *The Roots of Fundamentalism: British
and American Millenarianism 1800-1930* Chicago: University of

Chicago Press, 1970), pp. 140-41. The text of this creed appears in Sandeen, pp. 273-77. In footnote No. 19 on p. 141 Sandeen asserts that Steward G. Cole in *The History of Fundamentalism* (New York: Richard R. Smith, 1931), p. 34, was mistaken in stating that Niagara adopted a five-point creed in 1895.

[12]Robert D. Linder in David F. Wells and John D. Woodbridge, eds., *The Evangelicals: What They Believe, Who They Are, Where They are Changing* (Nashville: Abingdon, 1975), p. 196.

[13]For example, in the Baptist Church a significant number withdrew over a period of time, forming the General Association of Regular Baptist Churches (1932), the Baptist General Conference (1946), and the Conservative Baptist Association (1947). John Gresham Machen withdrew from the Presbyterian Church to found the Westminster Theological Seminary. See James DeForest Murch, *Cooperation Without Compromise: A History of the National Association of Evangelicals* (Grand Rapids: Eerdmans, 1956), pp. 32-37; and Bruce L. Shelley, *Evangelicalism in America* (Grand Rapids: Eerdmans, 1967), pp. 62-63.

[14]Carl F. H. Henry, *The Uneasy Conscience of Modern Fundamentalism* (Grand Rapids: Eerdmans, 1947), pp. 30, 33, 42, 45; cf. David O. Moberg, *The Great Reversal: Evangelism versus Social Concern* (Philadelphia: J. B. Lippincott, 1972), especially chapter 2, "The Great Reversal." For a renewed plea by Henry to evangelicals to undertake a more effective social witness, see *Evangelicals in Search of Identity* (Waco, Tx.: Word Books, 1976), pp. 57-72.

[15]C. Gordon Beacham, "The Jubilee of IFMA--Has God Used Us?" in *IFMA Study Papers, 1967. 50th Annual Meeting 25-28 September 1967 held at Grace Chapel, Havertown, Pennsylvania* (IFMA: mimeographed).

[16]See, "IFMA Policy on Relations"; Edwin L. Frizen, Jr., "The IFMA Story," and "Missionary Organizational Relations" (IFMA: mimeographed).

[17]*IFMA News*, Fourth Issue (1976): 7. The 1976 total of 9,483 personnel consisted of 7,188 from North America and 2,295 from other countries. The figure of 7,188 includes 782 home staff and 368 short-term missionaries.

[18]J. O. Percy, compiler; Mary Bennett, ed., *Facing the Unfinished Task. Messages delivered at the Congress on World Mission. Sponsored by the IFMA of North America* (Grand Rapids: Zondervan, 1961), p. 7. The Resolutions passed at the Congress appear in *IFMA News* (Jan. 1961): 6-7 and also in Denton Lotz, "'The Evangelization of the World in This Generation'": The

Resurgence of a Missionary Idea Among the Conservative Evangelicals" (Ph.D. dissertation at the University of Hamburg,
1970), pp. 505-506. Hereafter cited as *Evangelization*.

[19]Limited cooperation between the IFMA and the EFMA began
as early as 1957 when the Evangelical Committee on Latin America
was established. For a list of joint IFMA-EFMA meetings, see
Edwin L. Fritzen, Jr., "The IFMA Today" in *IFMA Study Papers*.

[20]See, for example, the presentations by John F. Walvoord,
President of Dallas Theological Seminary, on "The Theological
Basis for Foreign Missions," and by Charles J. Woodbridge on
"The Evangelical Answer to Ecumenism." The concern for lost
souls was highlighted by a traffic light suspended over the
entrance to the sanctuary, with a sign which read, "On each red
flash a lost soul enters eternity. Three every two seconds."

[21]*Facing the Unfinished Task*, pp. 7, 143, 149; Preamble to
the Congress Resolutions.

[22]Ibid., pp. 23, 25, 180, 262-63.

[23]The four nationals were Emilio Nuñez from Guatemala,
Akira Hatori from Japan, M. R. Rajnoor from India, and Stephen
Sitole from Rhodesia.

[24]*Facing the Unfinished Task*, pp. 211-212; cf. 10, 25-26,
and Resolutions.

[25]Ibid., p. 243.

[26]Ibid., pp. 261-63.

[27]Ibid., p. 269.

[28]Ibid., p. 215. An example of this issue was the withdrawal of the Wycliffe Bible Translators from the IFMA in early
1960 after anonymous accusations from within the IFMA that Wycliffe had assisted Roman Catholics in Latin America and shared
facilities and equipment with other Christian groups in some
areas. This was not openly mentioned at the Congress. See
James and Marti Hefley, *Uncle Cam: The Story of William Cameron
Townsend Founder of the Wycliffe Bible Translators and the Summer Institute of Linguistics* (Waco, Tx.: Word Books, 1974),
pp. 200-206. Cf. Harold Lindsell, "Faith Missions Since 1938"
in Wilbur C. Harr, ed., *Frontiers of the Christian World Mission
Since 1938. Essays in Honor of Kenneth Scott Latourette* (New
York: Harper and Brothers, 1962), pp. 221-223.

[29]*Facing the Unfinished Task*, p. 264.

³⁰Ibid., pp. 43, 44, 47, 52, 64-65, 181-87, 242.

³¹Lotz, *Evangelization*, p. 54.

³²Murch, *Cooperation Without Compromise*, pp. 51-52; Shelley, *Evangelicalism in America*, pp. 72-73.

³³Murch, *Cooperation Without Compromise*, p. 58.

³⁴Ibid., pp. 62-70.

³⁵In 1965 the NAE claimed a membership of 2,547,312 composed of 34 denominations, 8 conferences, 9 associations, and individually affiliated churches, with a service constituency of 10,000,000; see "The Ecumenical Movement Today," CT 9.9 (Jan. 29, 1965): 5, for a thorough statistical report.

³⁶Murch, *Cooperation Without Compromise*, p. 59.

³⁷Ockenga to the St. Louis Assembly, quoted in Shelley, *Evangelicalism in America*, p. 82.

³⁸Murch, *Cooperation Without Compromise*, pp. 58-59; Shelley, *Evangelicalism in America*, p. 82.

³⁹Murch, *Cooperation Without Compromise*, pp. 68-70.

⁴⁰*United Evangelical Action* (Mar. 15, 1957): 35.

⁴¹Murch, *Cooperation Without Compromise*, p. 102; Dayton, *Mission Handbook*, pp. 384-85; and a personal letter to the writer from Wade T. Coggins, Exec. Dir. of the EFMA (24 Feb., 1977).

⁴²See Article II of the "Constitution of the Evangelical Foreign Missions Association" (Feb. 1976: mimeographed).

⁴³Murch, *Cooperation Without Compromise*, p. 100; cf. Cavert, *Church Cooperation and Unity in America*, pp. 50-51.

⁴⁴"Constitution of the EFMA."

⁴⁵Tom Watson, "The Future of the IFMA" in *IFMA Study Papers*.

⁴⁶See Edwin L. (Jack) Frizen, "The IFMA Today" in *IFMA Study Papers*; and Harold Lindsell, "Faith Missions Since 1938," pp. 217-218 in Harr, *Frontiers of the Christian World Mission*.

⁴⁷Murch, *Cooperation Without Compromise*, p. 179.

⁴⁸Ibid., pp. 184-89; see also Everett L. Cattell, "National

Association of Evangelicals and World Evangelical Fellowship,"
CT 9.9 (Jan. 29, 1965): 12-14. The seven founding member
groups were from Ceylon, Cyprus, Great Britain, India, Japan,
Taiwan, and the USA. Cattell reports that more than twenty
national fellowships had joined the WEF by 1965.

[49]Cattell, "National Association of Evangelicals and the
World Evangelical Fellowship," p. 13.

[50]See Carl McIntire, *Servants of Apostasy* (Collingswood,
N.J.: Christian Beacon Press, 1955), pp. 357-66; J. Oliver
Buswell, Jr., "The American and the International Council of
Churches," CT 9.9 (Jan. 29, 1965): 9-11; and Ralph Lord Roy,
Apostles of Discord (Boston: Beacon Press, 1953), pp. 186-90.

[51]Accurate statistics for the ACCC are difficult to obtain.
McIntire, ibid., p. 380, lists the membership in 1954 as
1,183,977. Over one-third (440,161) were in the category of
Individual Auxiliary Membership, who belonged to churches in the
NCCC. Only 263,311 belonged to the 17 constituent bodies; but
Buswell, "The American and the International Councils of Christian Churches" (1965) gave a figure of 1.5 million, including
the total constituency of member denominations as 939,537, with
the added note "Not all the churches in these denominations are
in the ACCC"; cf. Roy, *Apostles of Discord,* pp. 196-98.

[52]McIntire, *Servants of Apostasy*, p. 359.

[53]Ibid., pp. 327-28; cf. Roy, *Apostles of Discord,*
pp. 223-27.

[54]McIntire, *Servants of Apostasy*, p. 195.

[55]Ibid., p. 106.

[56]Ibid., p. 386.

[57]See Dayton, *Mission Handbook*, 10th ed., pp. 413-15 and
Mission Handbook, 11th ed., pp. 375, 387-88 for an incomplete
list of TAM-ICCC; and a total of about 1,850 Fellowship of
Missions missionaries, with 1,364 listed as overseas personnel
in 1976.

[58]Richard Quebedeaux, *The Young Evangelicals: Revolution
in Orthodoxy* (New York: Harper and Row, 1974), p. 24.

[59]William H. Beahm, "Factors in the Development of the
Student Volunteer Movement for Foreign Missions" (Ph.D. disser-
tation, University of Chicago, 1941), p. 41; cf. David M. Howard,
Student Power in World Evangelism (Downers Grove, Ill.: Inter-

Varsity Press, 1970), p. 90.

[60]Rouse, *The World's Student Christian Federation* , pp. 93-94.

[61]Warren, *Crowded Canvas*, p. 40. J. C. Pollock in *A Cambridge Movement* (London: John Murray, 1954), p. 214, reports that Stephen Neill was also college representative of the CICCU and President of the SCM when at Cambridge.

[62]Douglas Johnson, ed., *A Brief History of the International Fellowship of Evangelical Students* (Lausanne: Intervarsity Fellowship of Evangelical Students, 1964), p. 44. IVFs were formed in Canada (1929), Australia (1936), and New Zealand (1936).

[63]Ibid., pp. 51, 72.

[64]Ibid., p. 173. In 1964 the IFES had twenty-four affiliated member movements. See ibid., pp. 115-164 for a brief description of the member movements.

[65]The dates, themes, and number of participants from 1946 to 1976 were:

Year	Theme	Participants
1946	Christ's Commission	575
1948	No information available	---
1951	By All Means Proclaim Christ	1,500
1954	Changing World--Unchanging Christ	3,200
1957	One Lord, One Christ, One World	5,300
1961	Commission, Conflict, Commitment	5,400
1964	Change, Witness, Triumph	7,000
1967	God's Men--From All Nations to All Nations	9,200
1970	Christ the Liberator	12,300
1973	Jesus Christ: Lord of the Universe, Hope of the World	14,000
1976	Declare His Glory Among the Nations	15,000

Compiled from the published Reports of the Conventions by Inter-Varsity Press and from Lotz, *Evangelization*, pp. 377-399. For further details of some of the Urbana Conventions see these reports and evaluations in CT and EMQ:

"Missionary Drive Paces Inter-Varsity Conclave," CT 6.8 (Jan. 19, 1962): 29-31.
"Youth in Search of a Mission," CT 9.8 (Jan. 15, 1965): 38-41.
"Inter-Varsity: A Reality that Can't be Faked," CT 12.8 (Jan. 19, 1968): 35-36.
"Evangelical Student Power: Urbana '70," CT 15.8 (Jan. 29, 1971): 29-30.

James W. Reapsome, "Urbana '70: Our Man's Impression," EMQ 7.3 (1971): 129-32.
"Urbana '73: 'A Way I Can Help'," CT 18.8 (Jan. 18, 1974): 41-43.
David M. Howard, "Urbana '73 Theme Emphasizes Positive View of Missions," EMQ 9.2 (1973): 118-21.
David M. Howard, "What Happened at Urbana?" EMQ 13.3 (1977): 141-48.

66Eric S. Fife and Arthur F. Glasser, *Missions in Crisis: Rethinking Missionary Strategy* (Chicago: Inter-Varsity Press, 1961).

67*Commission, Conflict, Commitment: Messages from the Sixth International Student Missionary Convention* (Chicago: Inter-Varsity Press, 1962), pp. 3-4; cf. pp. 115, 198; and Lotz, *Evangelization*, pp. 388-89.

68Quebedeaux, *The Young Evangelicals*, pp. 92-94.

69See P. F. Barkman, E. R. Dayton, and E. L. Gruman, *Christian Collegians and Foreign Missions* (Monrovia, Ca.: MARC, 1969), for a detailed analysis of the views of students at the 1967 Convention.

70J. W. Pickett, A. L. Warnshuis, G. H. Singh, D. A. McGavran, *Church Growth and Group Conversion*, 4th ed. (first published as *Christian Missions in Mid-India*, reprinted and expanded edition by William Carey Library, Pasadena, 1973).

71Especially during the 1960s McGavran took every opportunity to develop his views, conducting seminars for both IFMA and EFMA leaders, and participating in a consultation convened by Victor E. W. Hayward under WCC-CWME auspices at Iberville, Canada in 1963 on "The Growth of the Church." The IRM 57.227 (1968) on "Church Growth" carried the Iberville statement and discussion of church growth theology.

72Donald A. McGavran, *Understanding Church Growth* (Grand Rapids: Eerdmans, 1970), p. 82--McGavran's emphasis. See also A. R. Tippett, ed., *God, Man and Church Growth. A Festschrift in Honor of Donald Anderson McGavran* (Grand Rapids: Eerdmans, 1973), p. 38.

73The stimulus given to mission research, publication, and dissemination of literature through the Institute of Church Growth, the William Carey Library, and the Church Growth Bulletin and Book Club have all been notable practical expressions of these goals.

74Donald Anderson McGavran, *The Bridges of God. A Study*

in the Strategy of Missions (New York: Friendship Press, 1955);
Donald McGavran, "New Methods for a New Age in Missions," IRM
44.176 (1955): 394-403.

[75]"New Methods for a New Age in Missions," p. 402.

[76]*The Bridges of God*, p. 136; cf. the concept of Joint
Action for Mission proposed in the ecumenical movement, and
Orchard's *Out of Every Nation*.

[77]Donald Anderson McGavran, "After the First Flush of
Success," IRM 48.191 (1959): 271. A similar point appeared in
"Wrong Strategy: The Real Crisis in Missions," IRM 54.216
(1965): 451, 455.

[78]Donald A. McGavran, ed., *Crucial Issues in Missions
Tomorrow* (Chicago: Moody Press, 1972), p. 10 and *Understanding
Church Growth*, p. 34. The relationship of mission to church
planting in McGavran's thought closely resembles pre-Vatican II
Roman Catholic mission theology.

[79]For the development of the Institute of Church Growth to
1965 see Herbert Melvin Works, "The Church Growth Movement to
1965: An Historical Perspective" (D.Miss. dissertation, Fuller
Theological Seminary, 1974), chaps. 6-8.

[80]Alan R. Tippett, *Solomon Islands Christianity: A Study
in Growth and Obstruction* (London: Lutterworth, 1967; reprint
ed., South Pasadena: William Carey Library), p. 31; also A. R.
Tippett, *Church Growth and the Word of God. The Basis of the
Church Growth Viewpoint* (Grand Rapids: Eerdmans, 1970), passim.

[81]McGavran, *Understanding Church Growth*, p. 88.

[82]Ralph D. Winter, "Quality or Quantity?" in McGavran,
Crucial Issues in Mission Tomorrow, pp. 175-87.

[83]Donald McGavran, "The God Who Finds and His Mission,"
IRM 51.203 (1962): 304.

[84]*Church Growth Bulletin* 1.1 (1964): 2-3.

[85]Donald McGavran, "The Institute of Church Growth,"
IRM 50.200 (1961): 431.

[86]Donald McGavran, "Church Growth Strategy Continued,"
IRM 57.227 (1968): 334. This optimistic statement was tempered
somewhat by McGavran in *Understanding Church Growth* (pp. 56-57)
when he recognized that "it is true that some countries present
hindrances to mission--China, India, Egypt, Russia . . . . Well

over half the population of the world is still indifferent or even hostile to the Good News . . . compared to a time when everyone was hostile, now only some are."

[87]McGavran, *Understanding Church Growth*, pp. 62-63, and chapters 10-11; "Church Growth Strategy Continued," p. 340; "The Dimensions of World Evangelization" in *Lausanne, 1974.*

[88]Ralph D. Winter, "The Highest Priority: Cross-Cultural Evangelism" in *Lausanne, 1974*, p. 213.

[89]Ibid., pp. 213-41 for the full development of this argument.

[90]Ralph D. Winter, "Churches Need Missions Because Modalities Need Sodalities," EMQ 7.4 (1971): 193-200.

[91]See, for example, Donald A. McGavran, "World Evangelization at the Mercy of Church-Mission 'Disease'," EMQ 13.4 (1977): 333-37.

[92]McGavran, *The Bridges of God*, pp. 13-16.

[93]Donald McGavran, *How Churches Grow: The New Frontiers of Mission* (London: World Dominion Press, 1959), p. 93.

[94]See, for example, Donald A. McGavran and Winn C. Arn, *How to Grow a Church* (Glendale, Ca.: Regal Books (1973), pp. 89-97, where five classes of leadership in growing churches are described.

[95]*Understanding Church Growth*, p. 275; and the whole of chapter 14, "Halting Due to Redemption and Life"; cf. also "Wrong Strategy," pp. 450-58; "Church Growth Strategy Continued," pp. 338-39; Tippett, *God, Man and Church Growth*, pp. 28-30, 37. For similar position held by Tippett, see *Verdict Theology in Mission Theory* 2nd ed. (Pasadena: William Carey Library, 1973), pp. 64-65, 77-78.

[96]See, for example, two evangelical discussions by Jack E. Shepherd, "Continuity and Change in Christian Mission" in Tippett, *God, Man and Church Growth*, and John R. W. Stott, *Christian Mission in the Modern World* (London: Falcon, 1975).

[97]See further Costas, *The Church and Its Mission*, pp. 145-49.

[98]See J. Verkuyl, "The Mission of God and the Missions of the Churches," *Occasional Essays* (San Jose, Costa Rica: CELEP, Jan. 1977), pp. 32-33.

[99]See the report of a recent consultation touching this

point sponsored by the Lausanne Theology and Education Group in
Missiology 5.4 (1977):   507-513; and Victor E. W. Hayward and
Donald McGavran, "Without Crossing Barriers?   One in Christ v.
Discipling Diverse Cultures," *Missiology* 2.2 (1974): 203-224.

[100]See especially the work of Ralph D. Winter for this
latter point, "The Highest Priority: Cross-Cultural Evangelism"
in *Lausanne, 1974*, pp. 230-35 and "Who are the Three Billion?"
Church Growth Bulletin 13.5 and 6 (1977):   123-26, 139-44.
Eugene D'Souza made the same essential point at Vatican II; see
Council Speeches of Vatican II, ed. by Yves Congar, Hans Küng,
and Daniel O'Hanlon (Glen Rock, N.J.:   Paulist Press, 1964),
pp. 281-82.

5

Seeking to Engage a
Revolutionary World: 1966-1975

The emergence of a constructive and comprehensive conservative evangelical mission theology may best be seen in three
major gatherings of evangelicals between 1966 and 1974. The
first, at Wheaton in early 1966, drew together the EFMA and
IFMA as co-sponsors of a Congress on the Church's Worldwide
Mission which, while largely North American in composition, had
a worldwide focus. Later in 1966, the second meeting brought
evangelicals from around the world to Berlin for a genuinely
worldwide gathering at the World Congress on Evangelism. While
organized and sponsored by North American organizations, it
produced significant interaction from a broadly representative
group of evangelicals from many countries. This meeting at
Berlin engendered a number of regional evangelical gatherings,
as we shall see in the next chapter.

The Lausanne International Congress on World Evangelization in 1974 is certainly the most important evangelical meeting
to be held this century. In its size, scope, and vision, Lausanne showed the growing strength, diversity, and insight of
worldwide evangelicalism. The Congress sought to engage the
total church and world in an attempt to produce a comprehensive
understanding of the task facing evangelicals in the present
day. The Lausanne Covenant provides a summary of the evangelical understanding of mission which clearly demonstrates the
maturity of theological insight which has emerged among evangelicals since 1966.

These three meetings will be focal points through which
the development of evangelical mission theology in the decade

from 1966 to 1976 will be traced and analyzed.

THE CHURCH'S WORLDWIDE
MISSION: WHEATON, 1966

Between 9-16 April, 1966, 938 delegates from 71 countries met at Wheaton College, Wheaton, Illinois, at the Congress on the Church's Worldwide Mission.[1] Sponsored by the IFMA and the EFMA, the meeting was hailed by *Christianity Today* as "the largest ecumenical strategy conference of Protestant missionaries ever held in North America."[2]

"The Call to the Congress" cited several reasons for convening the meeting. The primary factor involved the dissatisfaction evangelicals felt regarding ecumenical mission theology and practice, especially following the integration of the IMC and the WCC in 1961. The Congress met to enable evangelicals to define their own distinctive position in relation to ecumenical theology, in the conviction that the time had come for "evangelical leadership to make plain to the world their theory, strategy and practice of the church's universal mission."[3] The developing relationship between the IFMA and the EFMA leaders pointed to the desire for closer fellowship among evangelicals.

The Congress reflected the growing confidence and maturity of the conservative evangelical forces based in North America. "Twenty-five years ago there could have been no Wheaton Congress," Lindsell wrote, but the "evangelical missionary endeavor has come of age in the 1960s."[4]

Ten major study papers and five biblical expositions constituted the main part of the Congress's agenda. The subjects covered in the papers indicate the major areas of concern:

Mission and . . .
Syncretism	Foreign Missions
Neo-Universalism	Evangelical Unity
Proselytism	Evaluating Methods
Neo-Romanism	Social Concern
Church Growth	A Hostile World

These papers provided the subject matter for the Wheaton Declaration which "was a consensus of the Congress, a faithful effort to reflect what the delegates wanted."[5] In accord with the nature of the gathering, the Declaration was not a binding document, but a challenge to all groups convinced of the truths it contained.[6]

Wheaton's basic understanding of mission related to evangelism. The Declaration stated: "we reaffirm unreservedly the

primacy of preaching the gospel to every creature." In the closing
act of dedication, delegates pledged to seek "THE MOBILIZATION
OF THE CHURCH, its people, its prayers, and resources, FOR THE
EVANGELIZATION OF THE WORLD IN THIS GENERATION."[7]

One major paper attempted to reclaim the word "proselytism,"
understood as those acts of evangelism which seek the conversion
of sinners, as a term to describe the biblical mandate to evangelize the world.[8] This included seeking people who already
belonged to some Christian church, especially of Roman Catholic
or Orthodox background. While decrying corrupt forms of witness
involving cajolery, bribery, undue pressure or intimidation, the
Declaration strongly affirmed the need for the type of proselytism
which leads all followers of Christ to disciple their fellow men.[9]

A particular understanding of scripture underlay most presentations at Wheaton. The Declaration affirmed a point made
many times:

> we appeal in the many issues that confront us to the
> Bible, the inspired, the only authoritative, inerrant
> Word of God. The Scriptures constitute our final rule
> of faith and practice.[10]

This strong emphasis on the authority of scripture as the basic
mandate for the Christian mission, characteristic of evangelical thought, was certainly maintained at Wheaton.

The Congress affirmed that "church planting has the priority among all other missionary activities."[11] The influence of
the church growth movement at this point is clear. Attention was
also given the closely related concept of Evangelism in Depth,
for that highlighted the total mobilization of the people and
resources of the churches in a continuous evangelistic outreach as
an indispensable element in the evangelization of the world.[12]

While aiming to present a positive and forthright declaration of evangelical convictions, Wheaton made a strong and sustained attack on the ecumenical movement, the WCC, and various
theological positions described as "liberal" or "modern." Among
Wheaton's delegates, Lindsell wrote, "the overwhelming majority
. . . [had] grave reservations about the Ecumenical Movement."[13]
As an observer from the WCC, Eugene L. Smith agreed, saying,
". . . the distrust of the ecumenical movement within this
group has to be experienced to be believed."[14]

Although graciously received personally, Smith found that
nine of the fifteen major papers carried attacks on the ecumenical movement. He concluded that:

There were frequent comparisons with the best in "evangelicalism" with what seems to them the worst in "ecumenism." It was carefully stated from the platform that
only the formal document voted on by the Congress was
to be taken as the "mind" of the meeting; but in the
heavy attacks upon the World Council of Churches, no
World Council documents were cited--except one paragraph on proselytism. Many of the attacks on the
Council focused on persons who have never, or only very
slightly, participated in any Council activities....

The most frequent charges against us were theological liberalism, loss of evangelical conviction, universalism in theology, substitution of social action
for evangelism, and the search for unity at the
expense of biblical truth.[15]

Horace L. Fenton, Jr., then Director of the Latin American
Mission, reported that many delegates were concerned by the
tone of this attack. He added:

there was a strong, popular reaction against this
negative emphasis, and the final draft of the Declaration, while strong in enunciating basic convictions, was
free from direct attacks on men and organizations.[16]

Wheaton, scoring the radical departure of the ecumenical
movement from evangelical principles and practice, made two
points: a marked contrast exists between the two understandings
of mission; and the Congress truly continued the nineteenth
century missionary movement and theology.

In a notable comparison, Lindsell said that Wheaton 1966 had
"inherited both the evangelical stance and the ecumenical orientation of the New York Ecumenical Missionary Conference of 1900."[17]
Significantly, the Declaration's use of the SVM watchword implied
that Wheaton was *the* legitimate successor in that tradition.

Why did the Wheaton delegates feel such strong antipathy
to the ecumenical movement? Lindsell offered an interesting
comment about the conviction of evangelicals on this point when
he wrote,

in the closing days of the age just prior to the
Second Advent of Jesus Christ the professing church
will be apostate.... It will be a worldwide
ecclesiastical organization under the sway of Satan,
persecuting true believers. This church will be made
up of apostate Romanism and Protestantism....
Because [evangelicals] believe this to be true, their

> distrust of ecumenism is not only built upon what they
> see now, but also upon that which they are confident
> will come to pass.[18]

This insight gives some indication of the reason behind the
depth and intensity of the evangelical hostility towards the
ecumenical movement, unsupported as it is by documentation from
official WCC sources, or from the writings of theologians
closely related to the ecumenical movement. This attitude
demands further attention if serious communication is to occur
in the future. Fortunately, evangelical theologians such as
John R. W. Stott and David Hubbard have entered into serious
conversation with people in the ecumenical movement.

Wheaton exhibited considerable uncertainty about the best
way of understanding the relationship between church and mission. Part of this confusion related to the different ways in
which the word "mission" was used to describe both a theological task (that is, evangelistic outreach), and an organizational
entity (the institution responsible for missionaries).

At the theological level the Congress stated that the
church is responsible for mission or evangelical outreach.
This was clearly emphasized in the Congress title "The Church's
Worldwide Mission" and by the statement in the Declaration that
"In obedience to the Great Commission, the church has a con-
tinuing responsibility to send missionaries into all the world."

The paper by R. P. Chavan, the Moderator of the General
Assembly of the Christian and Missionary Alliance in India,
noted that the emergence of the indigenous church called for a
change in policy regarding church and mission at the organizational level also. Previously missionaries "had controlled
everything including the supervision of the planning for the
church and institutions, and the use of finances and property."
That colonial era had now passed because "the new church has
grown to maturity . . . . It must be accepted the world over
that the indigenous church must be the norm."[19] Chavan also
indicated that subsidies for church workers should be discon-
tinued and that most properties should be transferred to the
local church.

This closely parallels the arguments used for the integration of church and mission in the ecumenical movement.
Indeed, the Declaration recognized the widespread acceptance
of this position:

> Currently many claim it is impossible to maintain on
> biblical grounds the concept of the missionary society
> as a sending agency distinct from any national organi-

zation of churches on the field.[20]

The Declaration envisaged church and mission sharing in a "cooperative partnership in order to fulfil the mission of the Church to evangelize the world in this generation." Yet, finally, it denied that church and mission should be integrated by arguing, "we recognize a continuing distinction between the church established in the field and the missionary agency."[21]

Why did Wheaton insist on a continuing distinction between church and mission at an organizational level, even while setting forth a theological viewpoint similar to that which prevailed in the ecumenical movement? The key is most likely to be found in the organizational structure of the sponsoring agencies. The IFMA is composed of independent mission boards which do not have any denominational affiliation, and the EFMA has a mixed constituency of independent and denominational boards. With that organizational structure it would be virtually impossible to seek for the integration or close internal relationship of church and mission.

The difficulty in this position did not pass unnoticed at the Congress. National church leaders especially noted the continued domination and financial influence of the mission vis-à-vis the church. James Bolarin of Kenya described this danger to the church as a form of "neo-colonialism and being tied to the mission apron strings."[22] Chavan reported that in India the position of a mission and its institutional strength had created a situation which made "the mission much more prominent than the church in the eyes of Christian and non-Christian, though this of course was not intended."[23] The foreignness of much evangelical mission work was also noted as a factor hindering church growth.[24]

The confessional section in the Declaration noted that by failing to trust fully the Holy Spirit's leadership in newly planted congregations, evangelicals were responsible for "perpetuating paternalism and provoking unnecessary tensions between national churches and missionary societies."[25]

Church-mission relations remain an unresolved issue at Wheaton. They posed a vital question to be worked through in the future by evangelical leaders from all nations, especially as national leaders develop their own distinctive contributions to the worldwide Christian community.[26]

There was and is no doubt about the primacy of evangelism in the evangelical understanding of mission. This emphasis at Wheaton has already been noted. But the relationship between evangelism and social involvement on the part of evangelicals seemed to be a sensitive issue at the Congress. The Declaration stated:

> Whereas evangelicals in the Eighteenth and Nine-
> teenth Centuries led in social concern, in the Twen-
> tieth Century many have lost the biblical perspective
> and limited themselves only to preaching a gospel of
> individual salvation without sufficient involvement
> in their social and community responsibilities.[27]

The Declaration's Confession noted that evangelicals had failed
to apply "Scriptural principles to such problems as racism,
war, population explosion, poverty, family disintegration,
social revolution, and communism."[28] Clearly the Congress
hoped to work towards a more balanced understanding of the
relationship between evangelism and social involvement.

In his paper, "Mission and Social Concern," Horace L.
Fenton, Jr. noted that Carl Henry had raised this question
nearly twenty years earlier in *The Uneasy Conscience of Modern
Fundamentalism.* Yet, "there is still plenty of evidence that
the basic issue remains unresolved among us."[29] Fenton argued
that further neglect of the issue could bring dire consequences.

In a strongly-worded warning based on his Latin American
experience, Fenton declared:

> In Latin America today a whole generation is turning
> away from religion and the church, because religion
> as they have known it has for four centuries been
> sublimely indifferent to many of the basic needs of
> the people . . . . Any evangelism which ignores
> social concern is by its nature an incomplete and
> unscriptural evangelism, and it will likely end up
> by being an unheeded evangelism.[30]

Fenton pointed to three practical demonstrations of the kind of
relationship he was advocating: "Good Will Caravans," literacy
campaings, and relief programs. For him, each of these was an
example of "proclaiming the Gospel, by word and deed, *together.*"[31]

The recognition of the close relationship between evangelism and social involvement found expression in the Declaration. It pointed to Old Testament witness on social justice,
the example of Jesus Christ in ministering to the physical and
social needs of people, and the life example of the disciples
and the evangelical heritage. The Declaration stated:

> Evangelicals look to the Scriptures for guidance as
> to what they should do and how far they should go in

> expressing this social concern, without minimizing
> the priority of preaching the gospel of individual
> salvation . . . . We reaffirm unreservedly the
> primacy of preaching the gospel to every creature,
> and we will demonstrate anew God's concern for
> social justice and human welfare.[32]

The stance of evangelicals in relation to the wider issues
of justice and human rights in all their various forms brought
an unequivocal response from Congress delegates. The Declaration urged "all evangelicals to stand openly and firmly for
racial equality, human freedom, and all forms of social justice
throughout the world." In a similar vein it stated "we shall
urge church and government leaders throughout the world to work
for the inalienable rights of full religious liberty everywhere."[33]

These forthright statements provide an indication of the
intention of evangelicals to be involved in matters of social
concern. They do this with an understanding of the close relationship of evangelism to social issues, while maintaining the
primacy of evangelism and verbal proclamation.

The Congress heard on several occasions about the resurgence of some traditional religions--Buddhism, Hinduism, and
Islam--as facts which had to be faced in the modern world. A
major reference to this facet of contemporary life came in the
paper on "Mission in a Hostile World."[34] The main suggestion
for a Christian response to other religions consisted of a
strong warning not to succumb to the approach which many felt
the ecumenical movement was espousing: syncretism and neo-
universalism.

Syncretism was defined as "the attempt to unite or recon-
cile biblically revealed Christian truth with the diverse or
opposing tenets and practices of non-Christian religions or
other systems of thought that deny it."[35] To counteract this
tendency the Wheaton Congress suggested seeking greater clarity
"in presenting the uniqueness of Jesus Christ and the precise
message of His saving work as revealed in the Bible."[36]

The Congress wished to repudiate universalism, understood
as teaching that "because Jesus died for all, He will sover-
eignly and out of love bring all men to salvation."[37] Arthur
M. Climenhaga in his paper, "Mission and Neo-Universalism,"
argued that this viewpoint logically must lead "to a new universalism of all religions and faiths--a veritable universalis-
tic syncretism of Christianity with other ethnic faiths."[38]
The Declaration recognized that denying universalism placed a
special responsibility on evangelicals, for

the repudiation of universalism obliges all evangelicals to preach the gospel to all men before they die
in their sins. To fail to do this is to accept in
practice what we deny in principle.[39]

Some delegates suggested that study centers should be
established to assist Christians better to understand other
religions because "forever gone is the day when one could con-
fine his preparation for the religious encounter to mastering a
few Bible texts, to be quoted to all and sundry with a 'that-
settles-it' finality."[40] The question of dialogue, however,
was only mentioned in passing.[41] The issue of the relationship
between religions at a theological and practical level was not
really developed adequately at Wheaton.

The question of unity and its relation to mission proved
to be one of the most sensitive at the Congress. The two major
evangelical mission groupings had undertaken sponsorship of the
Congress "in the desire for a closer fellowship of evangelicals." The Congress affirmed the theological basis of unity to
be that "we are one in Jesus Christ, members of His Body, born
again of His Holy Spirit, although we may be diverse in our
structural relationships."[42] Sponsorship of the Congress
itself involved something of a new departure for the IFMA and
the EFMA.

Fenton commented that:

The very fact that we gathered at all, on such a scale,
and under the sponsorship of these two groups, seemed
almost a miracle in itself. For there have been among
us strong differences in conviction that have kept us
apart--in spite of the basic theological unity we have
claimed. It seems safe to say that five years ago
such a Congress could not have taken place.[43]

Many delegates were conscious of the failure of the evangelical
community to exhibit real signs of unity within itself. The
Declaration included a confession that:

Evangelicals, however, have not fully manifested this
biblical oneness because of carnal differences and
personal grievances; and thus missionary advance and
the fulfillment of the Great Commission have been
hindered.[44]

Yet the Congress vehemently opposed the notion of unity
which it believed the ecumenical movement stood for. This
opposition was based on the idea that the ecumenical movement
sought organizational unity at the expense of doctrine. Many

feared that the WCC aimed at creating an ecclesiastical organization which would become a super-church, seeking a worldwide religious monopoly.[45]

Delegates at Wheaton clearly wanted far more cooperation between various groups and organizations. The Declaration gave explicit evidence of this desire when it stated:

> we will encourage and assist in the organization of
> evangelical fellowships among churches and missionary
> societies at national, regional, and international
> levels . . . . We will encourage evangelical mission
> mergers when such will eliminate duplication of adminis-
> tration, produce more efficient stewardship of personnel
> and resources, and strengthen their ministries.[46]

Yet Lindsell saw the remaining problem: "it remains for evangelical spokesmen to state more clearly how spiritual unity finds expression in visible organization."[47] Ecumenical and evangelical theologians are still struggling to discover how to express in some visible form the church's essential spiritual unity. All Christians--evangelicals and those associated with the ecumenical movement--must strive to fulfill Christ's petition in John 17 "that they may all be one" in order that "the world may know that thou hast sent me." This remained an unresolved issue at Wheaton.

The Congress gave a guarded and critical evaluation of "Neo-Romanism." While expressing satisfaction at some of the changes which have occurred within Roman Catholicism, especially at Vatican II, and rejoicing in the wider use of the scriptures among Roman Catholics, many at Wheaton held that Rome "has not modified nor will it modify essential dogmas." The Declaration therefore warned of the danger of regarding the Roman Catholic Church as "our great sister Church," and insisted that as evangelicals, the Congress must reaffirm basic Protestant principles, namely, "salvation is through faith in Christ alone and that the Bible is the only rule of faith and practice" in any contacts with Rome.[48] Perhaps the comment of Juan Isais of Mexico reflected the attitude of others: "The Catholic Church, with her gestures of friendship, represents an enigma for the evangelicals who have lived with her in the past."[49]

In summary, the achievements of Wheaton contributed to the development of evangelical mission theology in several notable ways.

The choice of subjects to be discussed, which subsequently and intentionally formed the central elements of the Declaration, made it obvious that the evangelical community wished to

respond to the flux and change of events and ideas throughout
the whole church and the world. Wheaton showed evangelicals
attempting to respond to the theological and secular context
in which the mission of the church is conducted.

Some who prepared papers examined developments within the
conservative evangelical community--such as the church growth
movement and changing church-mission relations--and sought to
define a broad policy and strategy in relation to these changes.
Other contributors considered changes within mainline Protestant denominations and the ecumenical movement. Wheaton repudiated the theological trends labelled as "syncretism" and
"neo-universalism," but showed little understanding of the
theological ideas which were being scored.

Novel elements in Roman Catholic attitudes and practices
were critically evaluated at Wheaton. The Congress also considered fleetingly the world, problems caused by nationalism,
other world religions, and communism. This became a part of
the process of evaluating and defining an evangelical perspective on the theory, strategy, and practice of the church's
universal mission.

Never before had evangelicals undertaken such a comprehensive agenda. This in itself suggested the growing maturity of
the evangelical missionary endeavor--its coming of age in the
1960s. It also indicated the need which evangelicals sensed
for concerted planning and action.

The Declaration is best understood as a major attempt to
elaborate a positive response to the changing context of mission. Inclusion of a confession concerning past evangelical
failures added to the sincerity and depth of the Congress's
statement. The basic evangelical understanding of mission--
primarily in terms of evangelism, by which it meant the
preaching of the gospel to every creature--remained the predominant thrust of the Wheaton statements. But the Congress
made a serious attempt to link evangelism with social action
and strongly affirmed its commitment to religious liberty for
all, racial equality, and social justice. This marked an important forward step by a major evangelical gathering.

Unity had long been a difficult issue for evangelicals.
Plagued by fragmentation and doctrinal differences, even when
in agreement on basic evangelical doctrines, the major missionary groups had had a poor record in regard to any kind of
cooperative ventures with other Christian groups, even of evangelical persuasion. The Congress itself was a notable achievement, in that it brought together a wide range of evangelicals
who produced a Declaration which received the unanimous support

of the delegates. Problems remained in finding ways of turning
declarations of intention into action, but Wheaton proved a
promising start for evangelicals concerned about finding better
and more effective ways to accomplish the Great Commission in
the contemporary world.

Wheaton represented the reaction and response of evangelicals to a changing world from a basically defensive position.
Yet it indicated a growing unity and maturity among evangelicals
and thus marked an important and necessary stage in the development of a theology and strategy of mission in that tradition.

WORLD CONGRESS ON EVANGELISM:
BERLIN, 1966

Sponsored by *Christianity Today* as its tenth anniversary
project, the World Congress on Evangelism met at Berlin from
October 25 to November 4, 1966, with Billy Graham (who first
envisioned it) as honorary chairman,[50] and *Christianity Today*
editor, Carl F. H. Henry as executive chairman. The Congress
attracted some 1,100 conservative evangelical leaders from more
than 100 countries. Under the theme "One Race, One Gospel, One
Task," they discussed global evangelism in the context of a
nuclear, space, and mass communications era.

The participants represented a wide and diverse group of
evangelicals, including Emperor Haile Selassi of Ethiopia (then
the Protector of the Ethiopian Orthodox Church), members of the
Mar Thoma Church in India, and two new Christian converts from
the Auca Indians of Ecuador, one of whom had taken part in the
murder of missionaries in 1956. Some delegates belonged to
churches associated with the ecumenical movement; others came
from independent churches.[51]

The daily program at Berlin included Bible studies, inspirational addresses, plenary presentations, and a large number
of small panel discussions on a variety of subjects. More than
200 papers were given at the Congress. The published Report
therefore represents a large cross-section of evangelical
thought and opinion.

As the name "World Congress on Evangelism" suggests, the
major purpose of the gathering related to a consideration of
the place of evangelism in the church and the world.[52] *Christianity Today* listed the more specific aims of the Congress as
being:

1) To define biblical evangelism, 2) to show the modern
world the relevance of Christ's mission, 3) to stress
the urgency of evangelistic proclamation throughout the

world in this generation, 4) to discover new methods of
relating biblical evangelism to our times, 5) to study
the obstacles to biblical evangelism and to propose the
means of overcoming them, 6) to consider the types of
evangelistic endeavor currently employed in various
lands, and 7) to summon the church to recognize the
priority of its evangelistic task.[53]

The same journal also sought to establish the identity and
theological perspective of the Congress:

In contrast to other recent ecumenical conferences, such
as the Vatican Council, World Council of Churches' assemblies, and the conferences on Faith and Order and on
Church and Society, [this Congress] assumes both the
Reformation principle of the final authority of the
Bible and the apostolic emphasis on the evangelization
of mankind as the primary mission of the church.[54]

While many of the presentations were largely inspirational
or horatory, the major addresses attempted a serious analysis
of the issues concerning evangelism.[55] This concentration on
evangelism pointed to the evangelicals' search for an identity
over against Roman Catholicism and Protestantism associated
with the ecumenical movement. As *Christianity Today* commented,
Berlin stood on "the final authority of the Bible and the apostolic emphasis on the evangelization of mankind as the primary
mission of the church,"[56] thereby affirming positions which
evangelicals felt were being neglected or denied by other
Christians.[57] A basic commitment to the authority of the Bible
and an emphasis on evangelism formed the basis for the Berlin
Congress.

While belief in the divine authority of scripture was not
developed at length, this constituted an underlying assumption
common to all participants. They had been invited to attend
Berlin as conservative evangelicals. The Closing Statement
approved by the Congress affirmed:

God's people are again being called upon to set God's
Word above man's word . . . . We reject all theology
and criticism that refuses to bring itself under the
divine authority of Holy Scripture.[58]

The theology of evangelism which the Congress affirmed
took its central motivation from obedience to the Great Commission. In a series of Bible studies led by John R. W. Stott,
the three forms of the Great Commission in John, Matthew, and
Luke provided the basic texts. Stott's opening words were:

It seems not only appropriate but indispensable that the
first three Bible Studies of the Congress should be concerned with the Great Commission which Christ our Lord
has given us. For, in the last resort, we engage in
evangelism today not because we want to or because we
choose to or because we like to, but because we have
been told to. The church is under orders. The risen
Lord has commanded us to "go," to "preach," to "make
disciples"; and that is enough for us.[59]

The Closing Statement of the Congress, "One Race, One Gospel, One Task," included the same sense of obligation to the
Great Commission. It went further, however, in seeking to
define evangelism by concentrating on its essential meaning:

Evangelism is the proclamation of the Gospel of the
crucified and risen Christ, the only Redeemer of men,
according to the Scriptures, with the purpose of
persuading condemned and lost sinners to put their
trust in God by receiving and accepting Christ as
Saviour through the power of the Holy Spirit, and
serve Christ as Lord in every calling of life and
in the fellowship of his church, looking toward the
day of his coming in glory.[60]

Several points emerge from this definition. It emphasized
the christological nature of evangelism by focusing on the crucifixion and resurrection of Christ, his work as Redeemer and
Saviour, his Lordship over life, and his eschatological return.
Anthropologically, it described the condition of people cut off
from God by sin as "condemned and lost sinners." The Statement
emphasized the authority of the Bible for presenting Christ.
The trinitarian basis for the whole process of salvation was
affirmed--by the power of the Holy Spirit, people put their
trust in God through Christ. The church arises as an evangelical fellowship.

Billy Graham claimed that one of the major reasons for
calling the Congress concerned the need to eliminate the confusion about and clarify the understanding of evangelism. He
dealt with this issue in the address, "Why the Berlin Congress?"[61]
Graham decried the way some Christians used evangelism to describe educational and social reform activities instead in its
true function, namely, the winning of people to a personal
relationship to Jesus Christ. Theologically, he identified the
greatest hindrance as the universalism which denies that people
are ultimately lost.

Schneider and Ockenga presented the basic theological
foundations for evangelism in greater detail. "Authority for

evangelism is grounded most deeply and finally in the risen
Lord's Great Commission," Schneider argued, pointing to the
major purpose of evangelism: "to win men for Christ."[62]

Ockenga developed a trinitarian basis for evangelism.
Briefly summarized, he explained, "that the Father elects, which
is predestination; that the Son redeems, which is atonement;
and that the Holy Spirit regenerates, which is salvation."[63]
Dealing with some of the theological disputes which had divided
evangelicals, Ockenga opted for a moderate, mediating position.
In the debate between Calvinists and Arminians, he concluded,
"I approve a practical synergism of affirming prevenient grace,
the responsibility of each individual, and the election in
Christ of all who believe."[64] He suggested that each of the
major theories of the atonement could be supported by scripture.
In assessing the work of the Holy Spirit, Ockenga argued that
Christians should be open to the charismatic movement and such
gifts as healing and speaking in tongues. He did not wish to
offer an opinion concerning ministers who offered invitations
at meetings, and those who did not.

As with previous evangelical gatherings, Berlin accepted
the SVM watchword as a goal and aim for evangelical planning.
Billy Graham first suggested this when he stated:

one of the purposes of this World Congress on Evangelism is to make an urgent appeal to the world church
to return to the dynamic zeal for world evangelization
that characterized Edinburgh 56 years ago.[65]

Graham hoped that a gift of spiritual fire would make the Congress "as significant in the history of the church as the World
Missionary Conference" in overcoming the lack of zeal and
passion for evangelism which characterized many churches.

The Closing Statement declared, "Our goal is nothing short
of the evangelization of the human race in this generation, by
every means God has given to the mind and will of men." And
again, "While not all who hear the Gospel will respond to it,
our responsibility is to see that every one is given the opportunity to decide for Christ in our time." Others echoed the
concern to support world evangelism in terms of the watchword,
including Carl F. H. Henry and Bishop Otto Dibelius. In his
final assessment of the Congress, Henry concluded that its
"goal was nothing short of the evangelization of the earth in
the remaining third of the twentieth century."[66]

To achieve this goal of world evangelization it seemed
obvious to some, especially Henry, that the place of the laity
in evangelism would have to be clearly delineated and emphasized.

Before the Congress began, *Christianity Today* editorialized that:

> the congress marks an effort by many mass evangelists
> to restore evangelism to the local congregation as a
> continuing individual concern, and thus to put them-
> selves out of business as a separate professional
> class. It is a concerted effort by leaders in evan-
> gelism to enlist every professing Christian in active
> evangelistic and missionary engagement.[67]

In an opening address, Henry argued that "one major weakness of modern evangelism lies in its abandonment of the heavy
burden of evangelism to a small company of professional super-
salesmen."[68]

The issue of the role of the laity in evangelism could not
have been raised more clearly. Indeed, it was the same problem
which the WCC study on "The Missionary Structure of the Congregation" had isolated and attempted to rectify by emphasizing
the evangelical significance of the laity in their daily occupations and secular lives.

The Congress Statement pointed to the same need for involvement by the laity when it called on "all believers in
Christ to unite in the common task of bringing the word of salvation to mankind . . . . We seek to enlist every believer and
to close the ranks of all Christians for an effective witness
to our world."[69] Beyond this general challenge, the specific
role of the laity in evangelism was never outlined. This
important issue remains one of the urgent and necessary points
for further study.

Berlin's participants assumed the place of the church in
the total process of evangelism. The church received little
attention in the theological addresses. Yet probably most
would have agreed with the theological presuppositions made by
Künneth about the church when he stated: "'Gospel' and 'Church'
. . . . stand in an indissoluble relationship. The Gospel
points to the Church, and the Church derives from the Gospel."[70]

From this basic assumption that the church exists because
of the gospel and for the sake of the gospel, the Congress's
Statement declared that evangelism constitutes the primary task
of the church. The participants proclaimed their "unswerving
determination to carry out the supreme mission of the church,"
recognizing that this included the responsibility "to baptize
. . . into the fellowship of his Church." The final section
appealed: "We implore the world church to obey the divine commission to permeate, challenge, and confront the world with the
claims of Jesus Christ."[71]

The Congress implied rather than stated that primarily it would be Christians in each place who would accept and act on the divine commission. A preliminary *Christianity Today* article stressed that Berlin "brings together nationals who themselves carry the burden of evangelism on home terrains around the earth."[72]

Probably the most important expression of this point came from those leaders from Africa, Asia, and Latin America who spoke at various sessions; 34 of the brief addresses recorded in the second volume of the Berlin Report were from these countries. Samuel Escobar pleaded for missionaries to overcome "the paternalistic, imperialistic and colonialistic mentality so that indigenous churches will rise that are well established in the faith, have a well-trained national leadership," and be able to live effectively in their local situation.[73]

Roland Allen's proposal of evangelical awakening through the spontaneous expansion of the church by the natural witnessing of the people of God was viewed with general approval.[74]

Berlin recognized the importance of the relationship between evangelism and social action. Participants made evident their widespread dissatisfaction with the prevailing opinions perceived to be operative in the WCC-related churches and gatherings. Both Henry and Graham denounced opinions judged to invert the New Testament by placing emphasis on "the revolutionizing of social structures rather than on the regeneration of individuals," and which "look upon evangelism as social action only."[75] Such a viewpoint suggested only one thing: "the evangelistic paralysis of the ecumenical movement."[76] Indeed, Henry concluded,

that conciliar ecumenism's long-standing neglect of evangelism as a primary concern was what had shaped the rising demand in the world Church for a global platform devoted to obedient fulfillment of the Great Commission.[77]

But while the Congress paid particular attention to evangelism, as we have seen, it still had to overcome a neglect concerning the social implications of the gospel amongst evangelicals which Henry had already noted as early as 1947 in his book, *The Uneasy Conscience of Modern Fundamentalism*. Henry wrote again in 1967:

in its wise rejection of the social gospel in the forepart of this century, the evangelical movement reacted to the unwise neglect of the larger social implications of the Gospel . . . . Christian denial of neighbor love may in fact become an offense to the world that prevents effective hearing of the Gospel.[78]

Racism especially was seen to be contrary to the gospel, and a report of a group discussion stated that "many delegates felt that racial tension is today a major deterrent to the evangelistic enterprise."[79] José D. Fajardo complained that:

> the ministry of the Protestant church in Latin America has been limited almost wholly to preaching and teaching, while it has done almost nothing about the physical needs of millions of people in every country.[80]

How was this issue handled at the Congress? In his opening address, Henry tersely set forth his own distinctive view of the relationship between evangelism and social action:

> The God of the Bible is the God of justice and of justification. The Christian evangelist has a message doubly relevant to the modern scene: he knows that *justice* is due to all because a just God created mankind in his holy image, and he knows that all men need *justification* because the Holy Creator sees us as rebellious sinners. The Gospel is good news not simply because it reinforces modern man's lost sense of personal worth and confirms the demand for universal justice on the basis of creation, but also because it offers rebellious men as doomed sinners that justification and redemption without which no man can see God and live.[81]

No other speaker at the Congress achieved the balance of this statement. Most seemed content with the traditional conservative evangelical position which Graham presented:

> I am convinced that if the Church went back to its main task of proclaiming the Gospel and getting people converted to Christ, it would have a far greater impact on the social, moral and psychological needs of men than any other thing it could possibly do. Some of the greatest social movements of history have come about as a result of men being converted to Christ.[82]

Yet others were not satisfied with this position. William E. Pannell, the black American evangelist, challenged the delegates when he said:

> being an evangelical . . . . has meant, at least in my lifetime, not only passivity in social matters, but also by default, a tacit support of the status quo . . . . To declare that morality cannot be

legislated is worse than spitting into the wind.
Apparently it cannot be experienced in the church
either. I am speaking now as a Negro, and frankly
I am a bit weary of hearing that Lord Shaftesbury
and Wilberforce effected social change in England.[83]

Another black American, Baptist minister Louis Johnson, was
reported as saying that the "law did for me and my people in
America what empty and highpowered evangelical preaching never
did for 100 years."[84]

The Closing Statement, under the heading of "One Race,"
confessed past evangelical failures in regard to racism, and
spoke of "the biblical unity of the human race." On this basis
it declared that all who are in Christ "can recognize no distinctions based on race or color and no limitations arising out
of human pride or prejudice," either in the church or in the
proclamation of the gospel to all people. This indictment of
racism was hailed by Graham as "the strongest that ever came
out of a Protestant church gathering."[85]

Despite this concern about evangelism and social involvement, the subject was never adequately handled at the Congress.
The *Christianity Today* evaluation of Berlin reported that:

the most common complaint seemed to be that daily
discussion groups opened up great issues without
striving to arrive at a consensus. The relation
of evangelism to social concern--to cite the major
example--was a recurring theme, and many delegates
felt there should have been more of an attempt to
crystallize thinking on it.[86]

Henry concurred at this point. He noted that evangelical
thought concerning the pressing social concerns "reflected significant divisions within the evangelical community touching
Christian responsibility at some of the major frontiers of contemporary social concern."[87]

In his analysis of this point in relation to human rights,
Henry made a valuable summary which has a wider application in
relation to the broader question. He concluded:

one gets three theses that Evangelicals everywhere
fully accept: (1) that whatever measure of freedom
for the Gospel exists anywhere should be used maxi-
mally for the fulfillment of the Great Commission;
(2) that the power to change human nature and to
transform society lies wholly in the Gospel and not
in political or secular power; (3) that political

power has shown itself historically to be mainly
corrupt and hostile to the claims of God. But a
fourth premise--that Christians therefore are divert-
ing their energies from legitimate priorities when
they seek to promote human rights in relation to
government and law--is often sheltered by the third
thesis, and Evangelical disagreement over its propri-
ety points to one of the most important frontiers of
contemporary discussion over social engagement.[88]

This summary carefully evaluated the position of the Congress, and pointed to an area of continuing discussion and
debate in the evangelical community. The voices of blacks and
some evangelical leaders from Africa, Asia, and Latin America
had been especially insistent in this debate. The Congress did
no more than raise the issues involved. Important as that step
was in the development of evangelical mission theology, it
marked one of the weakest aspects of the Congress.

The relationship of Christianity to other religions received
scant attention at Berlin. The main point made concerned the
repudiation of universalism. Universalism seemed to imply to
delegates that every individual will be saved, regardless of
their religion, thereby condoning syncretism.[89] Others called
for "a deeper and sympathetic understanding of world religions"
in order to improve the effectiveness of Christian evangelism,
and some asked for a number of Study Institutes to be set up.[90]

The issue of Christian unity proved to be one of the most
important subjects discussed at Berlin. But, as in other
gatherings which have been interested in this topic, the question was: What kind of unity? A number of people expressed
dissatisfaction with the prevailing state of disunity among
evangelicals. Carl Henry spoke of "the ugly barriers that
separate us as believers" and of the need for "the full cooperation of evangelical centers around the world."[91] The Anglican
Bishop Chandu Ray of Pakistan expressed dismay at the "bicker-
ings and squabbles, of the disunity even among evangelicals."[92]

Christianity Today reported that Billy Graham departed
from his text of the first address to say, "divisions contribute to the Church's tragic confusion today." He later added
that the Congress met a long-felt need for worldwide consultation among evangelicals.[93]

Yet there was an even stronger feeling that the search for
Christian unity represented by the ecumenical movement was
entirely wrong in its orientation. Graham emphatically denied
the Congress represented any move toward organizational unity
by evangelicals.[94]

Rather, the Congress described itself as an "evangelical
ecumenical gathering," referring to a shared belief in evangelism and the authority of the Bible as the true basis of Christian unity. This pointed to a unity in fellowship, not organization. Henry later argued that "mutuality in doctrine and
mission is the real key to Christian unity."[95] Surprisingly,
the doctrinal basis for unity was never clearly delineated at
the Congress, although there can be no doubt that a conservative
evangelical perspective underlay all that the Congress did.

Christianity Today argued that,

> perhaps the most encouraging aspect of the congress
> [was] that without proposing new structures, its
> participants fanned out over the world with fresh
> determination to win the lost for Christ.[96]

The impetus which Berlin generated among evangelicals resulted in a number of regional conferences on evangelism--in
Africa, Asia, Latin America, North America, and Europe.[97]
These regional gatherings may be the most tangible expressions
of the desire for unity. They were called to fulfill the aim
of the Congress to stimulate evangelism without any concern for
organizational or ecclesiastical unity.

A strong anti-Roman Catholic feeling was evident in the
remarks of some speakers, especially the Spanish and Latin
American participants. Some, however, noted the change of
attitude among Roman Catholics towards "separated brethren"
following Vatican II.

One new venture mentioned several times at Berlin concerned
the idea of forming interracial and international teams of evangelists. The purpose behind the proposal was to put the Christian missionary enterprise on an international basis, and thus
free it from the restrictions of race and culture which sometimes hindered evangelism.[98]

Carl Henry wrote the book, *Evangelicals at the Brink of
Crisis*, to pinpoint the critical issues still facing evangelicals after Berlin. The World Congress on Evangelism had made
some significant initial steps toward meeting the theological,
evangelistic, social, and ecumenical crises which Henry outlined,
but he still contended that the Congress had made no more than
a beginning. The crises still had to be met.

Perhaps the most significant thing about the Congress was
that it happened at all--drawing together conservative evangelicals from around the world for a free expression of views
and opinions. That made it a unique event. It gave a new sense

of identity and strength to the worldwide evangelical community.
The inclusion and participation of evangelical leaders from
Africa, Asia, and Latin America marked a new stage in the development of relations between the dominant Western group and
nationals struggling to assume responsibility in their own
situations.

The focus on evangelism gave solid theological backing to
the evangelical understanding of mission--primarily the verbal
proclamation of the gospel. Berlin deliberately attempted to
concentrate attention on evangelism, something which evangelicals felt had been neglected, distorted, and possibly abandoned
by others--most of all by the ecumenical movement. But little
was done specifically, apart from recommending the primacy of
evangelism to other Christians.

The desire to formulate a better understanding of the
relationship between evangelism and the social responsibility
of Christians made that subject an important focus for discussion in the international evangelical forum Berlin provided.
The confession about racism in the Closing Statement, the aspiration towards a better policy, and the commitment to act more
responsibly in the future were marks of a growing consciousness
of racism among evangelicals. Yet no real consensus emerged at
Berlin; these issues were raised, but not adequately answered,
as the reports by the evangelicals themselves recognized.

The nature and form of Christian unity remained an unresolved issue at Berlin. While clearly opposing the ecumenical
movement's emphasis on visible and organizational unity, the
Congress was not able to formulate adequately a conception of
unity which could overcome the divisions evident within the
evangelical community.

The issues raised at Berlin became part of the continuing
agenda for the whole evangelical fellowship. Regional conferences met after Berlin to stimulate evangelism and foster
fellowship among evangelicals.

The next global meeting of evangelicals took place at
Lausanne in 1974, and this gathering attempted to draw together
some conclusions regarding the issues which Berlin had raised.

INTERNATIONAL CONGRESS ON WORLD
EVANGELIZATION: LAUSANNE, 1974

The International Congress on World Evangelization which
met from 16-25 July, 1974, at Lausanne, Switzerland, crystallized
fourteen years of planning and work by Billy Graham and continued
and expanded the work of previous evangelical meetings.[99] Berlin

had been a Congress on Evangelism. Lausanne addressed the task of *world evangelization* which, as the agenda demonstrated, included the total range of concerns embraced by the word "mission."[100] The presentations and discussion at Lausanne showed a spirit of openness, diversity of viewpoint, and depth of analysis never before achieved at an evangelical gathering.

One major influence on the depth and breadth of Lausanne's work came through the contributions of evangelical leaders from Africa, Asia, and Latin America. Among the 2,473 participants from 150 countries and 135 Protestant denominations, about 1,200 came from non-Western countries.[101] More than one-third of the plenary papers were given by non-Western leaders, and the impact of such people as René Padilla and Samuel Escobar on the Congress through the Radical Discipleship group was of particular importance.

The fruit of Lausanne's deliberations came in the form of a fifteen-point Covenant.[102] As with previous evangelical gatherings, the Congress had no legislative mandate; but the leadership at Lausanne hoped that through the Covenant the influence of the Congress could be extended as others joined the 2,200 participants who signed the document to commit themselves to the task of world evangelization. While not a binding document, the Covenant expressed "a consensus of the mind and mood of the Lausanne Congress," and certainly represents an authoritative statement of the evangelical position.[103]

With such noted evangelical leaders as Billy Graham and John R. W. Stott providing key presentations, the theological orientation of Lausanne remained firmly evangelical, stressing the authority of the Bible, the uniqueness of Christ, and the need for evangelism. However, Lausanne also produced some marked changes in evangelical mission theology. This occurred through broadening the focus of the Congress from evangelism to mission--a move in which Stott played a decisive role.

When evangelism was set in the wider context of the whole life and mission of the global church in the world, new emphases emerged. The Radical Discipleship group challenged the Congress to face the implications of discipleship concerning the total needs of humanity. Ecclesiological questions were pressed with great urgency. The result of these forces produced a Covenant which went far beyond traditional evangelical affirmations "to show that biblical evangelism is inseparable from social responsibility, Christian discipleship and church renewal."[104]

John R. W. Stott undertook to define biblically a cluster of words about which there has been much debate: mission, evangelism, dialogue, salvation, and conversion.[105] The definitions which Stott offered seem to have been widely accepted at Lausanne, and provide a good basis for future use and debate.

In the section relating to mission, Stott argued:

> "mission" is an activity of God arising out of the
> very nature of God. The living God is a sending God,
> which is what "mission" means. He sent the prophets
> to Israel. He sent his Son into the world. His Son
> sent out the apostles, and the seventy, and the
> church. He also sent the Spirit to the church and
> sends him into our hearts today. So the mission of
> the church arises from the mission of God and is to
> be modeled on it. "As the Father has sent me," Jesus
> said, "even so I send you" (John 20:20) . . . . Our
> mission, like his, is to be one of service.[106]

The trinitarian basis of the *missio Dei* in which the church participates, following the incarnational model of Jesus Christ, provides close links with theological ideas developed in the ecumenical movement.

From this theological foundation Stott concluded that "'mission' . . . describes everything the church is sent into the world to do,"[107] as a servant following the example of Jesus Christ. He argued that a proper understanding of loving service includes both evangelism and social action as authentic expressions of the task Christians are sent into the world to accomplish.

In a candid confession, Stott stated that he had changed his mind on this point since the Berlin Congress in 1966. Recalling that many evangelicals, including himself, had argued that on the basis of the Great Commission, mission consisted exclusively in a preaching, converting, and teaching ministry, Stott stated:

> Today, however, I would express myself differently . . .
> I now see more clearly that not only the consequences of
> the commission but the actual commission itself must be
> understood to include social as well as evangelistic
> responsibility, unless we are to be guilty of distorting
> the words of Jesus.[108]

On the basis of this new understanding of the Great Commission and the commands of Christ, Stott argued that the relationship between evangelism and social action could best be described in this way:

> social action is a *partner of evangelism*. As partners
> the two belong to each other and yet are independent

of each other. Each stands on its own feet in its own
right alongside the other. Neither is a means to the
other, or even a manifestation of the other. For each
is an end in itself.[109]

This comprehensive understanding of mission, flowing from
the activity and purpose of God, provided a new orientation for
evangelical mission theology. Closely related to ecumenical
mission theology at several points (e.g., mission derives from
the *missio Dei*; the comprehensive understanding of mission involving evangelism and social action; and the turn towards the
world as the arena for mission), this new notion invites a continuing discussion between evangelical and ecumenical theologians.

"Evangelism," Stott argued, "may and must be defined only
in terms of the *message*," which must be shared with others.[110]
By refusing to allow either results or methods to dominate the
discussion of evangelism, he hoped to concentrate on the christological foundations and content of the good news which Christians are to share.

Stott's presentation on dialogue indicated Lausanne might
come to a fresh appreciation of the need for dialogue between
Christians and other people. While immediately rejecting any
form of syncretism, he welcomed the kind of dialogue in which
committed Christians could enter "with loving sympathy inside
the doubts of the doubting, the questions of the questioners,
and the loneliness of those who lost their way."[111]

In assessing the range of ideas associated with salvation,
Stott rejected the idea that salvation could be interpreted to
mean psycho-physical health, or political liberation. He
understood salvation as "personal freedom from sin and its consequences, which brings many wholesome consequences in terms of
health and social responsibility,"[112] which a person accepts
and receives through conversion, understood as a total response
of repentance and faith.

The ideas which Stott presented in his address, "The Biblical Basis of Evangelism," profoundly influenced the final
shape of the Congress Covenant. A number of key ideas developed
at Lausanne can be directly related to Stott's presentation.
His support of the statement produced by the Radical Discipleship group helped promote the acceptance of the concerns presented by that committee.[113]

Ecclesiology has frequently been one of the weakest points
in evangelical theology. Howard A. Snyder presented an incisive
and illuminating paper on "The Church as God's Agent in Evangelism,"[114] which sought to direct attention to the ecclesiologi-

cal aspects of mission theology. He argued that the church is
the only divinely appointed means for spreading the gospel, and
the community of God's people normally grows through proclamation of the gospel, the multiplication of local congregations,
the building of Christ-centered communities, and the exercise
of spiritual gifts. Making a distinction between the church
and para-church structures (boards, schools, denominations,
associations, crusades, et cetera), Snyder argued that some
structures of the community of God's people (for example,
spiritual leadership, worship, and small groups) are always
cross-culturally relevant. Other para-church structures, including denominations, must be tested by the criteria of functional relevancy for building up the church in one of its areas
of growth. Different cultural situations require different
structures.[115]

      The strength of Snyder's theological position lay in its
integration of several diverse elements of evangelical theology,
namely, the emphasis on personal witness of Christians, the need
for church growth (in quantity and quality), with an appreciation of the charismatic gifts necessary for church leadership.
This marked a significant change from earlier evangelical statements which placed primary emphasis on the witness of evangelical Christians.

      The Lausanne Covenant incorporated Snyder's contribution
in paragraph 6, "The Church and Evangelism," when it stated:

      the church is at the very center of God's cosmic
      purpose and is his appointed means of spreading
      the Gospel . . . . The church is the community
      of God's people rather than an institution; and
      must not be identified with any particular culture,
      social or political system, or human ideology.

      Church-mission relations concerned many delegates at the
Congress. At the end of a thorough discussion of the issues
involved in cross-cultural evangelization, one group reported
that:

      it was clearly recognized that the initiative for
      evangelization in the Third World is being trans-
      ferred to the church and that the mission must now
      serve in a subordinate role, always provided that
      such a role does not usurp the sense of call and
      obedience of the missionary to his Lord.[116]

      Yet problems remained in defining the appropriate relation-
ship between church and mission, as had occurred at previous
evangelical meetings. While the same group confirmed the need

for two separate bodies, some "Third World delegates apparently
desire a closer relationship than dichotomy offers. Much was
heard concerning a preference for 'merger,' 'marriage,' or
'integration.'"[117] Indeed, many expressed the view that church
and mission should become involved in a pooling and distributive
relationship, in which centralized funds and personnel could be
applied to the shared task of evangelism. This closely parallels
the thinking of ecumenically-related churches involved in mission.

The radical change in missionary strategy brought about by
the growth of national churches lay behind the assertion in
paragraph 8 of the Covenant on "Churches in Evangelistic Partnership" that "a new missionary era has dawned." With the
dominant role of Western missions fast disappearing, Lausanne
looked at the need to develop strong indigenous churches and at
the necessity of internationalizing the missionary enterprise.[118]

Paragraph 10 of the Covenant, "Evangelism and Culture,"
called for the use of "imaginative pioneering methods," which
under God could produce "churches deeply rooted in Christ and
closely related to their culture."[119] In accomplishing this
goal, paragraph 11 confessed that "some of our missions have
been too slow to equip and encourage national leaders to assume
their rightful responsibilities," and clearly stated that evangelicals are "committed to indigenous principles, and long that
every church will have national leaders who manifest a Christian
style of leadership in terms not of domination but of service."
Through the development of indigenous churches many participants hoped the offence of the foreignness of Western Christianity could be removed.[120]

The moratorium debate received little direct attention at
Lausanne. But the essential points regarding the need to ensure
mature relationships between churches, and the desire to encourage strong indigenous churches able to exist without external resources were heeded. Paragraph 9 of the Covenant on
"The Urgency of the Evangelistic Task," pointed to the withdrawal of missionaries as one possible prelude to more effective evangelism when it stated:

A reduction of foreign missionaries and money in an
evangelized country may sometimes be necessary to
facilitate the national church's growth in self-
reliance and to release resources for unevangelized
areas.

The call to understand mission as a six-continent enterprise, in which each church and all churches must contribute,
participate and share, received strong emphasis. The Covenant
expressed this at a number of points:

world evangelization requires the whole church to take
the whole Gospel to the whole world (paragraph 6).

God is raising up from the younger churches a great
new resource for world evangelization, and is thus
demonstrating that the responsibility to evangelize
belongs to the whole body of Christ. All churches
should therefore be asking God and themselves what
they should be doing both to reach their own area
and to send missionaries to other parts of the
world . . . . Thus a growing partnership of churches
will develop and the universal character of Christ's
Church will be more clearly exhibited (paragraph 8).

Missionaries should flow ever more freely from and
to all six continents in a spirit of humble service
(paragraph 9).

the Holy Spirit is a missionary spirit; thus evangelism should arise spontaneously from a Spirit-filled
church . . . . We, therefore, call upon all Christians
to pray for such a visitation of the sovereign Spirit
of God that all his fruit may appear in all his people
and all his gifts may enrich the body of Christ
(paragraph 14).

An important example of the international character of the
Christian mission mentioned several times was the 201 Asian
missionary agencies involved in sending out some 2,971 missionaries.[121]

The theological considerations raised by the issue of
church-mission relations, the practical changes demanded by the
rapid development of indigenous churches, and the growth of missionary consciousness by Asian and African Christians expressed
through new missionary agencies, point to even greater changes
in this area in the coming years, as the "new missionary era"
unfolds.

Billy Graham predicted that the relationship of evangelism
and social action would be a matter of vital concern at the
Congress.[122] And he was right! Frequently during the Congress,
participants affirmed that they had a deep and abiding interest
in social action on behalf of the poor and needy, even to the
point of working to change social structures.[123]

The first major point established had been made often
before in evangelical gatherings, but received even stronger
emphasis here: that a concern for and involvement in the
social needs of humanity is a necessary part of the witness and

responsibility which Christians have for the world. This came
out most strongly in the presentations of the Latin American
spokesmen. René Padilla stated:

> There is no place for statistics on "how many souls
> die without Christ every minute," if they do not
> take into account how many of those who die, die
> victims of hunger.[124]

Samuel Escober warned that:

> A spirituality without discipleship in the daily
> social, economic, and political aspects of life is
> religiosity and not Christianity . . . . Once and
> for all we should get rid of the false notion that
> concern for the social implications of the Gospel
> and the social dimensions of witnessing comes from
> false doctrine or lack of evangelical conviction.
> Contrariwise, it is concern for the integrity of
> the Gospel that motivates us to stress its social
> dimension.[125]

In his analysis of "Depth in Evangelism," Orlando E. Costas
spoke of the "incarnational" growth of the church, by which he
meant:

> Her prophetic, intercessory and liberating action on
> behalf of the weak and destitute must be more and
> more efficacious. Her preaching to the poor, the
> brokenhearted, the captives, the blind and the
> oppressed must constantly experience greater depth.
> Otherwise she will not be able to effectively en-
> lighten the path of life, nor adequately give flavor
> to the earth nor leaven the structures of society.
> In this case, she will become practically and
> functionally a walking corpse.[126]

The case for involvement in the needs of people in society was
firmly made at Lausanne.

 Yet some stressed that such an involvement should not be
confused with evangelism. Otherwise evangelicals would succumb
to their complaint made against the ecumenical movement.[127]

 The understanding of the relationship between social action
and evangelism most widely accepted at Lausanne seemed to be
the two-mandate position. W. Stanley Mooneyham summarized this
in the presentation, "Acts of the Holy Spirit '74":

> There are two mandates in the New Testament. One is

witness; the other is service. To ignore or deny either
of them is to seriously cripple the church. Social action is certainly not Christian evangelism, but to engage in evangelism of souls without recognition that
these souls also have bodies is foolish and unreal.

Neither is the changing of social structures to be
equated with evangelizing a country, but to ignore
political injustice and economic abuse while we talk
about the transforming power of Jesus Christ is to
weaken and discredit our message.[128]

The Covenant confirmed this position and set out some of
the underlying theological convictions. The positive obligation to support both mandates found clear expression in paragraph 5 on "Christian Social Responsibility":

Although reconciliation with man is not reconciliation
with God, nor is social action evangelism, nor is
political liberation salvation, nevertheless we affirm
that evangelism and socio-political involvement are
both part of our Christian duty. For both are necessary expressions of our doctrines of God and man, our
love for neighbour and our obedience to Jesus Christ.

This was qualified, or interpreted, in paragraph 6, "The Church
and Evangelism," which affirmed that, "in the church's mission
of sacrificial service evangelism is primary." The Covenant
then used an expression widely accepted as embracing the whole
scope of mission in the ecumenical movement, and applied it to
the task of evangelization by stating, " . . . world evangelization requires the whole church to take the whole Gospel to
the whole world."[129]

On the basis of the affirmation that God is Creator and
Judge, paragraph 5 declared that a Christian "should share his
concern for justice and reconciliation through human society
and for the liberation of men from every kind of oppression."
It further added that because all people are made in the image
of God they should never be exploited, but respected and served.
A proper understanding of salvation "implies also a message of
judgment upon every form of alienation, oppression and discrimination," for "the salvation we claim should be transforming us
in the totality of our personal and social responsibilities."
Two sentences at the conclusion of paragraph 9 spoke of the
enormous need in the world:

All of us are shocked by the poverty of millions and
disturbed by the injustices which caused it. Those
of us who live in affluent circumstances accept our

duty to develop a simple life-style in order to contribute more generously to both relief and evangelism.

The responsibilities of governments in relation to human
rights--including religious liberty--formed part of the substance of paragraph 13, "Freedom and Persecution." The Congress
expressed its "deep concern for all who have been unjustly
imprisoned, and especially for our brethren who are suffering
for their testimony to the Lord Jesus." Also, in paragraph 13,
the participants pledged

> to pray and work for their freedom. At the same time
> we refuse to be intimidated by their fate. God helping
> us, we too will seek to stand against injustice and to
> remain faithful to the Gospel, whatever the cost.

The Radical Discipleship group focused attention on the
need for a serious examination of the implications of discipleship, especially in relation to social concerns. Through their
efforts particularly, paragraph 5 was altered so that

> the statement on social responsibility was consider-
> ably strengthened by (a) the replacement of the ex-
> pression 'social action' with 'socio-political involve-
> ment,' (b) the addition of direct references to aliena-
> tion, oppression and discrimination and to the denun-
> ciation of evil and injustice, and (c) the promotion of
> the whole section from No. 7 to No. 5 [in the Covenant].[130]

In "A Response to Lausanne," the Radical Discipleship group
strongly affirmed that "we must repudiate as demonic the attempt
to drive a wedge between evangelism and social action." Stott
also supported this stand in his exposition of the phrase, "the
church's mission of sacrificial service," with the comment, "it
normally includes both evangelistic and social action, so that
normally the church will not have to choose between them."[131]

The Congress used traditional evangelical terms to define
evangelism. Paragraph 4, "The Nature of Evangelism," stated
that "evangelism itself is the proclamation of the historical,
biblical Christ as Saviour and Lord, with a view to persuading
people to come to him personally and be reconciled to God."
The results of evangelism include "obedience to Christ, incorporation into his church and responsible service in the world."

The significant points Lausanne raised concerning evangelism touched on the analysis of specific areas. Ralph Winter's
distinction between the types of evangelism, and the worldwide
concentration of missionaries has already been mentioned.[132]
The use of the mass media for evangelism received particular

attention.[133] Sociological data about the rapid growth of
cities and urban communities pointed to a trend of major significance for the future of evangelism.[134] The role of the
laity in evangelism was noted but not developed. Some women
delegates commented on the small number of women at the Congress
in comparison with the proportion of women in churches.[135]

The most notable aspect of Lausanne's approach to the
question of Christianity's relationship to other faiths concerned the positive emphasis on the kind of dialogue "whose
purpose is to listen sensitively in order to understand" (paragraph 4). Stott's attitude to this question was an important
factor. David Gitari, General Secretary of the Bible Society
of Kenya, strongly supported this emphasis on dialogue in his
paper, "Theologies of Presence, Dialogue, and Proclamation."[136]
The Covenant's paragraph 3, "The Uniqueness and Universality of
Christ," firmly repudiated other tendencies associated with
some forms of dialogue, specifically, "every kind of syncretism
and dialogue which implies that Christ speaks equally through
all religions and ideologies."

Any approach to people of other faiths on the basis of a
universalist theology which would assert that "all men are
either automatically or ultimately saved, still less to affirm
that all religions offer salvation in Christ," was completely
rejected in paragraph 3. Concerning universalism, Harold Lindsell specifically attacked the WCC for not declaring that "some
men are lost, that there is a hell, and that those who die
without having personally made a profession of faith in Jesus
Christ are lost."[137] The subject of universalism remains an unresolved issue between the evangelical and ecumenical communities.

Through papers and discussions Lausanne raised the issue
of evangelism in relation to adherents of specific faiths:
Jews, Muslims, Buddhists, Confucianists, animists, and atheists.
Also, people involved in some traditional "hard places" for
evangelism discussed these areas, especially China, Muslim
countries, India, and Communist countries. The suggestions
common to most of these discussions concerned the need for adequately prepared Christians, and the importance of fostering
churches which would be able to relate closely to the cultural
context in which they are situated.[138] Paragraphs 10 and 11 of
the Covenant underlined the need for using imaginative methods
and national leaders to spearhead the communication of the gospel in culturally relevant ways to the people to be evangelized.

One of the most urgent needs felt by evangelicals at Lausanne concerned the desire to foster a kind of unity which
would enable the task of evangelism to proceed more rapidly.
Billy Graham listed this as one of his major objectives for the

Congress when he looked forward to

> a new "koinonia" or fellowship among evangelicals of all
> persuasions . . . . Let's go forward together in a world-
> wide fellowship in evangelism, in missions, in bible trans-
> lation, in literature distribution, in meeting world
> social needs, in evangelical theological training.[139]

Harold Lindsell commenting on this desire for fellowship said:

> the participants at Lausanne want a fellowship of
> true believers created as an instrument for world
> evangelication. But they do not want an ecclesi-
> astical machine or hierarchical structure.[140]

A number of papers addressed the theme of unity. Henri
Blocher spoke on "The Nature of Biblical Unity," and Jonathan
T'ien-en Chao on "The Nature of the Unity of the Local and Universal Church in Evangelism and Church Growth." Howard Snyder's
paper on "The Church as God's Agent in Evangelism" had an
implied concern for unity in the church.

Yet the issue of unity in relation to mission did not
receive proper attention at Lausanne. Blocher's contribution
aimed at showing that, on the basis of the New Testament,
spiritual unity does not have to be an all or nothing approach,
as has often occurred within the evangelical community. He
drew no practical conclusion from the study. Chao's study
appealed for recognition of the validity of the emerging church
in church-mission relations.

What the Congress had in mind, therefore, in paragraph 7's
affirmation that "the church's visible unity in truth is God's
purpose" is not entirely clear. What would constitute "visible"
unity? Participation in a Congress such as Lausanne? Or was
more implied? What does "unity in truth" mean? Does it refer
primarily to individuals who can share together in prayer and
fellowship, or does it have ecclesiological implications?
Snyder asked,

> What does "one Lord, one faith, one baptism" mean
> in practical terms when we are confronted with the
> reality of the church in history? I suggest that
> evangelicalism's difficulty at this point attests
> to the fundamental theological problem which evan-
> gelicals have yet to deal with adequately: the
> problem of the church . . . . The question of the
> church--in relation either to evangelism or to
> unity--was scarcely touched upon at Lausanne.[141]

The Covenant contained a note of confession for past evangelical failures in relation to unity. It acknowledged that "our disunity undermines our gospel of reconciliation," and "our testimony has sometimes been marred by sinful individualism and needless duplication" (paragraph 7).

In fact, the heading for paragraph 7, "Cooperation in Evangelism," best summarizes what the participants most likely had in mind for the future of evangelicalism at this point. Having affirmed that "evangelism also summons us to unity," the Covenant then suggested that

> we who share the same biblical faith should be closely
> united in fellowship, work and witness . . . . We
> pledge ourselves to seek a deeper unity in truth, wor-
> ship, holiness and mission.

It then elaborated what this might mean in practice:

> We urge the development of regional and functional
> cooperation for the furtherance of the church's mis-
> sion, for strategic planning, for mutual encourage-
> ment, and for the sharing of resources and experience.

In response to this request and following the Congress, the Lausanne Committee for World Evangelization was inaugurated to encourage the task of evangelism throughout the world. With Gottfried Osei-Mensah of Kenya as the Executive Secretary, the forty-eight person committee has functioned as a coordinating communication and information center. It has published an *Information Bulletin*, giving reports from sources around the world on the progress of evangelism in many countries. The formation and functioning of this committee may well be one of the most important products of Lausanne, and is reminiscent of the formation of the Continuation Committee which preceded the IMC in relation to the Edinburgh WMC (1910).[142]

Lausanne viewed the Roman Catholic Church much more positively than had some earlier evangelical gatherings. A paper by Ramez Atallah of the Canadian Inter-Varsity Christian Fellowship on "Some Trends in the Roman Catholic Church Today" openly commended certain changes, particularly the reinterpretation of dogma, the new emphasis on scripture, the renewed awakening of religious experiences through the liturgy and the charismatic movement, and the decentralization of authority suggested by the doctrines of the People of God and of Collegiality.

While not unaware of important differences still remaining between evangelicals and Roman Catholics, Lausanne's participants expressed appreciation for the changes which had occurred and recognized the theological contribution of such Roman Catholic scholars as Küng, Rahner, and Schillebeeckx. That marked a significant change in emphasis on the part of the evangelical community.[143]

The Lausanne Congress marks the highpoint in the development of evangelical mission theology.

The meeting itself symbolized the emergence of a worldwide community of evangelicals in which "50% of the participants, and also of the speakers and the Planning Committee, were from the Third World."[144] Lausanne was one of the most geographically representative gatherings of Christians ever held, and for that reason could speak with an authority and power never before achieved in a meeting of evangelicals.

The Covenant is the most mature and comprehensive statement produced by evangelicals. The attention given to the theological basis of mission, and to the analysis of evangelism, Christian social responsibility, and the church and its unity, and the serious consideration of the political and cultural context of mission, make this a document of major significance not only for evangelicals but the whole church.

The overarching designation "world evangelization" gave far greater scope to Lausanne's papers and discussions than those at earlier gatherings. Moreover, the papers were generally superior to those produced at previous meetings. The Lausanne presentations, high in quality, thoroughly documented, and broad-ranging, stand in contrast to the high proportion of devotional and hortatory papers given in earlier gatherings The pre-Congress materials sent to participants provided more solid background material than had ever before been available for an evangelical gathering. Lausanne's preparation and output stand unique among evangelical assemblies.

The analysis of evangelism perhaps best showed the strength and diversity of the Congress. Winter's paper on the types of evangelism, the scope of the evangelistic task still remaining, and graphic presentation of the concentration of missionary personnel gave new depth to the whole discussion of evangelism. The presentation by Costas on the types of In-Depth Evangelism currently being used in different parts of the world provided a healthy reminder of the wide range of possibilities open to achieve the goal of effective evangelism. The plea for different types of evangelistic activity related to diverse cultural situations reminded participants that "a new missionary era has dawned."

The strong emphasis on the need for social action in rela-

tion to evangelism, evident at so many points throughout the
Congress, gives some hope that Mooneyham's comment, "the debate
which has gone on for nearly a century is really a non-issue,"
may be true.[145] The part played by Latin American leaders and
by the Radical Discipleship group in insisting on the importance of social action marked one of the most influential contributions at the Congress, notably fulfilling the prophetic
words which Carl F. H. Henry had first uttered to the evangelical community in 1947.

Lausanne's major weakness appeared in its limited concern
with ecclesiology--a matter of worldwide, growing, and urgent
concern to evangelicals in this new missionary era. Church-
mission relations have become crucial now that churches have
been established in almost every country and national leaders
have emerged to take primary responsibility for the outreach
of the church.[146]

Moreover, the forms of unity and cooperation which must
emerge to fulfill the desire for fellowship and planning among
evangelicals will require close attention. The need for concerted and united effort by evangelicals in social action will
demand para-church structures yet to be evolved. Fruitful
relations between evangelicals and other Christians--Protestant,
Roman Catholic, and Orthodox--(now perhaps possible for the
first time) have barely begun. All these require immediate
discussion and action.

Evangelical mission theology has not yet adequately faced
the challenge of cross-cultural communication, including the
need for interreligious dialogue. The bare rejection of syncretism provides no satisfactory theological basis for new
kinds of witness demanded in a changing world, especially for
mission in Asian and Muslim countries. George Peters has drawn
fresh attention to this problem in calling for an adequate con-
figuration, conceptualization, and contextualization of the
gospel in evangelical mission theology.[147]

The WCC's sub-unit on Dialogue with People of Living
Faiths and Ideologies has been wrestling with these very issues.
The resulting sharp differences that have emerged in the WCC
over these questions suggest that both evangelical and ecumenical theologians must focus with new creativity on this area of
mission theology in coming years.[148]

Lausanne's attitude of penitence contrasts with the tri-
umphalism and the polemical tone often evident at Wheaton and
Berlin. The participants at Lausanne seemed more willing to
enter into dialogue in order to understand. This change in
attitude is a good sign that the diversity and newly expressed

maturity of the worldwide evangelical fellowship presented at
the Congress will be better able to meet the challenge of the
new era in which all Christians now find themselves.

SUMMARY

The years from 1966 to 1974 saw a remarkable development
in the emergence of a worldwide evangelical community. The
1966 meetings at Wheaton and Berlin provided an opportunity for
evangelicals to interact with each other and begin the process
of formulating a coherent theological position and identity in
distinction to but in some creative engagement with the long-
established ecumenical movement.

Several characteristics may be noted concerning the 1966
Congresses. The theological basis emphasized the authority of
the Bible and reaffirmed the primacy of evangelism among the
tasks committed to the church. American evangelical leaders
and organizations, such as Carl F. H. Henry, Harold Lindsell,
and Billy Graham, and *Christianity Today*, the IFMA and the EFMA
mission agencies, proved decisive in the organization of these
gatherings. Many evangelicals recognized the need to address
the serious lack of social action within evangelical theology
and practice. The Congresses themselves indicated evangelicals
were keen to find ways to improve fellowship among themselves
and to seek new forms of cooperation and unity, although many
expressed a polemical attitude towards other branches of the
Christian church.

In the period after 1966, evangelicals came together in a
number of regional gatherings,[149] and began to participate
freely in the ongoing debate within the ecumenical movement and
among evangelicals concerning the mission of the church. New
voices became evident in the evangelical community which began
to press the issue of social responsibility, and the role of
national churches in evangelism. Lausanne addressed the inclusive subject of world evangelization, which referred to the
total ministry and mission of the church.

The influence of people such as John R. W. Stott and Latin
American evangelicals like Samuel Escobar and René Padilla
proved important at this point. Lausanne certainly continued
the evangelical interest in evangelism, but now set that subject
in the wider context of mission and began to struggle with what
changes might be necessary in "a new missionary era" brought
about by the growing strength of churches in Asia, Africa, and
Latin America.

Some of the major weaknesses of evangelical mission theology relate to ecclesiology. Evangelical missionary agencies

are organized on an independent basis (even if related to an
accreditation body such as the IFMA or the EFMA), and this
makes it difficult to arrive at mutually satisfactory church-
mission relations. The congregational structure of church
organization favored by many evangelicals does not easily
accommodate itself to visible forms of church unity. Instead,
spiritual unity or loose cooperative arrangements seem best
suited to express the form of unity desired by evangelicals.
Many evangelicals continue to fear that the ecumenical movement's goal of visible unity means monolithic organic union and
will stifle evangelical theology. For these theological and
practical reasons, evangelicals have found great difficulty in
discovering new forms to improve effective cooperation, or give
expression to the affirmation that "the church's visible unity
in truth is God's purpose."

The diversity of views expressed at Lausanne emerged when
evangelicals from other continents besides North America began
to express themselves. This suggests the need to trace the
development of regional evangelical organizations and groups
and their distinctive emphases.

NOTES

¹Harold Lindsell, ed., *The Church's Worldwide Mission:
Proceedings of the Congress on the Church's Worldwide Mission
9-16 April [1966] at Wheaton College, Wheaton, Illinois* (Waco,
Tx.: Word Books, 1966), p. 4. Hereafter cited as *Wheaton, 1966.*

²Harold Lindsell, "Precedent-Setting in Missions Strategy,"
CT 10.15 (Apr. 29, 1966): 43.

³*Wheaton, 1966,* p. 3. This statement is paralleled by an
amplification given on the title page: "an analysis of the
current state of evangelical missions, and a strategy for
future activity."

⁴Ibid., pp. 7, 8.

⁵Ibid., p. 84.

⁶The evangelical gatherings discussed in this chapter were
conferences of individuals. In contrast, WCC Assemblies have a
more official character because most delegates are official
representatives of churches. Yet the actual weight and influence of the statements produced in evangelical and ecumenical
conferences is quite similar. We have already noted (p. 39)
that "the authority of the [WCC] consists only in the weight
which it carries with the churches by its own wisdom"; WCC

documents are commended to the member churches for study, comment and action as the churches determine. In effect, evangelical and ecumenical statements have a similar status, and face the same difficulties!

[7]Ibid., pp. 235, 237.

[8]Ibid., pp. 111-123, Jacques Blocher, "Mission--And Proselytism." Cf. the WCC document, "Christian Witness, Proselytism and Religious Liberty," received by the Third Assembly in 1961.

[9]*Wheaton, 1966*, pp. 225-26.

[10]Ibid., p. 221; see also, pp. 1, 11, 20, 30, 32, 36, 185, 223, 227.

[11]Ibid., p. 228; on church growth see ibid., pp. 140-49, 227-29.

[12]On Evangelism in Depth, see ibid., pp. 154, 172, 190, 256-57. A detailed analysis of Evangelism in Depth will be found in the next chapter.

[13]Ibid., p. 11. Negative evaluations of the ecumenical movement abound; see, for example, pp. 2-3, 4, 10-11, 27, 68, 69-72, 89, 91, 97, 109, 114, 116, 118, 140, 149, 163, 166-69, 170, 179, 180, 220, 231, 241, 243.

[14]Eugene L. Smith, "The Wheaton Congress in the Eyes of an Ecumenical Observer," IRM 55.220 (1966): 480.

[15]Ibid., p. 481.

[16]Horace L. Fenton, Jr., "Debits and Credits--the Wheaton Congress," IRM 55.220 (1966): 478. But the Declaration has some thinly veiled attacks; see *Wheaton, 1966*, pp. 229, 223, 225, 231.

[17]*Wheaton, 1966*, p. 10. The 1900 Conference used the word "ecumenical" not because it represented all churches, but "because the plan of campaign which it proposes covers the whole area of the inhabited globe," *Ecumenical Missionary Conference, New York, 1900* (New York: American Tract Society), vol. 1, p. 10.

[18]*Wheaton, 1966*, p. 9-10.

[19]Ibid., p. 151.

[20]Ibid., p. 229.

[21]Ibid., p. 230, "Mission--And Foreign Missions."

[22]Ibid., p. 240.

[23]Ibid., p. 156.

[24]Ibid., p. 142.

[25]Ibid., p. 220.

[26]This point was stressed in the critical analysis of Wheaton in the *Christian Century*, "Evangelical Congress on Worldside Mission" by Maynard Shelley, 83.21 (May 25, 1966): 695-97.

[27]*Wheaton, 1966*, p. 234.

[28]Ibid., p. 220.

[29]Ibid., p. 194.

[30]Ibid., p. 198.

[31]Ibid., p. 200.

[32]Ibid., pp. 234-35.

[33]Ibid., p. 235.

[34]Ibid., pp. 208, 210; also pp. 259-60.

[35]Ibid., p. 222.

[36]Ibid.

[37]Ibid., p. 223.

[38]Ibid., p. 106.

[39]Ibid., p. 225.

[40]Ibid., p. 210; see also pp. 50, 94-95.

[41]Ibid., pp. 137, 209, 212.

[42]See ibid., pp. 3, 232.

[43]Fenton, "Debits and Credits--the Wheaton Congress," p. 477.

[44]*Wheaton, 1966*, p. 231.

[45]For references of this kind see pp. 2, 6-7, 9-10, 67-72, 89-90, 105-106, 117-18, 149, 163-71, 220, 230-32, 241-42.

[46]Ibid., p. 232. For further expression of this desire for evangelical cooperation and organizational efficiency, see pp. 8, 13, 16, 62-63, 138, 149, 158, 171-76, 188, 220, 243, 246, 255, 266.

[47]Ibid., p. 14.

[48]Ibid., p. 227. Lindsell repeated the view that Rome was "apostate" and declared that until it accepts Reformation principles "it cannot be called a true church," p. 7.

[49]Ibid., p. 254.

[50]W. Stanley Mooneyham spoke of "the nearly three years of careful planning and organization required to fashion Billy Graham's dream of such a Congress into reality" in the Introduction to the two-volume report of the Congress in Carl F. H. Henry and W. Stanley Mooneyham, eds., *One Race, One Gospel, One Task. World Congress on Evangelism, Berlin 1966*, 2 vols. (Minneapolis: World Wide Publications, 1967), p. 4. Hereafter cited as *Berlin* I or *Berlin* II. Sponsored by Billy Graham and *Christianity Today*, Berlin emerged from what Quebedeaux has called "Establishment Evangelicalism." Graham also preached at an eight-night crusade in Berlin just prior to the Congress. The CT report 11.4 (Nov. 25, 1966): 34-35, "The World Congress: Springboard for Evangelical Renewal," stated that the total number of delegates and observers (including Roman Catholics, several WCC officials, and a Jewish rabbi) numbered 1,111.

[51]No breakdown of delegates into geographical or ecclesiastical groupings appears. No women were speakers, and few were present as delegates. Carl McIntire was not given credentials to attend the meeting, and vigorously denounced the gathering when he arrived in Berlin.

[52]*Berlin* I, p. 9.

[53]"Good News For a World in Need," CT 11.1 (Oct. 14, 1966): 34.

[54]Ibid.

[55]See *Berlin* II sections: "The Authority for Evangelism," Johannes Schneider; "The Basic Theology of Evangelism," Harold John Ockenga; "Hinderances to Evangelism in the Church," Walter Künneth; "Obstacles to Evangelism in the World," Harold B. Kuhn; "Methods of Personal Evangelism," Richard C. Halverson; "The

Methods of Group Evangelism," A. W. Goodwin Hudson.

[56]"Good News For a World in Need":   34.

[57]For examples of evangelical criticisms of the ecumenical movement and "liberal" theology, see *Berlin* I, pp. 16, 24, 27, 41, 151, 272, 276; *Berlin* II, pp. 4, 7-9, 95, 178-79, 258.

[58]*Berlin* I, p. 6.

[59]*Berlin* I, p. 37.

[60]Ibid., p. 6. This Statement was not put to a vote since the Congress was not intended to be a deliberative gathering; but it was received by acclamation with no publicly expressed dissent.

[61]Ibid., pp. 22-34.

[62]*Berlin* II, pp. 1, 6.

[63]Ibid., p. 96.

[64]Ibid., p. 99.

[65]*Berlin* I, p. 22.

[66]Carl F. H. Henry, *Evangelicals at the Brink of Crisis: Significance of the World Congress on Evangelism* (Waco, Tx.: Word Books, 1967): p. 2.

[67]"Good News For a World in Need":   34; cf. also "The Surging Wave of the Future," CT 11.2 (Oct. 28, 1966): 32.

[68]*Berlin* I, p. 11; cf. the similar analysis made earlier by Strachan at the 1960 Congress on World Missions and more extensively in Evangelism in Depth literature, as we shall see in the next chapter.

[69]Ibid., pp. 5, 6.

[70]*Berlin* II, p. 173.

[71]*Berlin* I, pp. 5-6.

[72]"The Good, Glad News," CT 11.2 (October 28, 1966):   3.

[73]Samuel Escobar, "The Totalitarian Climate," *Berlin* II, p. 290. A similar concern, although not so strongly worded, was expressed by some others; see ibid., pp. 21, 307.

74Ibid., pp. 343, 350, 418, 478.

75*Berlin* I, pp. 16, 24; Henry, *Evangelicals at the Brink of Crisis*, pp. 34-36, 39, 58-59, 64, 74, 97.

76*Berlin* I, p. 16.

77Henry, *Evangelicals at the Brink of Crisis*, p. 81.

78Ibid., p. 54.

79*Berlin* II, p. 205.

80Ibid., p. 500; for other examples of this concern with the social implications of the gospel, see *Berlin* I, pp. 281, 306-309; *Berlin* II, pp. 198, 205-206, 256-57, 306, 313, 376-78, 499-501, 523.

81*Berlin* I, p. 16; cf. *Evangelicals at the Brink of Crisis*, p. 71. Compare this with the *Bangkok, 1973* Report which includes this phrase, "God's justice manifests itself both in the justification of the sinner and in social and political justice," *Bangkok, 1973*, p. 88.

82*Berlin* I, p. 28. For other similar arguments see *Berlin* I, pp. 51, 156; *Berlin* II, pp. 263-67, 501-502.

83*Berlin* II, pp. 376-378.

84Reported in *Christianity Today*, "The World Congress: Springboard for Evangelical Renewal": 35.

85Quoted in Henry, *Evangelicals at the Brink of Crisis*, p. 57. But cf. *Jerusalem 1928*, vol. 4, pp. 195-202; *The Churches Survey Their Task: The Report of the Conference at Oxford July 1937 on Church, Community and State* (London: Allen & Unwin, 1937), pp. 46, 213-218; *Evanston, 1954*, pp. 151-60.

86"The World Congress: Springboard for Evangelical Renewal": 34.

87Henry, *Evangelicals at the Brink of Crisis*, p. 56.

88Ibid., p. 69.

89See, for example, *Berlin* II, pp. 185-87; Henry, *Evangelicals at the Brink of Crisis*, pp. 24-25.

90*Berlin* II, pp. 275, 280, 286.

91*Berlin* I, pp. 11, 18.

92*Berlin* II, p. 286. Other similar expressions can be found throughout the Congress Report; see *Berlin* I, pp. 192, 196; *Berlin* II, pp. 103, 347.

93"A Call for Evangelical Unity," CT 11.3 (Nov. 11, 1966): 49.

94*Berlin* I, pp. 9, 10, 32.

95Henry, *Evangelicals at the Brink of Crisis*, p. 92.

96"The World Congress: Springboard for Evangelical Renewal": 34.

97These will be discussed in the next chapter.

98*Berlin* I, p. 17; *Berlin* II, pp. 278, 286, 317, 482, 491.

99*Lausanne, 1974*, p. 16.

100See *Lausanne, 1974*, p. 34, for Graham's hopes for the meeting; and the four goals outlined by the Director of Lausanne, Donald E. Hoke in "Lausanne May Be a Bomb," CT 18.12 (March 15, 1974): 669-670.

101Figures given by C. René Padilla in *The New Face of Evangelicalism. An International Symposium on the Lausanne Covenant* (Downers Grove, Ill.: Inter-Varsity Press, 1976, p. 9. Hereafter cited as *Evangelicalism*. EMQ 10.4 (1974): 260 reported the total number present at Lausanne, including wives, media reporters, and stewards, was 4,051. Waldron Scott, "The Task Before Us," *Lausanne, 1974*, p. 8, gave this geographical breakdown for delegates: 660 from Asia and Australia; 370 from Africa; 219 from Latin America; 360 from North America; and 562 from Europe.

102*Lausanne, 1974*, pp. 3-9. Future references to the Covenant in this chapter will be by paragraph number.

103For background on the three drafts of the Covenant prepared some months before the Congress, see John Stott, *The Lausanne Covenant: An Exposition and Commentary* (Minneapolis: World Wide Publications, 1975), p. 1, and Padilla, *Evangelicalism*, p. 10.

104Padilla, *Evangelicalism*, p. 11.

105John R. W. Stott, "The Biblical Basis of Evangelism,"

Lausanne, 1974, pp. 65-78; see also Stott's *Christian Mission in the Modern World* for an expanded version of the Lausanne address.

[106]*Lausanne, 1974*, pp. 66-67.

[107]Ibid., p. 68.

[108]Stott, *Christian Mission in the Modern World*, p. 23.

[109]Ibid., p. 27.

[110]*Lausanne, 1974*, p. 69.

[111]Ibid., p. 72. Stott was quoting Michael Ramsey at this point.

[112]Ibid., p. 74.

[113]The statement of the Radical Discipleship group is entitled, "Theology [sic] Implications of Radical Discipleship," in *Lausanne, 1974*, pp. 1294-1296; it also circulated separately as "A Response to Lausanne," and can be found in Anderson and Stransky, *Mission Trends No. 2*, pp. 249-52.

[114]*Lausanne, 1974*, pp. 327-60.

[115]For further elaboration of Snyder's views see Howard A. Snyder, *The Problem of Wineskins: Church Structure in a Technological Age* (Downers Grove, Ill.: Inter-Varsity Press, 1975).

[116]*Lausanne, 1974*, p. 524; see also pp. 201, 341-42, 501-503, 508-523, 1108-1111; cf. the similar sentiment expressed at Edinburgh WMC, *WMC, 1910*, vol. 9: 110.

[117]*Lausanne, 1974*, p. 524.

[118]Cf. Whitby's statement on "Partners in Obedience."

[119]This is remarkably close to the EACC's Faith and Order Conference (1966) formulation of "confessing church," *Confessing the Faith in Asia Today*, p. 14.

[120]There are many references throughout *Lausanne, 1974* on the need to encourage indigenous churches free from Western patterns. See, for example, pp. 18, 30, 125, 136, 250-54, 262, 431, 436, 510, 524, 662, 767, 770, 826, 842, 934, 1229, 1236, 1242-1248, 1252, 1263, 1270.

[121]See James Wong, ed., *Missions From the Third World*,

(Singapore: Church Growth Study Center, 1973), p. 38. For
further discussion of this, cf. *Lausanne, 1974*, pp. 21, 97,
110, 149, 525, 629, 669, 1302-1305, 1323.

122*Lausanne, 1974*, p. 29.

123See the major papers by Samuel Escobar on "Evangelism
and Man's Search for Freedom, Justice and Fulfillment"; George
Hoffman on "The Social Responsibilities of Evangelization"; and
Carl F. H. Henry, "Christian Personal and Special Ethics in
Relation to Racism, Poverty, War, and Other Problems." For
other examples see ibid., pp. 31, 94, 103, 130-31, 144-45,
303-326, 445-46, 475, 679, 696, 698-712, 898, 916, 920, 928,
1077, 1091, 1163-1182, 1294-1296, 1306-1307.

124*Lausanne, 1974*, "Evangelism and the World," p. 131.

125Ibid., pp. 310-311.

126Ibid., p. 679.

127For example, ibid., p. 31, where Billy Graham obviously
had the WCC in mind when he said, "Evangelism has been reinter-
preted in some circles to mean primarily 'changing the structures of society in the direction of justice, righteousness
and peace.'"

128Ibid., p. 445. This is identical to Stott's position
that mission involves evangelism and social action.

129Cf. the WCC's Rolle definition of "ecumenical," in
The First Six Years, p. 126; and *Nairobi, 1975*, pp. 45, 52-53.

130Padilla, *Evangelicalism*, p. 11.

131Stott, *The Lausanne Covenant*, p. 31.

132See p. 193.

133*Lausanne, 1974*, pp. 526-73, 598-600, 1311-1312.

134Ibid., pp. 898-922, 938-47.

135Ibid., pp. 765-75, 977-80.

136*Lausanne, 1974*, pp. 1116-1126; cf. also pp. 71-73, 186,
1295; also Padilla, *Evangelicalism*, pp. 60-61, 78-79.

137*Lausanne, 1974*, p. 1209; cf. also pp. 76, 118, 1058,
1095, 1138, 1214-1215.

138Ibid., pp. 464-73, 790-99, 808-871.

139Ibid., p. 34.

140Harold Lindsell, "Lausanne 74: An Appraisal," CT 18.24 (Sept. 13, 1974): 26.

141Snyder in Padilla, *Evangelicalism*, pp. 131, 138.

142For further information on the work of the Continuation Committee see EMQ 11.2 (1975): 133-37 and EMQ 12.2 (1976): 74; also *Information Bulletin* of the Lausanne Committee for World Evangelization.

143*Lausanne, 1974*, pp. 872-82, 1071-1082, 1332.

144Stott, *The Lausanne Covenant*, p. 3.

145*Lausanne, 1974*, p. 445.

146This point has been emphasized by George W. Peters, "Issues Confronting Evangelical Missions," in Wade T. Coggins and E. L. Frizen, Jr., eds., *Evangelical Missions Tomorrow* (South Pasadena: William Carey Library, 1977), pp. 158-159.

147Ibid., pp. 166-70.

148A recent consultation held at Pasadena, CA., May-June, 1977, sponsored by the International Congress on World Evangelization touched on some of the problems noted here. See the report, "The Pasadena Consultation," in *Missiology* 5.4 (1977): 507-513.

149See Chapter 6.

6

Regional Evangelical Developments: Interaction and Independence

Evangelicals on each continent began developing new programs and organizations in the 1960s. The most important of these, Evangelism in Depth in Latin America, created a new vision of the possibilities for evangelism in that continent, drawing together evangelicals as they shared in this enterprise. The African program, New Life For All, received its initial stimulus from Evangelism in Depth, but then evolved as an independent project designed to relate to the African situation. These new methods of evangelism attracted the attention of evangelicals around the world.

Following the Berlin World Congress on Evangelism in 1966, regional gatherings were held to infuse other national leaders with the enthusiasm and vision participants at Berlin had discovered. The regional congresses held in Africa, Asia, Latin America, Europe, and North America contributed to the growth of regional evangelical self-identity and independence stimulated by interaction with Christians from other continents. These regional meetings gave evidence of the emergence of different approaches to the primary work of evangelism.

The vitality of the regional groups found expression in a number of different organizations and agencies. In Africa, an Association of Evangelicals was formed. Latin American evangelicals participated in a series of Evangelism in Depth campaigns which were directed by nationals. A number of missionary groups emerged in Asia to foster and focus the desire of Asians to share in the task of evangelism throughout the region and the world.

These regional developments provided a variety of theological approaches to the work of mission, ranging from an exclusive emphasis on evangelism in terms of verbal proclamation to a comprehensive mission program designed to meet the physical, intellectual, and spiritual needs of people. This chapter will trace and analyze the emerging variety of regional evangelicalism.

EVANGELISM IN DEPTH

The development of new forms of evangelism in Latin America and Africa in the 1960s began especially through the reflection and work of one person: R. Kenneth Strachan. As the Director of the Latin America Mission (LAM) from 1950 to 1965, Strachan concerned himself with several issues: the indigenization of the LAM by incorporating Latin American personnel into staff positions; rethinking the whole approach to evangelism, including new insights on the place of laity; a reappraisal of the church-mission relationship; and a serious concern for the internal life and disunity of the church in relation to the world.[1] These were similar to the issues being discussed on the ecumenical theological agenda, although Strachan sometimes criticized the WCC.[2] While involved in regular evangelical activities, including the Billy Graham Caribbean Crusade in 1958,[3] Strachan later reported that "I began to analyze the relative stagnation of our churches in many parts of Latin America." This prompted him to make a special study of several growing movements (Communism, Jehovah's Witnesses, the Pentecostal Movement), to discover the source of their growth. Strachan arrived at this conclusion: "the expansion of any movement is in direct proportion to its success in mobilizing its total membership in continuous propagation of its beliefs."[4] This key insight became the foundation for a new strategy of evangelism. In contrast to crusade evangelism, which attempted to draw people in to hear the Christian message from a small group of professional witnesses at a special time, Strachan proposed that Christians must go out to the people in a continuing program of outreach in order to be successful. He sought

> the mobilization of the entire forces in continuous evangelism . . . . It means that the laymen will have to function properly as God intended--as the pattern of Acts describes--which is that every solitary Christian is a witness, every Christian witnessing in proper relationship to his church community, every solitary Christian a missionary . . . . The full-time Christian worker is the trainer to train the laymen to get out and do the job.[5]

From this fresh conception of evangelism emerged the Evangelism in Depth program of the LAM, which became an innovative strategy

and methodology for conservative evangelicals throughout Latin
America during the 1960s, and which stimulated a similar revolution in evangelism in many other parts of the world.

In contrast with the old methods of evangelism, four points
stood out: First, the church, rather than the visiting evangelistic team, became the central element in the program of
evangelistic outreach. Second, the key to effective, widespread
witness involved the mobilization of the laity. Third, the
churches must work together in harmony to accomplish the task of
evangelism in a given area, meaning that the leadership of local
Christians must be united. Strachan hoped this would break
down the prevailing weakness and disunity of many existing
Protestant congregations. Fourth, the goal must be total and
complete outreach, to "every creature," "in all the world."
All of this was summarized in the phrase: "total mobilization
for total evangelization."[6]

Strachan never claimed that Evangelism in Depth represented
anything new, but he considered it to be

> a formal effort to relate in a long-range programme the
> best elements of personal witness and mass evangelism,
> integrated in the continuous testimony of the local
> church and linked to the total witness of the entire
> Body of Christ.[7]

The organization of the Evangelism in Depth ministry always
sought leadership from the country sponsoring the program. The
general objectives were understood to be total mobilization of
the Christian community and total evangelization of a given area.

Evangelism in Depth hoped thereby to achieve particular
objectives, namely, to awaken interest in the local church, to
develop a strong national leadership, to develop a strong
national church, and to evangelize every stratum and facet of
national life.[8]

Toward the end of the 1960s several assessments of the
Evangelism in Depth programs produced some insights which led
to some changes. Strachan died in February, 1965, and Ruben
Lores became director of Evangelism in Depth. The LAM began a
process of internal reevaluation which brought about a complete
restructuring of the LAM in 1971 into a group of autonomous
entities known as the Latin American Community of Evangelical
Ministries (CLAME), with Evangelism in Depth a separate
affiliate organization.[9] Orlando E. Costas became Secretary
for Studies of the Institute of In-Depth Evangelism.

George W. Peters, Professor of World Missions at Dallas

Theological Seminary, investigating several types of evangelistic methodologies including Evangelism in Depth, concluded that although Evangelism in Depth programs have reached many people and registered many professions of faith, "no appreciable, immediate and measurable acceleration in church growth [was] evident in most churches . . . in the years following the campaigns."10

With growing interest in programs of "saturation evangelism," as Evangelism in Depth and a closely-related African scheme, New Life For All, came to be characterized, a consultation sponsored by the IFMA and the EFMA met in Leysen, Switzerland, in 1969.11 At this gathering, Ruben Lores refined the principles behind saturation evangelism, revolving around the key term "mobilization."12 In Lores' thinking, that term referred to the spiritual renewal of Christians, the motivation of each believer for evangelism, and the use of a thorough program for coordinating available resources for the task of Christian proclamation.

To achieve these desired goals, Lores formulated four principles: first, the mobilization of every Christian in witness; second, mobilization within the framework of the church; third, mobilization by local leadership; and fourth, mobilization with comprehensive, global objectives. This systematization of basic principles helped to give conceptual clarity to the objectives and methodology of a program which had emerged by a process of trial and testing throughout Latin America.

Orlando E. Costas presented a paper to the Lausanne Congress on "Depth In Evangelism--An Interpretation of 'In-Depth Evangelism' Around the World."13 Costas argued that In-Depth Evangelism represents "a dynamic evangelistic concept, a comprehensive strategic methodology, and a coordinated, functional program" designed to mobilize the church of Jesus Christ with all her resources for a comprehensive witness in the world. Using the term "comprehensive" as the key to describe the program, Costas broadened and deepened the analytical and theological dimensions of In-Depth Evangelism in relation to the world, the message, the church, and the methodology.

What major theological insights emerge from Strachan's Evangelism in Depth and its subsequent development by Lores and Costas? As might be expected, evangelism has remained the central thrust. However, by making the individual Christian and the local congregation the central foci, instead of a professional evangelist, Evangelism in Depth developed a theology of the laity. As Lores pointed out:

While traditional evangelism seeks to multiply the

number of listeners, through the mobilization of the
church we seek to multiply the number of evangelists
by getting into the experience, motivation and service
of each believer.[14]

The strong and consistent emphasis in the various types of
Evangelism in Depth has centered on the church as a key factor
in evangelism. Church-mission relations were clearly defined:
Mission, as an organization, is the servant of the church. It
is the church which has a mission to fulfill. By directing
attention to the use and development of local leadership, responsible for the whole task of evangelism, Evangelism in Depth
has been committed to the creation of vital and responsible
indigenous churches. As in the WCC study, "The Missionary
Structure of the Congregation," Evangelism in Depth recognized
the need for renewal and change in the structural forms of
church life.[15] Lores argued that

> the life and activities of many congregations center
> around the church building. Meetings multiply, and
> church life is *come-structured*. This psychology must
> change if the world is to be evangelized. The church
> must shift from a *come-structure* to a *go-structure*.[16]

The use of an intensive and intentional methodology, designed
to focus on certain goals and then direct the life of the congregation towards fulfilling those aims, has been a prominent
feature of this type of program.

Some changes can be discerned in the understanding of the
relationship between evangelism and social action in the evolution of Evangelism in Depth thought. Strachan stressed evangelism as the major task which must be undertaken. Lores modified this by indicating that evangelism occurs in a social,
ethical, and ecclesiastical context.[17] The approach of Costas
to church growth has stressed its multidimensional character in
which incarnational growth points to the church's "prophetic,
intercessory and liberating action on behalf of the weak and
destitute." Costas challenged evangelical Christians to give
more intensive witness at this point so that the church can
"effectively lighten the path of life," adequately give "flavor
to the earth," and "leaven the structures of society."[18]

One of the strongest themes evident in Evangelism in Depth
continues to be a concern for the unity of the church. Strachan
deplored the divisions so evident in the Christian community in
Latin America and pleaded for unity on the grounds that "the
relationship of member to member is obligatory and not optional
(I Cor. 12:15-16, 21) . . . Unity (defined always in scriptural
terms) is an indispensable requirement, cooperation in evange-

lism between members is binding and not voluntary."[19] In the same vein, Lores urged Christians to seek unity in "at least the cooperative effort of all true children of God to proclaim the gospel."[20] This restricted, but serious, call to unity among Christians produced significant results in gathering Christians together for witness, especially in Latin America.[21]

The impact of Evangelism in Depth thought and practice has been significant in Latin America and Africa. Based on the conviction that evangelism is the task of the whole church through its total membership mobilized and trained for witness, Evangelism in Depth has challenged evangelicals to rethink mission theology. Costas summarized the challenge it presents in this way:

> In-Depth Evangelism calls attention to the imperative of a comprehensive approach to the involvement of the church in the fulfillment of her witnessing vocation. The issue . . . is how we can get this dynamic organism to *grow integrally*, how we can get this community to be at the same time a living-worshipping-fellowship, a dynamic training center, and an effective team in a complicated world; and how we can put all of her structures at the service of the Gospel of the kingdom so that evangelism--the proclamation of the Gospel, and the subsequent invitation to confess Jesus Christ as Lord and Saviour and be incorporated into the life of his kingdom--will no longer be a superficial, commercial, manipulative whitewash, but a comprehensive enterprise where the Gospel is shared in depth, and out of the depth of man's needs and multiple life situations.[22]

CONFRONTING LATIN AMERICA WITH THE GOSPEL

1. Evangelism in Depth

Evangelism in Depth campaigns have profoundly influenced and shaped the evangelistic outreach of the small evangelical churches in Latin America since 1960. With many denominations taking part, the program was brought to most Latin American countries.[23]

These campaigns resulted in several major achievements. First, they mobilized evangelicals in a planned program of outreach touching significant segments of the total population in countries where Protestants constitute a tiny proportion of the whole population. Second, they trained the laity for witness. This helped create a trained leadership, a stewardship of time and resources, and a general mood of expectation in congregations. Third, they achieved a measure of cooperation through

the participation of many churches in a shared endeavor, creating
bonds which have persisted in the period after the evangelistic
phase of the programs.

Despite the criticisms levelled at Evangelism in Depth,[24]
it created a new spirit of faith, courage, and optimism in many
churches throughout Latin America. "This new zeal, this new
enthusiasm, this new boldness to speak the Word of God . . . is
one of the most significant products of an Evangelism-in-Depth
effort."[25] Undoubtably this formed an important part of the
preparation and background of the Latin American Congress on
Evangelism in 1969.

2. Latin American Congress on Evangelism: Bogota, 1969

As part of the follow-up from the Berlin Congress (1966),
the first Latin American Congress on Evangelism (CLADE) met in
Bogota, Colombia, between November 21-29, 1969.[26] Guided by
the co-presidents, Clyde Taylor and Efrain Santiago (invited by
Billy Graham to organize CLADE), 920 delegates from 25 countries
attended the meeting which had the motto, "Action in Christ For
a Continent in Crisis."[27]

Of its twenty-eight major addresses, Wagner reported that
Samuel Escobar's presentation on social action received the most
enthusiastic attention at the Congress.[28] Escobar argued that
both evangelism and social action are necessary for Christian
witness. This thrust found a place in the Declaration which
stated, "the time has come for us evangelicals to take seriously
our social responsibility." Participants affirmed "Christ's
example must be incarnated in the critical Latin American
situation of underdevelopment, injustice, hunger, violence, and
despair" if Christians were to faithfully witness in that
social-cultural context.[29]

Those present at Bogota were concerned to find practical
ways in which indigenous Christians could fulfill the mission
of the church in Latin America. While grateful for their past
heritage, Congress members wanted to look forward,

> conscious of new responsibilities, new tasks, and
> new structures which form a true challenge to Latin
> American believers and to the indigenous leadership
> in all dimensions of the ministry.[30]

Bogota affirmed its thorough and wholehearted acceptance
of the basic evangelical faith. It focused on evangelism as
the first task of the church, "not something optional." Evangelism is "the very essence of the Church: it is her supreme
task." To be faithful to that mandate "we need to reevaluate

our present evangelistic methods in the light of amazingly rapid growth in some denominations," especially among Pentecostals.

The Declaration's proposals sought to overcome the problems hindering outreach. This included Evangelism in Depth's theme: "the total mobilization of the Church for the evangelistic task . . . beginning with the local congregation." Recognizing the church's weakness in using the mass media, the Declaration emphasized the "obligation to understand and employ modern means of communication," to enable the gospel to speak intelligently and convincingly through the media.

In assessing the renewal within the Roman Catholic Church, participants saw both the risk and opportunity, and called for an informal dialogue on the part of evangelicals to ascertain how future relations with Roman Catholics should be developed.

The most valuable results of Bogota may flow from the opportunity which it provided "for each delegate to establish a new web of friendships and contacts and a subsequent feeling of evangelical unity,"[31] something which had never occurred before for many of the evangelicals in Latin America. As with the ecumenical organizations in Latin America, there is no continent-wide evangelical agency.

Some Latin American developments may be noted. First, evangelical leaders from Latin America, such as Orlando Costas and Samuel Escobar, have made significant contributions to the worldwide evangelical community. Second, the sustained growth of Pentecostal churches on that continent makes Pentecostalism by far the most important segment of Protestantism in Latin America. Third, relations between evangelicals and Roman Catholics have improved greatly in many areas of Latin America, with joint prayer groups and Bible studies. Catholic approval of Bible distribution by Protestants, among other acts, has brought about cordial fraternal relations between Catholics and evangelicals in many places.[32]

Latin America remains in a state of upheaval and transition--politically, socially, and religiously. Evangelical mission theology shares in and reflects that flux.

AFRICA FOR CHRIST

Independence for most African countries in the past twenty-five years has stimulated evangelicals to seek new methods of evangelism and to convene continent-wide gatherings. While these African developments have been closely related to the influence of evangelical mission thought, theology, and practice from outside Africa (most notably to Evangelism in Depth and

the Berlin World Congress on Evangelism), the African context
has shaped and formed these contributions to suit their new
environment.

1. New Life For All

New Life For All (NLFA) began as the brain-child of Gerald
O. Swank of the Sudan Interior Mission. Intrigued by reports
of Evangelism in Depth, Swank met in 1962 with W. Dayton Roberts
of the LAM. Subsequently Swank developed the NLFA proposals
which were adopted in 1963 by a group of churches--Anglican,
Baptist, Methodist, Assemblies of God, and Sudan Interior Mis-
sion--as a means of evangelism in northern Nigeria. They
agreed to implement a mission as quickly as possible.[33]

The basic principles of NLFA involve the total mobilization of all believers in obedience to the Great Commission, a
united evangelistic effort by all the cooperating churches in a
given area to present the gospel to every person. The formula
"Total Mobilization = Total Evangelization" summarized the conviction that the total membership of the church must be trained
and involved in a continuing evangelistic movement.[34]

The NLFA plan involves six steps during the course of a
year, and these can be repeated again and again. They are:
(1) Preparation (leadership and program development); (2) Information (retreat for leaders); (3) Instruction (training
Christians for witness); (4) Evangelization (reaching every
person); (5) Consolidation (follow-up of new converts); and
(6) Continuation (assessment and planning for the future).[35]

Major programs using the general NLFA strategy have been
implemented in Nigeria (beginning in 1964), Zaire (called
Christ Pour Tous/Christ For All, 1966-68), Cameroon (*Vie Nouvelle Pour Tous*/New Life For All, 1969), and more limited
efforts in Rhodesia, Chad, Tanzania, and the Central African
Republic.[36]

2. Association of Evangelicals of Africa and Madagascar

In February, 1966, with the formation of the Association
of Evangelicals of Africa and Madagascar (AEAM), the first
continent-wide fellowship of evangelicals came into existence.
Sponsored by the joint Africa Working Committee of the IFMA and
the EFMA, 189 delegates from 23 African nations gathered in
Kenya and decided to form the AEAM. Its purpose was to provide
a closer fellowship and cooperation in the task of evangelism
and to establish evangelical churches; to unify evangelicals on
the basis of belief in the infallibility of the written Word of
God; to alert Christians to current spiritual dangers; and to

assist evangelicals with emergency relief.[37]

A strong antipathy towards the ecumenical movement appeared to be a major influence motivating the formation of the AEAM. The Constitution declared that "no full member may at the same time be affiliated with the World Council of Churches, or its associated organizations." This tone has continued to characterize the image of the AEAM, even among African Christians.[38]

The AEAM has provided a forum to raise questions regarding the place and role of Western missionaries in Africa, but its main emphasis has been to encourage evangelism, to contend for the authority of the Bible, and to maintain strong opposition to syncretism. With the aim of fostering evangelical theological education and scholarship, the AEAM has sponsored the Evangelical Theological Society of Africa, an Accrediting Council for Theological Education in Africa, and the Bangui Evangelical School of Theology in French-speaking Africa.[39]

3. West African Congress: Ibadan, 1968

The West African Congress on Evangelism convened at Ibadan, Nigeria, in July, 1968, to discuss more effective means of evangelism in West Africa. This became the first regional Congress called to follow up the work of the Berlin Congress (1966). Some 460 participants from about 30 African countries and overseas were present.[40]

Presentations of the New Life For All movement aroused wide interest, and constituted the most important contribution to the Congress. Peters reported that

> Unanimously and enthusiastically the delegates accepted the principles and methodology of NLFA, with the intention of carrying home their impressions and understanding of the program in order to kindle the fires of evangelism in their home constituencies.

> Invitations were received from South, East and Central Africa. In response, the Reverend Wilfred Bellamy and the Reverend Yakubu Yako toured large parts of Africa in November and December of 1968, and shared their experiences and knowledge in retreats and workshops with leaders of eighteen key centers. NLFA is becoming a pattern of evangelism for large parts of Africa.[41]

The relationship of Christianity to social conditions in Africa could not be ignored with Nigeria and Biafra at war, and with Hausa and Ibo Christians present at the Congress. The Congress prayed for peace. Other questions, for example concerning

the drift of young people to the cities, were explored under
the leadership of David Calcott of the International Labor
Organization.

The Congress authorized no statement and its chief success
appears to have been in stimulating and encouraging the wide
use of the NLFA model for evangelism in Africa.

4. Pan African Christian Leadership Assembly:
    Nairobi, 1976 (PACLA)

At Lausanne the African participants began to plan an all-
Africa Conference. Two years later, from December 9-21, 1976,
some eight hundred Africans gathered at Nairobi. The chairman
of PACLA, Gottfried Osei-Mensah, welcomed representatives from
evangelical, ecumenical, and African independent churches.

Michael Cassidy of South Africa, the program director,
listed four basic goals for the meeting:

> to build into Africa a network of Christian relations
> based on Jesus Christ, that will survive no matter what
> happens politically; to face issues before the church
> in Africa; inspiration and renewal; and evangelization
> --taking the gospel to every corner of Africa.[42]

The meeting provided a valuable arena of interaction for those
present in which

> distances between churches were overcome, confessions
> of past offences toward one another were made, and
> new resolves were taken to grapple together with the
> total agenda of Africa in the days ahead.[43]

Festo Kivengere, Anglican Bishop of Uganda, argued that denomi-
nationalism was second only to apartheid as a hindrance to the
gospel in Africa.[44]

Nearly 750 persons signed the seven-point PACLA pledge,
which sought to set out the main theological points of a comprehensive view of mission and evangelism. These included the
triune God, the scripture as "God's authoritative and inspired
Word," the Great Commission, relating the whole gospel "to all
forms of human need," and the love commandment activating the
ministry of reconciliation across every dividing barrier.

Some implications of these main points were made explicit.
These included resisting any undermining of the "deity, uniqueness and saving power" of Christ, and all forms of "syncretism
and universalism." Participants pledged to "resist all forms

of discrimination, oppression or exploitation," and any separation of "the personal and social dimensions of the Gospel."
Christian fellowship requires sharing "resources of means and
manpower," and "transcending denomination, colour, race and
tribe."

PACLA's widely representative character and the broad consensus it engendered on previously divisive issues gave hope
that much more could be accomplished by evangelical Christians
in Africa through further cooperative efforts. No further
meetings were planned. Yet the possibility of local action
based on the PACLA pledge would seem to offer hope for imple-
menting action.

Evangelicals in Africa show evidence of a growing maturity
and independence from Western influence. The vigorous way many
churches have approached evangelism through such programs as
NLFA and the leadership which has developed in Africa--evident
in the Congress on Evangelism, AEAM, and PACLA--demonstrate
that new developments in mission theology, strategy, and practice may certainly be expected from African evangelicals in
the future.

THE CHALLENGE OF EVANGELISM IN ASIA

The development of Asian evangelical organizations has not
progressed far, despite the strength of evangelicalism in India,
Korea, Taiwan, and Indonesia. Yet the desire to evolve structures and a theology related to the Asian context can be seen
in several events which have taken place since 1968.

1. Christ Seeks Asia: Singapore, 1968

Some 1,000 participants shared in the Berlin follow-up
meeting, the Asia-South Pacific Congress on Evangelism which
met in Singapore between November 5-13, 1968.[45] Essentially
practical in orientation, the Congress sought to encourage an
effective and vigorous policy of evangelism in the Asian context, taking into account the two billion population, the high
proportion of youth, rapid urbanization, widespread poverty,
and the like.

The Congress aimed to be both evangelical and Asian. As
one observer noted:

> from the outset, the Asians said plainly they wanted
> to stand on their own feet and be independent of the
> West . . . . The congress did not break new ground
> theologically . . . The theology that did emerge,
> however, was evangelical, for delegates whose churches

are both in and out of the WCC.[46]

The major thrust of the Congress as expressed in its
Declaration called for Asians to unite for the furtherance of
the gospel in Asia, "since the evangelical witness must appeal
to the mind of Asia as the way to Asia's heart." The Declaration proposed that international teams of Asians should be
exchanged across national and denominational frontiers.[47]

2. All-Asia Mission Consultation: Seoul, 1973

Twenty-five Asian evangelicals met from August 27 to September 1, 1973, in Seoul, Korea, to discuss the participation
of Asian churches in the missionary enterprise.[48] Two concerns
emerged from the discussion. First, the leaders wanted the
consultation to be an Asian gathering; consequently, the Western
guests were not invited to attend or share in the meeting until
the fourth day. Second, a number of participants were highly
critical of the ecumenical movement, and saw the Seoul Consultation as an evangelical answer to the CWME Bangkok Assembly.

The Consultation elected a Continuation Committee, with
Philip Teng of Hong Kong as Chairman and David J. Cho of Korea
as General Secretary, to promote the main concerns of the
gathering: to form evangelical mission associations in each
country of Asia; to develop a regional missionary agency; to
establish a mission research center in cooperation with the
Korea International Mission (KIM), of which Cho was Director;
and to examine relations between Asian churches and Western
missionaries.[49] The Consultation pledged to send at least two
hundred new Asian missionaries into the field by the end of
1974, a goal which was nearly accomplished.[50]

3. Asian Missions Association: Seoul, 1975

Through the work of that Continuation Committee, the Inauguration Convention of the Asia Missions Association (AMA) met
at Seoul from August 28 to September 1, 1975. Fifty participants from twelve Asian and four Western nations were present
to adopt a Constitution and "The Declaration on Christian
Mission."[51]

The Declaration made a number of points of significance
for an understanding of evangelical mission theology in Asia.
In an examination of the role of Western missionaries, participants suggested that many Asians regarded the "Christian mission as a vehicle of Western imperialism," especially in view
of the over-dependence on Western churches by Asian Christians.
To counteract this situation, the Asian evangelicals declared
their willingness to accept "our heavy responsibility for

carrying out the unfinished task" of evangelism, and appealed
for close cooperation with Western missionary agencies:

> Do not any longer go your own way. Do not any longer
> compete with each other and with us. Do cooperate
> with the growing evangelical leadership in Asia.

> Let us establish a united front of East and West,
> North and South, to carry out the unfinished task of
> the Christian mission.[52]

In attacking "modern liberalism," evidently associated
with the ecumenical movement, the Declaration condemned the
"socio-politically oriented *missio Dei*," liberation, "the ideological deviation of modern ecumenical mission," dialogue, and
moratorium. These comments indicated a hostility and attitude
reminiscent of the Wheaton and Berlin Congresses of 1966, with
little appreciation of the intent or significance of ecumenical
mission theology, especially as it has developed in the EACC/CCA.

The AMA appeared to be struggling to define itself theologically and organizationally against all other Asian Christians,
and for that reason ignored others working for similar ends and
against similar problems (dependence on Western churches,
Christians in a minority situation in Asia, the need to study
Asian conditions, failure to coordinate Christian resources for
maximum effectiveness), all of which have been continuing questions in Asian ecumenical discussions for nearly thirty years.
One can only hope that in view of the expressed willingness of CCA
leaders to open conversations with evangelical leaders in Asia,
honest and charitable discussions may be possible in the future.

NORTH AMERICAN FOCUS ON EVANGELISM

1. US Congress on Evangelism: Minneapolis, 1969

About 5,000 delegates from all states in the USA gathered
in September, 1969, at Minneapolis for the US Congress on Evangelism. This event proved to be a profoundly shaking experience
for many participants. Those present found a new freedom in
faith, attitude, and insight, especially in relation to evangelism through the Congress's "freedom from old cliches, freedom
from narrow loyalties, freedom from restricted fellowship,
freedom in Christ to proclaim the Gospel in love to the family
of mankind."[53]

The attention of the Congress focused largely on the relationship of evangelism to the social concerns of American society (Vietnam and peace, racism, law and order, revolution, and
civil rights). Leighton Ford expressed a view reflected in the

presentations of many other speakers when he spoke of evangelism
and social action as both belonging to God's work in the world:

> As Christians we have to be concerned both for love and
> justice. Love goes beyond justice, and only the saving
> power of Jesus Christ can produce real love. But love
> is not a substitute for justice, and since not all men
> are or will be converted to Christ, and since even we
> Christians have imperfect love, we have a responsibility
> to seek justice in society. A Christian politician who
> seeks to pass laws that create guidelines for justice
> is doing God's work just as truly as a Christian pastor
> who seeks to win the lost to Christ.[54]

The Conference called for a new relationship between the
church and the world, challenging Christians to leave their
ecclesiastical ghettos to participate fully in the social
structures of the community, while continuing to be fully
obedient in Christian discipleship. Myron S. Augsburger summed
up this challenge:

> If the Church today is awake to the full authority
> and splendor of her evangelizing mission, she must
> realize that her evangelism consists as truly of what
> she is, as it does of what she says. She is Christ's
> holy presence in the world of the unholy, different
> from the world because delivered from it, yet all the
> while redemptively linked with it.[55]

The US follow-up to the Berlin Congress drafted no resolutions, but demonstrated a new spirit among American evangelicals. Open to the issues facing American society and frankly
calling for compassionate outreach by Christians, those present
discovered new insights into the meaning of Christian integrity
and faithfulness as they struggled with other Christians to discover how to communicate the gospel in the context of American
society.

2. Key 73

This new spirit of cooperation among evangelicals perhaps
made many responsive to Carl F. H. Henry's call for a nation-
wide evangelistic campaign embracing evangelicals in all denominations. This led to the "Key 73" program, in which almost
"one hundred fifty nationally identifiable denominations and
organizations joined in an effort to call the continent to
Christ."[56]

Participation in Key 73 reflected something of the diversity of American evangelism. Of an estimated thirty to forty

million evangelicals in the USA in the mid-1970s, some fourteen million may be in NCCC-related denominations. Others belong to denominations unaffiliated with either evangelical or ecumenical organizations--the Southern Baptists with 12.5 million and the Lutheran Church-Missouri Synod with 2.7 million being the largest two groups in this category. The remainder are identified with a large number of small denominations. Key 73 attempted to draw all these various segments of evangelicalism into a united evangelistic endeavor.

Responses among different denominations varied. Some evangelicals refused to participate in any effort which involved NCCC-related churches. The National Association of Evangelicals refused to cooperate. Of the major denominations, the United Methodist Church funded Key 73 activities within Methodism with about $1,000,000, while Southern Baptists disengaged to concentrate on their own evangelistic program. Roman Catholics shared with Protestants in scripture distribution and Bible studies in some areas.

The national impact of Key 73 proved much less than its organizers had hoped, and relied mainly on mass media advertising.[57] At the local level in many places evangelical Christians joined across denominational lines to participate on a community basis in evangelistic outreach. This may well have been the most fruitful result of the whole program.

The debates which Key 73 aroused within the Protestant churches in the USA pointed to the difficulty of drawing together under any common umbrella a large proportion of the total evangelical community. It therefore emphasized the cleavages between ecumenically-related churches and a large part of evangelicalism, and the great differences among evangelicals themselves in the pluralism American society encourages. It seems likely that evangelicals in America will continue to support a number of different conceptions of mission.

One of these options concerns a renewed emphasis on the necessity for social action as an indispensable part of the witness evangelicals present, which received strong support in the Chicago Declaration of 1973.

3. Evangelicals for Social Action

The Thanksgiving Workshop on Evangelicals and Social Concern held at Chicago in November, 1973, coordinated by Ronald J. Sider, drew together some fifty evangelicals. As the first step in moving evangelicals toward a stronger commitment to social action as integral to evangelical witness, they sought to draft a statement. Younger evangelicals, like Sider, Lewis

Smedes, and Jim Wallis, were joined by Frank Gaebelein, Carl F. H. Henry, Rufus Jones, and Paul Rees in this endeavor, which aimed at building on the foundation laid at the Minneapolis Congress (1969) for more involvement in society by evangelicals.

A wide and diverse range of interests soon appeared. The blacks were unhappy with the proposed statement on racism. The women believed their concerns had not been adequately considered. Peace church representatives protested the absence of any statement on war. Through a long process of discussion, debate, and redrafting, the Chicago Declaration was finally adopted.[58]

The Chicago Declaration pointed directly to the inseparable relationship between evangelism and social action. Sider summarized the point this way:

> Evangelistic proclamation is fully biblical only when
> it calls for repentance from all types of sin and
> urges a biblical discipleship in which all relation-
> ships, both personal and societal, are transformed.
> And prophetic social criticism is fully biblical only
> when it announces both that participation in structural
> evil is a damnable sin against God Almighty and also
> that divine forgiveness is bestowed on those who repent
> and turn from all their sins.[59]

The Declaration confessed the failure of evangelicals in the past in relation to social action, and called for justice for the poor and racially oppressed, attacked materialism and militarism, and supported "that righteousness which exalts a nation."

The Chicago Declaration became an important statement for evangelicals in America. Never before had such an explicit and serious commitment been given by evangelical leaders to the social responsibility of evangelical Christians.

Yet as those present at Chicago in 1973 realized, the Declaration was merely the first step in communicating that message to the wider evangelical constituency before priorities could be established and concrete action undertaken. That task has not yet been accomplished.[60] However, some groups have emerged to give tangible form to the concerns expressed in the Chicago Declaration.

4. Radical Evangelicals

Although signs of diversity among evangelicals began to appear in the 1960s especially in relation to the authority of the scriptures,[61] it is the issue of Christian discipleship which has become the critical focus of the various groups of

Radical evangelicals.[62]

The relationship of evangelism and social action is of great importance to Radical evangelicals. In a characteristic statement, John Alexander wrote:

> We believe that personal redemption and social action are both important. But not only are both important; they are part and parcel of each other. To say only that both are important makes them sound like they are related to each other like the layers of a piece of plywood--no essential connection though they can be glued together. We believe that they are much more intertwined than that. Their relation is more like the grain and the rest of the wood in a piece of lumber; if you try to separate them all you get is a pile of splinters.[63]

This view of evangelism and social action as interrelated and necessary tasks is the key to understanding the style of Christian discipleship which the Radical evangelicals are advo- cating. For them a major form of evangelism is the Christian community which by its witness, love, and outreach draws others into a new relation with God and other people. Consequently, conversion involves much more than the acceptance of right doc- trine; it must find concrete expression in a life lived for God and neighbor.

The Christian community is the focal point of discipleship for Radical evangelicals. Close-knit fellowship groups or some form of communal life and activity give a distinctive quality to the Radical evangelical perspective--the Christian life must be lived as well as believed. The concerns expressed in many activities--justice, racism, minority rights, poverty, and human need--are addressed in a practical way by the life style of the Radical evangelicals who attempt to face these issues within their communities.

> It really has become our conviction that more cen- tral than anything we do is who we are; that God's purposes are carried primarily in history through the life of a people, and it's in the quality of life that they share and then lay down for the sake of the world that God's purposes of justice and healing and libera- tion come to pass in history.[64]

The political stance of the Radical evangelicals is mark- edly different from the alliance of conservative religion and politics which has frequently characterized evangelicalism in this century.[65] *Sojourners* and *The Other Side* stand for a position calling for Christians to stand against the materialism

274 CONSERVATIVE EVANGELICAL MISSION THEOLOGY

of American culture pervading society, politics, and the institutional church (conservative and liberal). On this view the Christian mission and discipleship involves the formation of alternative Christian communities that model a simple life style, genuine concern for the poor in the USA and in the developing countries,[66] commitment to one another as sisters and brothers in Christ, and a prophetic critique of many ecclesiastical and political policies and institutions.[67]

The Radical evangelicals constitute a small but disciplined and articulate group. Their influence on evangelicalism in the USA could be very significant as they enter into an informed dialogue with other Christian traditions and with the larger evangelical community.

5. Southern Baptist Foreign Missions[68]

After the breach between northern and southern Baptists in 1845, Foreign and Domestic Mission Boards were established by the Southern Baptists. China and Liberia soon became the main fields for foreign missionary work.[69] The general aims of mission policy were the promotion of indigenous churches and the establishment of educational institutions. By 1885, the Southern Baptist Board began to emphasize a policy of "self-support of native churches." Missionaries were instructed that:

> the oral communication of the gospel, the formation
> of churches, the training and ordination of a native
> ministry, the translation and circulation of the
> scriptures, and the extension of missionary work by
> the aid of native laborers supported, as far as prac-
> ticable by the natives themselves, should be regarded
> as the chief business of our missionaries.[70]

Southern Baptists have consistently refused to share in comity agreements with other missionary agencies, or to become involved in cooperative educational or medical institutions. They believe that Baptists should devote their

> energies and resources with singleness of heart to
> fostering and multiplying denominational schools and
> other agencies at home and abroad in full denominational
> control and in full harmony with the spirit and doctrine
> of the churches contributing funds to our boards.[71]

Although individual Southern Baptists have frequently shared in evangelical gatherings, the convention has not joined in any cooperative organizations, even those with which it could identify closely theologically (for example, the EFMA).

Southern Baptists experienced much financial hardship in the early part of this century. Following World War II their mission policy called for greatly increased personnel and finance under the Program of Advance proposed by successive executive secretaries M. Theron Rankin and Baker James Cauthen. Basic objectives in the expanded program in 1958 were summarized thus:

> The ultimate purpose of foreign missions is to do all possible to bring every man in every land around the world to a saving knowledge of Jesus Christ as rapidly as possible, and to involve them in Christian service . . . . The greatest effectiveness will be realized in terms of the developing of Christian life and the cultivating of church resources in mission lands themselves. Therefore, the central objective in each land is the planting, multiplying, and strengthening of churches.[72]

A vigorous, planned church growth strategy has remained a central element in Southern Baptist mission theology. To achieve this objective, city-wide evangelistic gatherings in all Baptist churches in a local area, as well as other programs of outreach, have been extensively used.

In the late 1960s, Cauthen called for more flexible and innovative methods to relate Baptist missionary work to the global problems of the population explosion, food shortages, the threat of nuclear warfare, and other dimensions of the changing world situation. This process of reevaluation culminated in a request by the Southern Baptist Convention in 1974 for the Home and Foreign Mission Boards to develop bold new plans for the last quarter of this century.

These plans evolved through two major efforts. Three hundred Southern Baptist leaders, missionaries, and nationals from other countries met in Miami, Florida in June, 1975, for a consultation and study of world mission. The Foreign Mission Board then evaluated suggestions made at Miami and adopted ten "Bold New Thrusts in Foreign Missions 1976-2000." The selected goals are:

1. Great overarching objective: To preach the gospel to all the people in the world.
2. One hundred percent increase in missionary staff-- more than 5,000 by A.D. 2000.
3. Missionaries at work in at least 125 countries as God may lead.
4. Accelerated tempo of volunteer lay involvement over- seas--up to 3,000 per year now, and up to 10,000 per year by A.D. 2000.

5. Greatly expanded efforts in evangelism--major
   thrusts in urban areas and among students and
   other young people.
6. Tenfold multiplication of overseas churches--with
   concomitant increases in baptisms and church
   membership.
7. Extraordinary efforts in leadership training--
   through strengthened seminaries, Theological
   Education by Extension, and lay leadership
   training.
8. Vastly increased use of radio, television, and
   publications on mission fields, and penetration
   by way of mass media of areas not presently open
   to missionary activity.
9. Accentuated attention to human need--through
   health care, disease prevention, benevolent
   and social ministries.
10. Vigorous, appropriate, and prompt responses to
    world hunger and disasters.[73]

As with other conservative evangelical groups, evangelism
and church growth remain central aspects of the Southern Baptist
program. James Cauthen again emphasized this when he stated
that the Board has "one central objective--that of establishing
in each country many strong indigenous churches and a strong
Baptist denomination."[74] However, the need to encourage indigenous leaders to formulate local policy was also recognized by
Cauthen, who affirmed that as work matures in a particular area,
indigenous leadership must become more and more prominent, with
missionaries assuming a helping role.[75]

Southern Baptist plans envisage "a unified program"
involving all aspects of mission. Mission promotional literature in 1976 affirmed that

the overseas task includes evangelism, church development, theological and leadership training programs,
mass media ministries, publications ministries, health
care ministries, benevolent and social ministries, and
disaster relief and world hunger programs.[76]

The Southern Baptist program is the most ambitious of any
large mission board, calling for an increase of nearly doubling
the 2,667 missionaries it had in 1975 by A.D. 2000. Its attempt
to develop a flexible, comprehensive list of objectives, at the
same time obedient to the gospel imperative and responsive to
the context of the world, make this one of the most significant
evangelical missionary projects developed in the USA.

In surveying the American scene, one can see from the

strength and variety of American evangelicalism that no one
pattern of mission theology is likely to predominate. With
large denominations like the Southern Baptists and Lutheran
Church-Missouri Synod maintaining separate programs and with
the theological span stretching from separatist fundamentalists
to evangelicals within the NCCC-related churches, a variety of
approaches to mission will continue to exist.

Two main trends may be noted: First, evangelicals have
become better known and are willing and able to articulate
their concerns for evangelism and biblical authority. The
bitterness and divisiveness which have sometimes characterized
relations between some evangelicals and other Christians in the
past is lessening. Key 73 may be seen as one example of such
cooperative interaction.

Second, a small but significant group of evangelical
leaders has attempted to redress the balance between evangelism
and social action in the thought and practice of the evangelical community. The stimulus of such documents as the Chicago
Declaration, the support given to evangelical agencies like
World Vision, and the comprehensive mission of the Southern
Baptist denomination are all indications of this emphasis.

Some 35,000 Protestant missionaries out of the estimated
total of 55,000 worldwide come from North America. Evangelicals comprise about eighty-five percent of the total from North
America in 1976 (up from sixty-nine percent in 1968).[77] These
facts alone make evangelicals in the USA one of the most important sources of mission activity and thought in the world today.

THE SECULAR CHALLENGE TO EVANGELISM IN EUROPE

1. European Congress on Evangelism, 1971

Over 1200 delegates and observers from 35 countries
attended the 1971 European Congress on Evangelism in Amsterdam
to discuss practical ways of promoting evangelism in Europe.[78]
Presentations and workshops on various kinds of evangelism, and
brief national meetings, constituted the main agenda. No
official statement was issued.

The major addresses contained little new material theologically. Henri Blocher presented a paper on "The Lost State of
Mankind." Finland's Paavo Kortegangas spoke on "The Social
Implications of Evangelism," and noted that in many places the
spiritual and physical needs of people and the individual and
social consequences of evangelism cannot be separated.

Two presentations produced particular response from the

Congress. Emphasizing the importance of understanding youth, a
dramatic multimedia production, "The Revolutionaries," startled
some delegates with its attempt to portray the mood of contemporary European youth. Jan van Cappelleveen, "Communicating
the Gospel Through the Local Church," stirred delegates with
his argument that most local churches are ill-equipped for
evangelism because they are clerically dominated and are involved with people inside the church rather than those in the
world. Thus most churches in effect hinder effective evangelism.

The European Congress provided a useful gathering point
for evangelicals in Europe to discuss the problems and challenges of evangelism in the 1970s. It developed no strategic
proposals and limited its goal to challenging and inspiring
individual participants.

2. The Frankfurt Declaration, 1970

Following the WCC Assembly at Uppsala in 1968, Peter Beyerhaus, Professor of Mission at Tübingen, expressed great concern
about the direction of recent ecumenical mission theology. He
characterized the trend as the "radical displacement of the
center from God to man and the replacement of theology by
anthropology" in which the focus on the human situation represented a "conscious and definite turning away from God as the
absolute and ultimate Reference-Point for all Christian thought
and service."79

Beyerhaus concluded that a conservative evangelical
response in the style of the Wheaton Declaration might awaken
the German Protestant missionary societies to the danger.
Accordingly, he formulated the "Frankfurt Declaration on the
Fundamental Crisis in Christian Missions" to call attention to
"an insidious falsification of the basic assumptions of the
Christian faith."80

At this point Beyerhaus associated himself with the No
Other Gospel movement (*Kein anderes Evangelium*), and at its
Theological Convention in Frankfurt on March 4, 1970, it adopted
(with minor amendments) the Beyerhaus draft Declaration.81
English translations soon appeared in *Christianity Today* and the
Church Growth Bulletin with enthusiastic recommendations from
Harold Lindsell and Donald McGavran.

The Declaration listed "Seven Indispensable Basic Elements
of Mission":

1. "Mission is grounded in the nature of the Gospel."
2. The supreme goal of mission is the glorification of
    God's name, and the "proclamation of the lordship

of Jesus Christ."
3. Mission challenges non-Christians to believe in
   Christ and be baptized in order to be saved.
4. Mission is the presentation of salvation obtained
   through the sacrificial crucifixion of Jesus Christ,
   which calls for decision and baptism.
5. Mission's "primary visible task" is "*to call out the
   messianic, saved community* from among all people,"
   which results in the creation of a witnessing congregation.
6. The offer of salvation in Christ is directed to all
   people, who receive it only through faith.
7. The mission, God's saving activity, continues from
   the resurrection to Christ's return. All people
   will be "called to decision for or against Christ."[82]

Following the format of the Barmen Declaration, the Frankfurt Declaration cites a verse of scripture, expresses its
affirmative theses, and then states its rejections ("We reject
. . ."). It opposed what were judged to be the erroneous trends
of ecumenical mission theology, including socio-political analysis, humanization, universalism, syncretism, and the identification of salvation with progress, development, and social
change.[83]

As a polemical document, the Frankfurt Declaration stated
a case. As a contribution to the process of reformulating mission theology, it added to the polarization of opinion between
some evangelicals and those in the ecumenical movement. Beyerhaus himself recognized that the viewpoints he opposed represented "neither the majority of Christians in the [WCC] member
churches nor of the General Assembly delegates."[84] His chosen
method of communication contributed little to the process of
mature theological reflection, but his position has been widely
influential among some conservative evangelicals.

3. The Berlin Ecumenical Declaration, 1974

Beyerhaus's attack on the WCC continued and, indeed, intensified following the Bangkok Conference on "Salvation Today."
Prior to the meeting of the WCC's Central Committee in Berlin
in 1974, Beyerhaus and Walter Künneth convened a Conference of
Confessing Christians from Germany which issued a Declaration
entitled, "Freedom and Unity in Christ."[85] The title clearly
parallels the theme of the then forthcoming Fifth Assembly of
the WCC, "Jesus Christ Frees and Unites."

The twelve theses of the Declaration, divided into five
sections, indicate the major points:[86]

   I.   The Decisive Hour of Ecumenism
       1. The new humanism as an anti-Christian
           temptation
       2. The new polarization as the inescapable
           division in the church
       3. The new watchword as a command to
           responsibility

  II.   The Liberation Program of Ecumenism
       4. True freedom is only revealed by the Holy Bible
       5. True freedom comes only from Jesus Christ
       6. True freedom is only mediated by the Gospel

 III.   The vision of unity of Ecumenism
       7. No one-world church
       8. No one-world religion
       9. No one-world community

  IV.   The Powerful Influence of Ideological Ecumenism
     10. Ecumenism as a wrong spirit
     11. Ecumenism as a conquering strategy

   V.   The Confessing Community Answers Ecumenism
     12. Spiritual understanding and opposition,
         gathering and sending

     A vehemently anti-ecumenical spirit pervades this Declaration. As Beyerhaus himself acknowledged when analyzing the six different groups present at Lausanne--all under the general title of "evangelical"--those who produced the Frankfurt and Berlin Declarations belonged to the "confessing Evangelical" group, which differed markedly from others present at Lausanne.[87] The Berlin Declaration lacks the positive, open character of the Lausanne Covenant produced a few months later.

     Despite Beyerhaus's comment, "I judge the Lausanne Covenant to be a good document, to which I consent," he also thought that "Berlin needs Lausanne, Lausanne needs Berlin."[88] Yet the difference in attitude is so marked that the Berlin Declaration will not help either the worldwide evangelical community or the ecumenical movement come to a better understanding of the issues involved, unless one accepts the contention that the entire ecumenical movement is motivated by a kind of heresy akin to the gnosticism of the second century, as the Berlin Declaration suggests.[89]

SUMMARY

     This survey of evangelical regional developments has demonstrated that while North America certainly continues to be the

strongest and most influential segment of evangelicalism, significant advances have also taken place in other parts of the
world.

As the title of this chapter indicates, considerable
interaction has occurred between the various sections of the
evangelical community. Evangelism in Depth stimulated evangelistic programs in Africa and North America. A new depth and
perspective in evangelical discussions of mission theology and
practice have been evident through the contributions of people
such as Ruben Lores and Orlando Costas. American evangelical
leaders, among them Carl F. H. Henry, Stanley Mooneyham, Harold
Lindsell, and George Peters, have encouraged the growth of the
worldwide evangelical community, assisting in the discussions
and meetings taking place in other parts of the world.

Yet signs of independence can also be noted in several
areas. The Evangelism in Depth movement, begun by Kenneth
Strachan, emerged in response to conditions in Latin America
and, while it has stimulated similar types of programs in other
places, it has continued to grow and develop under the leadership of Lores and Costas. In Africa, New Life For All and the
AEAM have largely been developed and led by Africans. The
effort to establish the Asian Missions Association and the
East-West Center for Missions Research and Development in
Seoul grew out of the concern of some Asians to organize and
encourage this aspect of evangelical life. The follow-up Congresses on Evangelism held after Berlin in Africa, Asia, Latin
America, the USA, and Europe were basically organized by people
in those regions to foster evangelism suited to the local
conditions.

The major point developed in these regional movements
relates to evangelism. Evangelism in Depth proved a valuable
model capable of working throughout Latin America, and able to
be reproduced in other situations. While not replacing mass
rallies, Evangelism in Depth and New Life For All concentrate
far more heavily on the local congregation as the most important
focal point for evangelism. The goal is to assist all Christians to become involved in the process of evangelism, frequently in concert with evangelical Christians of other denominations in a planned program of outreach, coordinated under the
leadership of local Christians. The various programs developed
from Evangelism in Depth have all been based on these principles.

The relationship between evangelism and social action
received specific attention in Latin America and North America.
South America's social turmoil has made evangelical spokesmen
aware of the need to relate Christianity to the issues facing
society. Samuel Escobar and Orlando Costas have given prophetic

leadership on this point. Similarly, in North America the need
to involve evangelicals in social action has been widely recognized by the evangelical community, as the strong emphasis on
this issue at the Minneapolis Congress on Evangelism, and in
the Chicago Declaration (1973) demonstrates.

Evangelicals have begun to seek ways to cooperate across
denominational boundaries. The significant number of evangelical denominations joining in Evangelism in Depth programs was a
major breakthrough in Latin America. NLFA activities in Africa
achieved considerable success at this point. Key 73 produced
more cooperation among evangelicals than had been achieved previously at the national level. The PACLA in Africa indicated a
move for Christian unity in that continent. The rather more
defensive position adopted by evangelicals in Asia, and by the
German group which produced the Frankfurt and Berlin Declarations, indicates the division of opinion among evangelicals.
Some stress purity of doctrine above all other considerations,
while evangelicals who cooperate in evangelistic programs do so
in the conviction that it is an important witness to the spiritual unity of Christians.

There is undoubtably a growing diversity among those who
call themselves "evangelicals." The continued development of a
variety of programs, concerns, and issues should be expected.
Interaction between the segments of the worldwide evangelical
community will continue, with Americans providing strong leadership and financial support. Yet increased independence among
different groups will also become more evident, as the situations in various places require different responses.

NOTES

[1]R. Kenneth Strachan, "Call to Witness," IRM 53.210
(1964): 192-93; R. Kenneth Strachan, *The Inescapable Calling*
(Grand Rapids: Eerdmans, 1968), pp. 106-108; W. Dayton Roberts,
Strachan of Costa Rica. Missionary Insights and Strategies
(Grand Rapids: Eerdmans, 1971), pp. 72-75.

[2]Roberts, *Strachan*, p. 68. Strachan would not support the
WCC "because of its liberalism and unscriptural basis of fellowship, and unscriptural centralization of ecclesiastical power,
its dedication to other tasks and concerns than those which
legitimately concern the church of Christ." However, the important Strachan-Hayward debate on evangelism in IRM 53.210 (1964)
indicates that Strachan was open to serious conversation
between evangelical and ecumenical spokesmen.

[3]John Pollock in *Crusades: 20 Years With Billy Graham*

(Minneapolis: World Wide Publications, 1966), p. 188, claimed
that Evangelism in Depth emerged from the discussions Graham
and Strachan had at this time. This must be considered very
unlikely in view of the quite different approaches to evangelism
which Strachan and Graham employed.

[4]Strachan, "Call to Witness," p. 194.

[5]Roberts, *Strachan*, p. 87.

[6]Strachan, *The Inescapable Calling*, p. 109-111.

[7]Strachan, "Call to Witness," p. 197.

[8]George W. Peters, *Saturation Evangelism* (Grand Rapids:
Zondervan, 1970), p. 57.

[9]W. Dayton Roberts, "Mission to Community--Instant
Decapitation," IRM 62.247 (1973):   338-45.

[10]Peters, *Saturation Evangelism*, p. 72.   See also Ray S.
Rosales, *The Evangelism in Depth Program of the Latin America
Mission*. *Sonedeos* No. 21 (Cuernavaca: CIDOC, 1968).   This
M.Th. thesis, completed in 1966, also pointed to the same weak-
ness in the follow-up phase of Evangelism in Depth. See chap-
ter 7, pp. 16-22; cf. the similar conclusions by C. Peter Wagner,
Frontiers in Missionary Strategy (Chicago: Moody Press, 1971).

[11]See the published report, Clyde W. Taylor and Wade T.
Coggins, eds., *Mobilizing For Saturation Evangelism* (Wheaton:
Evangelical Missions Information Service, n.d.).

[12]The following points are taken from his address, ibid.,
pp. 43-67, "Mobilization of Believers and Churches for Evangelism."

[13]*Lausanne, 1974*, pp. 675-94.

[14]Lores, "Mobilization of Believers and Churches for Evangelism," p. 48.

[15]See *The Church For Others*, pp. 18-19.

[16]"Mobilization of Believers and Churches for Evangelism,"
p. 49; cf. W. Dayton Roberts, *Revolution in Evangelism. Evangelism-in-Depth in Latin America* (Chicago: Moody Press, 1967),
pp. 104-105; and Costas, "Depth In Evangelism," pp. 685-86.

[17]Lores, "Mobilization of Believers and Churches for Evangelism," p. 53.   Consider, too, the use of Goodwill Caravans in

Latin America; see Eugenio Orellana, Introduction by Jonas
Gonzales, "Goodwill Caravans," IRM 64.256 (1975): 386-90;
and Rosales, *The Evangelism in Depth Program*, chapter 5, p. 8.

[18]Costas, "Depth in Evangelism," p. 679; cf. Orlando E.
Costas, "Evangelism in a Latin American Context," *Occasional
Essays: Latin American Evangelical Center for Pastoral Studies*
4.142 (Jan. 1977): 9-10, 12.

[19]Strachan, *The Inescapable Calling*, pp. 100-101.

[20]Lores, "Mobilization of Believers and Churches for Evangelism," p. 45.

[21]See Peters, *Saturation Evangelism*, pp. 70-71. "The
success in involving churches has been phenomenal and has ranged
from sixty-five to eighty-five percent" in an area where "united
efforts and unified strategy even among evangelicals were practically out of the question."

[22]Costas, "Depth In Evangelism," p. 681.

[23]For details of specific programs see Paul E. Pretiz,
ed., *In-Depth Evangelistic Movements Around the World: A Special
Report for ICOWE, 1974* (San Jose, Costa Rica: Publicaciones
Indef, 1974); Rosales, *The Evangelism in Depth Program of the
Latin American Mission*; Peters, *Saturation Evangelism*; W. Dayton
Roberts, *Revolution in Evangelism*; W. Dayton Roberts, *Strachan*,
chaps. 6, 7, 8; and Malcolm R. Bradshaw, *Church Growth Through
Evangelism in Depth* (Pasadena: William Carey Library, 1969).
Evangelism in Depth programs have been held in Nicaragua (1960),
Costa Rica (1961), Guatemala (1962), Honduras (1963-4), Ven-
ezuela (1964-5), Bolivia (1965), Dominican Republic (1965-6),
Nicaragua-Atlantic Coast (1965), Peru (1967), Colombia (1968),
Mexico (1969-70), Ecuador (1969-70), Paraguay (1970), and Chile
(1973-4).

[24]For a summary list see Pretiz, *In-Depth Evangelistic
Movements Around the World*, pp. 19-22.

[25]Roberts, *Revolution in Evangelism*, p. 84.

[26]See the published report, *Acción en Cristo para un
Continente en Crisis* (San Jose: Editorial Caribe, 1970).

[27]From the report by C. Peter Wagner, "Latin American Congress on Evangelism," EMQ 6.3 (1970): 167-71. Orlando E. Costas
in *Theology of the Crossroads*, p. 78, reported that some charismatic Christians were not invited, and a leader of the Argen-
tinian Pentecostals--Juan Ortiz--was refused permission to speak

to other evangelicals at CLADE by a group of anticharismatic, theologically conservative Argentinians. (Ortiz was a contributor to the Lausanne Congress in 1974). However, about one-third of the Congress delegates were from Pentecostal groups-- still a relatively small proportion considering about two-thirds of the total Protestant community in Latin America is Pentecostal. See also Elden Rawlings, "Bogotá: Latin Liaison," CT 14.6 (Dec. 19, 1969): 33; and C. Peter Wagner, *Look Out! The Pentecostals are Coming* (Carol Stream, Ill: Creation House, 1973), p. 149.

28Samuel Escobar, "The Social Responsibility of the Church in Latin America, EMQ 6.3 (1970): 129-52.

29From "The Evangelical Declaration of Bogota," EMQ 6.3 (1970): 172-75.

30Ibid., p. 172.

31Wagner, "Congress on Evangelism," p. 170.

32See some examples given by a LAM missionary, Charles Troutman, in *Everything You Want to Know about the Mission Field But are Afraid You Won't Learn Until You Get There* (Downers Grove, Ill: Intervarsity Press, 1976), pp. 87-90.

33Peters, *Saturation Evangelism*, pp. 88-91; Pretiz, *In-Depth Evangelistic Movements Around the World*, p. 57.

34*Principles and Practice in New Life For All* (Jos, Nigeria: New Life For All, 1968), pp. 8-9, 12-16; see also Wilfred A. Bellamy, "New Life For All" in Taylor and Coggins, *Mobilizing For Saturation Evangelism*, pp. 12-42.

35*Principles and Practice in New Life For All*, p. 18.

36See Pretiz, *In-Depth Evangelistic Movements*, pp. 57-67, for brief summaries of these NLFA projects; also Costas, "Depth In Evangelism," pp. 687-88 for an analysis of the Cameroon program.

37For basic information on the founding of the AEAM, see W. Harold Fuller, "Evangelicals Join in Africa," EMQ 3.3 (1967): 170-77; and "Association of Evangelicals," CT 10.11 (Mar. 4, 1966): 47-48.

38See, for example, the article, "'Evangelicals' deny fighting WCC Assembly" in *Target* Nairobi (Oct. 19-26, 1975), in which the AEAM General Secretary, Byang Kato defended the AEAM against charges of negativism and dependence on European conservativism made by African church leaders in Kenya.

[39]See "Evangelicals in Africa," CT 21.22 (Aug. 26, 1977): 38-39.

[40]For basic information on the Congress, see Wilfred A. Bellamy, "African Congress on Evangelism Faces Issues Confronting Church," EMQ 5.2 (1969): 112-114; CT 12.22 (Aug. 16, 1968): 46-47; and Peters, *Saturation Evangelism*, pp. 115-116.

[41]Peters, *Saturation Evangelism*, p. 116.

[42]*Information Bulletin of the Lausanne Committee for World Evangelization* 6 (Feb. 1977): 1. Cassidy had previously been involved in a similar kind of inclusive gathering through his leadership in the Congress on Mission and Evangelism in South Africa, which was sponsored by African Enterprise (directed by Cassidy) and the South African Council of Churches; see Michael Cassidy, et al., eds., *I Will Heal Their Land . . . Papers of the South African Congress on Mission and Evangelism. Durban 1973* (Pietermaritzburg: Africa Enterprise, 1974) and Michael Cassidy, *Prisoners of Hope* (Pietermaritzburg: Africa Enterprise, 1974).

[43]"Nairobi, December 1976," *Missiology* 5.2 (1977): 241. The PACLA Pledge is found on pp. 241-42 of this reference.

[44]*Partnership* 8 (Mar. 14, 1977). This is a bulletin produced by Partnership in Mission of Abington, Pennsylvania.

[45]W. Stanley Mooneyham, ed., *Christ Seeks Asia: Official Reference Volume, Asia-South Pacific Congress on Evangelism. Singapore 1968* (Hong Kong: Rock House, 1969).

[46]"Sharp Word for the West from Asian Evangelicals," CT 13.5 (Dec. 6, 1968): 44; cf. Carl F. H. Henry, "An Assessment" in *Christ Seeks Asia*, p. 10.

[47]*Christ Seeks Asia*, p. 9.

[48]The report of this Consultation and the 1975 Asian Missions Association meeting can be found in David J. Cho, ed., *New Forces in Missions: The Official Report of the Asian Missions Association* (Seoul, Korea: East-West Center for Missions Research and Development, 1976). The twenty-five participants came from thirteen Asian countries.

[49]See ibid., pp. 245-46 for "The Statement of the All-Asia Mission Consultation, Seoul '73." The marked influence of Cho and the KIM on this whole gathering should be noted. Cho was responsible for calling together the Consultation, ibid., pp. 13, 16, 24. As soon as the Consultation concluded, the KIM sponsored Summer Institute of World Mission began, and the East-West

Center for Missions Research and Development began as a project
sponsored by Cho and the KIM, under the authority of the Continuation Committee. For a brief description of the KIM (and some
50 other Asian missionary societies) see Marlin A. Nelson and
Chaeok Chun, *Asian Mission Societies: New Resources for World
Evangelization* (Monrovia, Ca.: MARC, 1976).

[50]Cho, *New Forces in Mission*, p. 281.

[51]Ibid., pp. 392-402 for the Declaration.

[52]Ibid., pp. 400-401.

[53]"An Evaluation: What the US Congress on Evangelism
Means to the Future of the Church" in Geo. M. Wilson, ed.,
*Evangelism Now: US Congress on Evangelism--Minneapolis, 1969.
Official Reference Volume: Papers and Reports* (Minneapolis:
World Wide Publications, 1969), p. 232.

[54]Ibid., p. 62, "The Church and Evangelism in a Day of
Revolution."

[55]Ibid., p. 200, Augsburger acknowledged Paul Rees to be
the author of these words. See also the papers by Halverson,
Rees, Chafin, Larson, Hatfield, Skinner, Miller, and Abernathy
for similar comments.

[56]Carl F. H. Henry, "Looking Back at Key 73," *The Reformed
Journal* 24.9 (1974): 7.

[57]For a critical look at this aspect of Key 73, and the
concept of the program itself, see Deane A. Kemper, "Another
Look at Key 73," *The Reformed Journal* 25.1 (1975): 15-17.

[58]The Declaration is found on the front cover and pp. 1
and 2 of Ronald J. Sider, ed., *The Chicago Declaration* (Carol
Stream, Ill.: Creation House, 1974).

[59]Ibid., p. 30.

[60]See a report of the 1977 meeting of Evangelicals for
Social Action in CT 21.17 (June 3, 1977): 33, which acknowledged
that little had been done to implement the principles of the
1973 statement.

[61]See Harold Lindsell, *The Battle for the Bible* (Grand
Rapids: Zondervan, 1976), particularly his attack on the Fuller
Theological Seminary. For a helpful summary and evaluation of
developments, see Gerald T. Sheppard, "Biblical Hermeneutics:
The Academic Language of Evangelical Identity," *Union Seminary*

Quarterly Review 32.2 (1977): 81-94.

[62]For a brief overview of the Radical evangelical groups and some of their concerns see Richard Quebedeaux, "The Evangelicals: New Trends and New Tensions," *Christianity and Crisis* 36.14 (1976): 197-202; also Quebedeaux, *The Young Evangelicals*, pp. 37-41; 73-135. The views of the Radical evangelicals are best known through their publications. From the Jesus movement in California came *Right On*, now called *Radix*, associated with the Berkeley Christian Coalition of which Sharon Gallagher is a leader. On the East Coast of the USA, *The Other Side* (formerly *Freedom Now*), in Philadelphia, edited by John F. Alexander, and *Sojourners*, with Jim Wallis as editor (which began in 1971 as *The Post American*), produced by the People's Christian Coalition, a Christian commune now located in Washington, DC, and more recently the evangelical feminist journal, *Daughters of Sarah* (Chicago), edited by Lucille Sider Dayton.

[63]John F. Alexander, "Time Bombs," *The Other Side* 8.3 (May-June 1972): 3; cf. Ronald J. Sider, "Evangelism, Salvation, and Social Justice," IRM 64.255 (1975): 251-67; and Sider, "Evangelism or Social Justice: Eliminating the Options," CT 21.2 (Oct. 8, 1976): 26-29.

[64]"Crucible of Community," *Sojourners* 6.1 (1977): 21; cf. Donald G. Bloesch, *Wellsprings for Renewal: Promise in Christian Communal Life* (Grand Rapids: Eerdmans, 1974).

[65]See Donald W. Dayton, "The Social and Political Conservatism of Modern American Evangelicalism: A Preliminary Search for the Reasons," *Union Seminary Quarterly Review* 32.2 (1977): 71-80.

[66]On this point, see Ronald J. Sider, *Rich Christians in an Age of Hunger* (Downers Grove: Inter Varsity Press, 1977).

[67]See, for example, Stephen C. Knapp, "Mission and Modernization: A Preliminary Critical Analysis of Contemporary Understandings of Mission from a 'Radical Evangelical' Perspective" in Beaver, *American Missions in Bicentennial Perspective*, pp. 146-209.

[68]This brief summary of Southern Baptist Foreign Missions has been included because that denomination has conducted the largest independent missionary program in the world. Changes in Southern Baptist policy may be paralleled by similar moves in other evangelical groups.

[69]Baker J. Cauthen and Others, *Advance: A History of Southern Baptist Foreign Missions* (Nashville: Broadman Press,

1970), pp. 18-21.

[70]Jesse C. Fletcher, "Foreign Mission Board Strategy," *Baptist History and Heritage* 9.4 (Oct. 1974): 215.

[71]Ibid., p. 217. Two notable exceptions to this 1916 policy statement on educational work may be observed: Baptists have cooperated in Chung Chi University, Hong Kong, and in the Vellore Hospital and Medical School, India. This policy in some ways seems rather curious because Southern Baptists generally insist that they exercise no denominational control over autonomous congregations.

[72]Ibid., p. 220.

[73]*The Commission* (Nashville) 39.6 (June 1976): 1.

[74]*1976 Southern Baptist Convention Annual*, "One Hundred and Thirty-first Annual Report--Foreign Mission Board," p. 98.

[75]Ibid.

[76]*The Commission*, ibid., pp. 5-6.

[77]Dayton, "Current Trends in North American Protestant Ministries Overseas," p. 6; Dayton, *Mission Handbook*, p. 20.

[78]The report of this, the last regional follow-up Congress after Berlin, edited by the Congress Chairman, G. W. Kirby, *Evangelism Alert* (Minneapolis: World Wide Publications, 1972), has not been available to the writer. See also the summary of the Congress by Bill Yoder, "European Congress on Evangelism," EMQ 8.2 (1972): 102-113.

[79]Peter Beyerhaus, *Missions: Which Way? Humanization or Redemption*, trans. by Margaret Clarkson (Grand Rapids: Zondervan, 1971), pp. 86-87.

[80]Peter Beyerhaus, *Shaken Foundations: Theological Foundations for Mission* (Grand Rapids: Zondervan, 1972), p. 64.

[81]Ibid., p. 67; Beyerhaus, *Missions: Which Way?*, pp. 111-120 contains the text of the Declaration; also McGavran, *The Conciliar-Evangelical Debate*, pp. 287-93. Among the original signers were W. Künneth and Georg Vicedom.

[82]This represents a sharp condensation of the seven elements in the Frankfurt Declaration.

[83]Beyerhaus, *Missions: Which Way?*, pp. 113-120.

[84]Ibid., pp. 73-74.

[85]Walter Künneth and Peter Beyerhaus, eds., *Reich Gottes oder Weltgemeinschaft? Die Berliner Ökumene-Erklärung zur Utopischen Vision des Weltkirchenrates* (Badliebenzell: Verlag der Liebenzeller Mission, 1975), pp. 16-41. Two drafts were published--a shorter form on May 23, 1974, and an expanded version on July 1, 1974.

[86]The full text of the Declaration is to be found in ibid., pp. 16-41.

[87]Ibid., pp. 307-308.

[88]Ibid., pp. 296, 311.

[89]Ibid., p. 39.

Summary of Part II

The development of evangelical mission theology from a narrow concern for evangelism, often developed in a polemical manner, to a broader emphasis on mission with a particular interest in evangelism, has taken several decades. Two main stages are evident. In the early part of the twentieth century in the USA, where evangelicalism has been strongest, evangelicals became isolated from mainline Protestantism. The first stage saw the evangelicals emerge from that isolation, seeking to develop an identity and theology through a number of evangelical organizations. This occurred primarily after World War II and lasted until the mid-1960s. The second stage, in which evangelicals developed a truly global community with a comprehensive view of mission, may be traced from 1966, the year in which evangelicals sponsored two major world conferences on mission and evangelism.

THE FIRST STAGE: TO 1966

From an influential position in nineteenth century Protestantism, evangelicals suffered a great reversal in the early twentieth century, especially in North America. In the USA, the fundamentalist-modernist debates left many evangelicals isolated and inturned, with a narrow interest in evangelism as virtually the sole task of the church, having repudiated any emphasis on social action as an error associated with liberalism and the social gospel.

Many evangelicals became concerned with the image of fundamentalists as divisive bigots, especially when Carl McIntire formed the ACCC. Some among them began to plan for a more positive, irenic organization to give direction to the essential evangelistic thrust of the church's life, while still maintaining strong opposition to the NCCC. Carl F. H. Henry and Harold Lindsell provided leadership for these moves.

Following World War II several organizations became forums through which the distinctive evangelical mission theology could be articulated. Among these, the IFMA (1917) experienced a period of rejuvenation in the mid-1940s as independent "faith" mission groups gathered support. The NAE, organized in 1942, and its missionary agency, the EFMA (1945), rapidly evolved into strong bodies, gathering both denominational and independent missionary groups into affiliation. From the mid-1950s the IFMA and the EFMA joined together in a number of ventures, for example, joint missionary executives' retreats, and later sponsored service agencies such as the Evangelical Missions Information Service and the *Evangelical Missions Quarterly*.

Although many evangelical missions, including the Southern Baptists, remained outside their membership, the IFMA and the EFMA became important organizations for fostering an evangelical identity distinct from the ecumenical movement. These evangelical groups stressed strict adherence to a statement of faith covering at least the inerrancy of the Bible, the Virgin Birth of Christ, his substitutionary atonement and physical resurrection from the dead, and the Second Coming of Christ, and an emphasis on evangelism (usually understood primarily in terms of verbal proclamation), as the most important aspect of the church's mission. The IFMA Congress on World Missions in 1960 began to approach the task of evangelism from a worldwide perspective.

The main evangelical group working with students, the Inter Varsity Christian Fellowship, sponsored mission conventions which have met triennially at Urbana, Illinois, since 1948. These gatherings, which have grown in size from some 600 students to over 15,000 in 1976, have drawn evangelical leaders from around the world for lectures and discussions. The growth of the Urbana Conventions indicates a vital interest among evangelical students in mission activities.

The Church Growth Movement, initiated by Donald McGavran (1960), has become one of the most influential developments in evangelical mission theology in the post-war period. McGavran and those associated with him in the Church Growth Institute, located at the Fuller Theological Seminary since 1965, have made church growth a major criterion for assessing mission policy.

Using interdisciplinary research tools (including anthro-

pology, sociology, and statistics), the Church Growth Movement
has encouraged intensive research into the factors hindering or
promoting church growth. McGavran and Alan Tippett have focused
attention on "people movements" among homogeneous groups
responsive to the gospel as one significant factor in seeking
to improve the effectiveness of evangelism in the world today.
Ralph Winter's work on different types of evangelism, distinguished by degrees of cultural identity or difference between
the missionary and the group being evangelized, has aroused new
questions about the kind of missionary agencies most needed in
the world today.

THE SECOND STAGE: 1966-1975

Evidence of the growing maturity of evangelical organizations, and of their deepening interest in and concern for mission
theology, came in 1966 with the Wheaton and Berlin Congresses.
These indicated a new stage in the emergence of an evangelical
identity, as evangelicals from around the world began to share
together in an analysis of the situation facing those involved
in mission and evangelism in every continent.

The Wheaton Congress on the Church's Worldwide Mission,
jointly sponsored by the IFMA and the EFMA, analyzed and responded to crucial issues in the church and the world from an
evangelical perspective. Several important characteristics
should be recalled. First, many presentations demonstrated a
continuing hostility towards the ecumenical movement. Second,
the beginnings of a widely representative evangelical theology
of mission are apparent in the Wheaton Declaration. It reflects
the early struggle on the relationship between evangelism and
social action in the witness of the Christian Community. Third,
ecclesiological issues surfaced concerning church-mission relations, and also the kind of unity which evangelicals should
seek. The strong impact of church growth thought on evangelical mission theology also became apparent.

Later in 1966 the Berlin World Congress on Evangelism,
sponsored by *Christianity Today* with the assistance of the
Billy Graham organization, drew together some 1200 delegates
from over 100 countries for the first large meeting of evangelicals from around the world in the twentieth century. Evangelism remained the particular focus of the Congress, although
many other questions and issues were addressed in the numerous
panel discussions.

The predominant influence of Billy Graham, Carl F. H. Henry,
and other American leaders characterized the meeting. But a
growing number of evangelical voices from outside North America
were heard at Berlin. The Congress stimulated regional

congresses on evangelism in Africa, Asia, Latin America, the USA, and Europe. These gatherings strengthened the witness and impact of evangelicals in these areas, and may be one of the most important results of Berlin, 1966.

Development of a regional consciousness among evangelicals began in Latin America with the emergence of Kenneth Strachan's Evangelism in Depth program. Widely used throughout Latin America from 1960 onwards, Evangelism in Depth programs drew together many evangelicals in an unprecedented manner. Its principles focused attention on the local congregation as the primary level for evangelism, with every Christian sharing in the task of witness and outreach in a given area. While the results of Evangelism in Depth in terms of church growth were disappointing, the stimulus given to local churches and Christian leadership training across denominational lines proved invaluable.

The Latin American Congress on Evangelism (1969) helped to consolidate this interaction between evangelicals on that continent. Leaders such as Ruben Lores and Orlando Costas helped those who wished to use the Evangelism in Depth principles in other countries.

The African New Life For All movement drew heavily on Evangelism in Depth experience. Beginning in Nigeria in 1963, it has evolved as a continuing program in that country and other African countries have adopted similar schemes, especially following the West African Congress on Evangelism in 1968.

In 1966, African evangelicals organized a continent-wide association, the AEAM, as a vehicle for sponsoring cooperative evangelical ventures, especially relating to theological studies and education. The PACLA (1976) attracted both evangelical and ecumenical church leaders, and its pledge may prove a valuable basis for drawing together all Christians in some common endeavors in the future.

Evangelicals in Asia gathered for the Asia-South Pacific Congress on Evangelism in 1968. Later plans evolved for an Asian Missions Consultation, largely organized by David J. Cho of Korea. The Asian Missions Association, formed in 1975, is attempting to encourage Asian evangelical churches and Christians to undertake more responsibility for mission and evangelism.

The situation in North America demonstrates the diversity of opinion and emphasis among evangelicals. The US Congress on Evangelism (1969) emphasized the importance of evangelicals becoming more involved in the life of the nation and its social

problems. The Chicago Declaration (1973) strongly endorsed
this position. Several Radical evangelical groups continue to
stress the place of evangelism and social action as key elements in discipleship.

Key 73 aroused considerable debate among the evangelical
community and showed how difficult it is to gather all evangelicals under one umbrella in the USA. However, as the major
supporters of evangelical missionary efforts worldwide, American evangelicals will continue to influence strongly the shape
and direction of evangelical mission theology in the future.

Diversity is evident among European evangelicals. John R.
W. Stott of England has provided strong leadership for evangelicals around the world, and initiated spirited but open
debate with ecumenical theologians and leaders. Peter Beyerhaus and the German evangelical group, No Other Gospel, express
quite a different attitude in the Frankfurt Declaration (1970)
and the Berlin Declaration (1974).

All of these regional voices contributed to the Lausanne
Congress on World Evangelization (1974). As no other meeting
had done, Lausanne evoked expressions of opinion from the whole
evangelical community as participants struggled with the issues
of mission theology in the world today. The fruit of the discussions in the Lausanne Covenant show that evangelicals have
developed a mature, positive, and well-rounded theology of mission. While continuing to stress the authority of the Bible
and evangelism, the Covenant also focuses on Discipleship and
church renewal as key elements in the total mission of the
church. The strength of evangelical voices from Latin America,
Africa, and Asia at Lausanne demonstrates that debate within
the worldwide evangelical community will be diverse and varied,
yet with all bound together in the task of involving "the whole
Church to take the whole Gospel to the whole world."

Evangelism is the task of the whole church, and the Roman
Catholic Church has been involved in reassessing its understanding of the primary mission of the church, as the evangelical community has been engaged in developing its mission theology. We must now seek to trace developments within the Roman
Catholic Church.

Part III

Roman Catholic
Mission Theology

7

The Revolution in Catholic
Mission Theology

This study has concentrated thus far largely on developments within Protestantism. But recent events in the Roman
Catholic Church, as well as the growing dialogue between all
branches of the church, make this brief chapter on Roman Catholic mission theology an essential part of the survey being
undertaken here. The field is vast and this chapter can do no
more than highlight some of the major trends in Catholic mission theology.

At least three reasons may be offered for including this
chapter. First, the Roman Catholic Church's understanding of
mission theology has developed in a way which closely parallels
movements in Protestantism. Second, the full Catholic contribution to the ecumenical movement through its involvement in
Faith and Order discussions, CWME meetings, SODEPAX, and in many
national and regional Councils and Conferences of Churches,
makes it necessary for other branches of the Christian church
to understand the perspective and insights which Catholics
bring to this ongoing discussion. Third, there has been a convergence by Roman Catholics and Protestants on certain issues,
especially concerning evangelism, justice, interreligious dialogue, and unity. The Catholic viewpoint about these questions
should receive adequate attention if the convergence is to
result in a fruitful interchange of ideas.

Beginning with a short summary of Roman Catholic mission
theology in this century prior to Vatican II, this chapter will
then study the impact of the Council. The Synod of Bishops'
meetings on Justice and Evangelism provided new insights into

Catholic thought on these issues. The question-of "anonymous
Christianity," much debated within the Catholic Church, will be
explored. Charismatic Catholics are a new phenomenon within
Roman Catholicism whose contribution should be noted. Regional
developments in Latin America (especially the Episcopal Conference at Medellin in 1968 and liberation theology), and the Asian
encounter theology will be analyzed. A brief summary will draw
together the salient points of this survey of recent developments in Roman Catholic mission theology.

CONVERSION AND CHURCH PLANTING:
PRE-VATICAN II MISSION THEOLOGY

     Roman Catholic missionary activity has increased enormously
this century as successive popes in the first six decades encouraged support for and new methods of mission.

     Five encyclicals on mission constitute the major sources
for understanding modern Roman Catholic mission theology before
Vatican II. They are:

> *Maximum Illud*, 1919 . . . . Benedict XV
> *Rerum Ecclesiae*, 1926 . . . Pius XI
> *Evangelii Praecones*, 1951 . Pius XII
> *Fidei Donum*, 1957 . . . . . Pius XII
> *Princeps Pastorum*, 1959 . . John XXIII[1]

     The primary understanding of mission informing these docu-
ments relates to preaching the gospel among all people, especially those in non-Christian countries, in order to accomplish
the establishment or planting of the church throughout the
world.[2] Pius XII summarized the Roman Catholic approach to
mission when he wrote:

> The primary object of missionary activity as every-
> one knows, is to bring the shining light of Christian
> truth to new peoples and to form new Christians. To
> attain, however, this object, the ultimate one, mis-
> sionaries must unremittingly endeavor to establish the
> Church firmly among the peoples and to endow them with
> their own native hierarchy.[3]

     Roman Catholic mission before Vatican II assumed these
aims. The developments in this period occurred in emphasizing
different aspects and ways of accomplishing these goals. Three
broad issues were involved. First, how to encourage an adequate
flow of missionaries from all sections of the church who would
place the gospel above national and western cultural values.
Second, how to foster the formation of an adequately trained
hierarchy and clergy. Third, how to increase the support and

involvement of the laity in missionary activities.

The future of Roman Catholic missionary work in this century depended on broadening the missionary force. France had
been the main contributor of money and personnel in the nineteenth century and, in 1900, about seventy percent of Roman
Catholic missionaries were from France. By 1930, however, less
than half were of French nationality.[4] Since 1930, the number
of missionaries from France has remained practically unchanged,
with the main increases coming from North America and other
European countries.[5]

The influx of new missionaries from outside France tended
to alleviate problems caused by the close relationship between
French colonial policy and Catholicism in some areas, for
example, in China and Tahiti. Benedict XV sought to create conditions in which Catholic missionaries of any country could work
together, free from colonial politics and policies. He wrote:

> It would be tragic indeed if any of our missionaries
> forgot the dignity of their office so completely as to
> busy themselves with the interests of their terrestrial
> homeland instead of with those of their homeland in
> heaven. It would be a tragedy indeed if an apostolic
> man were to spend himself in attempts to increase and
> exalt the prestige of the native land he once left
> behind him. Such behavior would infect his apostolate
> like a plague.[6]

The fostering of an indigenous clergy has been a high
priority in Catholic mission policy in this century. Benedict
clearly set out the reasons for this when he instructed those
in charge of mission parishes to train a local clergy because
they could most effectively communicate the gospel.[7] The
effects of this policy became apparent in the consecration of
national bishops by Benedict, Pius XI, Pius XII, and John XXIII.
In one year, John XXIII named fourteen missionary bishops, and
noted that by 1959,

> we count 68 Asian and 25 African bishops. The remain-
> ing native clergy grew in number from 919 in 1918 to
> 5,553 in 1957 in Asia, and during the same period in
> Africa from 90 in 1918 to 1,811 in 1957.[8]

Seminaries were also established to train the clergy in these
areas.

The contribution of the laity to mission suggested by
Benedict in his encyclical concerned prayer, personnel, and
finance. Pius XII added another dimension by encouraging Cath-

olic Action, so that "the apostolate of the laity" could be used
to advance the cause of religion and to improve the social conditions of nations with the laity and clergy working together.[9]
Missionary organizations for lay people have drawn substantial
support from the laity for Catholic mission around the world.

The emerging understanding of mission as a task for which
the whole church is responsible, and to which all should contribute,[10]--clergy and laity, and Christians in all continents
--closely paralleled developments in the ecumenical movement,
as church and mission became theologically and organizationally
integrated.

OPEN WINDOWS TO THE WORLD: VATICAN II

The spirit of *aggiornamento*, evident in the calling of the
Second Vatican Council by John XXIII, and which subsequently
informed its life, had two main dimensions: first, an internal
renewal of the church in order to be increasingly faithful to
the gospel of Christ and the scriptures; and, second, a revi-
talization of the church's approach to the modern world with
the aim of making the church more effective in its mission to
all people.[11]

The struggle to fulfill this vision of renewal, while remaining faithful to the heritage of the past, pervaded all the
Council's actions.[12] The search for genuine renewal became
evident as the carefully prepared preliminary documents were
sent back for major revision and amendment. In many instances
the final documents contained a mixture of the old and new side
by side. The history of the text on missions clearly demonstrates this process.

The Preparatory Commission on Missions, under the Prefect
of the Propaganda, Cardinal Agagianian produced a draft schema
under seven main headings, which represented some of the chief
concerns of the previous papal encyclicals on mission. This
initial draft did not reach the floor of the Council in either
the first or second sessions. During 1964 the original schema
was drastically reduced to a series of thirteen propositions
and on Friday, November 6, 1964, Pope Paul VI presided over a
working session of the Council and introduced the revised text
with the recommendation that "We hope that, while you may
decide on improvements in some parts, you will approve the
present text."[13] Yet the two and one-half days of debate made
it clear that the schema would be sent back for rewriting.

Bishop Lamont of Rhodesia compared the propositions to
Ezekiel's "dry bones." Bishop Riobé of France (a member of the
Missionary Commission itself) explained that the commission had

been torn for three years between a theological and a juridical
view of mission. The decisive vote in favor of sending the
document back for revision gave added emphasis to the need for
a more adequate theological statement to be included, as many
of the fathers requested.[14]

The Fourth Session received a thoroughly revised document,
which had been produced with the benefit of consultation with
several theologians and missiologists such as Yves Congar, the
Jesuits Grasso and Buijs, Andre Seumois, J. Ratzinger, and J.
Glazik.[15] In this final draft of *Ad Gentes*, a new chapter on
"Doctrinal Principles" provided a theological basis for mission
which linked it to other conciliar documents, especially *Lumen
Gentium*. The decree also contained proposals for the reorganization of the Propaganda.

What was the new understanding of missions which emerged
at Vatican II? It is to *Lumen Gentium* that we must turn, a
document described as "*the* masterpiece of Vatican II," which by
its "emphasis on the Church and her renewal for mission in the
world," gave Vatican II "its most distinctive character as a
Council."[16] *Lumen Gentium* is fundamental to all the other
documents of the Council, and crucial for understanding the new
emphasis on mission in the Roman Catholic Church.

The Dogmatic Constitution on the Church developed several
main conceptions of the church. It described the church as the
mystical body, the People of God, and an hierarchical institution.[17]

Chapter 1, "The Mystery of the Church," points to the
intimate union of the church with Christ, the light of all nations. By this relationship, "the Church is a kind of sacrament
of intimate union with God, and of the unity of all mankind,
that is, she is a sign and an instrument of such union and
unity." The Council wished to explain to Christians and the
world "the nature and encompassing mission of the Church,"
namely, "of bringing all men to full union with Christ."[18] As
a sacramental mystery, the church communicates the very purpose
and will of the triune God, from whom she "receives the mission
to proclaim and to establish among all peoples the kingdom of
Christ and of God. She becomes on earth the initial budding
forth of that Kingdom."[19] The universal scope of the mission
which God has given the church consists in pointing all people
to Christ, for "all men are called to this union with Christ,
who is the light of the world, from whom we go forth, through
whom we live, and toward whom our journey leads us."[20]

The motif of "the People of God" in Chapter 2 describes
the church as "that messianic people [which] has for its head

Christ." This messianic people does not include all people, but it "is nonetheless a lasting and sure seed of unity, hope, and salvation for the whole human race."[21] The universal implications of this doctrine became clear when *Lumen Gentium* declared that,

> This characteristic of universality which adorns the People of God is a gift from the Lord Himself. By reason of it, the Catholic Church strives energetically and constantly to bring all humanity with all its riches back to Christ its Head in the unity of His Spirit.[22]

The argument goes on to explore how Catholics, Protestants, Orthodox, and non-Christians must all be included within the scope of the church's universal mission.[23]

Lumen Gentium developed a two-fold argument in its understanding of the necessity of the church for salvation. On the one hand the Council affirmed a traditional viewpoint in declaring on the basis of scripture and tradition that for all Catholics, "the Church, now sojourning on earth as an exile, is necessary for salvation."[24] On the other hand, it also asserted that for people who have not received the gospel,

> Those also can attain to everlasting salvation who through no fault of their own do not know the gospel of Christ or His Church, yet sincerely seek God and, moved by grace, strive by their deeds to do His will as it is known to them through the dictates of conscience.[25]

The church must foster its missionary work among all people, and especially those ignorant of God's way and will, to promote the glory of God, to seek the salvation of all people, and in obedience to Christ's command to "preach the gospel to every creature."

Chapter 3, "The Hierarchical Structure of the Church, With Special Reference to the Episcopate," emphasized the particular responsibility of bishops for mission. It stated:

> As successors of the apostles, bishops received from Him the mission to teach all nations and to preach the gospel to every creature, so that all men may attain salvation by faith, baptism, and the fulfillment of the commandments (cf. Mt. 28:18; Mk. 16:15-16; Acts 26:17f.)[26]

This concept of mission as the primary duty of the hierarchy constituted a continuing thrust evident in the pre-Vatican II encyclicals on mission. Yet this also became the starting point

for major curial reform. Paul VI instituted a body of twenty-
four bishops, drawn from the whole church to exercise authority
over the Sacred Congregation for the Propagation of the Faith.
With twelve of the prelates to be drawn from missions, the
responsibility and involvement of representatives from all parts
of the church has been clearly established.27 One other out-
growth of the bishops' responsibilities for mission may be
noted. The Synod of Bishops, which Paul VI called to give tangible form to the doctrine of collegiality, took up the question
of evangelization in 1974, as we shall see.

The People of God motif, which underlay Chapter 4 on "The
Laity," directed attention to the particular work of the laity
in mission in which "by their very vocation [they] seek the
Kingdom of God by engaging in temporal affairs and by ordering
them according to the plan of God."28 As with the priesthood,
the ministry of the laity revolved around the prophetic,
priestly, and royal offices.29 Through the witness of the
laity "the world is permeated by the spirit of Christ and more
effectively achieves its purpose in justice, charity and peace."30

Chapter 7 on "The Eschatological Nature of the Pilgrim
Church and Her Union with the Heavenly Father," set the mission
of the church in an eschatological perspective, drawing attention both to its present and future dimensions. While ultimately all will be re-established in Christ,

the promised restoration which we are awaiting has
already begun in Christ, is carried forward in the
mission of the Holy Spirit, and through Him continues
in the Church.31

The themes relating to the mission of the church in *Lumen
Gentium* form the theological foundation for *Ad Gentes*, and are
evident in many of the Vatican II documents, most notably in
*Gaudium et Spes, Apostolicam Actuositatem, Unitatis Redinte-
gratio,* and *Nostra Aetate.*

The theological basis of *Ad Gentes* established mission as
part of the essence of the church's life. As "the universal
sacrament of salvation" the church participates in mission in
order "that all things can be restored in Christ, and in Him
all mankind can compose one family and one people." The missionary nature of the church derives from the triune God, "for
it is from the mission of the Son and the mission of the Holy
Spirit that she takes her origin, in accordance with the decree
of God the Father." For this reason *Ad Gentes* declared, "the
whole Church is missionary, and the work of evangelization is a
basic duty of the People of God."32

Side by side with the conception of mission as an essential part of the church's life undertaken in accordance with the nature of God by the whole people of God directed towards the whole world, one also discovers in *Ad Gentes* some quite different notions. For example, the Decree on Missions also focused on the responsibility of bishops for mission. The task of mission itself no longer described the church's participation in God's plan to unite all things in Christ, but was defined as "church planting" by a particular group, that is,

> those particular undertakings by which the heralds of the gospel are sent out by the Church and go forth into the whole world to carry out the task of preaching the gospel and planting the church among peoples or groups who do not yet believe in Christ.[33]

In seeking to improve relations with those outside the Roman Catholic Church, the Council drew heavily on John XXIII's instructions that "the Spouse of Christ prefers to make use of the medicine of mercy rather than that of severity," by using apologetics rather than condemnation in addressing those outside the Catholic Church.[34] This emphasis stressed dialogue as a fruitful method of communication with people of other faiths and ideologies, even with atheists and communists. Dialogue became one of the principal thrusts of Vatican II's approach to the world.[35]

The theme of unity received particular attention at the Council. Pope John spoke of the unity which Christ implores for his church and the human family involving the unity of Catholics, the desire among some separated brethren for closer links with the Catholics, and the unity in esteem and respect for Catholics found among non-Christians.[36] *Ad Gentes* called for cooperation in some aspects of mission and witness between Catholics and other Christians.[37]

As one part of the renewal of the church for mission, the Council exhorted bishops and episcopal conferences to foster interest in missionary activities through pastoral councils, priestly zeal, educational activities, and lay organizations, thus promoting involvement in mission because "the whole Church is missionary, and the work of evangelization is a basic duty of the People of God."[38]

EVANGELIZATION: THE
SYNOD OF BISHOPS, 1974

Following Vatican II, Paul VI established the Synod of Bishops to act as a representative and consultative group to the papacy from the church throughout the whole world.[39] Its intended

functions include offering the pope advice on topics selected
by mutual agreement.

The Third General Conference of the Synod of Bishops met
between September 27-October 23, 1974, with over 200 bishops
from 95 countries present to discuss "The Evangelization of the
Modern World." The Synod used a preparatory study in its
deliberations, and issued a Declaration on Evangelism, but was
unable to approve a final document because of the large amount
of material put forward. Consequently the Pope distilled the
essence of the Synod's discussion in an Apostolic Exhortation.[40]

Both the Synod and the Pope reaffirmed that evangelism is
central to the task of the church: "We wish to confirm once
more that the task of evangelizing all people constitutes the
essential mission of the Church."[41] The Synod explored many
facets of evangelization--its source, content, methods, objectives, personnel, and motivating spirit, as the chapter headings
of *Evangelii Nuntiandi* reveal.

After some debate about several different meanings of the
word "evangelization" (including changing the world, building
the church, awakening faith, and proclaiming the gospel to non-
Christians),[42] Pope Paul proposed an inclusive definition:

> For the Church, evangelizing means bringing the Good
> News into all the strata of humanity, and through its
> influence transforming humanity from within and making
> it new: "Now I am making the whole of creation new."
> But there is no new humanity if there are not first of
> all new persons renewed by Baptism and by lives lived
> according to the Gospel. The purpose of evangelization
> is therefore precisely this interior change, and if it
> had to be expressed in one sentence the best way of
> stating it would be to say that the Church evangelizes
> when she seeks to convert, solely through the divine
> power of the Message she proclaims, both the personal
> and collective consciences of people, the activities
> in which they engage, and the lives and concrete
> milieux which are theirs.[43]

As the Pope's exposition of this definition made clear,
evangelization is a complex process involving the renewal of
humanity, the witness of Christian living, explicit proclamation of the gospel, the entry of converts into the Christian
community through an inner adherence to the message of Christ
and the church, and sharing in the church's ministry of evangelism.[44] The Lausanne Congress viewed the task of evangelization in a similar way. The comprehensive scope of evangelization is akin to what the WCC means by "mission."

The Synod exhibited the same attitude of openness to the world which characterized Vatican II. The bishops addressed particular attention to those who had never heard the gospel, to people baptized but living outside the Christian life, as well as to Christians who need to have their faith deepened and nourished to enable them to become more mature. The problems posed by secularization, atheism, and the widespread violation of human rights, including religious liberty, all received attention.

To answer the question "Who has the mission of evangelizing?" Pope Paul and the Synod referred to Vatican II which explicitly stated in *Ad Gentes* that "the whole Church is missionary, and the work of evangelization is a basic duty of the People of God." Paul noted the specific responsibilities to be undertaken by bishops, priests, religious, and the laity in evangelism, again following the lead of Vatican II in its exposition of the mission of the church.[45]

The ecclesial nature of evangelization received special emphasis. The focus on the communal nature of the church, in which an individual's witness becomes a representative act on behalf of the whole church, in which small communities exist within the wider church, individual churches participate in the church universal, and the whole church is incarnate in individual churches, developed important aspects of ecclesiology. This understanding of the individual and the universal church "will enable us to perceive the richness of this relationship between the universal Church and the individual Churches."[46]

Recognizing that the church must exist in specific locations, the question of indigenization became an important consideration. Individual churches

> have the task of assimilating the essence of the
> Gospel message and of transposing it, without the
> slightest betrayal of its essential truth, into the
> language that these particular people understand,
> then of proclaiming it in this language.[47]

The influence of the concern for liberation which had arisen so markedly in the Conference of Latin American Bishops at Medellin became apparent in the Synod's discussions. The Declaration by the bishops pointed to

> the mutual relationship between evangelization and
> integral salvation or the complete liberation of man
> and of peoples. In a matter of such importance we
> experienced profound unity in reaffirming the intimate
> connection between evangelization and such liberation.[48]

This deep concern for total liberation evident in the Declaration affirmed what Vatican II had declared and Medellin had advocated even more strongly. It also reiterated the 1971 Synod of Bishops' statements about justice.[49]

The relationship between evangelization and social action outlined by the Synod pointed to both the example of Jesus Christ and the demands of love as reasons for the church to be active in seeking the liberation of people from all oppressive forces, for example, famine, chronic disease, illiteracy, poverty, injustices in international relations, and situations of economic and cultural neo-colonialism. The Synod Declaration affirmed that,

> Faithful to her evangelizing mission, the Church as a truly poor, praying and fraternal community can do much to bring about the integral salvation or the full liberation of men. She can draw from the gospel the most profound reasons and ever new incentives to promote generous dedication to the service of all men--the poor especially, the weak and the oppressed--and to eliminate the social consequences of sin which are translated into unjust social and political structures.[50]

Pope Paul also emphasized the theme of liberation, but noted the particular spiritual vocation of the church to proclaim the gospel of the kingdom of God as the essential completion of a truly evangelical understanding of man involving communion with God as the final goal of life. The relationship between these elements in a full understanding of liberation was finely expressed by Pope Paul in this way:

> The Church considers it to be undoubtably important to build up structures which are more human, more just, more respectful of the rights of the person and less oppressive and less enslaving, but she is conscious that the best structures and the most idealized systems soon become inhuman if the inhuman inclinations of the human heart are not made wholesome, if those who live in these structures or who rule them do not undergo a conversion of heart and of outlook.[51]

The church could best work towards achieving the goal of liberation by encouraging large numbers of Christians to devote themselves to the work of liberation, the Synod argued. The need for religious liberty to be recognized as a fundamental human right was also recognized, especially in face of widespread oppression, persecution, and hardship, which many Christians suffer for the sake of the Christian faith.[52]

In considering unity in relation to evangelism, the Pope
spoke of the present disunity and division among Christians as
"perhaps one of the greatest sicknesses of evangelization
today."[53] The depth of this conviction found expression in the
desire

> for a collaboration marked by greater commitment with
> the Christian brethren with whom we are not yet united
> in perfect unity, taking as a basis the foundation of
> Baptism and the patrimony of faith which is common to
> us. By doing this we can already give a greater common
> witness to Christ before the world in the very work of
> evangelization. Christ's command urges us to do this;
> the duty of preaching and of giving witness to the
> Gospel requires this.[54]

The power and influence of the Holy Spirit in the whole
process of evangelization, and in the search for unity,
received clear recognition in the statement that "the Holy
Spirit is the principal agent of evangelization."

The Synod of Bishops's strong affirmation of evangelization as central to the church's mission confirmed an emphasis
which Vatican II had endorsed. Nothing essentially new emerged
from the Synod's deliberations, but the stress on the whole
church's responsibility for mission, which seeks the liberation
of all people from oppressive forces, by a church itself seeking
unity in common witness with all other Christians gave added
emphasis to some of the most important aspects of the Second
Vatican Council's theological concerns.

ANONYMOUS CHRISTIANS

The question of the possibility of salvation for those
outside the church, and the implications of the answer to that
question for missionary activity, have become disputed issues
in the Roman Catholic Church. A letter from the Holy Office to
Archbishop Cushing of Boston in 1949 made clear that the dictum
"outside the Church there is no salvation" must *not* be interpreted to mean that only those persons actually incorporated
into the church as members can be saved. Rather, it argued,

> To gain eternal salvation it is not always required
> that a person be incorporated in fact as a member of
> the Church, but it is required that he belong to it
> at least in desire and longing.[55]

This letter was mentioned in an official footnote in *Lumen
Gentium*, no. 16,[56] when the Council acknowledged that:

> Those also can attain to everlasting salvation who
> through no fault of their own do not know the gospel
> of Christ or His Church, yet sincerely seek God and,
> moved by grace, strive by their deeds to do His will
> as it is known to them through the dictates of con-
> science. Nor does divine Providence deny the help
> necessary for salvation to those who, without blame
> on their part, have not yet arrived at an explicit
> knowledge of God, but who strive to live a good life,
> thanks to His grace.

Other documents of Vatican II make the same essential point, that all people who, aided by God's grace, seek to do his will, can attain salvation, at least in principle, when inculpably ignorant of the gospel and without explicit knowledge of or membership in the church. The major references are found in *Gaudium et Spes*, no. 22, and *Ad Gentes*, no. 7, while *Nostra Aetate*, no. 2 recognized that other religions "often reflect a ray of that Truth which enlightens all men."

Several theologians have provided arguments to support the assertion that many outside the visible church are in fact anonymous Christians because they have experienced and responded to God's grace, and thus are in some sense related to the church, although not juridically.[57]

This position involves a number of theological considerations. First, since God wills the salvation of all people, his grace and unbounded love cannot be limited only to those who explicitly belong to the church. Second, it is the very essence of human nature to be open to the transcendental dimension of God's unbounded love in which every person lives within the environment of the salvific will of God, revealing itself in the enduring offer of grace. Third, the response of a person to grace necessarily involves an implicit acceptance of Christ, for Christianity is "only the explication of what we already are by grace and what we experience at least incoherently in the limitlessness of our transcendence."[58] Fourth, in under-standing its mission,

> the Church will not so much regard herself today as the
> exclusive community of those who have a claim to salva-
> tion but rather as the historically tangible vanguard
> and the historically and socially constituted explicit
> expression of what the Christian hopes is present as a
> hidden reality even outside the visible Church.[59]

The church's vocation is to make explicit what is implicit and ever become more fully the universal and sacramental and eschatological sign of salvation for all people.

A number of voices have been raised against this kind of understanding of the vocation of Christianity in the world to-day. Some at the Council expressed concern that after these ideas had been presented at the Bombay Eucharistic Congress in 1964 many thought that the church would no longer insist as much on missionary work and the missionary's task would hence-forth be not to baptize and preach the gospel, but rather to promote conditions that would help people find Christian values in the non-Christian religions.[60]

A long-time missionary to Japan, Henry van Straelen, com-plained that this notion of "anonymous Christians" had been formulated by theologians who had never been involved in inter-religious and intercultural situations, and thus lacked any practical experience to test and evaluate such ideas.[61] Hans Küng objected that any theological statement which identified Buddhists, Hindus or any other people as "anonymous Christians" when in fact they would strenuously deny any such designation, is quite inadequate and suspect.[62]

The relationship of Christianity to other religions, the status and destiny of those outside the visible church, and the implications of the answers to these questions for mission theology and practice remain some of the most disputed areas in mission theology. The WCC has begun to grapple with these issues in discussions about dialogue, but with little success in arriving at any consensus; the conservative evangelicals have hardly touched on these questions at all, apart from a denunciation of universalism and syncretism; and the debate continues in the Roman Catholic Church.[63]

THE CATHOLIC CHARISMATIC MOVEMENT

Members of the Roman Catholic Church have become involved in the charismatic movement, along with Christians in many other denominations in North America, Europe, and especially in Africa and Latin America.

In the USA the charismatic renewal began at Duquesne Uni-versity in February, 1967, and rapidly spread throughout the continent.[64] A gathering of Catholic Charismatics at Notre Dame in 1974 brought over 30,000 people together, with a sig-nificant number of bishops and priests involved in the movement.[65]

At the local level, many barriers have been broken down in a genuine lay movement drawing together Christians from many denominations in worship and fellowship. The strength of the movement within the Catholic Church lies in its self-recognition as a creative new dimension of life *within* the church. It has led many into a fuller and more active participation in the liturgical life of the church.

The specific influence of the charismatic movement on the theology of mission in the Catholic Church, as yet limited, will unfold as it continues to develop and articulate a theological understanding intended to enrich the wider church.[66]

REGIONAL DEVELOPMENTS IN
LATIN AMERICA AND ASIA

1. Medellin and Liberation Theology in Latin America

Roman Catholicism has long been the dominant religious force in Latin America. With a population of some 335,000,000 in 1977, of whom the vast majority are Catholic, the church has suffered from a dearth of priests during most of this century throughout the region.[67]

The Latin American Episcopal Conference (CELAM) was organized in 1955 in close cooperation with the Pontifical Commission for Latin America to meet some of the urgent needs facing Catholics throughout the area. As a permanent organization, its members authorized CELAM to encourage the propagation and defense of the faith, especially against Protestantism; to promote the welfare of diocesan clergy and religious; to foster education of the clergy and laity; and to help improve Catholic social action and charities.[68]

A Latin American movement to seek renewal in the church and build a new relationship between church and society drew inspiration from John XXIII's encyclicals *Mater et Magistra* (1961) and *Pacem in Terris* (1963). Public statements by the hierarchy in Brazil and Chile sought to promote the process of social transformation in relation to social justice, land reform, and the distribution of wealth.[69] Christian Democratic parties favored social reform.[70] Some Catholic priests, like Camilo Torres, came to espouse revolutionary action by Christians in Latin America.[71]

Against this background of a growing movement for the transformation of church and society, the bishops of Latin America decided to hold a CELAM meeting "to define the presence of the Church in the actual transformation of Latin America in light of Vatican Council II."[72] The Second CELAM met at Medellin between August 24-September 6, 1968, with Pope Paul VI present at the opening. The Pope endorsed the strong pleas for basic renewal and reform in church and society which had characterized the preparatory documents.[73] The position papers of the bishops at Medellin all dealt with the fundamental need to relate the church's life and work to the context of Latin America.

Medellin demonstrated a remarkable change in the focus of
the Roman Catholic Church in Latin America. Traditionally the
Catholic hierarchy had been closely allied with the ruling oli-
garchy in many countries. Medellin decisively turned away from
this alliance by encouraging and supporting the aspirations of
the masses for seeking greater justice and participation in
society. The church turned toward the world in a new way.[74]
The first five Final Documents on "Human Promotion" dealt with
Justice, Peace, Family and Demography, Education, and Youth.
Then followed the reports on "Evangelization and Growth in
Faith"; with a third section, "The Visible Church and its Structures," examining the implications of the discussions for the
forms of church life.

The bishops were deeply aware of the flux and ferment
stirring throughout Latin America and, in the words of Pope
Paul, felt impelled to strive towards fulfilling "a vocation to
create a new and ingenious synthesis of the old and the new,
the spiritual and the temporal, that which others have bequeathed
us and that which is our own creation."[75] The urgent necessity
of such a vocation began with the recognition that

> we are on the threshold of a new epoch in the history
> of our continent. It appears to be a time full of zeal
> for full emancipation, of liberation from every form
> of servitude, of personal maturity and of collective
> integration. In these signs we perceive the first
> indications of the painful birth of a new civilization.
> And we cannot fail to see in this gigantic effort
> towards a rapid transformation and development an
> obvious sign of the Spirit who leads the history of
> man and of peoples toward their vocation.[76]

The fundamental insight of Medellin for the mission of the
Roman Catholic Church in Latin America involved the recognition
that the church must be involved in the process of transforming
people who could then complete the transformation of society in
accordance with God's will.

Medellin dealt with the "dependence" of Latin America on
"external neocolonialism" as one important element in the life
of the continent, especially in regard to economic domination.[77]
The document on Justice argued that the way to overcome oppression must be through "concientization"--the indispensable
awakening and formation of a "social conscience and a realistic
perception of the problems of the community and of social
structures."[78] Yet it affirmed that the final goal God desires
for all people involves liberation for it is

> God who in the fullness of time, sends his Son in the

flesh, so that he might come to liberate all men from
the slavery to which sin has subjected them: hunger,
misery, oppression and ignorance, in a word, that injustice and hatred which have their origin in human
selfishness.

Thus, for our authentic liberation, all of us need a
profound conversion so that "the kingdom of justice,
love and peace," might come to us.[79]

In linking justice and peace Medellin followed Vatican II
and John XXIII's encyclicals. The distinctive task of the
church in reaching these objectives involved the denunciation
of all injustice and oppression, and the inspiring of a vision
of peace based on justice as the fruit of love [80] The report
on Justice affirmed that

The Church--the People of God--will lend its support
to the down-trodden of every social class so that they
might come to know their rights and how to make use of
them. To this end the Church will utilize its moral
strength and will seek to collaborate with competent
professionals and institutions.[81]

The growth of a Christian humanism became identified as
part of the mission of the church, involving the transformation
of society on the basis of justice and peace as a necessary
component.

Our mission is to contribute to the integral advance-
ment of man and of human communities of the continent
. . . . Our peoples seek their liberation and their
growth in humanity . . . .[82]

Each of the Medellin documents reflected the influence of
the seminal principles of "the challenge of a liberating and
humanizing commitment." Education was described as "liberating
education." Catechetical renewal involved "the integral development of man and of social change" as a part of the faithful presentation of the Word. Lay movements were seen as "a
sign of liberation, of humanization and of development." The
servant role of the church and the priesthood, and the vision
of an "evangelical poverty" were offered as signs of the
church's commitment to liberation as well as a call to personal and corporate renewal.

The major result of Medellin has been well summarized by
Segundo Galilea in these words:

the Church obtained a sharper consciousness of its

prophetic mission in the present historical moment:
a mission that is conceived of as the transmission of
a great evangelical mystique to the mighty movement
of liberation, as the prophetic denunciation of all
attempts that try to impede the integral vocation of
the Latin American man, and as a disinterested promotion of everything that fosters it.[83]

Medellin provided the stimulus for the development of what
has become known as the Theology of Liberation. The elements
which dominated CELAM's conclusions--dependence and injustice,
liberation and humanization, conscientization, and renewal--have
each been taken up and interpreted in what liberation theologians insist is a new method of doing theology. The growing
and diverse literature on liberation theology cannot be analyzed
here, but some of the issues raised do have a direct bearing on
a theology of mission.

The prophetic stance of Medellin openly raised the question
of the need for structural change in society. The process of
conscientization, involving economic, social, and political
analysis, has brought many Latin American Christians to a new
awareness of the importance of the struggle for liberation. In
the face of repression, violence, and the widespread denial of
human rights which Christians have had to suffer in seeking to
work towards justice in society, the importance of liberation
has been increasingly recognized. The Roman Catholic hierarchy
in Peru, Chile, Argentina, and Brazil, and groups of Christians,
such as the Church and Society Movement in Latin America (ISAL),
have raised this as one of the most important tasks of the
church in the 1970s.[84]

The liberation movement has become closely related to
socialism since 1968. Medellin explicitly denounced both
"liberal capitalism" and "Marxism," but since that time Christian socio-political analysis has increasingly used the cate-
gories of Marxism to interpret the Latin American situation.
Miguez-Bonino identified four elements in this analysis: an
understanding of history as ultimately dependent on man's organization of the process by which goods are produced; the communal dimension of social formations; the fact of class struggle
and the revolutionary role of the proletariat; and the significance of praxis as the test of theory.[85] There can be no doubt
that the validity and the necessity of using Marxist theory as
a tool for socio-political analysis is now one of the important
issues that liberation theology raises for mission.

It is now widely recognized that the whole People of God
must be involved in the process of transforming society.
Liberation theology affirms "the *solidarity of the Church* with

the Latin American reality."[86] While the gifts and tasks of the
laity, priests, religious, and bishops may vary, the commitment
to change is common to all. Gutierrez and Segundo have interpreted the distinctive task of the church as that of a sign:

> the Church must be a visible sign of the presence
> of the Lord within the aspirations for liberation
> and the struggle for a more human and just society.
> Only in this way will the message of love which
> the Church bears be made credible and efficacious.[87]

But that still leaves open the question of how the church
can best fulfill its function as a sign. Miguez-Bonino identified four levels of action: the pastoral role of a community
of faith, alert to the problems of the world and committed to
encouraging Christian discipleship in the world; the prophetic
role of statement and pronouncement which point to specific
issues and problems; the conscientization role through education and lay formation; and direct action in the political and
social sphere.[88] There has been a move to more direct action
by many lay people and some priests, and this has certainly
raised the question of what methods are legitimate and appropriate as expressions of love in the mission of the church.
Liberation theology raises issues similar to those which surfaced during the WCC study, "The Church for Others," and the
Geneva Conference on Church and Society. Attention has turned
to movements for humanization outside the church as primary
targets for understanding God's mission in the world today
which, in Latin America, includes movements explicitly linked
with revolutionary, Marxist-oriented, groups.

Gutierrez explored the relationship between evangelism and
social action in liberation theology in terms of their fundamental unity.

> Political liberation, the liberation of man through
> history, liberation from sin and admission to commun-
> ion with God . . . are all part of a single, all-
> encompassing salvific process.[89]

This integral and comprehensive understanding of the levels of
liberation which together constitute salvation is similar to
the notion of salvation which the Bangkok Conference on Salvation Today attempted to develop.

The greatest danger liberation theology faces has been its
intense preoccupation with social analysis and action to change
structures, a response no doubt elicited by the reality of the
conditions in Latin America.

Liberation theology has become an ecumenical endeavor in which Catholics and Protestants join together freely. For example, Protestants Rubem Alves and José Miguez-Bonino have collaborated with Catholics Gustavo Gutierrez, Juan Luis Segundo, Hugo Assmann, and Dom Helder Camara to interpret and publicize the deep concerns of the Latin American people. Some Pentecostals also have taken part in efforts to assist the educational and social aspirations of oppressed people as a part of their total ministry, and to that extent share in the concerns of liberation theology.[90]

Liberation theology grew out of the Latin American context where great structural changes are needed in society if people are to be truly liberated from oppressive social, economic, and political conditions, and thus become free people who are able to respond fully to God and one another. The task of liberation theology is to make people aware of that possibility through conscientization and by supporting every movement for liberation--comprehensively understood--in which Christians of all denominations who support this goal join together in tackling a common task with all others in society, including revolutionary socialists who seek, at least in part, the same ends.

2. Indian Encounter Theology

The question of the universal possibility of salvation, which Vatican II had addressed, contained another issue: the relationship of Christianity to other faiths.

To take only one example from the Hindu-Christian encounter in India, Raymond Panikkar suggested that one discovers "Christianity and Hinduism both meet in Christ. Christ is their meeting-point. The real encounter can only take place in Christ, because only in Christ do they meet."[91] Arguing that God's universal providence embraces all people, and that Christ is the fullness of his revelation, Panikkar developed the thesis that there must also be a link between the religions of the world and the religion of his Son. For Hinduism this meant,

it is a kind of Christianity in potency, because
it has already a Christian seed, because it is the
desire of fullness, and that fullness is Christ,
is already pointing towards it, already contains,
indeed, the symbolism of the Christian reality.[92]

For this reason, the appropriate understanding of the relationship between Christianity and other religions in Panikkar's view could not be truth versus falsehood nor light versus darkness, but must be seen in terms of analogies like seed-fruit, forerunner, real presence.[93]

In a later meditative essay, *The Trinity and World Religions*,[94] Panikkar attempted to show that the universal structure of all religions could best be understood in trinitarian terms because this formula most adequately incorporated the essential elements of humanity and transcendence which every spirituality contains. He defined the fundamental essence of the nature of man as "theandric," that is, "the realization that man possesses an infinite capacity which links him up to the asymptotic limit called God; or to put it the other way round, that God is the end, the boundary of man."[95]

The basic motive behind Panikkar's analysis of the forms and essence of religion related to his desire to foster a creative dialogue between adherents of different religions which could finally "permit each religion and each believer to come in theandric synthesis to the plentitude and perfection of faith and mystical experience" in a new self-awareness of the possibilities and limits of life. Through this encounter of religions, all people could discover the divine mystery of human existence.

SUMMARY

The pre-Vatican II twentieth century papal encyclicals on mission brought into clear focus the importance of mission, understood primarily as the conversion of non-Christians and the planting of the church in places where it previously had not existed. The encyclicals stressed the need for the indigenization of the church, particularly of the hierarchy and clergy, to achieve this goal, together with an appeal for wider support from the whole church for the missionary enterprise with its desperate shortages of personnel and finance.

The Second Vatican Council added some new dimensions to the Roman Catholic understanding of mission based on a new theological understanding of the church and its relationship to the world. The emphasis on the whole church as the People of God gave a new thrust to the ministry of the laity in the witness and outreach of the church into the world. The attitude of pastoral sympathy and openness to the world and other Christians which the Council fostered encouraged the use of dialogue and ecumenism as ways to create strong relations between Catholics and others. In some places Vatican II spoke of the task of the church as that of a "sign of salvation" throughout the world, flowing from the will and purpose of the triune God. The needs of the world became evident in the discussions about the promotion of peace and justice as part of the church's work in society.

The newly constituted Synod of Bishops considered the question of evangelization in 1974. Drawing upon the previous

thrusts of Vatican II, and supporting the commitment to liberation as part of the church's task of evangelization which
Medellin had espoused, the insights of the Synod were gathered
together in Pope Paul VI's Apostolic Exhortation *On Evangelization in the Modern World*.

With its acute social, political, and economic problems,
the Latin American situation provided the background for the
Conference of Latin American Bishops at Medellin in 1968. This
gathering sought to move the church towards a deeper understanding
of the whole context within which it needed to work and bring
about change. The basic commitment to justice and social change
laid down at Medellin provided the foundation for the theology
of liberation which developed through the work of theologians
such as Gustavo Gutierrez and Juan Luis Segundo. Liberation
theology articulated the need for the church to participate in
the process of conscientization as a basic step in the liberation of all people from oppressive forces in a move towards a
comprehensive salvation, involving political and social, human
and spiritual freedom.

Several of the issues which Roman Catholic mission theology developed were strikingly similar to those being debated in
the ecumenical movement represented by the WCC, and in the
evangelical Lausanne World Congress on Evangelization. The
attitude of openness to the world and a vital concern for the
needs of humanity characterized the Second Vatican Council, the
WCC in the 1960s and 1970s, and the Lausanne Congress (1974).
The question of evangelism in the modern world was, and remains,
a common concern. The issue of liberation and the need for
structural changes in society has been raised for all traditions, especially by Christians in Latin America and Asia. The
relationship of Christianity to other faiths has become an important point in theological discussions in the WCC and Roman
Catholic circles.

In the early part of this century Roman Catholic mission
theology revolved around church planting and conversion by a
small group of missionaries in non-Christian countries. The
developments which occurred at Vatican II, and which emerged
with greater clarity at Medellin and in the Synod of Bishops
meetings on Justice and Evangelization, focus on the involvement of the whole People of God in the transformation and renewal of all people and of the total social context for the
complete liberation of humanity. That constitutes a revolution
in Roman Catholic mission theology.

With an attitude of openness toward each other, and a deep
involvement and concern for the world in which the church must
fulfill its mission, the various Christian traditions can now

fruitfully interact with each other in seeking to clarify, comprehend, and act upon a theology of mission determined by God's purpose for the church in the world today.

The final section of this survey will explore some of the developments and tensions in mission theology.

NOTES

[1]English translations of the first four are available in Thomas J. M. Burke, ed., *Catholic Missions: Four Great Missionary Encyclicals* (New York: Fordham University Press, 1957). The fifth appears in *The Encyclicals and Other Messages of John XXIII* (Washington, D.C.: TPS Press, 1964), pp. 168-97. Hereafter cited as *John XXIII*.

[2]See the discussion of this point by Eugene Hillman, *The Church as Mission* (New York: Herder & Herder, 1965), pp. 19-37; Mission "referred always and exclusively to foreign missions, or to the apostolate among the non-evangelized peoples outside of Europe," p. 37.

[3]*Evangelii Praecones* par. 32; W. Richey Hogg, "Some Background Considerations for *Ad Gentes*," IRM 56.223 (1967): 287, noted how this drew together the emphases of Joseph Schmidlin on evangelization and of Pierre Charles on the planting of the church in new lands. See also the errata and corrections of printer's errors in Hogg's article in IRM 56.224 (1967): 513.

[4]Latourette, *Expansion*, vol. VII: *Advance Through Storm*, p. 42.

[5]See figures in Rene Pierre Millot, *Missions in the World Today*. Trans. by J. Holland Smith (New York: Hawthorn, 1961), pp. 30-31. Dayton, ed., *Mission Handbook*, 11th ed., 1976, pp. 20, 24, 28, estimated the world Catholic missionary force at 49,000 in 1975, with 11,903 from North America (about 24%), 7,100 of whom came from the USA; cf. the estimated world Protestant missionary total of 55,000 with approximately 37,000 from North America (about 67%).

[6]*Maximum Illud*, par. 19; cf. also *Evangelii Praecones*, par. 30 and *Princeps Pastorum*, "ultra-nationalism" in *John XXIII*, pp. 180-81.

[7]*Maximum Illud*, pars. 14 and 15; cf. also *Rerum Ecclesiae*, pars. 22-25; *Evangelii Praecones*, pars. 36-42, and *Princeps Pastorum*, Section II.

[8]*Princeps Pastorum,* Section I; cf. also Millot, *Missions in the World Today,* pp. 34-36; Latourette, *Expansion,* vol. VII, p. 22, and Hogg, "Some Background Considerations for *Ad Gentes,*" pp. 287-88.

[9]*Evangelii Praecones,* pars. 55-58.

[10]See Marie-Joseph Le Guillou, "Mission as an Ecclesiological Theme" in *Re-Thinking the Church's Mission, Concilium,* vol. 13 (New York: Paulist Press, 1966), pp. 81-130, and Ronan Hoffman, "Ecumenism and Mission Theology," *Worldmission* 15.3 (1964): 48-64.

[11]For two expressions of this spirit, see "Pope John's Opening Speech to the Council," and "Message to Humanity," in Walter M. Abbott, ed., *The Documents of Vatican II.* Trans. ed. Joseph Gallagher (New York: Geoffrey Chapman, 1966), pp. 3-7, 710-719. Hereafter cited as *Vatican II.*

[12]Paul M. Minus, Jr., *The Catholic Rediscovery of Protestantism: A History of Roman Catholic Ecumenical Pioneering* (New York: Paulist Press, 1976), has noted the tension between the preservationist and the transformationist patterns of ecumenism, a distinction which helps illuminate the forces at work in Vatican II.

[13]Quoted in Xavier Rynne, *Vatican Council II* (New York: Farrar, Straus and Giroux, 1968), p. 384.

[14]Ibid., pp. 383-87.

[15]Ibid., pp. 511-20; 548-49.

[16]Albert C. Outler in *Vatican II,* p. 102.

[17]See John Deschner, "Concerning *Lumen Gentium*" in *Studies in Vatican II,* Senior Colloquy, Perkins School of Theology, Southern Methodist University, 1966 (mimeographed), pp. 2-4.

[18]*Lumen Gentium,* no. 1.

[19]Ibid., no. 5.

[20]Ibid., no. 3.

[21]Ibid., no. 9.

[22]Ibid., no. 13; cf. *Apostolicam Actuositatem,* nos. 2 and 4; and *Dignitatis Humanae,* no. 11, regarding the christological center of mission.

[23]*Lumen Gentium*, no. 16; cf. *Unitatis Redintegratio*, nos. 1, 3, 7, 20.

[24]*Lumen Gentium*, no. 14.

[25]Ibid., no. 16.

[26]*Lumen Gentium*, no. 24; cf. *Christus Dominus*, nos. 6, 11, 12, 13.

[27]See Paul VI, *Ecclesiae Sanctae*, 6 August, 1966, found in part in Austin P. Flannery, ed., *Documents of Vatican II*, (Grand Rapids: Eerdmans, 1975), p. 860.

[28]*Lumen Gentium*, no. 31; also *Apostolicam Actuositatem*, nos. 2, 5, 7, 13, 29.

[29]*Lumen Gentium*, nos. 34-36.

[30]Ibid., no. 36.

[31]Ibid., no. 48.

[32]*Ad Gentes*, nos. 1, 2, 35; cf. *Lumen Gentium*, nos. 1-4, 13, 33, 48.

[33]*Ad Gentes*, no. 6.

[34]"Pope John's Opening Speech to the Council."

[35]See, for example, *Gaudium et Spes*, nos. 19-21, 23, 43; *Unitatis Redintegratio*, nos. 4, 9, 18, 21, 22; *Ad Gentes*, nos. 11-12, 16; *Nostra Aetate*, nos. 2, 14. Also Anton Paul Stadler, "Mission-Dialogue. A Digest and Evaluation of the Discussion in the Roman Catholic Church and Within the World Council of Churches 1965-1975" (Ph.D.: Union Theological Seminary, New York, 1977).

[36]"Pope John's Opening Speech to the Council."

[37]*Ad Gentes*, nos. 15, 36; cf. *Unitatis Redintegratio*, nos. 8-12, 23.

[38]*Ad Gentes*, no. 35.

[39]Established by Paul VI in *Apostolica Sollicitudo* 15 September, 1965, and mentioned in *Christus Dominus*, no. 5. The text of *Apostolica Sollicitudo* may be found in Abbott, *Vatican II*, pp. 720-24.

[40]The preparatory document, furnished by the Vatican, was *The Evangelization of the Modern World* (Vatican City, 1973); the Synod statement "A Declaration From the Synod" can be found in IRM 64.255 (1975): 311-14; the Pope's summary exhortation was *On Evangelization in the Modern World (Evangelii Nuntiandi*, 8 December, 1975), (Washington, D.C.: US Catholic Conference, 1976). See also the comments of Archbishop S. E. Carter, "The Synod of Bishops--1974," IRM 64.255 (1975): 295-301.

[41]Paul VI, *On Evangelization*, p. 12.

[42]*The Evangelization of the Modern World*, pp. 5-6.

[43]*On Evangelization*, pp. 15-16.

[44]Ibid., pp. 16-19.

[45]Ibid., pp. 43, 49-51.

[46]Ibid., p. 45.

[47]Ibid., p. 46.

[48]"A Declaration From the Synod," p. 313.

[49]See Synod of Bishops, *Justice in the World* (Washington, D.C.: National Conference of Catholic Bishops, 1972), pp. 33-52, especially p. 42; also Carter, "The Synod of Bishops--1974," pp. 298-99; Paul VI, *On Evangelization* pp. 22-25.

[50]"A Declaration from the Synod," p. 313.

[51]Paul VI, *On Evangelization*, p. 25.

[52]Ibid., p. 26.

[53]Ibid., p. 59.

[54]Ibid., p. 60.

[55]English trans. of the letter found in *The Church Teaches: Documents of the Church in English Translation* (St. Louis, Mo.: B. Herder Book Co., 1955), pp. 119-21.

[56]Abbott, *Vatican II*, p. 35, footnote no. 59.

[57]See, for example, Karl Rahner, *Theological Investigations* (Baltimore: Helicon/London: Darton, Longman and Todd, 1966-1969), vols. V, pp. 97-134; VI, 390-98; Eugene Hillman, *The Church as Mission* (New York: Herder and Herder, 1965),

The Wider Ecumenism: Anonymous Christianity and the Church
(London: Burns and Oates, 1968), and "'Anonymous Christianity
and the Missions," *The Downside Review* 84.277 (1966): 361-79;
and Heinz Robert Schlette, *Towards a Theology of Religions*
(New York: Herder and Herder, 1966).

[58]Rahner, "Anonymous Christians," *Theological Investigations*, vol. VI, p. 394.

[59]Rahner, "Christianity and the Non-Christian Religions,"
Theological Investigations, vol. V, p. 133.

[60]Xavier Rynne, *Vatican Council II*, p. 515; cf. W. E.
Hocking's notion of the reconception of all religions.

[61]Henry van Straelen, "Our Attitude Towards Other Religions," *Worldmission* 16.1 (1965): 71-98.

[62]Hans Küng, *The Church* (New York: Sheed and Ward, 1967),
pp. 317-18; and *On Being a Christian* (New York: Doubleday,
1976), pp. 97-98.

[63]Stadler, "Mission-Dialogue," in his constructive conclusion defines mission as "dialogical apologetics," with rami-
fications for a whole range of systematic theological questions.

[64]Kevin and Dorothy Ranaghan, *Catholic Pentecostals* (New
York: Paulist Press, 1969), pp. 20-21; cf. W. J. Hollenweger,
The Pentecostals (Minneapolis: Augsburg Publishing House,
1972), pp. 8-9.

[65]Léon Joseph Cardinal Suenens, *A New Pentecost?* (New
York: Seabury Press, 1975), p. 78.

[66]See, for example, Donald Gelpi, *Pentecostalism: A Theo-
logical Viewpoint* (New York: Paulist Press, 1971); Simon Tug-
well, *Did You Receive the Spirit?* (New York: Paulist Press,
1972); Kilian McDonnell and others, *Theological and Pastoral
Orientations on the Catholic Charismatic Renewal* (Ann Arbor:
Word of Life, 1974); and the thorough bibliographical summary in
Edward D. O'Connor, ed., *Perspectives on Charismatic Renewal*
(Notre Dame: University of Notre Dame, 1975), pp. 145-84.

[67]See, for example, John J. Considine, *Call for Forty
Thousand* (New York: Longmans, 1946) and John J. Considine, ed.,
The Church in the New Latin America (Notre Dame: Fides Publi-
cations, 1964); William J. Coleman, *Latin American Catholicism:
A Self Evaluation* (Maryknoll: Maryknoll, 1958); and Latourette,
Expansion, vol. VII, pp. 167-71.

[68]On the formation and functions of CELAM see Hellmut Gnadt Vitalis, *The Significance of Changes in Latin American Catholicism Since Chimbote 1963. Sonedos* No. 51 (Cuernavaca: CIDOC, 1969), especially chapter 4.

[69]Vitalis, *Changes in Catholicism*, chap. 7, pp. 6-16; and José Miguez-Bonino, "The Church and the Latin American Social Revolution" in *The Church and Social Revolution*, Senior Colloquy, Perkins School of Theology, 1967 (mimeographed).

[70]José Miguez Bonino, *Christians and Marxists: The Mutual Challenge to Revolution* (Grand Rapids: Eerdmans, 1976), pp. 22-23.

[71]John Gerassi, ed., *Camilo Torres, Revolutionary Priest* (New York: Random House, 1971); José Miguez Bonino, *Doing Theology in a Revolutionary Situation* (Philadelphia: Fortress, 1975), pp. 43-45.

[72]Juan Cardinal Landazuri Ricketts in *Latin American Episcopal Council, Second General Conference of Latin American Bishops, Medellin 1968: The Church in the Present-Day Transformation of Latin America in the Light of the Council.* vol. I: *Position Papers*; vol. II: *Conclusions* (Bogota: CELAM, 1970), vol. I, p. 23. Hereafter cited as *Medellin I* or *Medellin II.* Cf. Gustavo Gutierrez, *A Theology of Liberation: History, Politics and Salvation*, trans. by Sister Caridad Inda and John Eagleson (Maryknoll: Orbis, 1973), pp. 134-35, and Enrique Dussel, *History and the Theology of Liberation*, trans. by John Drury (Maryknoll: Orbis, 1976), pp. 113-115.

[73]Some preparatory documentation can be found in *Between Honesty and Hope: Documents from and about the Church in Latin America. Issued at Lima by the Peruvian Bishops' Commission for Social Action*, trans. by John Drury (Maryknoll: Maryknoll, 1970), pp. 171-200.

[74]José Miguez-Bonino had prophetically called for just such a change in the church's life in 1967; see his "Main Currents of Protestantism" in Samuel Shapiro, ed., *Integration of Man and Society in Latin America* (Notre Dame: University of Notre Dame Press, 1967).

[75]*Medellin II*, pp. 49-50.

[76]Ibid., p. 48.

[77]Ibid., p. 73.

[78]Ibid., pp. 65, 79.

[79]Ibid., p. 58.

[80]Ibid., pp. 76-77, 80-81.

[81]Ibid., p. 66.

[82]Ibid., pp. 38-39.

[83]Segundo Galilea, *Reflexiones,* pp. 11-13; quoted in Orlando E. Costas, *Theology of the Crossroads,* p. 72.

[84]Miguez-Bonino, *Doing Theology in a Revolutionary Situation,* pp. 46-56.

[85]Miguez-Bonino, *Christians and Marxists,* pp. 92-93. See, for example, the statements issued by the First Latin American Encounter of Christians for Socialism held in Santiago, Chile in 1972, noted in Miguez-Bonino, *Doing Theology in a Revolutionary Situation,* pp. xxi-xxiv; and Costas, *Theology of the Crossroads,* pp. 74-77. Several Catholic episcopates disassociated themselves from this meeting.

[86]Gutierrez, *Theology of Liberation,* p. 108.

[87]Ibid., p. 262; cf. Juan Luis Segundo, *A Theology For Artisans of a New Humanity;* vol. II: *The Community Called Church* (Maryknoll: Orbis, 1974), p. 15.

[88]Miguez-Bonino, "The Church and the Latin American Social Revolution," pp. 7-8.

[89]Gutierrez, *Theology of Liberation,* p. 176; cf. pp. 36-37.

[90]For example, Manoel de Mello, the leader of the Brazilian Igreja Evangelica Pentecostal "Brasil para Cristo," has consistently been engaged in educational and social reform activities. See Manoel de Mello, "Participation is Everything," IRM 60.238 (1971): 245-48, and "The Gospel and the Bread" in *Jesus Christ Frees and Unites,* sect. I: "Confessing Christ Today."

[91]Raymond Panikkar, *The Unknown Christ of Hinduism,* p. 6.

[92]Ibid., pp. 59-60.

[93]Ibid., p. 35; cf. also Raymond Panikkar, "The Relation of Christians to their Non-Christian Surroundings," in Joseph Neuner, ed., *Christian Revelation and World Religions* (London: Burns and Oates, 1967), pp. 170-72.

[94]Raymond Panikkar, *The Trinity and World Religions*

(Madras: CLS, 1970).

   [95]Ibid., p. 72.

Part IV

A Theological Analysis of Developments and Tensions in Mission Theology

8

A New Consensus?

This final section offers an evaluation of the major
developments and tensions in mission theology as they have
evolved from the mid-1940s to 1975, drawing on the theological
material which has been developed in the earlier parts of this
study. The chapter will be organized around the five key issues
which have been used to analyze the thought and contributions
of the various gatherings, publications, and people, involving:
1) the theological basis of mission, 2) church-mission relations, 3) evangelism and social action, 4) Christianity and
other faiths, and 5) mission and unity.

The major thesis of this chapter can be briefly summarized:
The three traditions considered in this study have developed a
significant convergence on the main issues in mission theology.
Yet considerable differences remain in the several approaches
to these questions and in their implications for mission. These
give rise to tensions both within and among the three streams,
i.e., the ecumenical movement as represented by the WCC, conservative evangelicalism, and Roman Catholicism.

THE THEOLOGICAL BASIS OF MISSION

The most significant point to have developed concerning
the theological basis of mission from 1948 to 1975 has been the
change from a church-centric to a trinitarian understanding of
the nature of the missionary enterprise.

For most of the first half of the twentieth century the
primary emphasis in the ecumenical movement and in Roman Catho-

lic mission theology concerned the church--building up its life
and witness, especially in Africa and Asia. The Oxford (1937),
Edinburgh (1937), and Madras (1938) cluster made this evident
in the ecumenical movement, as did the encyclicals of Benedict
XV and Pius XI in the Roman Catholic Church. After the war,
the IMC meeting at Whitby (1947), with its theme "Partnership
in Obedience" for evangelism, and Roman Catholic efforts to
encourage an indigenous hierarchy and clergy as part of the
effort to foster evangelism and the growth of the church pointed
to the dominant ecclesiological factor in mission theology.

Evangelical mission thought revolved essentially around
evangelism, often understood in terms of individual conversions,
with the implied aim of gathering believers into self-supporting,
self-governing, and self-propagating churches on the basis of a
closely defined basis of faith.

The change towards a trinitarian basis for mission occurred
over a period of time. Within the ecumenical movement, Hoekendijk's adverse criticism of church-centric thinking had an
effect, as did the intensive investigation for new theological
roots in the study, "The Missionary Obligation of the Church."
From these studies emerged a concern for a trinitarian grounding, which pointed to the *missio Dei* as the basis of the church's
mission. This viewpoint became widely accepted during the 1960s,
especially through the study, "The Missionary Structure of the
Congregation," which stressed *missio Dei* as the primary reality
in which Christians and congregations participate. The Uppsala
Report, "Renewal in Mission," adopted an implicit trinitarian
form in its opening paragraphs, and the Fifth Assembly at Nairobi
spoke of Christ as the mediator of God's new covenant in the
power of the Holy Spirit in "Confessing Christ Today."

The five Roman Catholic encyclicals on mission in the pre-
Vatican II period dealt principally with the practical problems
and needs of the missionary enterprise. However, the documents
of Vatican II, especially *Lumen Gentium* and *Ad Gentes*, proceed
immediately from a trinitarian basis, as the opening paragraphs
of the Constitution on the Church make clear. This emphasis was
reaffirmed in Paul's Apostolic Exhortation, *Evangelii Nuntiandi*.

The conservative evangelical understanding of mission has
usually stressed the authority of Scripture, and especially the
Great Commission as the basic source of the obligation God
places on all Christians who, in obedience to God's command,
must go into all the world to seek lost souls. Certainly this
continued to be the main position at the Wheaton and Berlin
Congresses in 1966. The Lausanne Congress in 1974 affirmed
this basis for mission too, but also spoke in the first paragraph of the Covenant on "the Purpose of God" in trinitarian

terms. It affirmed that God calls together a people for himself, and sends his people back into the world as his servants
and witnesses to build up Christ's body in the power of the Holy
Spirit. A trinitarian basis for mission, therefore, also
emerged at Lausanne.[1]

Of what theological significance is this convergence on a
trinitarian foundation for the missionary enterprise? It marks
a decisive shift from understanding mission as one part of the
church's task, involving the sending of special personnel to a
particular geographic location, to recognizing that mission is
a task of the whole church involving all God's people participating in the fulfillment of God's purposes throughout the whole
world. The latter also allows for the specially commissioned
and sent, but recovers the meaning of the Royal Priesthood of
all believers (I Pet. 2:9).

The trinitarian basis significantly broadens the whole
context and perspective of mission from one of *looking at* the
church's work to understanding mission as the *participation* by
the people of God *in* his work. To affirm "God the Father
Almighty, maker of heaven and earth" involves seeking God's
purpose and will for the whole created order. God is still
active in all things, for "in him we live and move and have our
being," and what God purposed in creation is what he will accomplish in his kingdom when his will is done on earth as it is in
heaven.[2] The church's mission arises out of God's mission to
the world.

God's creative power continues to work throughout the world
and cannot be confined to the boundaries of the church. As God
used Israel and the nations beyond to fulfill his purposes in
the Old Testament, so all nations and peoples still come within
the orbit of his control. The universality of God's mission,
embracing the whole world, is crucial to the church's understanding of the horizons of mission.[3] This means the people of
God must be alert to discern God's ways in the world, and seek
to participate in the process of consummation which God has
initiated, especially in the revelation given through Christ.

Such a perspective takes the world seriously as the arena
for mission. As God is involved in the whole created order,
seeking to accomplish his purposes, so the church will be *in*
the world (created order), but not *of* the world (fallen in sin)
in its hostility to God,[4] as it shares in God's work of restor-
ing all things through Christ.

The emphasis on Jesus Christ in a trinitarian basis for
mission theology involves several considerations. First, the
incarnation exemplifies the methodology to be used in fulfilling

God's work. Second, Jesus Christ is the norm by which God's
presence in the world is discerned. Third, Jesus Christ's
ministry indicates the nature of the church's ministry.

The principle of the incarnation points to an involvement
in the world by Jesus Christ which the church seeks to emulate
as it strives to penetrate into the very life and existence of
those to whom it ministers and serves, even as "the Word became
flesh" (Jn. 1:14), and "he made him to be sin who knew no sin"
(2 Cor. 5:21). Just as Jesus of Nazareth sought out publicans
and sinners, the outcasts and the needy, so Christians must
reach out to those to whom they go in God's name as they follow
the example of Jesus in coming to seek and to save the lost.

In his ministry Jesus used both word and deed to minister
to people in announcing the coming of the kingdom of God. Prophetic exhortation and judgment, as well as announcement and
invitation, were used by Christ to bring people to the renewal
of their relationship with God and others in his kingdom. His
healing and helping deeds became visible signs of ministry. The
church now shares in this ministry of word and deed in the
world, offering these as signs of God's presence.

In Lk. 4:18-19, Jesus described his own ministry in terms
of addressing the physical and spiritual needs of people. The
comprehensive understanding of ministry which that involved has
become the model which the church follows in its mission in the
world. The church remains faithful to the task which Jesus
gave to his disciples as it follows his example and lives in
obedience to his command to love God and neighbor, and his commission to go into all the world with the gospel.

The charismatic movement has brought the work of the Holy
Spirit into prominence in recent years. Several important emphases for mission theology flow from the Holy Spirit's activity. The gifts of the Spirit are available for the whole people
of God. The laity, inspired by the gifts of grace through the
Holy Spirit, are the main witnesses of God in the world. The
emergence of people movements in which the laity bear primary
responsibility for evangelism is one example of this phenomenon.
The growth of urban and industrial mission activities is also
built on a theology of the laity as active witnesses through
the power and presence of the Spirit.

The movements for justice, peace, liberation, and humanization may also be seen as evidence of the work of the Holy
Spirit in people's lives. Insofar as these movements are motivated by a desire to help the oppressed, the poor, and to meet
human need, they may be seen as evidence of God's work through
the Holy Spirit. Jesus spoke of such actions in the parable of

the Good Samaritan and in Mt. 25:31-46. No human effort which moves towards the realities of love, justice, and truth, which Christians identify with God's kingdom, can be outside the boundaries of God's activity.

A deep renewal of life for many people and churches has come through the charismatic movement. Devotion to God and service to neighbor in close fellowship with other Christians across denominational boundaries has become a powerful means for evangelism, witness, and service in some places. The Spirit has opened new ways for Christians to grow in obedience and grace through the charismatic movement. These experiences have given insight into the meaning of unity for those who participated in such activities.

The emergence of a trinitarian basis for mission has deepened and broadened the interpretation of the Great Commission. Whereas this mandate, especially in its Marcan form (Mk. 16:15), has often been used to support the position that evangelism (meaning verbal proclamation) is the main task of mission, the recent emphases on the Trinity have drawn attention to the trinitarian formula in the Matthean account, and to the Johannine parallel between the Father's sending the Son and the sending of the disciples. This exegetical development, evident in John R. W. Stott's writings for example,[5] has been one factor in producing the consensus that mission is a comprehensive task which the church undertakes arising from the mission of God in Christ, by the power of the Holy Spirit, in the world.

Mission, understood as God's purpose for the church in relation to the world, was variously described as "confessing Christ," and "witness" at the Fifth Assembly of the WCC in Nairobi; as "world evangelization" at the Lausanne Congress; and as "evangelization" at the 1974 Synod of Bishops of the Roman Catholic Church. Each of these gatherings pointed to the triune God as the source of the church's life and task: Because God is a sending God, the church is involved in the work of proclaiming Christ in word and deed by the power of the Holy Spirit to all people. While evangelicals still insist on a clear distinction between evangelism and social action, they affirm that "evangelism and socio-political involvement are both part of our Christian duty,"[6] and thus share a comprehensive understanding of the mission which God has given his people.

The place of the church in mission theology is an important issue about which significant differences can be noted among the different groups. Within the IMC/WCC the church-centric view of mission evident until the 1950s faded rapidly in the 1960s, when the main focus moved to the world. However,

Uppsala (1968) also pointed to the importance of local congregations in the total missionary enterprise. Nairobi (1975) strongly affirmed "the confessing community" as an essential element in Christian witness.

Yet the church has an ambivalent place in ecumenical mission theology. It is in need of renewal because its very structures and divisions obscure its witness to Christ; yet it is also the community of God's people committed to participating in God's mission. The tension between these two insights, both of which are valid, is likely to remain.

Evangelical mission theology has stressed evangelism as the first priority for God's people. In fulfilling that goal, local congregations are understood to be "God's primary agents for the widespread dissemination of the gospel,"[7] because "the church is at the very center of God's cosmic purpose and is his appointed means of spreading the Gospel."[8] The unstated presupposition behind this position is that outside the church there is no salvation--the growth of local congregations of believers is therefore of the utmost importance. The Lausanne Covenant acknowledged, however, that the church may also become a stumbling block to evangelism.

In Roman Catholic mission theology a new emphasis has emerged alongside the notion of church planting, namely, the understanding of the church as "a sign and an instrument" of God's saving purpose for all people. As the discussion concerning "anonymous Christianity" showed,[9] this sometimes leads to the conclusion by some Catholic theologians that Christianity and the church are the extraordinary means of salvation,[10] and that the function of the church is to make itself a convincing sign of the kind of peace and joy available for all people through God's saving love as manifested in Jesus Christ. The church, then, becomes primarily a sign, yet remains an agent of God's love and saving will.

The key issue about which there is no consensus in mission theology at present concerns the relationship between God's economy of salvation in Jesus Christ and his presence and activity in the whole world, including other faiths.[11] The question may be rephrased: How and where does God act, and of what significance is his action in the world?

At virtually every major meeting of the IMC/WCC this question has been raised and the comment made that "opinions differed." *That* God is at work outside the church has been widely accepted. But the significance and meaning to be attributed to that affirmation has caused considerable tension. This tension becomes most evident in such questions as that of the relation

between the mission of the church and the search for community
among groups and nations. The meaning to be attributed to
these activities remains an unresolved question in the ecumenical movement.[12]

Evangelicals at Lausanne recognized that "all men have some
knowledge of God through his general revelation in nature. But
we deny that this can save." The implication which follows is
that some knowledge of God may be open to all people, but salvation is restricted to those who acknowledge Jesus Christ as
Lord and Savior, and therefore are members of the church.

The Roman Catholic attitude towards God's work outside the
church, especially in the light of Vatican II, has been to affirm that all who are moved by grace and respond to God's will
known through the dictates of conscience, are able to attain
salvation.[13] The quests for truth, justice, goodness, and
freedom are viewed as impulses which originate in the divinely
given nature of human existence, and are therefore to be encouraged and supported. Catholic theology sees such impulses
as an authentic sign of God's presence and purpose.[14]

Discerning the presence of God in the world, and the meaning to be attributed to that general revelation, raises difficult problems for mission theology. On the basis of the shared
conviction that the mission of the church rests in the triune
God, more progress may be made in the future towards resolving
the differences which exist on this issue at the present time.

CHURCH-MISSION RELATIONS

It is now widely accepted that the missionary nature of the
church flows from the purpose and will of God, and that mission
is the basic duty of the people of God. The theological integration of church and mission is widely completed. Mission is
not some activity to be undertaken only by those interested in
preaching, teaching or helping others, but is a fundamental
responsibility and obligation which the whole church undertakes
because God wants all people to be saved, to know and accept
the truth of his holy love. Mission is part of the work of the
whole church in which all participate in some way if the church
is to be faithful to its essential nature.

A number of theological insights regarding mission flow
from this basic point. These include undertaking mission as a
six-continent enterprise; recognizing the importance of fostering indigenous churches; accepting the role of the laity in
mission; and being open to fuller and richer interpretations of
the gospel and of Christian devotion, worship, and life that
reflect the gifts of all peoples and all cultures.

The IMC Assembly report from Mexico City (1963) spoke of "Witness in Six Continents" as one of the new insights to emerge from the ecumenical movement at that time. At least two major thrusts contributed to this development. First, it had become quite obvious that no continent could be called "Christian." The missionary frontier between belief and unbelief faces churches in every place.[15] Second, the growing maturity of the churches in Africa and Asia resulted in their sending mission-aries as well as receiving them from other countries.[16] Both these factors indicated that the Christian mission involves all six continents.

The importance of developing indigenous churches, firmly rooted in the culture in which they seek to grow, has been al-most universally accepted now as a principle of mission theol-ogy.[17] The foreignness of the form of Christianity introduced by missionaries, especially those from Western countries, has been a frequent refrain in many meetings concerned with the growth of strong indigenous churches.

The popes recognized this when they required the ordination of local clergy as a prerequisite for further missionary ad-vances and hence embarked on a program to increase rapidly the number of indigenous hierarchy and clergy. The point has been made in the ecumenical movement from the WMC (1910) onwards. Movements such as Evangelism in Depth in Latin America and New Life For All in Africa have made this emphasis clear from the evangelical side.

In broad outline the aim of developing churches deeply rooted in Christ and closely related to their culture is accepted by all. But the difficulty in achieving this goal produces a major point of tension in mission theology at the present time. In Africa the vast number of independent churches, ranging from orthodox (in terms of adherence to the Scripture and creeds) to those groups with virtually no Christian links highlights the problem vividly. The situation in Latin America is complex, too, with charismatic churches at one end of the spectrum and some very conservative Roman Catholics at the other end, each of which would claim to be "indigenous" churches. The inter-action of Christians with people of the living faiths of Hin-duism and Buddhism has raised the same problem in Asia.[18] The principle of indigenous churches may be widely accepted; how to achieve that goal remains a point of great tension.

The role of the laity in mission has received considerable attention in recent mission theology. This development evolved from the insight that if the whole people of God are involved in the mission of the church, rather than a small group specifi-cally called "missionaries," then the focus of mission must concentrate on those people who are involved in the world, because they are the chief witnesses for Christ.

"The Missionary Structure of the Congregation" study in the WCC laid great stress on this point in the 1960s, and the subsequent WCC Assemblies at Uppsala and Nairobi continued to reiterate the same point, that is, "the whole church," the total body of Christ, bearing responsibility for the mission of the church.

Much of the program of evangelical outreach in Evangelism in Depth and New Life For All is built around the witness of individual Christians. The Lausanne Covenant called upon all Christians to pray that the Holy Spirit's fruit would "appear in all [God's] people and that all his gifts may enrich the body of Christ. Only then will the whole church become a fit instrument in his hands."[19]

At the Second Vatican Council, the role of the laity in mission received particular emphasis, for they "by their very vocation, seek the kingdom of God by engaging in temporal affairs and by ordering them according to the plan of God."[20] The Latin American Conference of Bishops at Medellin devoted one whole section to lay movements, and strongly endorsed the lead which Vatican II had taken at this point.[21]

The major problem regarding the laity in mission involves the training and effective utilization of the whole church. Most churches lamented their failure to implement what is accepted at a theological level, that "to each is given the manifestation of the Spirit for the common good" (I Cor. 12:7).

While the church growth movement first defined church growth in a systematic way,[22] the realities to which McGavran and Tippett pointed in analyzing the factors which help or hinder church growth have been widely accepted by many other Christians concerned with the mission of the church. The importance of numerical church growth, which could also be called church planting, has continued to find a place in ecumenical, evangelical, and Roman Catholic mission theology. What Tippett called qualitative growth, referring to the increase of spiritual gifts such as grace, maturity, and the fruits of the Spirit, is an aspect of church life endorsed by all. Organic church growth, or the renewal of church life through structural changes designed to improve its outreach and methods of operation, has occupied the attention of church leaders of all branches of the church in recent decades.

Orlando E. Costas added another element to this analytical scheme when he called for incarnational church growth, by which he meant the involvement of the church in the life and problems of society through its prophetic, intercessory, and liberating action on behalf of the weak and oppressed.[23] Again, the need for this type of church growth is accepted by all Christian groups.

The sharpest point of tension involves the setting of priorities between these various elements of church growth. Conservative evangelicals consistently declare that numerical or quantitative growth should have first priority in a world where three billion people are not Christian. The main thrust of the WCC's concern has been on organic and incarnational growth. The Roman Catholic emphasis has included both church planting and organic growth. The tensions both within and between groups involved in mission concerning priorities for different kinds of church growth make this one of the most widely debated topics of great practical importance in all churches today. Yet it seems clear that a balance must be maintained between all the dimensions of church growth in any comprehensive mission program.

The question of structures arises from any serious reflection on the relationship between church and mission, and the most effective means of fulfilling mission. A wide variety of means and structures has emerged throughout history to express and direct the missionary impulse.

Ralph D. Winter identified two major historical structures --modalities (a fellowship in which there is no distinction of sex or age), and sodalities (a group with a clearly identified membership determined by age, sex or purpose), which have each shared in the transmission of Christianity.[24] Sodalities have been the most vital sources for renewal and achievement in missionary activity, Winter argued. He concluded that sodality structures are necessary in order for church people to reach out in vital initiatives in cross-cultural mission. Yet a balance needs to be maintained between sodalities and modalities.

Difficult problems still remain in trying to achieve such a balance. Many evangelical mission groups function as service agencies involving literature, radio, aviation, and the like, and therefore do not directly contribute to building churches. Other independent bodies form individual congregations which do not easily relate to other churches--the problems created by this situation in Latin America, for example, have been quite undesirable, as many evangelicals testify.[25] In the opinion of George Peters, church-mission relations still constitute the primary problem in many areas.[26]

Ecumenical mission boards must face the issue, too, but from a different perspective. In the USA, ecumenical churches

with the admirable goal of involving the whole church in mission
have included mission activity in unified budgetary, planning,
and administrative procedures. Yet many lay people and missionaries believe this has stifled flexibility, initiative, and
close personal relations between missionaries, congregations,
and the areas of missionary engagement. This must be considered
at least as part of the reason for the startling decrease in
missionaries among DOM affiliated boards from 10,042 in 1968 to
5,010 in 1976 in the USA.[27] Groups seeking more freedom within
denominations, such as the Good News Movement in the United
Methodist Church, have pointed up the problems ecumenical denominations face in church-mission relations.

In the Roman Catholic Church, reforms instituted by Pope
Paul VI in accordance with the principles enunciated in *Ad
Gentes* have sought to improve church-mission relations in that
church. The restructuring of the Propaganda to include representatives from missions and prelates from "mission areas"
indicates the importance attributed to this matter.[28]

At the national and international level both ecumenical
and evangelical groups have called for better ways to implement
mission strategy. At least since Willingen (1952), ecumenical
gatherings have spoken about Joint Action for Mission in an
effort to evolve structures for joint planning and action in
particular areas, and to make available resources of personnel
and finances to enable the church to fulfill its mission more
effectively. The challenge has met with some success, and perhaps the work of Inter-Church Aid has become the most widespread example of large scale cooperation ever to have occurred
among churches.[29]

Evangelicals have also expressed the hope that Christians
could share together in joint efforts, especially for evangelism.[30] The regional Congresses on Evangelism, held after
Berlin (1966), were tangible results of that hope--but little
specific action seems to have emerged from these gatherings.
The post-Congress Lausanne Committee for World Evangelization
has attempted to maintain a consultative and information dis-
seminating function among evangelicals around the world.[31] The
hope for new structures has yet to become a reality among the
evangelical community.

The changes in the churches and the world in the years
since World War II make new church-mission relations imperative.
The emergence of mature churches in many countries which are
now independent means that besides finding suitable structures
for churches to express their missionary concern, new relationships between churches in different countries and regions must
also be developed. The advent of regional ecumenical and evan-

gelical organizations and leaders has highlighted this issue.
Roman Catholic membership in some regional bodies will give new
impetus to the search for new relationships among Christians.

Old bonds formed in colonial times are inadequate now; but
new commitments and structures only evolve with difficulty. The
growing missionary responsibility accepted by churches in Asia,
Africa, and Latin America makes this a truly global issue involving Christians in all parts of the world. Church-mission
relations have changed and developed enormously. Finding satisfactory solutions to the problems which exist now is one of the
difficulties still to be faced in mission thought and practice.

EVANGELISM AND SOCIAL ACTION

Developments in mission theology in the past decade have
at last substantially removed the acrimony between evangelicals
and ecumenical theologians regarding the relationship between
evangelism and social action. At Lausanne, Stanley Mooneyham
concluded that "the debate which has gone on for nearly a century is really a non-issue."[32] Certainly it is now widely
agreed that evangelism and social action are both essential
elements in the mission of the church, although distinctive
differences remain in the way evangelicals and ecumenists have
arrived at this common conclusion.

At least since the IMC meeting at Jerusalem (1928), the
ecumenical movement has laid considerable emphasis on active
involvement in society by Christians as an important part of
the mission of the church. Evangelism and social action have
been viewed as integral elements in a comprehensive Christian
witness to God's love and concern for the whole person and the
whole of society. Both testify to the personal and social renewal of life which God wants, that people may be freed from
the bondage of sin, oppression, and injustice. Lesslie Newbigin offered this summary:

> The preaching of the Gospel and the service of men's
> needs are equally authentic and essential parts of the
> Church's responsibility . . . . Not all are preachers
> and not all are technical experts, administrators,
> healers or teachers; but when all these differing gifts
> are seen to belong together in the life of the one com-
> munity, then the word illuminates the deed, and the
> deed authenticates the word, and the Spirit takes them
> both to bear His own witness to the Resurrection.[33]

Precisely this kind of integral approach to the relationship of evangelism and social action informs the ecumenical
movement's distinctive approach to this question. Thus, the

Bangkok Conference on "Salvation Today" affirmed that "God's justice manifests itself both in the justification of the sinner and in social and political justice."[34] In the same spirit the Fifth Assembly declared, "We are commissioned to proclaim the gospel of Christ to the ends of the earth. Simultaneously, we are commanded to struggle to realize God's will for peace, justice, and freedom throughout society."[35]

Conservative evangelicals have arrived at the same general conclusion from another theological basis. While the evangelicals of the 1940s turned away from the negativism associated with fundamentalism, Carl Henry's plea in *The Uneasy Conscience of Fundamentalism* for a more active involvement in social action showed that much still needed to be done by evangelicals to rectify past neglect of this issue. The Congresses of Wheaton and Berlin in 1966 detailed the position most evangelicals espouse, arguing that Christians are bound by two mandates--the cultural and the evangelical.[36]

The cultural mandate calls Christians to responsible participation in human society, including working for social justice and the healing and compassion ministries undertaken to foster human welfare. The evangelistic mandate refers to the commission to announce the good news of salvation through Jesus Christ that through the Holy Spirit people may come to repentance and faith. Both mandates are binding. Yet evangelicals overwhelmingly consider evangelism the more important of the two, although the weight given to the cultural mandate in the past decade is noteworthy. The Wheaton Declaration stated, ". . . we affirm unreservedly the primacy of preaching the gospel to every creature, and we will demonstrate anew God's concern for social justice and human welfare."[37] Lausanne also endorsed a two-mandate approach in paragraph 5 of the Covenant:

> Although reconciliation with man is not reconciliation with God, nor is social action evangelism, nor is political liberation salvation, nevertheless we affirm that evangelism and socio-political involvement are both part of our Christian duty. For both are necessary expressions of our doctrines of God and man, our love for our neighbour and our obedience to Jesus Christ.[38]

Yet, paragraph 6 of the Covenant asserted that "In the church's mission of sacrificial service evangelism is primary."

Lausanne confirmed the main approach established by evangelicals at Wheaton. However, two other points should also be noted. First, the question of social action received far more attention at Lausanne than at any previous evangelical gathering. Second, at least some of the participants moved towards a more integrated view of evangelism and social action in a comprehensive view of mission. The papers by John R. W. Stott, Orlando E. Costas, René Padilla, and the report of the Radical Discipleship group all indicate such a trend, and are evidence of a growing diversity in the ranks of evangelicals, with the influence of "establishment" leaders such as Billy Graham and Harold Lindsell waning somewhat.

To summarize briefly: Statements from both the ecumenical movement and from evangelical gatherings display an agreement that both evangelism and social action are part of the church's mission. The ecumenical viewpoint tends to stress the complementary character of each in a comprehensive understanding of mission. The evangelical position sees evangelism and social action as quite separate activities, with a preference for the evangelistic mandate.

The words "evangelism" and "social action" themselves are capable of bearing a wide range of meanings, and differences at this point are apparent. Evangelicals tend to use a precise definition of evangelism, largely in terms of the verbal proclamation of the gospel. The Wheaton Declaration affirmed that "God's primary method for evangelism and church planting is the ministry of Spirit-gifted and empowered men and women preaching and teaching the Word of God."[39] A similar statement appeared in the Lausanne Covenant: "evangelism itself is the proclamation of the historical, biblical Christ as Savior and Lord, with the view to persuading people to come to him personally and so be reconciled to God."[40] This emphasis flows directly from the evangelicals' understanding of the evangelistic mandate of the church.

Evangelism has not been understood in this way in the ecumenical movement. Rather, as evangelism and social action have been considered integral aspects of the church's mission, evangelism has been defined in a broad and comprehensive manner. The definition offered at the IMC meeting at Willingen reflects this:

> Evangelism is witness for Christ directed towards all men and seeking to claim for him every department of life both personal and public. This witness is given by proclamation, fellowship and service.[41]

The Fifth Assembly of the WCC at Nairobi used the term "confessing Christ" to describe the comprehensive nature of witness or evangelism.[42] In describing the content of the confession of Christians and churches in word and deed, the report declared:

> The gospel always includes: the announcement of God's

kingdom and love through Jesus Christ, the offer of
grace and forgiveness of sins, the invitation to repentance and faith in him, the summons to fellowship in
God's Church, the command to witness to God's saving
words and deeds, the responsibility to participate in
the struggle for justice and human dignity, the obligation to denounce all that hinders human wholeness,
and a commitment to risk life itself.[43]

This inclusive definition of what is to be communicated through
the total life and outreach of the whole church is congruent
with the ecumenical movement's integral approach to evangelism
and social action.[44]

The Roman Catholic Church also supports a broad view of
evangelization, as may be seen from the definition offered in
Pope Paul VI's Apostolic Exhortation:

The Church evangelizes when she seeks to convert, solely
through the divine power of the Message she proclaims,
both the personal and collective consciences of people,
the activities in which they engage, and the lives and
concrete milieux which are theirs.[45]

The Pope spoke of the complex process of evangelization involving the renewal of humanity, witness, explicit proclamation,
inner adherence to revealed truth, entry into the community of
faith, acceptance of the sacramental life of the church, and
participation in the witness and outreach of the church.[46]

The difference between the more narrowly defined understanding of evangelism among conservative evangelicals and the broader
and more inclusive definitions advanced by the ecumenical movement and the Roman Catholic Church indicates the difficulties
to be faced in arriving at a common understanding of evangelism
for all those concerned with mission theology.

A similar problem arises in relation to defining "social
action." At least four different levels of activity can be
distinguished.[47] On the pastoral level the church is involved
in creating an informed membership, conscious of the Christian
faith and its implications, alert to the problems of society,
and committed to Christian discipleship by means of personal
involvement in movements for renewal and through the support of
ecclesiastical, humanitarian and compassionate ministries and
services. This is clearly the most widespread type of social
action supported by churches.

The prophetic level refers to official statements which
point to changes needed in society, directing the attention of

churches and secular agencies to their responsibilities in
meeting the challenges or problems thus outlined. Some of the
pastoral letters of the papacy and the bishops, and the resolutions of various ecumenical bodies, would be examples of this
activity.

The third level of social action by the church is described
by Miguez-Bonino as "conscientization." This refers to programs
of popular education aimed at awakening people's consciences to
an awareness of their human dignity and of the need to organize
themselves in order to protect or protest particular policies
and activities involving the violation of human rights via
economic, social, and political injustice. The WCC's Programme
to Combat Racism belongs in this category.

Finally, the fourth level involves the direct action of
individuals and congregations in the political and social arena.
Participation of Christians in revolutionary movements--for
example, Camilo Torres in Colombia and Nestor Paz in Bolivia,
and the leadership given by Abel Muzorewa and N. Sithole in the
struggle by blacks for liberation in Zimbabwe, constitute examples of this type of action.

While it is now generally agreed by evangelicals, members
of the WCC, and the Roman Catholic Church that social action
has a legitimate place in the total mission of the church, tension revolves around these questions: What level or kind of
activity? What priority and proportion of funds and personnel
should be allocated to social action in relation to other important aspects of mission?

In the ecumenical movement the decisive shift towards the
world during the 1960s marked an important development in ecumenical mission theology. Greater emphasis on the pastoral
level of social action, together with more specific resolutions
and statements on socio-political issues, were evident, especially at the Geneva Conference on Church and Society (1966).
The Uppsala Assembly (1968), and SODEPAX (the Committee on
Society, Development and Peace jointly sponsored by the WCC and
the Roman Catholic Church), highlighted developmental issues.
The Programme to Combat Racism, which began in 1970, constitutes
a small but symbolically important development in the WCC's
level of involvement in social action. The major part of the
WCC's finances and program activities continues to be committed
to traditional types of Inter-Church Aid projects--disaster
relief, rehabilitation work, and refugee support.[48] A greater
emphasis on justice, development, and self-reliance is evident
in the projects and activities which the WCC now supports, but
there is little change in the level of activity which remains
basically pastoral in orientation.

Evangelicals have come to support pastoral social action as a Christian responsibility. The Congresses at Wheaton and Berlin expressed this unequivocally, and the Lausanne Covenant affirmed that socio-political involvement is a part of the duty of the Christian. The World Vision organization is the largest evangelical agency involved in humanitarian and relief work. Only the Radical Evangelicals have made any attempt to move into the prophetic level of social action principally through articles in their publications.[49]

Considerable differences still exist between evangelicals and members of the ecumenical movement about the place and importance of social action in Christian mission. John R. W. Stott summarized the problem in this way in an address to the Fifth Assembly of the WCC:

> Ecumenical leaders genuinely question whether evangelicals have a heartfelt commitment to social action. We evangelicals say we have, but I personally recognize we have got to supply more evidence than we have. On the other hand, evangelicals question whether the WCC has a heartfelt commitment to world-wide evangelism. They say they have, but I beg this Assembly to supply more evidence that this is so.[50]

The Roman Catholic Church has long supported a strong program of social action at the pastoral level, especially through such groups as Catholic Action. Some papal encyclicals and episcopal statements have sounded a prophetic note, too, with calls for justice, peace, and human rights. In Latin America a number of Roman Catholics have been involved in "conscientization" programs--Dom Helder Camara, for example. Direct political activity, although seldom officially sanctioned, has also been seen.

Liberation theologians in Latin America have used Marxist socio-economic-political analysis freely in their work. What is the relationship of Christianity to Marxism? Is an alliance between Marxists and Christians also evident outside Latin America?

An extensive analysis of these questions cannot be made here, but several comments seem appropriate. Miguez-Bonino has identified a number of elements which Marxism contributes to an understanding of revolutionary activity.[51] Marxism teaches that history is dependent on the human organization of the process through which goods are produced, a process which can be altered; humanity involves "a communal unity in the form of a concrete social formation with its structures, relationship and self-understanding (ideology)"; basic structural changes in

society will occur only through the struggle of those who suffer
from the present organization of society; and praxis is the
true test of any theory.

"The Christian alliance with Marxist socialism is . . . .
always an uneasy alliance," Miguez-Bonino has argued, because
the source and power of each derives from fundamentally different philosophies.[52] Yet the Marxist contribution is valuable
to Christians, he believes, because it provides

> a set of analytical tools, a concrete political and
> social programme and a coherent ideological view
> which permits men to embrace and carry forward the
> struggle for human liberation.[53]

The goal of human liberation has certainly been widely
accepted. The AACC Assembly in Lusaka (1974) called Christians
to an "identification with the complex of liberation struggles
that are going on in Africa" as churches recognize their "need
to be set free by Christ in order to share in His liberating
and renewing activity in Africa."[54] In Asia, the CCA Assembly
in 1973 challenged Christians to recognize that, "now is the
time for action. Christian Action in the Asian Struggle will
take place concretely as Christians participate in the struggles
of the peoples of Asia for the total liberation and fullness of
life promised by God."[55] Among Roman Catholic documents emphasizing human dignity and freedom in a social order "founded on
truth, built on justice, and animated by love," *Gaudium et Spes*
devoted particular attention to the rightful place which these
aspirations have in God's providence.[56]

Many Christians throughout the world share in the concern
for human liberation and seek to promote the social, political,
and economic policies which enable this hope to become a reality.
In this process "all men, believers and unbelievers alike,
ought to work for the rightful betterment of this world in which
all alike live."[57] Such cooperation between Christians and
others, including Marxists, involves in some situations a temporary alliance for particular ends, but does not indicate any
particular endorsement of Marxist ideology and strategy by
Christians. It may be, however, that Marxist analysis and criticism of society in some places has awakened Christians to
their responsibilities to stand with the poor and needy in
striving to achieve justice, human liberation, and freedom in
all of its dimensions.

Evangelism and social action, and the relationship between
the two, has been the focus of much debate in mission theology
in the past. The developments which have occurred, especially
in the evangelical understanding of the place of social action

in mission, have produced a consensus concerning the importance
of both. Yet tensions remain about precisely what is meant by
each of these terms, and the priority which should be placed on
each in the total mission of God's people.

CHRISTIANITY AND OTHER FAITHS

The issues raised in understanding the relationship of
Christianity to other religions are particularly difficult.
Charges of universalism and syncretism, and questions concerning the purpose and aims of dialogue, have frequently been
raised with little careful attention to what is in fact being
affirmed or denied by these terms.

Discussion of "universalism" frequently begins with the
biblical witness pointing to God's love for all people, and
his desire and will to save all. Several texts clearly indicate this:

Have I any pleasure in the death of the wicked, says
the Lord God, and not rather that he should turn from
his way and live? (Ezek. 18:23).

God our Saviour, who desires all men to be saved and
to come to the knowledge of the truth (I Tim. 2:3-4).

For the grace of God has appeared for the salvation of
all men (Titus 2:11).

The Lord is not slow about his promise as some count
slowness, but is forbearing toward you, not wishing
that any should perish, but that all should reach
repentance (II Pet. 3:9).

. . . we have an advocate with the Father, Jesus
Christ the righteous; and he is the expiation for our
sins, and not ours only but also for the sins of the
whole world (I John 2:1-2).

From this point a number of different arguments have been
advanced. In the ecumenical movement the major trend has been
to acknowledge that God wants all people to be saved. Christians are called then to share in the task of making God's love
in Jesus Christ known, that all people may confess and obey
God's will and way. The fate and destiny of those who do not
know of God's love in Christ is to be left in God's hands as the
Judge of all people.[58] The stress is on the responsibility the
church has to participate in God's mission, for Christians are

commissioned to carry the gospel to the whole world

> and allow it to permeate all realms of human life
> . . . . The world requires, and God demands, that we
> recognize the urgency to proclaim the saving word of
> God--today.[59]

The oft repeated evangelical charge that universalism
(understood in the sense that "ultimately all men will be
saved") is widely found in the ecumenical movement is certainly
not based on any official statements of the IMC-WCC.[60] Rather,
they appear to arise from a particular reading by some evangelicals of the stated willingness by Niles[61] and others to leave
the question of the salvation and judgment of all people in
God's hands, and from a disagreement with certain positions advanced by Vatican II in *Lumen Gentium*, no. 16, for example,
concerning the destiny of those outside the church. Both these
views are considered wrong.

Some theologians associated with WCC member churches may
have affirmed universal salvation, but the question of the eternal destiny of those who have not come to explicit faith in
Christ has not been explored in recent ecumenical mission theology.

Evangelical mission theology acknowledges the universal
character of God's will to save all people, but frequently also
asserts that only explicit faith in Christ makes God's intention
effective. The Lausanne Covenant states the contention this way:

> All men are perishing because of sin, but God loves all
> men, not wishing that any should perish but that all
> should repent. Yet those who reject Christ repudiate
> the joy of salvation and condemn themselves to eternal
> separation from God. To proclaim Jesus as "the Savior
> of the world" is not to affirm that all men are either
> automatically or ultimately saved, still less to affirm
> that all religions offer salvation in Christ. Rather
> it is to proclaim God's love for a world of sinners and
> to invite all men to respond to him as Savior and Lord
> in the wholehearted personal commitement of repentance
> and faith.[62]

The distinctive evangelical emphasis has been on the need
for repentance and faith as the decisive step in accepting what
God offers in Christ. From this premise it is further argued
that those who do not have explicit faith must suffer eternal
damnation--such is the implicit presupposition of the statement
that "the repudiation of universalism obliges all evangelicals
to preach the gospel to all men before they die in their sins."[63]

Roman Catholic mission theology also affirms that God wills
all people to be saved. Moreover, as we have seen,[64] Catholic

theology recognizes the possibility of salvation for those

> who through no fault of their own do not know the
> gospel of Christ or His Church, yet sincerely seek
> God and, moved by grace, strive by their deeds to
> do His will as it is known to them through the
> dictates of conscience.[65]

The Vatican II documents concerning mission do not contain material on the destiny of those who do not follow God's way as known to them through their conscience.

An appropriate understanding of the universality of the gospel remains one of the most difficult points of tension on the contemporary agenda concerning mission.[66] Those in the ecumenical movement would not accept the validity of most evangelical criticisms. The evangelical position, which apparently condemns some two-thirds of the world's population to no chance of salvation at all, is quite contrary to what other theologians understand of the will and intention of God. Yet many Protestants in varying degrees would find it difficult to support fully the Catholic position advanced at Vatican II; some would reject it believing that it does not adequately describe how salvation is brought about by Christ.

A closely related issue, dialogue, has become another important emphasis in mission theology. Understood as a way of communicating between groups, dialogue is now accepted as a necessary and helpful tool to enable people with different convictions to share together honestly and openly. Only in this way can differences based on ignorance, prejudice, and traditional antipathy be removed, especially between groups with a long history of hostility as has often prevailed between Christians and Muslims, and Christians and Jews.

At Bangkok in 1973, the CWME Assembly stated that "a desire to share and a readiness to let others share with us should inspire our witness to Christ rather than a desire to win a theological argument." Indeed, Bangkok noted with satisfaction that "mission is being carried on in a spirit of dialogue without the subsequent decrease in the sense of urgency in evangelism."[67] The Lausanne Congress also affirmed "that kind of dialogue whose purpose it is to listen sensitively in order to understand."[68] The importance Vatican II attributed to dialogue as the church's chosen means of communicating with people of other faiths and ideologies has already been noted.[69] The functional aspect of dialogue as a means of communication, enabling people of different convictions to meet freely in an atmosphere of mutual trust and respect, is the predominant emphasis in each of these affirmations.

Yet what of the theological relationship between dialogue and mission? Anton Stadler has pointed out that the approaches to mission and dialogue of both the WCC and the Roman Catholic Church failed to explore and clarify the relationship between the two.[70] Stadler's own thesis affirms that the most appropriate understanding views "mission as dialogical apologetics." In this definition dialogue allows Christians to give a coherent account of their convictions as a key to an interpretation of the world and of human existence. This thesis is based on a narrowly conceived idea of mission, shorn of any concern or desire for conversion, and is aimed at assisting Christians to become engaged "constructively and critically in the building of a more humane world thereby always witnessing to the God who promised a kingdom for all peoples."[71]

Stadler's presentation of mission as dialogue offers a proper understanding of the relationship between the two, if one recognizes that dialogue is not the *only* form of mission. Yet in fact a fuller and more adequate theological understanding of mission than Stadler presents is essential. In some situations proclamation is the most appropriate form of mission which God requires of his church and people. In others, social action holds primacy for missionary witness. So, too, in many cases dialogue has its proper place as a form--perhaps the chosen form--of Christian mission. The presuppositions of dialogue-- respect for persons, freedom to express one's own convictions, mutual trust, and honesty--are valid and important for all forms of mission. Yet to limit mission to dialogue alone unduly restricts the theological dimensions and operative patterns of mission. This whole concern for dialogue is of major practical importance in an era of mutual interdependence and interaction.

Grounding mission in God's triune nature enables one to incorporate dialogue into mission. Encounter in dialogue, as the biblical witness attests, is one pattern of God's work in the world. God is at work in the lives of all people, albeit in unknown ways, and dialogue enables the Christian to discern and respond to the realities of God's presence in the world. This in turn may help others to respond to the nature and meaning of that presence. The incarnation of Christ, in manifesting what God offers and commands, is the model for Christians' involvement in the world today.

In addition, what God has revealed in Christ is the norm for what Christians will look for in seeking to be open to the lives and religious expressions of other people. The Holy Spirit alone can convert other people to God. Christians cannot convert people--only God can do that, but they may be God's chosen instruments in that process. Yet the Spirit uses the witness which Christians offer in the encounter of dialogue.

They are admonished always to be "prepared to make a defence to
any one who calls you to account for the hope that is in you,
yet to do it with gentleness and reverence" (I Pet. 3:15).

In the greatly increased range of interreligious encounter
today, syncretism always poses a possible danger, against which
several mission conferences have warned. The Wheaton Declaration defined syncretism as

> the attempt to unite or reconcile biblically revealed
> Christian truth with the diverse or opposing tenets
> and practices of non-Christian religions or other
> systems of thought that deny it.[72]

In a similar vein, the Fifth Assembly of the WCC opposed any
"conscious or unconscious human attempts to create a new religion composed of elements taken from different religions."[73]
The basic presuppositions of syncretism, so understood, are that

> there is no unique revelation in history, that there
> are many different ways to reach the divine reality,
> that all formulations of religious truth or experience
> are by their very nature inadequate expressions of
> that truth and that it is necessary to harmonize as
> much as possible all religious ideas and experiences
> so as to create one universal religion for mankind.[74]

Hocking's notion of the reconception of all religions, "each
stimulating the other in growth toward the ultimate goal, unity
in the completest religious truth," would be an example of this
kind of syncretism.[75] There appears to be no support or move
toward such a goal among evangelicals, in the ecumenical movement, or within the Roman Catholic Church.[76]

Sometimes designated syncretism, a quite different problem
can become a pressing concern. Its essence: How can Christians communicate effectively with people who live in another
environment when this trans-cultural encounter requires expressions and concepts embedded in that other environment and religious world. This complex engagement should not be called syncretism

> if it is done with the desire to pass on the original
> message as clearly as possible and without greater
> modification of its original content than is inevi-
> table in any process of translation.[77]

This issue involves what E. A. Nida, Charles Kraft, and others
have called "dynamic equivalence" models for communicating.[78]

The final issue presented in this section concerns the
meaning of the phrase *extra ecclesiam, nulla salus* (outside the
church there is no salvation). Each of the three different
streams of mission theology have arrived at different understandings of this phrase. The evangelicals' response would be
that only those who explicitly acknowledge Christ as Lord and
Savior belong to the church and will be saved.[79] The WCC does
not have an agreed statement on this point. As the Fifth
Assembly's discussion on the extent and meaning of God's presence among people of other faiths indicated, a variety of
opinions continues to prevail among WCC members.[80] Among
these, some would support the evangelical viewpoint, while
others would affirm that some adherents of religions other than
Christianity may attain salvation.

On the Roman Catholic side, Vatican II affirmed that those
who, through no fault of their own, do not know the gospel of
Christ or his church can attain to salvation if they strive to
do God's will.[81] A major theological justification for this
view has been developed by Karl Rahner and others through the
concept of "anonymous Christians." This theological rationale
extends the bounds of the church to include all people who belong by desire or implicit faith. Clearly, on this issue no
consensus exists.

One possible answer has gathered significant support since
it was enunciated at Vatican II. It views the church as a sign
of God's saving purpose for all people, or as "the universal
sacrament of salvation."[82] On this view no other salvation
exists for the world than the one which the church proclaims
and embodies in its message and mission. Yet the church is not
understood as the only instrument or locus of salvation. Rather,
outside the saving grace of God, to which the church points in
its witness to Christ, there is no lasting hope of salvation
for humanity.

MISSION AND UNITY

That the unity of the church is a subject of major theological and practical significance is generally accepted, for
"the churches have achieved more unity in the last half century
than in at least the last nine centuries of division before
that."[83] The emergence of the ecumenical movement itself, involving the missionary movement and the movement towards unity;
the growing number of organic church unions; the mutual rediscovery of the Roman Catholic, Protestant, and Orthodox churches;
and the growing Christian fellowship in councils, groups, and
organizations--all these point to the importance unity holds
for the church today.

The close relationship between unity and mission in the
various strands of mission theology marks another point of convergence. The intertwining of the concern for mission and unity
has been evident in the ecumenical movement since the WMC in
1910, a reality which the Fifth Assembly reiterated when it recognized that "the call to evangelism, therefore, implies a . . .
commitment for visible unity."[84] The fundamental reason for
this became clear in the section report, "What Unity Requires":

> the purpose for which we are called to unity is "that
> the world may believe." A quest for unity which is not
> set in the context of Christ's promise to draw all peo-
> ple to himself would be false . . . . It is as a com-
> munity which is itself being healed that the Church can
> be God's instrument for the healing of the nations.[85]

The Lausanne Congress affirmed that "the church's visible
unity in truth is God's purpose." Linking evangelism and unity,
the Covenant stated:

> Evangelism also summons us to unity, because our one-
> ness strengthens our witness, just as our disunity
> undermines our gospel of reconciliation . . . . We
> pledge ourselves to seek a deeper *unity in truth,*
> worship, holiness and mission.[86]

Vatican II also stressed unity. The Decree *Unitatis Redintegratio* opens with the words "promoting the restoration of
unity among all Christians is one of the chief concerns" of the
Council. The Decree immediately linked this concern with mission in acknowledging that the discord of disunity "openly
contradicts the will of Christ, provides a stumbling block to
the world, and inflicts damage on the most holy cause of proclaiming the good news to every creature."[87]

These examples make clear that the concern for unity and
its close link with mission is shared by each of the traditions
under discussion. But as with other issues, understanding of
the theological nature of the point in question varies considerably. What is meant by "unity" in each instance?

The WCC has struggled with the question of unity since its
inception.[88] The Toronto Statement of 1950 declared that "membership of the World Council does not imply the acceptance of a
specific doctrine concerning the nature of Church unity." Some
churches in the WCC--notably the Orthodox--do not regard other
churches in the WCC as truly or fully valid. However, by 1961
at the Third Assembly of the WCC, the report on Unity proffered
a description of unity as a visible fellowship involving "all
in each place" and "the whole Christian fellowship in all

places and all ages."[89]   The Uppsala Assembly stressed the
"catholicity" of the church, in which Jesus Christ "constitutes
the Church which is his body as a new community of new creatures," and is thus "the sign of the coming unity of mankind."[90]
The Nairobi Assembly suggested "conciliar fellowship" as the
embodying form of this unity. This term embraced both the diversity of the church's life and the unity of the church in
Christ. As yet this unity is only partially expressed in present
interconfessional gatherings, because there is still no common
understanding of the apostolic faith, common ministry or common
eucharist.[91]

The Nairobi report recognized that "we describe this unity
in different ways." While the WCC therefore has no complete
definition of unity, it certainly envisages a visible unity of
churches in eucharist, ministry, and mission, centering in
Christ as the Head of the One Body.

The unity envisaged in the evangelical statements points to
quite a different conception. The Wheaton Declaration spoke of
the church's "essential spiritual unity." This unity is known
to Christians who have been "regenerated by the Holy Spirit and
who agree on the basic evangelical doctrines" and thus can "experience a genuine spiritual oneness," even while belonging to
different denominations.[92] No form of unity was mentioned as
an example of its "visible expression." A similar understanding
of unity appeared in the Lausanne Covenant. "Unity in truth"
means agreement on "the same biblical faith." It described
"cooperation" as the visible form of such unity involving planning, mutual encouragement, and the sharing of resources and
experience.[93]

Both Wheaton and Lausanne decried a stress on "organiza-
tional unity" which does not necessarily forward evangelism.
No one could doubt this referred to the ecumenical movement.
This has been a major criticism of the WCC by evangelicals.[94]

Considerable changes have taken place during this century
in the understanding of the Roman Catholic Church on the way in
which other Christians are to be regarded.[95] Pius XI's encyclical *Mortalium animos* (1928) declared that the only route to
Christian unity would be through the non-Catholics' acceptance
of all Catholic dogmas and return to the Roman Church. During
the next two decades, however, some interchanges between Roman
Catholics and Protestants occurred through the efforts of
scholars like Yves Marie-Joseph Congar, leading to unofficial
contacts in the 1950s,[96] before the full-fledged dialogue of the
1960s with official Roman Catholic observers at WCC meetings,
and Protestant observers participating actively in the Second
Vatican Council.

Unitatis Redintegratio marked the beginning of a new era in
the relation of the churches to one another. Instead of insisting on "return to Rome" as the only possible movement towards
unity, the Decree speaks of a movement towards Christ, in which
all participate. It is in Christ that the unity of the churches
and the entire human race will be re-established.[97] This is a
new approach to unity advanced at Vatican II, and offers considerable promise for a point of convergence in the future.

Some difficulties remain. One relates to the insistence
that through "Christ's Catholic Church alone, which is the
all-embracing means of salvation," can "the fullness of the means
of salvation . . . be obtained."[98] Specifically, "This Church,
constituted and organized in the world as a society, subsists
in the Catholic Church, which is governed by the successor of
Peter . . . ."[99] But the spirit of openness, and the recognition of the work of the Holy Spirit in other churches does encourage a joint effort to seek together "the restoration of
unity among all Christians."[100]

The differences among these views of unity are considerable.
The doctrine of the Trinity offers some insight into how these
conceptions of unity may be drawn together and related to mission. The divine providence of the Father, in which all things
will be drawn to their proper end in his Kingdom of grace and
truth, is active throughout the world and the church. The unity
of the church is given by God in Christ, who is the Head of the
Body. It is in Christ "from whom the whole body, joined and
knit together by every joint with which it is supplied, when
each part is working properly, makes bodily growth and upholds
itself in love" (Eph. 4:16), that the church finds its center
of unity. Faithfulness to Christ is essential. Yet that unity
is given as gift and task "so that the world may believe."
Unity is given and required for the sake of mission. The church
does not bring about the unity of mankind, but through its own
unity witnesses to its reality in Christ. Thus, the church,
embodying unity, becomes the servant of Christ through which the
Spirit can work. One should expect diversity in the church because of the gifts of the Spirit (I Cor. 12:1-13), yet find that
its very diversity contributes to the mission of God in Christ,
who is "reconciling the world to himself" (II Cor. 5:19).

CONCLUSION

The developments here surveyed in mission theology have
occurred as a result of external and internal forces at work in
the world and in the churches. Changing political circumstances
have made it evident that a new relationship between churches
in different parts of the world is necessary. The social context and intellectual climate in which the mission of the church

must take place have demanded new responses and forms of missionary activity. Within the churches, theological influences and the emerging strength and vitality of churches in Africa, Asia, and Latin America have called for different patterns of mission. All these forces will continue to create a dynamic situation requiring a continuing response in terms of mission theology.

The developments traced and analyzed in this work have led to the conclusion that there is a significant convergence on the importance of several issues in mission theology today. These relate to the trinitarian basis of mission theology, the importance of the church as the bearer of the *missio Dei*, a comprehensive understanding of mission involving evangelism and social action, and the need to use dialogue as a means of communication between Christians and people of other faiths and ideologies, and the conviction that unity and mission are closely related in God's plan for the church.

Considerable tension exists regarding each of these points, however, because there is much less agreement concerning the appropriate understanding and meaning involved at each point. Mission theology within the ecumenical movement, evangelicalism, and Roman Catholicism has developed a common agenda--the discussion of that agenda among (and within) the various traditions will now continue.[101]

The theological statements developed in the WCC, at Lausanne, and in the Roman Catholic Church are themselves each the result of discussion, debate, and compromise. There is no *one* position in any tradition, although the main pattern and trend of each of the three views is clear in contrast to the others.

Within each group a pluralism of opinion exists and this pluralism is now far more evident, especially in contrast to the monolithic character of each which seemed to have existed to the eyes of outside observers in recent years. The voices of Christians from Asia, Africa, and Latin America will continue to be heard more strongly and clearly in future discussions. They will bring further pluralism within each group.

Yet this debate concerning mission theology is merely a means of arriving at a clearer understanding of what the church must *be*. Theology has the task of criticizing and clarifying the church's witness of faith, thus enabling the church to be faithful to the gospel of Jesus Christ and responsive to the context in which that gospel is to be communicated. To participate in the *missio Dei* is the church's continuing vocation. It does so as a witness to that love which originates in the Father, is revealed in the Son, and is empowered by the Holy Spirit.

In fulfilling that mission Christians will do well to remember these words of Paul Althaus:

> The gospel is not an objective, universal truth,
> which one can pass on in the form of ideas, but
> rather the personal reality of God's sacrifice, the
> love that gives itself and bears our burden. So
> also this truth of the gospel can be proclaimed only
> in one's whole personal attitude toward people. The
> message of God's mercy, as it was a bodily, personal
> reality in Christ, must repeatedly become embodied
> in the love that seeks the lost. The credibility of
> the church when it preaches God's love for the lost
> depends on whether the church itself goes out to people
> in their lostness, identifies itself with them, and in
> a priestly way makes their predicament its own. In
> seeking, human love, God's love is understood. The
> incarnation can be preached and believed only in the
> degree to which it is lived in the preaching.
>
> The Word and its embodiment belong together, not
> only in the individual preacher, but also in the church
> as a whole. The preaching church is at the same time
> the serving church, which takes upon itself the need of
> people and in every way seeks to set up signs of the
> love of Christ in the world. This is precisely the
> meaning and intent of its service. It is intended
> to be understood as witness.[102]

Christian mission is embodied in the living obedience of faith of individuals and churches, as they share in God's plan to unite all things in Christ by the power of the Holy Spirit.

NOTES

[1]This may be an indication of the cross-fertilization of theological ideas from one tradition to another. The influence of people such as John R. W. Stott, who had been involved in the ecumenical debate on mission and presented the keynote address at Lausanne on "The Biblical Basis of Evangelism," may be important in improving such dialogue. See Stott, *Christian Mission in the Modern World*, p. 9.

[2]See John V. Taylor, *The Go-Between God: The Holy Spirit and the Christian Mission* (Philadelphia: Fortress Press, 1973), pp. 36-37.

[3]Carl E. Braaten, *The Flaming Center: A Theology of the Christian Mission* (Philadelphia: Fortress Press, 1977) noted

the importance of this point at several places.

[4]See the paper by René Padilla, "Evangelism in the World" in *Lausanne, 1974*, pp. 114-146, for an instructive outline of the ways in which the world is understood in the New Testament, and the role of evangelism in the world today.

[5]"The Biblical Basis of Evangelism" in *Lausanne, 1974*, pp. 66-68; and *Christian Mission in the Modern World*, pp. 22-25.

[6]*Lausanne, 1974*, p. 5.

[7]*Wheaton, 1966*, p. 228.

[8]*Lausanne, 1974*, p. 5.

[9]See pp. 310-12; cf. Braaten, *The Flaming Center*, pp. 105-106.

[10]See, for example, Avery Dulles, "Current Trends in Mission Theology," *Theology Digest* 20.1 (1972):   26-29.

[11]This issue has certainly been raised before. See Latham, *God for All Men*, p. 19; the Zurich "Aide Mémoire," par. 11; and the WCC Central Committee 1971, "Interim Policy Statement and Guide-lines" on Dialogue, par. 12.

[12]See, for example, the Appendix to "The Witness of Christians to Men of Other Faiths" in *Mexico City, 1963*, p. 149, and *Nairobi, 1975*, p. 76.

[13]*Lumen Gentium*, no. 16.

[14]See *Gaudium et Spes*, nos. 11-17, and *Dignitatis Humanae* nos. 3, 9.

[15]For example, Henri Godin and Yves Daniel's work, entitled *La France, Pays de Mission?* (*Is France a Mission Land?*); they answered "yes" in 1943.

[16]See Wong, *Missions From the Third World*, especially chap. 4, "Historical Perspectives," and Alan R. Tippett, *The Deep Sea Canoe: The Story of Third World Missionaries in the South Pacific* (Pasadena: William Carey Library, 1977).

[17]Some would prefer the term "contextualizing" to refer to this process of relating Christianity to a particular cultural situation. See *Mission Trends No. 3*, ed. by Anderson and Stransky, for essays by Shoki Coe, Jung Lee, E. W. Fashole-Luke, and Choan-Seng Song on this issue. The Theological Education

Fund has made this a major emphasis of its work. In a vivid
parable, D. T. Niles spoke of the seed of the gospel taking
root in European, African, Asian, and other soils.

[18]See the exchange between M. M. Thomas and Lesslie Newbigin, "Salvation and Humanization: A Discussion," in Anderson
and Stransky, *Mission Trends No. 1*, pp. 217-229, about the
meaning of phrases such as "a Christ-centered secular fellowship outside the Church."

[19]*Lausanne, 1974*, p. 8 in par. 14, "The Power of the Holy
Spirit."

[20]*Lumen Gentium*, no. 31; see the whole of chapter 4, "The
Laity," and *Gaudium et Spes*, no. 43.

[21]See *Medellín* II, no. 10, "Lay Movements."

[22]See p. 191-193, above.

[23]*Lausanne, 1974*, p. 679.

[24]See Ralph D. Winter, "The Two Structures of God's
Redemptive Mission," *Missiology* 2.1 (1974): 121-39; cf. "The
New Missions and the Mission of the Church," IRM 60.237 (1971):
89-100.

[25]See, for example, Peters, *Saturation Evangelism*, p. 70;
also Edward C. Pentecost, "Time for Faith Boards to Change
Goals and Strategies," EMQ 12.4 (1976): 211-217.

[26]Peters, "Issues Confronting Evangelical Missions,"
p. 158, in Coggins and Frizen, *Evangelical Missions Tomorrow*.

[27]Edward R. Dayton, "Current Trends in North American
Protestant Ministries Overseas," p. 6.

[28]See that part of Paul's *Ecclesiae Sanctae* relating to
missionary activity in Flannery, *Documents of Vatican II*,
pp. 857-62.

[29]See Johnson, *Uppsala to Nairobi*, pp. 162-77.

[30]See, for example, *Berlin* I, p. 5; *Lausanne, 1974*, p. 5.

[31]The Lausanne Committee has a "Strategy Working Group"
which hopes to develop comprehensive data on research and
strategy. For an introduction to this group's work, see
"Strategizing For World Evangelism" by C. Peter Wagner in
World Evangelization (Oct. 1977): 3-4, 9.

[32]*Lausanne, 1974*, p. 445.

[33]Lesslie Newbigin, "From the Editor," IRM 54.216 (1965): 422; cf. the concise statement on this subject by Visser 't Hooft to the Fourth Assembly in *Uppsala Report, 1968*, pp. 317-318.

[34]*Bangkok, 1973*, p. 88.

[35]*Nairobi, 1975*, p. 43.

[36]For a thorough analysis of these terms see Arthur F. Glasser, "Confession, Church Growth, and Authentic Unity in Missionary Strategy" in Norman A. Horner, ed., *Protestant Crosscurrents in Mission* (Nashville: Abingdon Press, 1968), pp. 178-88; cf. Mooneyham in *Lausanne, 1974*, p. 445.

[37]*Wheaton, 1966*, p. 235.

[38]*Lausanne, 1974*, p. 5.

[39]*Wheaton, 1966*, p. 233.

[40]*Lausanne, 1974*, p. 4; cf. John R. W. Stott's definition: "Evangelism is to preach the gospel," *Christian Mission in the Modern World*, p. 39.   Stott's discussion of evangelism in this book provides a helpful delineation of some aspects of the evangelistic task.

[41]*Willingen, 1952*, p. 220.

[42]Philip Potter has correctly noted the terms "mission," "witness," and "evangelism" have often been used interchangeably in ecumenical literature.   See "Evangelism and the World Council of Churches," ER 20.2 (1968):   176.

[43]*Nairobi, 1975*, p. 52.

[44]Ibid., p. 52.

[45]*Evangelii Nuntiandi*, p. 16.

[46]Ibid., p. 19.

[47]Suggested by José Miguez-Bonino in "The Church and the Latin American Social Revolution" in *The Church and Social Revolution*, Perkins School of Theology Senior Colloquy, 1967.

[48]On the Programme to Combat Racism and other WCC social action responsibilities, see Johnson, *Uppsala to Nairobi*, pp. 152-77, and Elizabeth Adler, *A Small Beginning* (Geneva: WCC, 1974).

[49]See Chapter VI, footnote 62, for a list of groups and publications.

[50]"Response to Bishop Mortimer Arias," IRM 65.257 (1976): 33.

[51]Miguez-Bonino, *Christians and Marxists*, pp. 92-94.

[52]Ibid., p. 116. This judgment is open to question in view of the Platonic philosophical background common to both Christianity and Marxism.

[53]Ibid., p. 119.

[54]*Lusaka, 1974*, p. 7.

[55]*Fifth Assembly*, p. 52.

[56]*Gaudium et Spes*, nos. 21, 23-32, 65-72.

[57]Ibid., no. 21.

[58]Niles, *Upon the Earth*, pp. 92-98, provides a good representative development of this argument.

[59]*Nairobi, 1975*, pp. 54-55. Such a view accepts completely Luther's statement that the Christian's "first and highest work of love is to bring others to faith even as he has come to it" --quoted by Schubert Ogden in the second of a lecture series entitled, "Faith and Freedom: Towards a Liberation Theology," at Perkins School of Theology, 1977.

[60]Harold Lindsell, "Universalism," *Lausanne, 1974*, p. 1206; cf. Arthur M. Climenhaga, "Mission--and Neo-Universalism," *Wheaton, 1966*, p. 96-110; and Louis L. King, "Neo Universalism: Its Exponents, Tenets and Threats to Missions," EMQ 1.4 (1964): 2-12.

[61]Niles, *Upon the Earth*, pp. 96-97. Many in the ecumenical movement would probably agree with John Wesley's point concerning the destiny of those who have never heard of Christ:

> that sentence, "He that believeth not shall be damned," is spoken of them to whom the Gospel is preached. Others it does not concern; and we are not required to determine anything touching their final state. How it will please God, then Judge of all, to deal with *them*, we may leave to God himself. But this we know, that he is not the God of the Christians only, but the God of the Heathens also; that he is "rich in mercy to all that call upon him," according to the light they have; and

that "in every nation, he that feareth God and worketh
righteousness is accepted of him."

From the Sermon "On Charity" (I: 3) in *The Works of John
Wesley*, vol. 7, (Grand Rapids: Zondervan, 1958-59), p. 48;
cf. also Wesley's sermon "On Living Without God," par. 14,
ibid., p. 353, where he stated: "I have no authority from the
Word of God 'to judge those that are without' [the Christian
dispensation]; nor do I conceive that any man living has the
right to sentence all the heathen and Mohametan world to
damnation."

Lindsell argued that Karl Barth's doctrine of election
leads to universalism. For a discussion of Barth's view of
universal salvation, see George Marvin Atkinson, "The Concept
of Christian Hope in Karl Barth's *Die Kirchliche Dogmatik*"
(Ph.D.: Southern Methodist University, 1975), pp. 251-55.

Charles Forman briefly outlines some changes in American
mission theology on this point in "A History of Foreign Mission
Theory in America," pp. 85-86 in Beaver, *American Missions in
Bicentennial Perspective*.

[62]*Lausanne, 1974*, p. 4; cf. p. 118.

[63]*Wheaton, 1966*, p. 225.

[64]See pp. 310-312, above.

[65]*Lumen Gentium*, no. 16.

[66]Braaten, *The Flaming Center*, p. 114, describes the tension as arising from an emphasis on particularity and universality, both grounded in the New Testament. His own constructive position is not clear, despite the claim that "the truth is
one which views the church as embodying *both* particular and
universal aspects" of the gospel.

[67]*Bangkok, 1973*, p. 79.

[68]*Lausanne, 1974*, p. 4.

[69]See p. 306.

[70]Stadler, *Mission-Dialogue*, esp. chapter 3. The questions
raised by the "Aide-Mémoire" of the Zurich Consultation in 1970,
prepared by ecumenical and Roman Catholic theologians, have
never been adequately addressed; see Samartha, *Living Faiths*,
pp. 36-40.

[71]Stadler, *Mission-Dialogue*, pp. 364-372.

[72]*Wheaton, 1966*, pp. 222.

[73]*Nairobi, 1975*, p. 73.

[74]W. A. Visser 't Hooft, *No Other Name: The Choice Between Syncretism and Christian Universalism* (Philadelphia: Westminster Press, 1963), p. 11.

[75]Hocking, *Re-Thinking Missions*, p. 44.

[76]Yet see William John Schmidt, "Ecumenicity and Syncretism: The Confrontation of the Ecumenical Movement with Syncretism in Special Reference to the International Missionary Council and World Council of Churches" (Ph.D: Columbia University, 1966).

[77]Visser 't Hooft, *No Other Name*, p. 11.

[78]See, for example, E. A. Nida, *Towards a Science of Translating* (Leiden: E. J. Brill, 1964); Charles Kraft, "Dynamic Equivalence Churches," *Missiology* 1.1 (1973): 39-57. For another approach to the same problem, see W. A. Visser 't Hooft, "Accommodation--True and False," *South East Asia Journal of Theology* 8.3 (1967): 5-18.

[79]Such a response is implied by the statement that "the repudiation of universalism obliges all evangelicals to preach the gospel to all men before they die in their sins. To fail to do this is to accept in practice what we deny in principle," *Wheaton, 1966*, p. 225.

[80]*Nairobi, 1975*, p. 76.

[81]*Lumen Gentium*, no. 16.

[82]Ibid., no. 48; cf. nos. 1 and 9.

[83]Barry Till, *The Churches Search For Unity* (Harmondsworth: Penguin Books, 1972), p. 523.

[84]*Nairobi, 1975*, p. 53.

[85]Ibid., p. 64.

[86]*Lausanne, 1974*, p. 5 (italics added).

[87]*Unitatis Redintegratio*, no. 1.

[88]See John Basil Meeking, "The Self-Understanding of the

World Council of Churches" (Ph.D.: Pontificiam Universitatem a St. Thoma, Rome, 1966); cf. Meredith B. Handspicker, "Faith and Order 1948-1968" in Fey, *Ecumenical Advance*, pp. 147-51.

[89]*New Delhi, 1961*, p. 116.

[90]*Uppsala Report, 1968*, pp. 13, 17-18.

[91]*Nairobi, 1975*, pp. 60-61. For some insight into the progress being made in Faith and Order studies, see *One Baptism, One Eucharist, and a Mutually Recognized Ministry: Three Agreed Statements* (Geneva: WCC, 1975). The ecclesiological significance of the various bodies of the ecumenical movement has not been adequately considered. A start has been made in *The Ecclesiological Significance of Councils of Churches* (National Council of the Churches of Christ in the U.S.A., 1963) and Lukas Vischer, "Christian Councils--Instruments of Ecclesial Communion," ER 24.1 (1972): 72-87.

[92]*Wheaton, 1966*, p. 231.

[93]*Lausanne, 1974*, p. 5.

[94]See Harald Christian Andreas Frey's study, "Critiques of Conciliar Ecumenism by Conservative Evangelicals in the United States," (Th.D.: Boston University School of Theology, 1961), pp. 53, 141; and J. Marcellus Kik, *Ecumenism and the Evangelical* (Philadelphia: Presbyterian and Reformed Publishing Co., 1958), pp. 4-5, 44, 90.

[95]See Paul M. Minus, Jr., *The Catholic Rediscovery of Protestantism: A History of Roman Catholic Ecumenical Pioneering* (New York: Paulist Press, 1976).

[96]Visser 't Hooft in his *Memoirs*, p. 328, tells of a secret meeting between himself and Cardinal Bea at a convent in Milan in 1960.

[97]*Unitatis Redintegratio*, no. 2; cf. *Lumen Gentium*, nos. 13, 48.

[98]*Unitatis Redintegratio*, no. 3.

[99]*Lumen Gentium*, no. 8.

[100]*Unitatis Redintegratio*, no. 1.

[101]One sign of this continuing conversation is a recent four-day consultation between Catholics and evangelicals in Venice which was reported in *Global Report of the World Evangelical Fellowship* (Nov. 1977).

[102]Paul Althaus, *Die Christlich Wahrheit*, vol. 2 (Gütersloh: C. Bertelsmann, 1949), p. 322.

Appendix

Bibliography

In addition to the works referred to in the text of this book, a number of related dissertations and other books directly concerned with mission theology have also been included in the bibliography.

The references are divided thus:

The primary sources have been arranged in chronological order; all secondary literature is in alphabetical order. Moreover, not all secondary materials in the text have been included in the bibliography.

PRIMARY SOURCES

1. Ecumenical

Edinburgh 1910

World Missionary Conference, 1910. 9 vols. Edinburgh: Oliphant, Anderson & Ferrier/New York: Revell, 1910.

International Missionary Council

Minutes of the International Missionary Council. London: International Missionary Council, 1921-1961; including Minutes of the Committee of the Council and of the *Ad Interim* Committee.

Beach, Harlan P., and Fahs, Charles H., eds. *World Missionary Atlas.* New York: Institute of Social and Religious Research, 1925.

The Jerusalem Meeting of the IMC March 24-April 8, 1928. 8 vols. London: International Missionary Council, 1928.

Kraemer, Hendrik. *The Christian Message in a Non-Christian World.* New York: Harper & Brothers, 1938.

The Madras Series. Presenting Papers Based upon the Meeting of the International Missionary Council at Tambaram, India, December 12 to 29, 1938. 7 vols. New York/London: International Missionary Council, 1939.

The World Mission of the Church. Findings and Recommendations of the International Missionary Council Tambaram, Madras, India, December 12 to 29, 1938. London: International Missionary Council, 1939.

Ranson, C. W., ed. *Renewal and Advance: Christian Witness in a Revolutionary World.* London: Edinburgh House Press, 1948.

Goodall, Norman, ed. *Missions Under the Cross. Addresses delivered at the Enlarged Meeting of the Committee of the International Missionary Council at Willingen, in Germany, 1952; with Statements issued by the Meeting.* London: International Missionary Council, 1953.

Payne, Ernest A., and Moses, David G. *Why Integration? An explanation of the proposal before the World Council of Churches and the International Missionary Council.* London: Edinburgh House Press, 1957.

Orchard, Ronald K., ed. *The Ghana Assembly of the International*

Missionary Council 28 December to 8 January, 1958. Selected Papers with an Essay on the Role of the International Missionary Council. London: Edinburgh House Press, 1958.

World Council of Churches

The Ten Formative Years: 1938-1948. Report on the activities of the World Council of Churches during its period of formation. Geneva: World Council of Churches, 1948.

Man's Disorder and God's Design. The Amsterdam Assembly Series. A one volume edition covering the four sections. New York: Harper & Brothers, n.d. [1948].

Visser 't Hooft, W. A., ed. *The Second Assembly of the World Council of Churches held at Amsterdam August 22 to September 4, 1948.* New York: Harper & Brothers, 1949.

Minutes of the Central Committee of the World Council of Churches. Geneva: World Council of Churches, 1948-1977.

The First Six Years: 1948-1954. A Report of the Central Committee of the World Council of Churches on the activities of the Departments and Secretariats of the Council. Geneva: World Council of Churches, 1954.

The Christian Hope and the Task of the Church: Six Ecumenical Surveys and the Report of the Assembly. New York: Harper & Brothers, 1954.

Visser 't Hooft, W. A., ed. *The Evanston Report. The Second Report of the World Council of Churches, 1954.* London: SCM, 1954.

A Theological Reflection on the Work of Evangelism. World Council of Churches Division of Studies Bulletin 5.1 and 2 (Nov. 1959).

Theological Reflections on the Missionary Task of the Church. World Council of Churches Division of Studies Bulletin 7.2 (1961): 1-17.

Evanston to New Delhi: 1954-1961. Report of the Central Committee to the Third Assembly of the World Council of Churches. Geneva: World Council of Churches, 1961.

Visser 't Hooft, W. A., ed. *The New Delhi Report: The Third Assembly of the World Council of Churches, 1961.* New York: Association Press, 1962.

Blauw, Johannes. *The Missionary Nature of the Church: A Survey of a Biblical Theology of Mission.* New York: McGraw-Hill, 1962.

Niles, D. T. *Upon the Earth: The Mission of God and the Missionary Enterprise of the Churches*. New York: McGraw-Hill, 1962.

Wieser, Thomas, ed. *Planning for Mission: Working Papers on the New Quest for Missionary Communities*. New York: US Conference for the World Council of Churches, 1966.

The Church for Others and the Church for the World: A Quest for Missionary Structures for Missionary Congregations. Final Report of the Western European Working Group and North American Working Group of the Department on Studies in Evangelism. Geneva: World Council of Churches, 1968.

Drafts for Sections. Prepared for the Fourth Assembly of the World Council of Churches, Uppsala, Sweden, 1968. Geneva: World Council of Churches, n.d.

New Delhi to Uppsala: 1961-1968. Report of the Central Committee to the Fourth Assembly of the World Council of Churches. Geneva: World Council of Churches, 1968.

Goodall, Norman, ed. *The Uppsala Report 1968: Official Report of the Fourth Assembly of the World Council of Churches, Uppsala, July 4-20, 1968*. Geneva: World Council of Churches, 1968.

Uppsala Speaks: Section Reports of the Fourth Assembly of the World Council of Churches, Uppsala, 1968. 2nd rev. ed. Geneva: World Council of Churches/New York: Friendship Press, 1968.

"Renewal in Mission." *Ecumenical Review* 21.4 (1969): 362-67. This is the final text of Uppsala, Section II.

The Humanum Studies: 1969-1975. A Collection of Documents. Geneva: World Council of Churches, 1975.

Jesus Christ Frees and Unites: Section dossiers for the Fifth Assembly of the World Council of Churches. Geneva: World Council of Churches, n.d.

Johnson, David Enderton, gen. ed. *Uppsala to Nairobi: 1968-1975. Report of the Central Committee to the Fifth Assembly of the World Council of Churches*. New York: Friendship Press/London: SPCK, 1975.

Paton, David M., ed. *Breaking Barriers. Nairobi 1975. The Official Report of the Fifth Assembly of the World Council of Churches, Nairobi 23 November-10 December 1975*. London:

SPCK/Grand Rapids: Eerdmans, 1976.

Commission on World Mission and Evangelism

Orchard, R. K., ed. *Witness in Six Continents: Records of the Meeting of the Commission on World Mission and Evangelism of the World Council of Churches held in Mexico City 8-19 December 1963.* London: Edinburgh House Press, 1964.

Latham, Robert O. *God for All Men.* London: Edinburgh House Press, 1964.

"Tell Out, Tell Out My Glory." *Risk* 9.3 (1972).

From Mexico City to Bangkok. Report of the Commission on World Mission and Evangelism, 1963-1972. Geneva: World Council of Churches, 1972.

Bangkok Assembly, 1973. Minutes and Report of the Assembly of the Commission on World Mission and Evangelism of the World Council of Churches December 31, 1972 and January 9-12, 1973. Geneva: World Council of Churches, 1973.

Faith and Order

Bate, H. N., ed. *Faith and Order: Proceedings of the World Conference, Lausanne, August 3-21, 1927.* New York: G. H. Doran, 1927.

Hodgeson, Leonard, ed. *The Second World Conference on Faith and Order held at Edinburgh August 2-18, 1937.* New York: Macmillan, 1938.

Tomkins, Oliver S., ed. *The Third World Conference on Faith and Order. Held at Lund August 15 to 28. 1952.* London: SCM, 1953.

Minear, Paul S., ed. *The Nature of the Unity We Seek: Official Report of the North American Conference on Faith and Order 3-10 September 1957, Oberlin, Ohio.* St. Louis: Bethany Press, 1958.

Vischer, Lukas, ed. *A Documentary History of the Faith and Order Movement 1927-1963.* St. Louis: Bethany Press, 1963.

Rodger, P. C., and Vischer, Lukas, eds. *The Fourth World Conference on Faith and Order, Montreal, 1963.* New York: Association Press, 1964.

New Directions in Faith and Order: Bristol 1967. Reports--Minutes--Documents.. Faith and Order Paper No. 50. Geneva: World Council of Churches, 1968.

*Faith and Order: Louvain 1971. Study Reports and Documents. Faith
    and Order Paper No. 59.* Geneva: World Council of Churches, 1971.

*Uniting in Hope: Accra 1974. Reports and Documents from the
    Meeting of the Faith and Order Commission, 23 July--5 August,
    1974. Faith and Order Paper No. 72.* Geneva: World Coun-
    cil of Churches, 1975.

                  The World's Student Christian Federation

Rouse, Ruth. *The World's Student Christian Federation.*
    London: SCM, 1948.

Thomas, M. M., and McCaughey, J. D. *The Christian in the World
    Struggle.* Geneva: WSCF, 1950.

*Witnessing in the University Communities: A Report on the Life
    of the WSCF and Related National SCMs During the Years
    1949-1952.* Geneva: WSCF, mimeographed.

*Witnessing to Jesus Christ the Reconciler: A Report on the
    Life of the WSCF and Related National SCMs During the Years
    1953-1956.* Geneva: WSCF, mimeographed.

The Life and Mission of the Church. Geneva: WSCF, mimeo-
    graphed, 0.763.VI.57.

History's Lessons for Tomorrow's Mission. Geneva: WSCF, [1960].

                          Church and Society

Bell, G. K. A., ed. *The Stockholm Conference 1925; the Offi-
    cial Report of the Universal Christian Conference on Life
    and Work held in Stockholm, 19-30 August 1925.* London:
    Oxford University Press, 1926.

The Church, Community, and State Series. 7 vols. London:
    George Allen & Unwin, 1937.

Oldham, J. H., ed. *The Churches Survey Their Task: The Report
    of the Conference at Oxford, July 1937 on Church, Community,
    and State.* London: George Allen & Unwin, 1937.

Albrecht, Paul. *The Churches and Rapid Social Change.* Garden
    City, N.Y.: Doubleday, 1961.

Bennett, John C., ed. *Christian Social Ethics in a Changing
    World: An Ecumenical Inquiry.* New York: Association
    Press/London: SCM, 1966.

Matthews, Z. K., ed. *Responsible Government in a Revolutionary Age*. New York: Association Press/London: SCM, 1966.

Munby, Denys, ed. *Economic Growth in World Perspective*. New York: Association Press/London: SCM, 1966.

de Vries, Egbert, ed. *Man in the Community: Christian Concern for the Human in Changing Society*. New York: Association Press/London: SCM, 1966.

World Conference on Church and Society: Christians in the Technical and Social Revolutions of Our Time. Geneva, July 12-16, 1966. The Official Report with a Description of the Conference by M. M. Thomas and Paul Abrecht. Geneva: World Council of Churches, 1967.

Dialogue

Hallencreutz, C. F. *New Approaches to Men of Other Faiths: A Theological Discussion, 1938-1968*. Research Booklet No. 18. Geneva: World Council of Churches, 1970.

Samartha, S. J., ed. *Living Faiths and the Ecumenical Movement*. Geneva: World Council of Churches, 1971.

_____. *Dialogue Between Men of Living Faiths: Papers Presented at a Consultation held at Ajaltoun, Lebanon, March 1970*. Geneva: World Council of Churches, 1971.

Samartha, S. J., and Taylor, J. B., eds. *Christian-Muslim Dialogue: Papers Presented at the Broumana Consultation, 12-18 July 1972*. Geneva: World Council of Churches, 1973.

Samartha, S. J., ed. *Living Faiths and Ultimate Goals. A Continuing Dialogue*. Geneva: World Council of Churches, 1974.

_____. *Towards World Community: The Colombo Papers*. Geneva: World Council of Churches, 1975.

The Wholeness of Human Life: Papers Presented at the Ibadan Consultation with Special Reference to African Traditional Religion. Ibadan: Daystar Press, n.d.

Africa

Smith, Edwin W. *The Christian Message in Africa. A Study Based on the Work of the International Conference at Le Zoute, Belgium 14-21 September 1926*. London: International Missionary Council, 1926.

*The Church in Changing Africa: Report of the All-Africa Church
Conference held at Ibadan, Nigeria January 10-19, 1958.*
New York: International Missionary Council, n.d.

*Drumbeats from Kampala: Report of the First Assembly of AACC.
Held at Kampala April 20 to April 30, 1963.* London:
Lutterworth, 1963.

Engagement: The Second AACC Assembly, 'Abidjan 1969.' Nairobi:
AACC, 1969.

*Evangelization of "Frontier Situations in Africa": Report of a
Consultation Organized by the AACC, 15-19 December 1973,
Nairobi, Kenya.* Compiled and edited by George K. Mambo and
Wanjiru Matenjwa. Nairobi: AACC, 1974.

*The Struggle Continues: Official Report of the Third Assembly
of the AACC Lusaka-Zambia 12-24 May 1974.* Nairobi: AACC,
1975.

*Structures of Injustice: A Report of a Consultation on Viola-
tions of Human Rights held in Khartoum, Sudan, 16-22 February 1975.* AACC: mimeographed copy, n.d.

A Time for Self-Reliance: AACC 1975-78. Nairobi: AACC, 1975.

                              Asia

*The Christian Prospect in East Asia: Papers and Minutes of the
Eastern Asia Christian Conference, Bangkok, December 3-11,
1949.* New York: Friendship Press, 1950.

*Christ--The Hope of Asia: Papers and Minutes of the Ecumenical
Study Conference for East Asia, Lucknow, India, December
27-30, 1953.* Madras: Christian Literature Society, 1953.

*The Common Evangelistic Task of the Churches in East Asia:
Prapat, Indonesia 17-26 March 1957.* EACC, n.d.

Than, U Kyaw, ed. *Witnesses Together: Being the Official Report of the Inaugural Assembly of the EACC, held at Kuala
Lumpur, Malaya, May 14-24, 1959.* Rangoon: EACC, 1959.

*A Decisive Hour for the Christian Mission: The EACC 1959 and
the John R. Mott Memorial Lectures.* London: SCM, 1960.

*Reports of Situation Conferences: Convened by the EACC
February-March, 1963.* EACC, n.d.

Fleming, John, ed. *Structures for a Missionary Congregation.*

Singapore: EACC, 1964.

Assembly of the East Asia Christian Conference held at Bangkok, Thailand from 25 February to 5 March 1964. Minutes. Part One. Bangkok: Van Chalerm Kanchanamongkol, n.d.

The Christian Community within the Human Community. Containing Statements from the Bangkok Assembly of the EACC February-March 1964. Minutes. Part Two. Bangalore: Christian Literature Society, 1964.

Confessing the Faith in Asia Today: Statement issued by the Consultation Convened by the EACC and held in Hong Kong October 25-November 3, 1966. Redfern: Epworth Press, 1967.

In Christ All Things Hold Together: Bangkok 1968. Statements and Findings of the Fourth Assembly of the EACC. EACC, n.d.

Than, U Kyaw. *Joint Laborers in Hope: A Report of the EACC 1968-1973.* Bangkok: CCA, 1973.

Christian Conference of Asia Fifth Assembly: 6-12 June 1973 Singapore. Bangkok: CCA, 1973.

Christian Action in the Asian Struggle. Singapore: CCA, 1973.

Latin America

Beach, Harlan P. *Renascent Latin America: An Outline and Interpretation of the Congress on Christian Work in Latin America, held at Panama, 19-29 February 1916.* New York: Missionary Education Movement of the US and Canada, 1916.

Speer, Robert E.; Inman, Samuel G.; and Sanders, K. Frank; eds. *Christian Work in South America at Montevideo, Uruguay, April 1925.* 2 vols. New York: Fleming H. Revell, 1925.

Hacia la Renovacion Religiosa en Hispano-Americo. A Report on the Congress Evangelico Hispano-Americano, Havana 1929. Mexico: CUPSA, 1930.

El Cristianismo en la America Latina. Buenos Aires: La Aurora, 1949.

Christians and Social Change in Latin America: Findings of the First Latin American Evangelical Consultation on Church and Society 23-27 July 1961, Huampani, Peru. Montevideo: Latin American Commission on Church and Society/Geneva: WCC, n.d.

Cristo, la esperanza para la America Latina. Buenos Aires: Confederacion Evangelica del Rio de la Plata, 1963 (CELA II).

Pacific

Beyond the Reef: Records of the Conference of Churches and Missions in the Pacific Malua Theological College, Western Samoa, 22 April-4 May 1961. London: International Missionary Council, 1961.

The Fourth World Meets: The Report of the Pacific Conference of Churches Assembly, Davui Levu, Fiji, 1-4 May 1971. Suva: Pacific Council of Churches, 1972.

Market Basket Media: The Report of the Evaluation Conference on Christian Communication in the Pacific, Suva, Fiji. Honoria: Provincial Press, n.d.

SPADES: South Pacific Action for Development Strategy. A Report of the Conference on Development in Vila, New Hebrides in January 1973. Pacific Council of Churches, n.d.

Report of the Third Assembly: The Pacific Council of Churches. Suva, Fiji: Pacific Council of Churches, 1976.

2. Evangelical

Interdenominational Foreign Mission Association

Kane, J. Herbert. *Faith, Mighty Faith: A Handbook of the Interdenominational Foreign Mission Association.* New York: IFMA, 1956.

Percy, J. O., compiler; Bennett, Mary, ed. *Facing the Unfinished Task. Messages Delivered at the Congress on World Mission. Sponsored by the IFMA of North America.* Grand Rapids: Zondervan, 1961.

IFMA Study Papers, 1967. 50th Annual Meeting 25-28 September 1967 held at Grace Chapel, Havertown, Pennsylvania. IFMA, mimeographed.

Evangelical Foreign Mission Association

Murch, James DeForest. *Cooperation Without Compromise: A History of the National Association of Evangelicals.* Grand Rapids: Eerdmans, 1956.

The Church's Worldwide Mission,
Wheaton, 1966

Lindsell, Harold, ed. *The Church's Worldwide Mission: Proceedings of the Congress on the Church's Worldwide Mission,
4-16 April (1966) at Wheaton College, Wheaton, Illinois.*
Waco, Tx.: Word Books, 1966.

World Congress on Evangelism,
Berlin, 1966

Henry, Carl F. H., and Mooneyham, W. Stanley, eds. *One Race,
One Gospel, One Task. World Congress on Evangelism,
Berlin, 1966.* 2 vols. Minneapolis: World Wide Publica-
tions, 1967.

International Congress on World Evangelization,
Lausanne, 1974

Douglas, J. D., ed. *Let the Earth Hear His Voice: International
Congress on World Evangelization Lausanne, Switzerland.
Official Reference Volume: Papers and Responses.* Minnea-
polis: World Wide Publications, 1975.

Intervarsity Christian Fellowship

Johnson, Douglas, ed. *A Brief History of the International
Fellowship of Evangelical Students.* Lausanne: Inter-
varsity Fellowship of Evangelical Students, 1964.

Church Growth

Pickett, J. W.; Warnshuis, A. L.; Singh, A. L.; and McGavran,
D. A. *Church Growth and Group Conversion.* 5th ed.
Pasadena: William Carey Library, 1973. (First published
in 1936.)

McGavran, Donald A. *The Bridges of God: A Study in the Strategy
of Mission.* New York: Friendship Press, 1955.

_____. *How Churches Grow: The New Frontiers of Mission.*
London: World Dominion Press, 1959.

_____. *Understanding Church Growth.* Grand Rapids: Eerdmans,
1970.

_____, ed. *The Conciliar-Evangelical Debate: The Crucial
Documents 1967-1976.* Pasadena: William Carey Library,
1977.

Africa

Principles and Practice in New Life For All. Jos, Nigeria:
New Life For All, 1968.

"Nairobi, December 1976." *Missiology* 5.2 (1977) contains the
Pan African Christian Leadership Assembly Pledge.

Asia

Mooneyham, W. Stanley, ed. *Christ Seeks Asia: Official Reference Volume Asia-South Pacific Congress on Evangelism,
Singapore 1968.* Hong Kong: Rock House, 1969.

Cho, David J., ed. *New Forces in Missions: The Official Report
of the Asian Missions Association.* Seoul: East-West
Center for Missions Research and Development, 1976.

Europe

Kirby, G. W., ed. *Evangelism Alert.* Minneapolis: World Wide
Publications, 1972.

Künneth, Walter, and Beyerhaus, Peter, eds. *Reich Gottes oder
Welt Gemeinschaft? Die Berliner Ökumene-Erklärung zur
Utopischen Vision des Weltkirchenrates.* Badliebenzell:
Verlag der Liebenzeller Mission, 1975.

Latin America

Strachan, R. Kenneth. *The Inescapable Calling.* Grand Rapids:
Eerdmans, 1968.

Accion en Cristo Para un Continente en Crisis. San Jose,
Costa Rica: Editorial Caribe, 1970.

"The Evangelical Declaration of Bogota." *Evangelical Missions
Quarterly* 6.3 (1970): 172-75.

Pretiz, Paul E., ed. *In-Depth Evangelistic Movements Around
the World: A Special Report for ICOWE.* San Jose, Costa
Rica: Publicaciones Indef, 1974.

North America

Wilson, Geo. M., ed. *Evangelism Now: US Congress on Evangelism
--Minneapolis, Minnesota, 1969. Official Reference Volume:
Papers and Reports.* Minneapolis: World Wide Publications,
1969.

Sider, Ronald J., ed. *The Chicago Declaration.* Carol Stream, Ill.: Creation House, 1974.

3. Roman Catholic

Pre-Vatican II

Burke, Thomas J. M. *Four Great Missionary Encyclicals.* New York: Fordham University Press, 1957.

The Encyclicals and Other Messages of John XXIII. Washington, D.C.: TPS Press, 1964.

Vatican II

Congar, Yves; Küng, Hans; and O'Hanlon, David. *Council Speeches of Vatican II.* Glen Rock, N.J.: Paulist Press, 1964.

Abbott, Walter M., ed. *The Documents of Vatican II.* Trans. ed. Joseph Gallagher. New York: Geoffrey Chapman, 1966.

Synod of Bishops

Justice in the World. Washington, D.C.: National Conference of Catholic Bishops, 1972.

The Evangelization of the Modern World. Synod of Bishops. Vatican City, 1973.

On Evangelization in the Modern World: Evangelii Nuntiandi, 8 December 1975. Washington, D.C.: US Catholic Conference, 1976.

Latin America

Latin American Episcopal Council, Second General Conference of Latin American Bishops, Medellin 1968: The Church in the Present-Day Transformation of Latin America in the Light of the Council. 2 vols. Bogota: CELAM, 1970.

Between Honesty and Hope. Documents from and about the Church in Latin America. Trans. by John Drury. Maryknoll, N.Y.: Maryknoll, 1970.

Gutierrez, Gustavo. *A Theology of Liberation.* Trans. by Sister Caridad Inda and John Eagleson. Maryknoll, N.Y.: Orbis, 1973.

Segundo, Juan Luis. *A Theology For Artisans of a New Humanity.* 5 vols. Maryknoll, N.Y.: Orbis, 1974.

Dussel, Enrique. *History and the Theology of Liberation.* Trans. by John Drury. Maryknoll, N.Y.: Orbis, 1976.

Asia

Panikkar, Raymond. *The Unknown Christ of Hinduism.* London: Darton, Longman & Todd, 1964.

_____. *The Trinity and World Religions.* Madras: Christian Literature Society, 1970.

Neuner, Joseph, ed. *Christian Revelation and World Religions.* London: Burns & Oates, 1967.

SECONDARY LITERATURE

1. Books

Adler, Elisabeth. *A Small Beginning.* Geneva: WCC, 1974.

Albert, Frank Joseph. "A Study of the Eastern Orthodox Churches in the Ecumenical Movement." Ph.D.: Harvard University, 1964.

Alexander, Calvert, S.J. *The Missionary Dimension: Vatican II and the World Apostolate.* Milwaukee: Bruce Publishing Company, 1967.

Althaus, Paul. *Die Christliche Wahrheit.* 2 vols. Gütersloh: Bertelsmann, 1949.

Alves, Rubem Azevedo. *A Theology of Human Hope.* New York: Corpus Books, 1969.

Andersen, Wilhelm. *Towards a Theology of Mission: A Study of the Encounter between the Missionary Enterprise and the Church and Its Theology.* IMC Research Pamphlet No. 2. London: SCM, 1955.

Anderson, Gerald H. "The Theology of Missions 1928-1958." Ph.D.: Boston University Graduate School, 1960.

_____, ed. *Christian Mission in Theological Perspective.* Nashville: Abingdon Press, 1967.

_____, ed. *Asian Voices in Christian Theology.* Maryknoll: Orbis, 1976.

Anderson, Gerald H., and Stransky, Thomas F., eds. *Mission Trends No. 1: Crucial Issues in Mission Today.* New York:

Paulist Press/Grand Rapids: Eerdmans, 1974.

Anderson, Gerald H., and Stransky, Thomas F., eds. *Mission Trends No. 2: Evangelization.* New York: Paulist Press/ Grand Rapids: Eerdmans, 1975.

_____. *Mission Trends No. 3: Third World Theologies.* New York: Paulist Press/Grand Rapids: Eerdmans, 1976.

Appleton, George. *On the Eightfold Path: Christian Presence Amid Buddhism.* New York: Oxford University Press, 1961.

Assman, Hugo. *Theology for a Nomad Church.* Maryknoll: Orbis, 1976.

Atkinson, George. "The Concept of Christian Hope in Karl Barth's *Die Kirche Dogmatik.*" Ph.D.: Southern Methodist University, 1975.

Barkman, P. F.; Dayton, E. R.; and Gruman, D. L. *Christian Collegians and Foreign Missions.* Monrovia, Ca.: MARC, 1969.

Barrett, David Brian. *Schism and Renewal in Africa.* Nairobi: Oxford University Press, 1968.

Barrett, David B.; Mambo, George K.; McLaughlin, Janice; and McVeigh, Malcolm J. *Kenya Churches Handbook: The Development of Kenyan Christianity 1498-1973.* Kisumu, Kenya: Evangel Publishing House, 1973.

Barth, Karl. *Church Dogmatics,* vol. 4, pt. 3, 2nd half: 830-901. Edinburgh: T. & T. Clark, 1962.

Bavinck, Johan H. *The Impact of Christianity on the non-Christian World.* Grand Rapids: Eerdmans, 1948.

_____. *An Introduction to the Science of Missions.* Philadelphia: The Presbyterian & Reformed Publishing Co., 1960.

Beahm, William H. "Factors in the Development of the Student Volunteer Movement for Foreign Missions." Ph.D.: University of Chicago, 1941.

Beaver, R. Pierce. *The World Christian Mission. A Reconsideration.* Calcutta: Baptist Missionary Press, 1957.

_____. *From Missions to Mission.* New York: Association Press, 1964.

_____. *The Missionary Between the Times.* New York: Doubleday, 1968.

Beaver, R. Pierce, ed. *The Gospel and Frontier Peoples: A Report of a Consultation, December 1973.* Pasadena: WCL, 1973.

_____, ed. *American Missions in Bicentennial Perspective.* Pasadena: WCL, 1977.

Bell, G. K. A. *The Kingship of Christ. The Story of the World Council of Churches.* Harmonsworth: Penguin, 1954.

Bergquist, James A., and Manickam, P. Kambar. *The Crisis of Dependency in Third World Ministries. A Critique of Inherited Missionary Forms in India.* Madras: CLS, 1974.

Beyerhaus, Peter. *Missions: Which Way? Humanization or Redemption.* Trans. by Margaret Clarkson. Grand Rapids: Zondervan, 1971.

_____. *Shaken Foundations: Theological Foundations for Mission.* Grand Rapids: Zondervan, 1972.

_____. *Allen Volkern zum Zeugnis.* N.p.: Brockhaus Verlag, 1972.

_____. *Bangkok 1973: The Beginning or End of World Mission?* Grand Rapids: Zondervan, 1974.

Beyerhaus, Peter, and Hallencreutz, Carl F., eds. *The Church Crossing Frontiers. Studie Missionalia Upsaliensia* XI. Uppsala: Gleerup, 1969.

Beyerhaus, Peter, and Lefever, Henry. *The Responsible Church and the Foreign Missions.* Grand Rapids: Eerdmans, 1964. English trans. of *Die Selbständigkeit der Jungen Kirchen als Missionarisches Problem.*

Biehler, Ekkhard. "Der Umbruch Theologischen Denkens in der Okumene zwischen Neu Delhi und Uppsala." Ph.D.: Berlin Kirchliche Hochschule, 1974.

Bigert, Irene. "Renewal and Unity. A Study of the 'renewal character' of the Ecumenical Movement with special reference to the World Council of Churches." Ph.D.: Leuven: Katholicke Universiteit, 1972.

Bloesch, Donald G. *The Evangelical Renaissance.* Grand Rapids: Eerdmans, 1973.

_____. *Wellsprings for Renewal: Promise in Christian Communal Life.* Grand Rapids: Eerdmans, 1974.

Boberg, John T., S.V.D., and Scherer, James A., eds. *Mission in the 1970s. What Direction?* Chicago: Chicago Cluster of Theological Schools, 1972.

Bock, Paul. *In Search of a Responsible World Society: The Social Teachings of the World Council of Churches.* Philadelphia: Westminster, 1974.

Braaten, Carl E. *The Flaming Center: A Theology of the Christian Mission.* Philadelphia: Fortress, 1977.

Bradshaw, Malcolm R. *Church Growth Through Evangelism-in-Depth.* Pasadena: WCL, 1969.

Bridston, Keith R. *Mission--Myth and Reality.* New York: Friendship Press, 1965.

Brown, Robert McAfee. *The Ecumenical Revolution.* New York: Doubleday, 1967.

Bruggeman, Antonio. "The Ecclesiology of Lesslie Newbigin." Ph.D.: Rome: Gregorian University, 1964.

Bühlmann, Walbert. *The Coming of the Third Church: An Analysis of the Present and Future.* Slough: St. Paul Publications, 1976.

Bürkle, Horst. *Dialog mit dem Osten: Radhakrischnan's Neuhinduistiche Botschaft im Lichte Christliche Weltsendung.* Stuttgart: Evangelisches Verlagswork, 1965.

Camara, Dom Helder. *Church and Colonialism.* London: Sheed & Ward, 1969.

_____. *Spiral of Violence.* London: Sheed & Ward, 1971.

_____. *Revolution Through Peace.* New York: Harper Colophon Books, 1972.

Carey, William. *An Enquiry into the Obligations of Christians to use Means for the Conversion of the Heathens.* Leicester, 1792; reprint. ed., London: Baptist Missionary Society, 1934.

Carpenter, George W. *Encounter of the Faiths.* New York: Friendship Press, 1967.

Cassidy, Michael. *Prisoners of Hope.* Pietermaritzburg: Africa Enterprise, 1974.

Cassidy, Michael; Fuevre, Charmain le; and Blanc, Anne, eds. *I Will Heal Their Land . . . Papers of the South Africa Congress on Mission and Evangelism Durban 1973.* Pieter-maritzburg: Africa Enterprise, 1974.

Castro, Emilio. *Amidst Revolution.* Trans. by James and Margaret Goff. Belfast: Christian Journals Limited, 1975.

Cauthen, Baker J., and others. *Advance: A History of Southern Baptist Foreign Missions.* Nashville: Broadman Press, 1970.

Cavert, Samuel McCrea. *On the Road to Christian Unity: An Appraisal of the Ecumenical Movement.* New York: Harper & Brothers, 1961.

_____. *The American Churches in the Ecumenical Movement 1900-1968.* New York: Association Press, 1968.

_____. *Church Cooperation and Unity in America 1900-1970.* New York: Association Press, 1970.

Change--Witness--Triumph. The Seventh Inter-Varsity Missionary Convention. Chicago: Inter-Varsity Press, 1965.

Chenu, Bruno. "La Signification Ecclesiologique du Conseil Oecuménique des Eglises, 1945-1963." Lyon: Facultes Catholiques, 1972.

The Christian Mission Today. Ed. by The Joint Section of Education and Cultivation of the Board of Missions of the Methodist Church. Nashville: Abingdon Press, 1960.

The Church and Social Revolution. Senior colloquy, Perkins School of Theology, Southern Methodist University, 1967. Mimeographed.

The Church Teaches: Documents of the Church in English Translation. St. Louis, Mo.: B. Herder Book Co., 1955.

Clark, Dennis E. *The Third World and Mission.* Waco, Tx.: Word Books, 1971.

Classified Catalogue of the Ecumenical Movement. 2 vols. Boston: G. K. Hall, 1972.

Coffele, Gianfranco. *Johannes Christiaan Hoekendijk. Da Teologia Missione ad una Teologia Missionaria.* Rome: Universita Gregoriana Editrice, 1976.

Coggins, Wade T., and Frizen, E. L., eds. *Evangelical Missions*

Tomorrow. Pasadena: WCL, 1977.

Cole, Stewart G. *The History of Fundamentalism.* New York: Richard R. Smith, 1931.

Coleman, William J., M.M. *Latin American Catholicism: A Self Evaluation.* Maryknoll: Maryknoll, 1958.

Coles, David J. "The Search for Methods in Contemporary Ecumenical Social Ethics." Ph.D: University of Manchester, 1973.

Commission, Conflict, Commitment: Messages from the Sixth International Student Missionary Convention. Chicago: Inter-Varsity Press, 1962.

Congar, Yves M-J., O.P. *Lay People in the Church.* Trans. by Donald Attwater. London: Bloomsbury Publishing, 1958.

_____. *Dialogue Between Christians: Catholic Contributions to Ecumenism.* Trans. by Philip Lorenz. Westminster, Md.: Newman Press, 1966.

Conn, Harvie M., ed. *Theological Perspectives on Church Growth.* Nutley, N.J.: Presbyterian & Reformed Publishing Company, 1976.

Considine, John J., M.M. *Call For Forty Thousand.* New York: Longmans, 1946.

_____, ed. *The Church in the New Latin America.* Notre Dame: Fides Publishers, 1964.

Conway, Gerald W. "An Exposition and Critical Analysis of the Theology of Missions as proposed by Hendrik Kraemer." Ph.D.: Rome: Pontifical Gregorian University, 1965.

Cook, Harold R. *Strategy of Missions: An Evangelical View.* Chicago: Moody Press, 1963.

Costas, Orlando. *The Church and its Mission: A Shattering Critique From the Third World.* Wheaton, Ill.: Tyndale House Publishers, 1974.

_____. *Theology of the Crossroads in Contemporary Latin America--Missiology in Mainline Protestantism: 1969-1974.* Amsterdam: Edition Rodopi, 1975.

Coston, Herbert Reece. "The World's Student Christian Federation as an Ecumenical Training Ground." Ph.D.: North-western University, 1963.

Cragg, Kenneth A. *Sandals at the Mosque: Christian Presence Amid Islam.* New York: Oxford University Press, 1959.

_____. *The Dome and the Rock.* London: SPCK, 1964.

_____. *Christianity in World Perspective.* London: Lutterworth Press, 1968.

Crow, Paul A., Jr. "The Concept of Unity in Diversity in Faith and Order Conversations from the Lausanne, 1927 to the Oberlin, 1957 Conferences." Ph.D.: Hartford, 1962.

Crowe, Philip, ed. *Keele 1967: The National Evangelical Anglican Congress Statement.* London: Church Pastoral Aid Society, 1967.

Danker, William J., and Kang, W. Jo., eds. *The Future of the World Christian Mission: Studies in Honor of R. Pierce Beaver.* Grand Rapids: Eerdmans, 1971.

Davies, J. G. *Worship and Mission.* London: SCM, 1966.

Dayton, Edward R., ed. *Mission Handbook: North American Protestant Ministries Overseas.* 10th ed. Monrovia, Ca.: MARC, 1973.

_____. *Mission Handbook: North American Protestant Ministries Overseas.* 11th ed. Monrovia, Ca.: MARC, 1976.

Derr, Thomas Sieger. "The Political Thought of the Ecumenical Movement 1900-1939." Ph.D.: Columbia University, 1972.

Devanandan, P. D. *Christian Issues in Southern Asia.* New York: Friendship Press, 1962.

Devanandan, Nalini, and Thomas, M. M., eds. *Preparation for Dialogue: A Collection of Essays on Hinduism and Christianity in the New India.* Bangalore: CISRS, 1964.

Devanesen, Chandran. *Asian Resurgence and the Church. The Cato Lecture, 1972.* Melbourne: Aldersgate, 1972.

de Vries, Egbert. *Man in Rapid Social Change.* London: SCM, 1961.

de Vries, Johannes Lukas. "Sending en Kolonialisme in Suidwes-Afrika. Die invloed van de Duitse Kolonialisme op die Sendingwerk van die Rynse Sendinggenootskap in die Vroeere Duits-Suidwes-Afrika." Ph.D.: Protestantse Theologische

Faculteit te Brussel, 1971.

Dhavamony, M., ed. *Evangelization, Dialogue and Development. Documenta Missionalia*-5. Rome: Universita Gregoriana, 1972.

_____. *Evangelisation. Documenta Missionalia.* vol. 9. Rome: Universita Gregoriana, 1975.

Dickinson, Richard D. N. "A Comparison of the Concepts of the State in Roman Catholicism and the Ecumenical Movement." Ph.D.: Boston University, 1959.

Dickson, Kwesi A., and Ellingworth, Paul, eds. *Biblical Revelation and African Beliefs.* Maryknoll: Orbis, 1969.

Douglas, J. D., ed. *Evangelicals and Unity.* Appleford: Marcham Manor Press, 1964.

Drummond, Richard Henry. *Gautama the Buddha: An Essay in Religious Understanding.* Grand Rapids: Eerdmans, 1974.

Duff, Edward, S.J. *The Social Thought of the World Council of Churches.* New York: Association Press, 1956.

Eagleson, John, ed. *Christians and Socialism. Documentation of the Christians for Socialism Movement in Latin America.* Trans. by John Drury. Maryknoll: Orbis, 1975.

Ellacuria, Ignacio. *Freedom made Flesh. The Mission of Christ and His Church.* Maryknoll: Orbis, 1976.

Elliott, Charles. *Patterns of Poverty in the Third World.* New York: Praeger, 1975.

Elwood, Douglas J., ed. *What Asian Christians are Thinking: A Theological Source Book.* Quezon City, Philippines: New Day Publishers, 1976.

Ewing, John W. *Goodly Fellowship. A Centenary Tribute to the Life and Work of the World's Evangelical Alliance 1846-1946.* London: Marshall, Morgan & Scott, 1946.

Facing Facts in Modern Missions: A Symposium. Chicago: Moody Press, 1963.

Fenton, Horace L. *Myths About Mission.* Downers Grove, Ill.: Inter-Varsity Press, 1973.

Ferre, Nels F. S. *The Finality of Faith, and Christianity Among the World Religions.* New York: Harper & Row, 1963.

Fey, Harold E., ed. *The Ecumenical Advance: A History of the Ecumenical Movement.* Vol. 2: *1948-1968.* Philadelphia: Westminster Press, 1970.

Fife, Eric S., and Glasser, Arthur F. *Missions in Crisis: Rethinking Missionary Strategy.* Chicago: Inter-Varsity Press, 1961.

Flannery, Austin P., ed. *Documents of Vatican II.* Grand Rapids: Eerdmans, 1975.

Flew, R. Newton, ed. *The Nature of the Church. Papers Presented to the Theological Commission appointed to the Continuation Committee of the World Conference on Faith and Order.* London: SCM, 1952.

Foreign Missions Conference of North America: Annual Reports 1893-1950. New York: Foreign Missions Conference of North America.

Freire, Paulo. *Pedagogy of the Oppressed.* New York: Herder & Herder, 1970.

Frey, Harald Christian Andreas. "Critiques of Conciliar Ecumenism by Conservative Evangelicals in the United States." Th.D.: School of Theology, Boston University, 1961.

Freytag, Walter. *Reden und Aufsätze.* Parts I and II. *Theologische Bucherei.* Vol. 13. München: Chr. Kaiser Verlag, 1961.

Freytag, W.; Hartenstein, K.; Lehmann, A.; et al. *Mission Zwischen Gestern und Morgen.* Stuttgart: Evangelischer Missionsverlag, 1952.

Fuerth, Patrick. "The Concept of Catholicity in the Documents of the World Council of Churches 1948-1968. An historical study with systematic-theological reflections." Rome: Pontificium Athenaeum Anselmianum, 1971. Two vol. mimeograph.

Gaines, David P. *The World Council of Churches: A Study of its Background and History.* Peterborough, N.H.: Noone House, 1966.

Gatti, Enzo. *Rich Church--Poor Church?* Maryknoll: Orbis, 1974.

Gaus, John E. "Analysis of the Changes in the Participation of Delegates to the Uppsala Assembly of the World Council of Churches, with Implications for International Organizations." Ph.D.: Morehead State University, 1970.

Gelpi, Donald. *Pentecostalism: A Theological Viewpoint.*
New York: Paulist Press, 1971.

Gensichen, Hans-Werner. *Living Mission: The Test of Faith.*
Philadelphia: Fortress Press, 1966.

_____. *Glaube für die Welt.* Gütersloh: Gütersloher Verlags-
haus Gerd Mohn, 1971.

Gerard, Francois Raymond Christian. *The Future of the Church:
The Theology of Renewal of Willem Adolf Visser 't Hooft.*
Ph.D.: Hartford, 1969. Pittsburg: Pickwick Press, 1974.

Gerassi, John, ed. *Camilio Torres, Revolutionary Priest.*
New York: Random House, 1971.

Germany, Charles H. *Protestant Theologies in Modern Japan: A
History of Dominant Theological Currents from 1920-1960.*
Tokyo: IISR Press, 1965.

Gill, David Muir. "The Concept of 'The World' in the Thought
of the World Council of Churches, 1948-1967." Ph.D.:
Hartford, 1968.

Glasser, Arthur F., ed. *Crossroads in Missions.* Pasadena:
WCL, 1971.

Glasser, Arthur F.; Hiebert, Paul G.; Wagner, C. Peter; and
Winter, Ralph D. *Crucial Dimensions in World Evangelization.* Pasadena: WCL, 1976.

Godin, Abbe Henri. *La France, Pays de Mission?* Lyon:
Editions de l'Abeille, 1943.

*God's Men: From All Nations to All Nations. The Eighth Inter-
Varsity Missionary Convention.* Chicago: Inter-Varsity
Press, 1968.

Goodall, Norman. *The Ecumenical Movement.* 2nd ed. London:
Oxford University Press, 1964.

_____. *Christian Mission and Social Ferment.* London:
Epworth Press, 1964.

_____. *Ecumenical Progress.* London: Oxford University
Press, 1972.

Günther, Wolfgang. "Von Edinburgh nach Mexico City. Die
Ekklesiologischen Bemühungen der Weltsmissionskonferenzen
1910-1963." Stuttgart: Universitat zu Erlangen, 1970.

Hallencreutz, Carl Fredrik. *Kraemer Towards Tambaram: A Study in Hendrik Kraemer's Missionary Approach.* Uppsala: Gleerup, 1966.

_____. *Dialogue and Community: Ecumenical Issues in Inter-religious Relationships. Studia Missionalia Upsaliensia XXXI.* Uppsala: Swedish Institute of Missionary Research/ Geneva: WCC, 1977.

Hammer, Raymond. *Japan's Religious Ferment: Christian Presence Amid Faiths Old and New.* New York: Oxford Univ. Press, 1962.

Harr, Wilber C., ed. *Frontiers of the Christian World Mission Since 1938: Essays in Honor of Kenneth Scott Latourette.* New York: Harper, 1962.

Hastings, Adrian. *Church and Mission in Modern Africa.* London: Burns & Oates, 1967.

Hayward, Victor E. W. *African Independent Church Movements.* London: Edinburgh House Press, 1963.

Hebblethwaite, Peter. *The Christian-Marxist Dialogue.* New York: Paulist, 1977.

Hefley, James and Marti. *Uncle Cam. The Story of William Cameron Townsend founder of the Wycliffe Bible Translators and the Summer Institute of Linguistics.* Waco, Tx.: Word Books, 1974.

Heimer, Haldor Eugene. "The Kimbanguists and the Bapostolo. A Study of two African Independent Churches in Luluabourg, Congo in relation to similar Churches in the context of Luiua traditional Culture and Religion." Ph.D.: Hartford, 1971.

Henry, Carl F. H. *The Uneasy Conscience of Modern Fundamental-ism.* Grand Rapids: Eerdmans, 1947.

_____. *Evangelicals at the Brink of Crisis: Significance of the World Congress on Evangelism.* Waco: Word Books, 1967.

_____. *Evangelicals in Search of Identity.* Waco: Word, 1976.

Henry, Paul B. *Politics for Evangelicals.* Valley Forge: Judson, 1974.

Hick, John. *God and the Universe of Faiths.* New York: Mac-millan, 1973.

_____, ed. *Truth and Dialogue. The Relationship between World Religions.* London: Sheldon Press, 1974.

Hillman, Eugene. *The Church as Mission.* New York: Herder & Herder, 1965.

_____. *The Wider Ecumenism: Anonymous Christianity and the Church.* London: Burns & Oates, 1968.

Hocking, W. E., chairman. *Rethinking Missions: A Layman's Inquiry After One Hundred Years.* New York: Harper & Brothers, 1932.

_____. *Living Religions and a World Faith.* London: Allen & Unwin/New York: Macmillan, 1940.

Hoekendijk, H. C. *Kerk en Volk in de Duitse Zendigswetenschap.* Amsterdam: Drukkerij Kampert en Helm, 1948.

_____. *The Church Inside Out.* Philadelphia: Westminster Press, 1966.

_____. *Horizons of Hope.* Nashville: Tidings, 1970.

Hogg, William Richey. *Ecumenical Foundations: A History of the International Missionary Council and Its Nineteenth-Century Background.* New York: Harper, 1952.

Hollenweger, Walter J. *Handbuch der Pfingstbewegung.* 10 vols. Ph.D.: Zürich, 1965.

_____. *The Pentecostals: The Charismatic Movement in the Churches.* Trans. by R. A. Wilson. Minneapolis: Augsburg, 1972.

_____. *Evangelism Today. Good News or Bone of Contention?* Belfast: Christian Journals, 1976.

Hollis, Michael. *Mission, Unity and Truth. A Study of Confessional Families and the Churches in Asia.* London: Lutterworth, 1968.

Horner, Norman A. *Cross and Crucifix in Mission.* Nashville: Abingdon, 1965.

_____, ed. *Protestant Crosscurrents in Mission: The Ecumenical Conservative Encounter.* Nashville: Abingdon, 1968.

Houghton, A. T. *Evangelicals and the World Council of Churches.* London: World Dominion Press, 1962.

Howard, David M. *Student Power in World Evangelism.* Downers Grove, Ill.: Inter-Varsity Press, 1970.

Howard, David M., ed. *Jesus Christ: Lord of the Universe, Hope of the World*. Downers Grove, Ill.: Inter-Varsity Press, 1974.

International Documentation on the Contemporary Church (IDOC): Future of the Missionary Enterprise:

In Search of Mission. No. 9. Rome: IDOC, 1974.

Uhuru and Harambee: Kenya in Search of Freedom and Unity. No. 14. Rome: IDOC, 1975.

Mission in America in World Context. No. 17. Rome: IDOC, 1976.

Idowu, E. Bolaji. *Towards an Indigenous Church*. London: Oxford University Press, 1965.

Johnston, Arthur P. *World Evangelism and the Word of God*. Minnesota: Bethany Fellowship, 1974.

Jones, E. Stanley. *Christ at the Round Table*. New York: Grosset & Dunlap, 1928.

Jones, Tracy K. *Our Mission Today: The Beginnings of a New Age*. New York: World Outlook Press, 1963.

Jurji, Edward J., ed. *The Ecumenical Era in Church and Society: Essays in Honor of John A. Mackay*. New York: Macmillan, 1959.

Kane, J. Herbert. *A Global View of Christian Missions*. Grand Rapids: Baker, 1971.

Kato, Byang H. *Theological Pitfalls in Africa*. Kisumu, Kenya: Evangel Publishing House, 1975.

Kik, J. Marcellus. *Ecumenism and the Evangelical*. Philadelphia: The Presbyterian & Reformed Publishing Co., 1958.

Kosmahl, Hans-Joachim. *Ethik in Ökumene und Mission. Das Problem der "mittleren Axiome" bei J. H. Oldham und in der christlichen Sozialethik*. Göttingen: Vendenhoeck & Ruprecht, 1970.

Koyama, Kosuke. *Waterbuffalo Theology*. Maryknoll: Orbis, 1974.

_____. *No Handle on the Cross*. Maryknoll: Orbis, 1977.

Kraemer, Hendrik. *Religion and the Christian Faith*. London:

Lutterworth, 1956.

Kraemer, Hendrik. *A Theology of the Laity*. London: Lutterworth, 1958.

_____. *World Cultures and World Religions*. Philadelphia: Westminster, 1960.

Krass, Alfred C. *Beyond the Either-Or Church: Notes Towards a Recovery of the Wholeness of Evangelism*. Nashville: Tidings, 1973.

Küng, Hans. *The Church*. New York: Sheed & Ward, 1967.

_____. *On Being a Christian*. Trans. by Edward Quinn. Garden City, N.Y.: Doubleday, 1976.

Lalive D'Epinay, Christian. *Haven of the Masses: A Study of the Pentecostal Movement in Chile*. London: Lutterworth, 1969.

Latourette, Kenneth Scott. *A History of the Expansion of Christianity*. 7 vols. New York: Harper & Row, 1937-1945; reprinted edition, Grand Rapids: Zondervan, 1970.

Latourette, Kenneth Scott, and Hogg, William Richey. *Tomorrow is Here: The Mission and Work of the Church as Seen from the Meeting of the International Missionary Council at Whitby. Ontario 5-24 July 1947*. New York: Friendship Press, 1948.

_____. *World Christian Community in Action: The Story of World War II and Orphaned Missions*. New York: IMC, 1949.

Le Guillou, Marie-Joseph. *Mission et Unite: Les Exigences de la Communion*. 2 vols. Paris: Les Editions du Cerf, 1961.

Lindsell, Harold. *A Christian Philosophy of Missions*. Wheaton: Van Kampen Press, 1949. Rev. ed. as *An Evangelical Theology of Missions*. Grand Rapids: Zondervan, 1970.

_____. *The Battle for the Bible*. Grand Rapids: Zondervan, 1976.

Lindquist, Martti. "Economic Growth and the Quality of Life. An Analysis of the Debate within the World Council of Churches 1966-1974." Helsinki: The Finnish Society for Missiology & Ecumenics, 1975.

Löffler, Paul. *The Layman Abroad in the Mission of the Church*. London: Edinburgh House Press for CWME, 1962.

Löffler, Paul. *Conversion to God and Man.* Geneva: WCC, 1964.

_____, ed. *Secular Man and Christian Mission.* Geneva: WCC, 1968.

Lotz, Denton. "'The Evangelization of the World in This Genera- tion': The Resurgence of the Missionary Idea among the Con- servative Evangelicals." Ph.D.: Universität Hamburg, 1970.

Luthuli, Albert. *Let My People Go.* New York: Meridian Books, 1962.

Luzbetak, Louis J., S.V.D. *The Church and Cultures: An Applied Anthropology for the Religious Worker.* Pasadena: WCL, 1975.

McDonnell, Kilian, and others. *Theological and Pastoral Orien- tations on the Catholic Charismatic Renewal.* Ann Arbor: Word of Life, 1974.

McFarland, H. Neill. "Theories of the Social Origin of Reli- gion in the Tradition of Emile Durkheim." Ph.D.: Colum- bia University, 1954.

McGavran, Donald Anderson, ed. *Church Growth and Christian Mission.* New York: Harper & Row, 1965.

_____, ed. *Crucial Issues in Mission Tomorrow.* Chicago: Moody Press, 1972.

McIntire, Carl. *Servants of Apostasy.* Collingswood, N.J.: Christian Beacon Press, 1955.

Mackay, John A. *Ecumenics: The Science of the Church Univer- sal.* Englewood Cliffs, N.J.: Prentice-Hall, 1965.

Mackie, Steven G., ed. *Can Churches be Compared?* Research Pamphlet No. 17. Geneva: WCC/New York: Friendship Press, 1970.

McQuilkin, J. Robertson, ed. *How Biblical is the Church Growth Movement?* Chicago: Moody Press, 1973.

Manecke, Dieter. *Mission als Zuegendienst: Karl Barth's Theo- logical Justification of Mission Compared with the Theories of W. Holsten, W. Freytag, and J. C. Hoekendijk.* Wuppertal: Brockhaus, 1972.

Margull, Hans Jochen. *Hope in Action: The Church's Task in the World.* Trans. by Eugene Peters. Philadelphia: Muhlenberg Press, 1962.

Margull, Hans Jochen, and Freytag, Justus. *Kein Einbahn-strassen*. Stuttgart: Evan. Missionsverlag, 1973.

Martin, Marie-Louise. *Kimbangu: An African Prophet and His Church*. Trans. by D. M. Moore. Grand Rapids: Eerdmans, 1975.

Marty, Martin E. *Church Unity and Church Mission*. Grand Rapids: Eerdmans, 1964.

Mathew, George. "A Christian Concern for Economic Development. A Study of the World Council of Churches from Amsterdam to Uppsala." Bangalore: United Theological College, 1970.

Mathews, Basil. *John R. Mott: World Citizen*. New York: Harper & Brothers, 1934.

Mbiti, John Samuel. *African Religions and Philosophy*. London: Heinemann, 1969.

Meeking, John Basil. "The Self-Understanding of the World Council of Churches." Ph.D.: Rome: Pontifician Universitatum St. Thomas in Urbe, 1961.

Merk, Frederick, and Kerm, Lois Bannister. *Manifest Destiny and Mission in American History: A Reinterpretation*. New York: Random House, 1966.

Metzler, David G. "The Concept of Catholicity in the Faith and Order Movement 1910-1938." Ph.D.: Boston University, 1973.

Miguez-Bonino, José. *Doing Theology in a Revolutionary Situation*. Philadelphia: Fortress, 1973.

_____. *Christians and Marxists. The Mutual Challenge to Revolution*. Grand Rapids: Eerdmans, 1976.

Millot, Rene-Pierre. *Missions in the World Today*. Trans. by J. Holland Smith. New York: Hawthorn Books, 1961.

Minus, Paul M., ed. *Methodism's Destiny in an Ecumenical Age*. Nashville: Abingdon, 1969.

_____. *The Catholic Rediscovery of Protestantism. A History of Roman Catholic Ecumenical Pioneering*. New York: Paulist, 1976.

Mission in Asia Today. Papers from Hong Kong, 1975. Singapore: Christian Conference of Asia, 1976.

The Missionary Obligation of the Church. Preparatory Studies. Committee on Research in Foreign Missions of the Division of Foreign Missions: NCCC in the USA, mimeograph, 1952.

Missionary Service in Asia Today. A Report on a Consultation held by the Asia Methodist Advisory Committee February 18-23, 1971. Kuala Lumpur: University of Malaya, 1971.

Moberg, David O. *Inasmuch: Social Responsibility in the Twentieth Century.* Grand Rapids: Eerdmans, 1965.

_____. *The Great Reversal: Evangelism versus Social Concern.* Philadelphia and New York: J. B. Lippincott Co., 1972.

Moltmann, Jurgen. *Theology of Hope: On the Ground and Implications of a Christian Eschatology.* New York: Harper & Row, 1967.

_____. *Religion, Revolution and the Future.* New York: Scribners, 1969.

_____. *The Crucified God: The Cross of Christ as the Foundation and Criticism of Christian Theology.* Trans. by R. A. Wilson & John Bowden. New York: Harper & Row, 1974.

_____. *The Church and the Power of the Spirit: A Contribution to Messianic Ecclesiology.* Trans. by Margaret Kohl. New York: Harper & Row, 1974.

Mott, John R. *Addresses and Papers of John R. Mott.* 6 vols. New York: Association Press, 1946-1947.

Müller-Fahrenholz, Geiko. *Heilsgeschichte zwischen Ideologie und Prophetie.* Freiburg: Herder, 1974.

Murch, James DeForest. *The World Council of Churches: An Analysis and Evaluation.* Washington, D.C.: NAE, 1962.

Myklebust, Olav Guttorm. *The Study of Missions in Theological Education: An Historical Inquiry into the Place of World Evangelization in Western Protestant Ministerial Training with Particular Reference to Alexander Duff's Chair of Evangelistic Theology.* Vol. 1 (to 1910). Vol. 2 (1910-1950). Oslo: Forlaget Land og Kirche, 1955.

Neill, Stephen C. *The Unfinished Task.* London: Edinburgh House Press, 1958.

_____. *Creative Tension.* London: Edinburgh House Press, 1959.

Neill, Stephen C. *Christian Faith and Other Faiths*. London: Oxford University Press, 1961.

_____. *A History of Christian Missions. Pelican History of the Church*. Vol. 6. Baltimore: Penguin Books, 1964.

_____. *Colonialism and Christian Missions*. London: Lutterworth Press, 1966.

_____. *Call to Mission*. Philadelphia: Fortress, 1970.

Neill, Stephen C., and Weber, Hans-Reudi, eds. *The Layman in Christian History*. London: SCM, 1963.

Neill, Stephen C.; Anderson, Gerald H.; Goodwin, John. *Concise Dictionary of Christian World Mission*. Nashville: Abingdon, 1970.

Nelson, Marlin A., and Chun, Chaeok. *Asian Mission Societies: New Resources for World Evangelization*. Monrovia, Ca.: MARC, 1976.

Nesmith, Richard Duey. "The Development of the Concept of the Responsible Society: Stockholm to Evanston." Ph.D.: Boston University, 1957.

Newbigin, J. E. Lesslie. *The Reunion of the Church: A Defence of the South India Scheme*. London: SCM, 1948; and 2nd rev. ed. London: SCM, 1960.

_____. *One Body, One Gospel, One World: The Christian Mission Today*. London: IMC, 1958.

_____. *A Faith For This One World?* New York: Harper & Brothers, 1961.

_____. *Trinitarian Faith and Today's Mission*. Richmond, Va.: John Knox Press, 1964.

_____. *The Finality of Christ*. London: SCM, 1969.

Nida, Eugene A. *Message and Mission: The Communication of the Christian Faith*. Pasadena: WCL, 1972.

_____. *Towards a Science of Translating*. Leiden: E. J. Brill, 1964.

Niebuhr, H. Richard. *The Purpose of the Church and Its Ministry*. New York: Harper & Row, 1956.

Niles, D. T., ed. *Why We Must Speak. Evangelism at the Third Assembly of the World Council of Churches.* Geneva: WCC, 1962.

_____. *Ideas and Services: A Report to the EACC 1957-67.* EACC, 1968.

Nishi, Shunji Forest. "The Unity of the Church. A Contemporary View with Reference to some Recent Doctrines of the Church." Ph.D.: Columbia University, 1950.

Nissen, Karsten. *Mission og Enhed: En Undersøgelse af de Strukturelle, Teologiske og Politiske Konsekvenser af det Internationale Missionsrads Integration med Kirkernes Verdensrad i 1961.* Aarhus Universitets Prisopgaver for Aret, 1972.

O'Connor, Edward D. *The Pentecostal Movement in the Catholic Church.* Notre Dame: Ave Maria Press, 1971.

_____, ed. *Perspectives on Charismatic Renewal.* Notre Dame: University of Notre Dame Press, 1975.

Ohm, Thomas, O.S.B. *Die Liebe zu Gott in den Nichtchristlichen Religionen.* Krailling vor München Wewel Verlag, 1950.

_____. *Asia Looks at Western Christianity.* Trans. from the German by Irene Marinoff. New York: Herder & Herder, 1959.

Oldham, J. H. *International Missionary Organization. For the Crans Meeting 22-28 June 1920.* London: Privately printed, n.d.

One Baptism, One Eucharist and a Mutually Recognized Ministry. Faith and Order Paper No. 73. Geneva: WCC, 1975.

Oosthuizen, G. C. *Theological Discussions and Confessional Developments in the Churches of Asia and Africa.* Franeker, Netherlands: T. Wever, 1958.

Orchard, Ronald Kenneth. *Out of Every Nation.* London: SCM, 1959.

_____. *Missions in a Time of Testing.* London: Lutterworth, 1964.

Orthodox Contributions to Nairobi. Geneva: WCC, 1975.

Outler, Albert Cook. *That The World May Believe: A Study of Christian Unity.* New York: Board of Missions of the

Methodist Church, 1966.

_____. *Methodist Observer at Vatican II.* New York: Newman, 1967.

_____. *Evangelism in the Wesleyan Spirit.* Nashville: Tidings, 1971.

_____. *Theology in the Wesleyan Spirit.* Nashville: Tidings, 1975.

Pache, René. *The Ecumenical Movement.* Dallas: Dallas Theological Seminary, 1950.

Padilla, C. René, ed. *The New Face of Evangelicalism. An International Symposium on the Lausanne Covenant.* Downers Grove, Ill.: Inter-Varsity Press, 1976.

Panikkar, K. M. *Asia and Western Dominance.* New York: John Day Book Co.: n.d. [1953].

Panikkar, Raymond. *The Trinity and the Religious Experience of Man.* New York: Maryknoll, 1973.

Pentecost, Edward C. *Reaching the Unreached. An Introductory Study on Developing an Overall Strategy for World Evangelization.* Pasadena: WCL, 1974.

Perkin, Noel, ed. *Facing Facts in Modern Missions.* Chicago: Moody Press, 1963.

Perry, Edmund. *The Gospel in Dispute. The Relation of Christian Faith to Other Missionary Religions.* Garden City, N.Y.: Doubleday, 1958.

Peters, George W. *Saturation Evangelism.* Grand Rapids: Zondervan, 1970.

Petty, Orville A., ed. *Laymen's Foreign Missions Inquiry. Supplementary Series.* 7 vols. New York: Harper & Brothers, 1933.

Philip, T. V. "Mission and Unity: Factors Contributing to the Integration of the International Missionary Council and the World Council of Churches." Ph.D.: Hartford, 1967.

Pollock, John Charles. *A Cambridge Movement.* London: John Murray, 1954.

_____. *Crusades: 20 Years with Billy Graham.* Minneapolis:

World Wide Publications, 1966.

Portman, John R. *The Concepts of Mission and Unity in the World Council of Churches. A Study of the Official Documents of the Central Committee from its Inception to the New Delhi Assembly, 1961.* Rome: Catholic Book Agency, 1966.

Quebedeaux, Richard. *The Young Evangelicals: Revolution in Orthodoxy.* New York: Harper & Row, 1974.

Rahner, Karl, S.J., ed. *Rethinking the Church's Mission.* Vol. 13: *Concilium.* New York: Paulist, 1966.

_____. *Theological Investigations.* Vols. 5 and 6. Trans. by Karl H. and Boniface Kruger. Baltimore: Helicon Press/ London: Darton, Longman & Todd, 1966-1969.

Ramsey, Paul. *Who Speaks for the Church? A Critique of the 1966 Geneva Conference on Church and Society.* Nashville: Abingdon, 1967.

Ranaghan, Kevin and Dorothy. *Catholic Pentecostals.* Paramus, N.J.: Paulist, 1969.

Ranson, C. W. *That the World May Know: A Call to Mission and Unity.* New York: Friendship Press, 1953.

Read, William R.; Monterroso, Victor M.; and Johnson, Harmon A. *Latin American Church Growth.* Grand Rapids: Eerdmans, 1969.

Reber, Robert Eldred. "The World Council of Churches and World Development: Proposals for Adult Education in the Churches." Ph.D.: Boston University, 1973.

Richardson, Robert Neville. "The World Council of Churches and Race Relations: A Study of Thought and Action 1960 to 1969." Ph.D.: University of Oxford, 1974.

Richardson, William J., ed. *The Modern Mission Apostolate.* New York: Maryknoll, 1965.

Roberts, W. Dayton. *Revolution in Evangelism: Evangelism-in-Depth in Latin America.* Chicago: Moody Press, 1967.

_____. *Strachan of Costa Rica. Missionary Insights and Strategies.* Grand Rapids: Eerdmans, 1971.

Röper, A. *The Anonymous Christians.* Trans. by Joseph Doncal. New York: Sheed & Ward, 1966.

Rosales, Ray S. *The Evangelism in Depth Program of the Latin America Mission. A Description and Evaluation. Sondeos* No. 21. Cuernavaca: CIDOC, 1968.

Rosin, H. H. *Missio Dei.* Leiden: Interuniversity Institute for Missiological Research, 1972.

Rossell, Jacques. *Mission in a Dynamic Society.* London: SCM, 1968.

Rouse, Ruth, and Neill, S. C., eds. *A History of the Ecumenical Movement 1517-1948.* 2nd ed. Vol. I. Philadelphia: Westminster Press, 1967.

Roy, Ralph Lord. *Apostles of Discord.* Boston: Beacon Press, 1953.

Rudersdorf, Karl-Heinrich. *Entwicklungsförderung und Christliche Kirchen: Entstehung und Entwicklung des Konzepts der Entwicklungsförderung im Weltrat der Kirchen (WCC).* Ph.D.: Philosopische Fakultat Berlin 1973.

Rütti, Ludwig. *Zur Theologie der Mission. Kritische Analysen und Neve Orientierungen.* München: Chr. Kaiser, 1972.

Rynne, Xavier. *Vatican Council II.* New York: Farrar, Straus & Firoux, 1968.

Samartha, Stanley J. *The Hindu Response to the Unbound Christ.* Madras: CLS, 1974.

Sandeen, Ernest R. *The Roots of Fundamentalism: British and American Millenarianism 1800-1930.* Chicago: University of Chicago Press, 1970.

Scherer, James A. *Missionary, Go Home! A Reappraisal of the Christian World Mission.* Englewood Cliffs, N.J.: Prentice-Hall, 1964.

Schlette, Heinz Robert. *Towards a Theology of Religions.* Trans. by W. J. O'Hara. New York: Herder & Herder, 1966.

Schlunk, Martin. *Die Weltmission der Kirche Christi.* Stuttgart: Evangelischer Missionsverlag, 1951.

Schmidt, William John. "Ecumenicity and Syncretism: The Confrontation of the Ecumenical Movement with Syncretism in Special Reference to the International Missionary Council and the World Council of Churches." Ph.D.: Columbia University, 1966.

Schulz-Ankermann, Friederike. "Die Boten Christi; und ihr nichchristliches Gegenüber auf die Weltmissionskonferenzen von 1910 bis 1963." Universität zu Erlangen, 1969.

Seabury, R. I. *Daughter of Africa.* Boston: Pilgrim Press, 1945.

Segundo, Juan Luis. *Liberation of Theology.* Trans. by John Drury. Maryknoll: Orbis, 1976.

Sell, Charles M. "A Critical Survey of the Theology of Missions of the International Missionary Council." Ph.D.: Dallas Theological Seminary, 1967.

Seumois, Andre V. *Introduction a la Missiologie.* Schöneck-Beckenried, Suisse: Administration de la Nouvelle Rerne de Science Missionnaire, 1952.

Shapiro, Samuel, ed. *Integration of Man and Society in Latin America.* Notre Dame: University of Notre Dame Press, 1967.

Sharpe, Eric J. *Faith meets Faith. Some Christian Attitudes to Hinduism in the Nineteenth and Twentieth Centuries.* London: SCM, 1977.

Shelley, Bruce L. *Evangelicalism in America.* Grand Rapids: Eerdmans, 1967.

Shenk, Wilbert R., ed. *The Challenge of Church Growth: A Symposium.* Elkart, Ind.: Institute of Mennonite Studies, 1973.

Sider, Ronald J. *Rich Christians in an Age of Hunger. A Biblical Study.* New York: Paulist Press/ Downers Grove, Ill.: Inter-Varsity Press, 1977.

Silvinskas, Petro P. "Protestant Concepts of Unity and Diversity in the Faith and Order Movement." Rome: Gregorian University, 1961.

Simonson, Conrad. *The Christology of the Faith and Order Movement. Oekumenische Studien* X. Leiden: Brill, 1972.

Sinclair, John H., ed. *Protestantism in Latin America: A Bibliographical Guide.* Pasadena: WCL, 1976.

Skoglund, John E., and Nelson, J. Robert. *Fifty Years of Faith and Order.* New York: WCC, 1963.

Smart, Ninian. *A Dialogue of Religions.* London: SCM, 1960.

Smart, Ninian. *World Religions and Dialogue*. Harmondsworth: Pelican, 1966.

Smith, Eugene L. *Mandate for Mission*. New York: Friendship Press, 1968.

Smith, Timothy L. *Revivalism and Social Reform in Mid-Nineteenth Century America*. New York: Abingdon, 1957.

Smith, Wilfred Cantwell. *The Faiths of Other Men*. New York: Mentor Books, 1965.

_____. *Questions of Religious Truth*. New York: Scribners, 1967.

Snowden, Glen Wenger. "The Relationship of Christianity to non-Christian Religions in the Theologies of Daniel T. Niles and Paul Tillich." Ph.D.: Boston University, 1969.

Snyder, Howard A. *The Problem of Wine Skins: Church Structure in a Technological Age*. Downers Grove, Ill.: Inter-Varsity Press, 1975.

Song, Choan-Seng. *Christian Mission in Reconstruction--An Asian Attempt*. Madras: CLS, 1975.

SPADES: South Pacific Action for Development Strategy. Suva, Fiji: PCC, Christian Education and Communications Programme, n.d.

Spennemann, Klaus. "Die Ökumenische Bewegung und der Kommunismus in Russland 1920-1956." Ph.D.: Universitat zu Erlangung, 1970.

Stadler, Anton Paul. "Mission-Dialogue. A Digest and Evaluation of the Discussion in the Roman Catholic Church and within the World Council of Churches, 1965-1975." Ph.D.: Union Theological Seminary, 1977.

Stauffer, Paul A. "The Meaning of Humanization: An Emerging Understanding of Man in World Council of Churches Discussions, 1965-1970." Ph.D.: Boston University, 1972.

Stockwell, Eugene L. *Claimed by God for Mission*. New York: World Outlook Press, 1965.

Stott, John R. W., and others. *Christ the Liberator*. Downers Grove, Ill.: Inter-Varsity Press, 1971.

Stott, John R. W. *The Lausanne Covenant: An Exposition and*

Commentary. Minnesota: World Wide Publications, 1975.

Stott, John R. W. *Christian Mission in the Modern World*. London: Falcon, 1975.

Stowe, David M. *When Faith Meets Faith*. New York: Friendship Press, 1963.

_____. *Ecumenicity and Evangelism*. Grand Rapids: Eerdmans, 1970.

Stratmann, Hartmut. *Kein anderes Evangelium. Geist und Geschichte der neuer Bekenntnisbewegung*. Hamburg: Furche Verlag, 1970.

Stroman, John Albert. "The American Council of Christian Churches: A Study of its Origins, Leaders, and Characteristic Positions." Ph.D.: Boston University, 1966.

Strothmann, Maynard Herman. "Eschatology and the Mission of Christianity (with Special Emphasis on Contemporary Protestant Thought)." Ph.D.: Columbia University, 1956.

Studies in Vatican II. Senior Colloquy, Perkins School of Theology, SMU, 1966, mimeographed.

Suenens, Leon Joseph. *A New Pentecost?* London: Darton, Longman & Todd, 1975.

Sundkler, Bengt. *The World of Mission*. Grand Rapids: Eerdmans, 1965.

Taylor, Clyde W., and Coggins, Wade T., eds. *Mobilizing for Saturation Evangelism*. Wheaton: Evangelical Missions Information Service, 1970.

Taylor, John Vernon. *The Primal Vision. Christian Presence Amid African Religion*. New York: Oxford University Press, 1963.

_____. *For All the World*. London: Hodder & Stoughton, 1966.

_____. *The Go-Between God*. London: SCM, 1972.

Temple, William. *Readings in St. John's Gospel*. First and Second Series. London: Macmillan, 1955.

Theurer, P. Wolfdieter. *Die Trinitarische Basis des Ökumenischen Rates der Kirchen*. Frankfurt: Verlag Gerhard Kaffke, 1967.

Thomas, M. M. *The Christian Response to the Asian Revolution.* London: SCM, 1966.

_____. *The Acknowledged Christ of the Indian Renaissance.* London: SCM, 1969.

_____. *Salvation and Humanization.* Madras: CLS, 1970.

_____. *Man and the Universe of Faiths.* Inter-religious *Dialogue Series* No. 7. Madras: CLS, 1975.

Thomas, M. M. and Devanandan, P. D., eds. *Christian Participation in Nation-Building.* Bangalore: CISRS, 1960.

Till, Barry, ed. *Changing Frontiers in the Mission of the Church.* London: SPCK, 1966.

_____. *The Churches Search for Unity.* London: Penguin Books, 1972.

Tillich, Paul. *Christianity and the Encounter of the World Religions.* New York: Columbia University Press, 1963.

Tippett, Alan Richard. *Solomon Islands Christianity: A Study in Growth and Obstruction.* London: Lutterworth, 1967; reprint. WCL.

_____. *Church Growth and the Word of God: The Biblical Basis of the Church Growth Viewpoint.* Grand Rapids: Eerdmans, 1970.

_____, ed. *God, Man and Church Growth: A Festschrift in Honor of Donald Anderson McGavran.* Grand Rapids: Eerdmans, 1973.

_____. *Verdict Theology in Missionary Theory.* 2nd ed. Pasadena: WCL, 1973.

_____. *The Deep Sea Canoe: The Story of Third World Missionaries in the South Pacific.* Pasadena: WCL, 1977.

Troutman, Charles. *Everything You Want to Know about the Mission Field, But are Afraid You Won't Learn Until You Get There.* Downers Grove, Ill.: Inter-Varsity Press, 1976.

Trueblood, Elton. *The Validity of the Christian Mission.* New York: Harper & Row, 1972.

Tugwell, Simon. *Did You Receive the Spirit?* New York: Paulist Press, 1973.

410   *SELECTED BIBLIOGRAPHY*

Turner, H. W. *African Independent Churches.* 2 vols. New York: Oxford University Press, 1968.

Vallée, Gerard. *Mouvement Oecumenique et Religions non Chretiennes: Un Debat Oecumenique sur la Recontre Interreligieuse de Tambaram a Uppsala (1938-1968).* Tourmai: Desclee & Cie/Montreal: Bellarmin, 1975.

Van Dusen, H. P. *One Great Ground of Hope: Christian Missions and Christian Unity.* Philadelphia: Westminster Press, 1961.

Van den Berg, Johannes. *Constrained by Jesus' Love. An Inquiry into the Motives of the Missionary Awakening in Great Britain in the Period between 1698 and 1815.* Kampen: J. H. Kok, 1956.

van Lin, J. J. E. *Protestante Theologie der Godsdiensten van Edinburgh naar Tambaram (1910-1938).* Assen: Van Gorcum, 1974.

van Straelen, Henry, S.V.D. *The Catholic Encounter with the World Religions.* London: Burns & Oates, 1966.

Vicedom, Georg F. *The Challenge of the World Religions.* Trans. by Barbara and Karl Hertz. Philadelphia: Fortress Press, 1963.

_____. *The Mission of God.* Trans. by Gilbert A. Thiele and Dennis Hilgendors. St. Louis, Mo.: Concordia, 1965.

Visser 't Hooft, W. A. *The Ecumenical Movement and the Racial Problem.* Paris: UNESCO, 1954.

_____. *The Pressure of our Common Calling.* Garden City, N.J.: Doubleday, 1959.

_____. *No Other Name: The Choice Between Syncretism and Christian Universalism.* Philadelphia: Westminster Press, 1963.

_____. *Memoirs.* London: SCM/Philadelphia: Westminster Press, 1973.

_____. *Has the Ecumenical Movement a Future?* Belfast: Christian Journals Limited, 1974.

Vitalis, Gnadt. *The Significance of Changes in Latin American Catholicism Since Chimbote 1963. Sondeos* No. 51. Cuernavaca: CIDOC, 1969.

Wagner, C. Peter. *Latin American Theology: Radical or Evan-*

gelical? Grand Rapids: Eerdmans, 1970.

Wagner, C. Peter. *Frontiers in Missionary Strategy.* Chicago: Moody Press, 1971.

_____. *Look Out! The Pentecostals are Coming.* Carol Stream, Ill.: Creation House, 1973.

Walker, Alan. *The New Evangelism.* Nashville: Abingdon, 1975.

Warren, Max A. C. *The Christian Mission.* London: SCM, 1951.

_____. *The Missionary Movement from Britain in Modern History.* London: SCM, 1965.

_____. *Crowded Canvas: Some Experiences of a Lifetime.* London: Hodder & Stoughton, 1974.

_____. *I Believe in the Great Commission.* London: Hodder & Stoughton, 1976.

_____, ed. *To Apply the Gospel: Selections from the Writings of Henry Venn.* Grand Rapids: Eerdmans, 1970.

Webber, George W. *The Congregation in Mission: Emerging Structures for the Church in an Urban Society.* New York: Abingdon, 1964.

Weber, Hans-Ruedi. *Asia and the Ecumenical Movement 1895-1961.* London: SCM, 1966.

Webster, Douglas. *Local Church and World Mission.* New York: Seabury Press, 1964.

_____. *Yes to Mission.* London: SCM, 1965.

Wells, David F., and Woodbridge, John D., eds. *The Evangelicals: What They Believe, Who They Are, Where They are Changing.* Nashville: Abingdon, 1975.

Wesley, John. *Works.* Vol. 7. Grand Rapids: Zondervan, 1958-1959.

Wietzke, Joachim. "Theologie im Modernen Indien--Paul David Devanandan." Ph.D.: Hamburg.

Williams, Colin W. *Where in the World? Changing Forms of the Church's Witness.* New York: NCC, 1963.

_____. *What in the World?* New York: NCC, 1964.

Williams, Colin W. *Faith in a Secular Age.* New York: Harper
& Row, 1966.

Winter, Ralph D. *The 25 Unbelievable Years 1945-1969.*
Pasadena: WCL, 1970.

_____, ed. *The Evangelical Response to Bangkok.* Pasadena:
WCL, 1973.

Wong, James, ed. *Missions From the Third World.* Singapore:
Church Growth Study Center, 1973.

Works, Herbert Melvin. "The Church Growth Movement to 1965:
An Historical Perspective." Doctor of Missiology dissertation: Fuller Theological Seminary, 1974.

World Development: Challenge to the Churches. Denys Munby,
ed. The official report and papers of the Conference on
Society, Development and Peace (SODEPAX) held at Beirut,
Lebanon 21-27 April 1968 under the joint auspices of the
Vatican Commission on Peace and Freedom and the World
Council of Churches. Washington, D.C.: Corpus Books, 1969.

Worsley, Peter. *The Trumpet Shall Sound: A Study of 'Cargo'
Cults in Melanesia.* London: MacGibbon & Kee, 1957.

Yap, Kim Hao. "Church Structure Issues in Asian Ecumenical
Thought with Particular Reference to Malaysia and Singapore." Ph.D.: Boston University, 1969.

2. Articles

Aagaard, Johannes. "Some Main Trends in Modern Protestant
Missiology." *Studie Theologica* XIX (1965): 238-68.

_____. "Trends in Missiological Thinking During the Sixties."
IRM 62.245 (1973): 8-25.

Anderson, Gerald H. "A Moratorium on Missionaries?" *Christian
Century* (Jan. 16, 1974): 43-45.

Arias, Mortimer. "That the World May Believe." IRM 65.257
(1976): 13-26.

Arthur, R. John. "Critical Questions about Christian Presence."
Student World 58.3 (1965): 236-39.

Association of Evangelicals in Africa and Madagascar. "Association of Evangelicals." CT X.11 (Mar. 4, 1966): 47-48.

Barrett, David B. "A.D. 2000: 350 Million Christians in Africa." IRM 59.233 (1970): 39-54.

Beaver, R. Pierce. "North American Thoughts on the Fundamental Principles of Missions." *Church History* 21 (1952): 345-64.

Beckmann, Johannes. "Roman Catholic Missions in the Light of the Second Vatican Council." IRM 53.209 (1964): 83-88.

Bellamy, Wilfred A. "African Congress on Evangelism Faces Issues Confronting Church." EMQ 5.2 (1969): 112-14.

Berkhof, Hendrikus. "Berlin versus Geneva: Our Relationship with the 'Evangelical.'" ER 28.1 (1976): 80-86.

Berkouwer, G. C. "What Conservative Evangelicals Can Learn from the Ecumenical Movement." CT 10.17 (May 27, 1966): 17-23.

Beyerhaus, Peter. "The Three Selves Formula." IRM 53.212 (1964): 393-407.

_____. "Mission and Humanization." IRM 60.237 (1971): 11-24.

Birch, Charles. "Creation, Technology and Human Survival: Called to Replenish the Earth." ER 28.1 (1976): 66-79.

Blauw, Johannes. "The Witness of Christians to Men of Other Faiths." IRM 52.208 (1963): 414-22.

Blocher, Jacques. "All-Africa Conference Put Under Evangelical Scrutiny." EMQ 6.3 (1970): 175-80.

Buswell, J. Oliver, Jr. "The American and the International Council of Churches," CT 9.9 (Jan. 29, 1965): 9-11.

Calian, C. Samuel. "Eastern Orthodoxy's Renewed Concern for Mission." IRM 52.205 (1963): 33-37.

de Campos Goncalves, Antonio. "Evangelism in Brazil Today: Its Significance and Results." IRM 48.191 (1959): 302-308.

Carter, Archbishop S. E., S.J. "The Synod of Bishops--1974." IRM 64.255 (1975): 295-301.

Cassidy, Michael. "The Third Way." IRM 63.249 (1974): 9-23.

Castro, Emilio. "Evangelism and Social Justice." ER 20.2 (1968): 146-50.

Castro, Emilio. "Salvation Today at Bangkok and After." *Study Encounter* 11.2 (1973): 4-11.

_____. "Mission Today." *Missiology* 2.3 (1974): 359-67.

_____. "Mature Relationships: Structures for Mission." IRM 64.254 (1975): 117-121.

Cattell, Everett L. "National Association of Evangelicals and the World Evangelical Fellowship." CT IX.9 (Jan. 29, 1965): 12-14.

Costas, Orlando E. "Evangelism in a Latin American Context." *Occasional Essays*. San Jose (1977): 3-51.

Crossley, John. "The Islam in Africa Project." IRM 61.242 (1972): 150-60.

Dayton, Donald W. "The Social and Political Conservatism of Modern American Evangelicalism." *Union Seminary Quarterly Review* 32.2 (1977): 71-80.

Dayton, Edward R. "Current Trends in North American Protestant Ministries Overseas." *Occasional Bulletin of Missionary Research* 1.2 (1977): 2-7.

De Silva, F. S. "The Significance of Prapat." IRM 46.183 (1957): 306-309.

Devanandan, Paul David. "The Bangkok Conference of East Asia Leaders: An Impression." IRM 39.154 (1950): 146-52.

_____. "Comments on the First Report of the Advisory Commission on the Theme of the Second Assembly." ER 4.2 (1952): 163.

"Dialogue with Men of Other Faiths." *Study Encounter* 3.2 (1967): 51-83.

Dulles, Avery. "Current Trends in Mission Theology." *Theology Digest* 20.1 (1972): 26-34.

_____. "The Church and Salvation." *Missiology* 1.2 (1973): 71-80.

"Edinburgh 1910-1960 and the World Council of Churches--Reflections on Edinburgh 1910." *Religion in Life* (1960): 329-401.

Escobar, Samuel. "The Social Responsibility of the Church in

Latin America." EMQ 6.3 (1970): 129-52.

Fenton, Horace L. "Debits and Credits--The Wheaton Congress." IRM 55.220 (1966): 477-79.

Fletcher, Jesse C. "Foreign Mission Board Strategy." *Baptist History and Heritage* IX.4 (1974): 210-222.

Ford, Leighton F. S. "Personal Evangelism, Conversion and Social Change." ER 20.2 (1968): 122-30.

Forman, Charles W. "The Missionary Force of the Pacific Island Churches." IRM 59.234 (1970): 215-226.

Freytag, Walter. "The Meaning and Purpose of the Christian Mission." IRM 39.153 (1950): 153-61.

_____. "Changes in Patterns of Western Missions." IRM 47.186 (1958): 163-70.

Fuller, W. Harold. "Evangelicals Join in Africa." EMQ 3.3 (1967): 170-77.

Gensichen, Hans-Werner. "The Second Vatican Council's Challenge to Protestant Mission." IRM 56.223 (1967): 291-309.

Gill, David M. "The Secularization Debate Foreshadowed. Jerusalem 1928." IRM 57.227 (1968): 344-57.

Glasser, Arthur F. "The Interdenominational Foreign Mission Association." CT IX (Jan. 29, 1965): 19-20.

_____. "What Has Been the Evangelical Stance, New Delhi to Uppsala." EMQ 5.3 (1969): 129-50.

Glazik, Josef. "The Meaning and Place of Missiology Today." IRM 57.228 (1968): 459-67.

Goodall, Norman. "The IMC and the WCC." IRM 37.145 (1948): 86-92.

_____. "'Evangelicals' and WCC-IMC." IRM 47.186 (1958): 210-215.

_____. "Evangelization and the Ecumenical Movement." ER 15.4 (1963): 399-409.

Greaves, L. B. "The All Africa Church Conference: Ibadan, Nigeria 10-20 January 1958." IRM 47.186 (1958): 257-64.

"The Growth of the Church: A Statement." Iberville Consultation, 1963. IRM 57.227 (1968): 330-34.

Gutierrez, Gustavo. "Notes for a Theology of Liberation."
Theology Digest 19.2 (1971): 141-47.

Havea, John A. "The Pacific Meets Beyond the Reefs." IRM
51.201 (1962): 72-74.

Hayward, Victor E. W. "Call to Witness, But What Kind of Witness?" IRM 53.210 (1964): 201-208.

_____. "Latin America--An Ecumenical Bird's Eye View." IRM
60.238 (1971): 161-85.

Hayward, Victor E. W., and McGavran, Donald. "Without Crossing
Barriers? One in Christ versus Discipling Diverse Cultures."
Missiology 2.2 (1974): 203-224.

Henry, Carl F. H. "From Mission to Missions." CT 4.22
(Aug. 1, 1960): 21-24.

_____. "A New Crisis in Foreign Missions?" CT 5.15
(Apr. 25, 1961): 3-14.

_____. "Looking Back at Key '73." *The Reformed Journal* 24.9
(1974): 6-12.

Hillman, Eugene. "'Anonymous Christianity' and the Missions."
Downside Review 84.277 (1966): 361-79.

_____. "Evangelism in a Wider Ecumenism: Theological
Grounds for Dialogue with Other Religions." *Journal of
Ecumenical Studies* 12.1 (1975): 1-12.

Hoedemaker, L. A. "Hoekendijk's American Years." *Occasional
Bulletin of Missionary Research* 1.2 (1977): 7-11.

Hoekendijk, J. C. "Call to Evangelism." IRM 39.154 (1950):
162-75.

_____. "The Church in Missionary Thinking." IRM 41.163
(1952): 324-36.

_____. "Christ and the World in the Modern Age." *Student
World* 54.1-2 (1961): 75-82.

_____. "Evangelization of the World in This Generation."
IRM 49.233 (1970): 23-31.

Hoffman, Gerhard. "The Crisis in World Mission." IRM 60.237
(1971): 39-49.

Hoffman, Ronan. "Ecumenism and Mission Theology." *Worldmission*
15.3 (1964): 48-64.

Hogg, W. Richey. "Some Background Considerations for
Ad Gentes." IRM 56.223 (1967): 281-90. See also corrections of printer's errors in IRM 56.224 (1967): 513.

Hoke, Donald E. "Lausanne May be a Bomb." CT 18.12
(Mar. 15, 1974): 669-70.

Honey, Floyd. "Joint Action for Mission: Historical Perspectives and Current Progress." *Missionary Research Library
Occasional Bulletin* 17.11 (1966): 1-9.

Howard, David M. "Urbana 73 Theme Emphasizes Positive View of
Missions." EMQ 9.2 (1973): 118-21.

_____. "What Happened at Urbana." EMQ 13.3 (1977): 141-48.

Hubbard, David Allen. "The Theology of Section II." CGB 5.2
(1968): 331-33.

Jackson, G. C. "Report from Bangkok." IRM 53.211 (1964):
307-317.

Johnson, R. Park. "Renewal of the Christian Mission to Islam:
Reflections on the Asmara Conference." IRM 48.192 (1959):
438-44.

Kemper, Deane A. "Another Look at Key 73." *The Reformed
Journal* 25.1 (1975): 15-20.

"The Kimbanguist Church in the Congo." ER 19.1 (1967): 29-36.

King, Louis L. "Neo Universalism: Its Exponents, Tenets and
Threats to Missions." EMQ 1.4 (1965): 2-12.

Kraemer, Hendrik. "Syncretism as a Religious and Missionary
Problem." IRM 43.171 (1954): 253-73.

Kraft, Charles H. "Dynamic Equivalence Churches." *Missiology*
1.1 (1973): 39-57.

Kromminga, John H. "Evangelical Influence on the Ecumenical
Movement." *Calvin Theological Journal* 11.2 (1976): 149-80.

Latourette, Kenneth Scott. "Re-Thinking Missions After

Twenty-Five Years." IRM 46.182 (1957): 164-70.

Lindsell, Harold. "An Appraisal of Agencies Not Cooperating with the IMC Grouping." IRM 47.186 (1958): 202-209.

_____. "Precedent Setting in Missions Strategy." CT 10.15 (Apr. 29, 1966): 43.

_____. "Attack Syncretism with Dialogue." EMQ 3.4 (1967): 203-208.

_____. "Uppsala 1968." CT 12.22 (Aug. 16, 1968): 43-46.

_____. "Lausanne 74: An Appraisal." CT 18.24 (Sept. 13, 1974): 26.

Löffler, Paul. "Laymen in World Mission." IRM 53.211 (1964): 297-306.

_____. "Conversion in an Ecumenical Context." ER 19.3 (1967): 252-60.

Lores, Ruben. "The Mission of Missions." EMQ 4.3 (1968): 140-47.

McFarland, H. Neill. "Christianity Confronts Other Faiths." *Christian Action* 19.1 (1964): 12-32.

_____. "Our Mission to Buddhists and Muslims." *Christian Action* 19.2 (1964): 17-38.

McGavran, Donald. "New Methods for a New Age in Missions." IRM 44.176 (1955): 394-403.

_____. "After the First Flush of Success." IRM 48.191 (1959): 265-75.

_____. "Institute of Church Growth." IRM 50.200 (1961): 431-34.

_____. "The God Who Finds and His Mission." IRM 51.203 (1962): 303-316.

_____. "Wrong Strategy--The Real Crisis in Missions." IRM 54.216 (1965): 451-61.

_____. "Church Growth Strategy Continued." IRM 57.227 (1968): 334-43.

_____. "Will Uppsala Betray the Two Billion?" CGB 4.5

(1968): 292-97.

McGavran, Donald. "The Right and Wrong of the Presence Idea of Mission." EMQ 6.2 (1970): 98-108.

_____. "The Great Debate in Missions." *Calvin Theological Journal* 5.2 (1970): 163-79.

_____. "World Evangelization at the Mercy of Church-Mission 'Disease.'" EMQ 13.4 (1977): 333-37.

Mackay, John A. "Ecumenical: The Word and the Concept." *Theology Today* 9 (1952): 1-6.

_____. "What the Ecumenical Movement Can Learn From Conservative Evangelicals." CT 10 (May 27, 1966): 17-23.

Macquarrie, John. "Christianity and Other Faiths." *Union Seminary Quarterly* 20.1 (1965): 39-48.

Manson, William. "Mission and Eschatology." IRM 42.168 (1953): 390-97.

Margull, Hans Jochen. "The Integration of the IMC-WCC." *Lutheran World* 8.3 (1961): 139-46.

_____. "Structures for Missionary Congregations." IRM 52.208 (1963): 433-46.

_____. "Evangelism in Ecumenical Perspective." ER 16.2 (1964): 133-45.

Maury, Philippe. "Evangelism--the Mission of the Church to Those Outside Her Life." ER 7.1 (1954): 29-35.

Mehl, Roger. "The Ecclesiological Significance of the World Council from the Roman Catholic Standpoint." ER 9.3 (1957): 240-52.

Meyendorff, John. "The Orthodox Church and Mission: Past and Present Perspectives." *St. Vladimir's Theological Quarterly* 16.2 (1972): 59-71.

Miguez-Bonino, José. "Our Debt as Evangelicals to the Roman Catholic Community." ER 21.4 (1969): 310-19.

_____. "Christian Unity and Social Reconciliation: Consonance and Tension." *Study Encounter* 9.1 (1973): 1-8.

_____. "A Latin American Attempt to Locate the Question of

Unity." ER 26.2 (1974): 210-223.

Miguez-Bonino, José. "Five Theses Towards an Understanding of the 'Theology of Liberation.'" *Expository Times* 87.7 (1976): 196-200.

Moses, D. G. "Mission and Unity--the Two Poles of the Ecumenical Movement." ER 5.3 (1953): 248-52.

_____. "Christianity and Non-Christian Religions." IRM 43.170 (1954): 146-54.

M'Timkulu, Donald G. S. "All African Church Conference." IRM 51.201 (1962): 63-66.

Müller-Fahrenholz, Geiko "Overcoming Apathy: The Church's Responsibilities in Face of the Threats to Human Survival." ER 27.1 (1975): 48-56.

Müller-Krüger, T. "Towards Church-Mission Integration in Germany." IRM 53.210 (1964): 182-90.

Neill, Stephen Charles. "Salvation Today?" *The Churchman* 17.4 (1973): 263-74.

Newbigin, J. E. Lesslie. "One Body, One Gospel, One World." ER 11.2 (1959): 143-56.

_____. "The Summons to Christian Mission Today." IRM 48.190 (1959): 177-89.

_____. "The Missionary Dimension of the Ecumenical Movement." ER 14.2 (1962): 207-215.

_____. "Joint Action for Mission." *National Christian Council Review* 83.1 (1963): 17-23.

_____. "From the Editor." IRM 54.215 (1965): 273-80.

_____. "Bangkok: A Taste of Salvation at Bangkok." *Indian Journal of Theology* 22.2 (1973): 49-53.

_____. "Nairobi 1975: A Personal Report." *National Christian Council Review* 96.6-7 (1976): 345-56.

_____. "Mission and Missions." *Expository Times* 88.9 (1977): 260-64.

_____. "The Basis, Purpose and Manner of Inter-Faith Dialogue." *Scottish Journal of Theology* 30.3 (1977): 253-70.

Nichols, Bruce J. "Towards an Asian Theology of Mission."
EMQ 6.2 (1970): 65-78.

Niebuhr, H. Richard. "Theological Analysis of Missionary Motivation." *Missionary Research Library Occasional Bulletin* 14.1 (1963).

Niles, D. T. "The Church's Call to Mission and Unity." ER 5.3 (1953): 244-47.

_____. "The All Africa Conference of Churches." IRM 52.208 (1963): 409-413.

Nissen, Karsten. "Mission and Unity." IRM 63.252 (1974): 539-50.

Nissiotis, Nikos A. "The Main Ecclesiological Problems of the Second Vatican Council and the Position of the Non-Roman Churches Facing It." *Journal of Ecumenical Studies* 2.1 (1965): 31-62.

Nunez, Emilio Antonio. "Perilous Ecumenical Overtures."
EMQ 5.4 (1969): 193-201.

Ockenga, Harold John. "Resurgent Evangelical Leadership."
CT 5.1 (Oct. 10, 1960): 11-15.

Orchard, Ronald Kenneth. "Joint Action for Mission." IRM 54.213 (1965): 81-94.

Orellana, Eugenio. "Goodwill Caravans." IRM 64.256 (1975): 386-91.

"Patterns of Relationships Between the Roman Catholic Church and the WCC." ER 24.3 (1972): 247-88.

Pentecost, Edward C. "Time for Faith Boards to Change Goals and Strategies." EMQ 12.4 (1976): 211-217.

Peters, George W. "The Primacy of Missions." *Bibliotheca Sacra* (1962): 335-41.

Potter, Philip. "Christian Presence." *Student World* 58.3 (1965): 209-214.

_____. "Evangelism and the World Council of Churches."
ER 20.2 (1968): 171-82.

_____. "The Third World in the Ecumenical Movement."
ER 24.1 (1972): 55-71.

Potter, Philip. "Evangelization in the Modern World." *Monthly Letter About Evangelism* No. 1 (1975).

Price, Frank W., and Orr, Clara E. "North American Protestant Foreign Missions in 1960." *Missionary Research Library Occasional Bulletin* 11.9 (1960): 1-41.

Quebedeaux, Richard. "The Evangelicals: New Trends and New Tensions." *Christianity and Crisis* 36.14 (1976): 197-202.

Ranson, Charles W. "Mexico City 1963." IRM 53.210 (1964): 137-46.

Rawlings, Elden. "Bogota: Latin Liaison." CT 14.6 (Dec. 19, 1969): 33.

Reapsome, James W. "Urbana '70: One Man's Impression." EMQ 7.3 (1971): 129-32.

Rembao, Alberto. "Protestant Latin America: Sight and Insight." IRM 46.181 (1957): 30-36.

Rhee, Jong Sung. "Significance of the Lausanne Covenant." *North East Asia Journal of Theology* (1975): 26-37.

Riesenhuber, Klaus. "Rahner's 'Anonymous Christian.'" *Theology Digest* 13.3 (1965): 163-71.

Roberts, W. Dayton. "Mission to Community--Instant Decapitation." IRM 62.247 (1973): 338-45.

Rossell, Jacques. "From a Theology of Crisis to a Theology of Revolution? Karl Barth Mission and Missions." ER 21.3 (1969): 204-215.

Samartha, Stanley J. "The Quest for Salvation and the Dialogue Between Religions." IRM 57.228 (1968): 424-32.

_____. "Christian Study Centers and Asian Churches." IRM 59.234 (1970): 173-79.

_____. "More Than an Encounter of Commitments." IRM 59.236 (1970): 392-403.

_____. "The WCC and Men of Other Faiths and Ideologies." ER 22.3 (1970): 190-98.

_____. "Dialogue as a Continuing Christian Concern." ER 23.2 (1971): 129-42.

Samartha, Stanley J. ". . . And Ideologies." ER 24.4 (1972): 479-86.

_____. "Dialogue: Significant Issues in the Continuing Debate." ER 24.3 (1972): 327-40.

_____. "Living Faiths and Ultimate Goals." ER 25.2 (1973): 137-47.

Scherer, James A. "Conservative Evangelicals and Missions." IRM 53.212 (1964): 483-86.

Schlette, Heinz Robert; Küng, Hans; and Rahner, Karl. "Anonymous Christianity: A Disputed Question." *Theology Digest* 24.2 (1976): 125-31.

Schmidt, William John. "Ecumenism and the Problem of Religious Syncretism." *Missionary Research Library Occasional Bulletin* 18.5 (1967).

Scott, Waldron. "Karl Barth's Theology of Mission." *Missiology* 3.2 (1975): 209-225.

Sharpe, Eric J. "New Directions in Theology of Mission." *The Evangelical Quarterly* 46.1 (1974): 8-24.

Shelley, Maynard. "Evangelical Congress on Worldwide Mission." *Christian Century* 83.21 (May 25, 1966): 695-97.

Sheppard, Gerald T. "Biblical Hermeneutics: The Academic Language of Evangelical Identity." *Union Seminary Quarterly Review* 32.2 (1977): 81-94.

Sider, Ronald J. "Evangelism, Salvation and Social Justice." IRM 64.255 (1965): 251-67.

_____. "Evangelism or Social Justice: Eliminating the Options." CT 21.1 (Oct. 8, 1976): 26-29.

Sinclair, Margaret. "The Christian Mission at This Hour: The Ghana Assembly of the IMC." IRM 47.186 (1958): 137-42.

Smith, Eugene L. "The Conservative Evangelicals and the World Council of Churches." ER 15.2 (1963): 182-91.

_____. "The Wheaton Congress in the Eyes of an Ecumenical Observer." IRM 55.220 (1966): 480-82.

Song, Choan-Seng. "Whither Protestantism in Asia Today?" *South East Asia Journal of Theology* II (1970): 66-76.

Spae, Joseph J. "SODEPAX: An Ecumenical and Experimental Approach to World Need." ER 26.1 (1974): 88-99.

Stadler, Anton P. "Dialogue: Does it Complement, Modify or Replace Mission." *Occasional Bulletin of Missionary Research* 1.3 (1977): 2-9.

Stockwell, B. Foster. "Latin American Evangelical Conference." IRM 39.153 (1950): 76-82.

Stott, John R. W. "Does Section II Provide Sufficient Emphasis on World Evangelism." CGB 5.2 (1968).

_____. "The Significance of Lausanne." IRM 64.255 (1975): 288-94.

Strachan, R. Kenneth. "New Emphasis on Missions." *Missionary Research Library Occasional Bulletin* 5 (1964): 1-6.

_____. "Call to Witness." IRM 53.210 (1964): 191-200.

_____. "Further Comment." IRM 53.210 (1964): 209-215.

Sundkler, Bengt. "Daring, in Order to Know: The IMC from Edinburgh to New Delhi." IRM 51.20 (1962): 4-11.

Taylor, John Vernon. "Bangkok and After." *CMS Newsletter* 370 (Apr. 1973).

Than, U Kyaw. "The Christian Mission in Asia Today." IRM 47.186 (1958): 153-62.

Thomas, M. M. "Issues Concerning the Life and Work of the Church in a Revolutionary World." ER 20.4 (1968): 410-19.

_____. "Salvation and Humanization." IRM 60.237 (1971): 25-38.

_____. "The Meaning of Salvation Today." IRM 62.246 (1973): 158-69.

Tippett, A. R. "Anthropology: Luxury or Necessity For Missions?" EMQ 5.1 (1968): 7-19.

_____. "The Suggested Moratorium on Missionary Funds and Personnel." *Missiology* 1.3 (1973): 275-280.

_____. "Conversion as a Dynamic Process in Christian Mission." *Missiology* 5.2 (1977): 203-221.

Troutman, Charles. "Evangelism and Social Action in Biblical

Perspective." EMQ 9.2 (1973): 100-110.

van den Heuvel, Albert H. "Uppsala--a Whimper or a Bang?" *Lutheran World* 16.2 (1969): 169-73.

_____. "The Fifth Assembly at Nairobi." ER 28.1 (1976): 97-104.

Van Dusen, H. P. "Christian Mission and Christian Unity." *Theology Today* (Oct. 1959): 319-28.

van Straelen, Henry, S.V.D. "Our Attitude Towards Other Religions." *Worldmission* 16.1 (1965): 71-98.

Verghese, Paul. "The Finality of Jesus Christ in the Age of Universal History." ER 15.1. (1962): 12-25.

_____. "Salvation." IRM 57.228 (1968): 399-416.

Verkuyl, Johannes. "The Mission of God and the Missions of the Churches." *Occasional Essays*. San Jose, Costa Rica: CELEP, Jan. 1977.

Vischer, Lukas, "The WCC and the Vatican Council." ER 14.3 (1962): 281-95.

_____. "Christian Councils--Their Future as Instruments of the Ecumenical Movement." *Study Encounter* 4.2 (1968): 97-108.

_____. "Christian Councils--Instruments of Ecclesial Communion." ER 24.1 (1972): 72-87.

_____. "The Unity of the Church: A Report." ER 25.4 (1973): 482-507.

Visser 't Hooft, W. A. "Asian Churches." ER 2.3 (1950): 229-40.

_____. "Various Meanings of Unity and the Unity Which the WCC Seeks to Promote." ER 8.1 (1955): 18-29.

_____. "The Super-Church and the Ecumenical Movement." ER 10.4 (1958): 365-85.

_____. "World Conference on Church and Society." ER 18.4 (1966): 417-25.

_____. "Accommodation--True and False." *South East Asia Journal of Theology* 8.3 (1967): 5-18.

Visser 't Hooft, W. A. "Is the Ecumenical Movement Suffering
    from Institutional Paralysis?" ER 25.3 (1973): 295-309.

_____. "Evangelism in the Neo-Pagan Situation." IRM 63.249
    (1974): 81-86.

Wagner, C. Peter. "Latin American Congress on Evangelism."
    EMQ 6.3 (1970): 167-71.

_____. "Evangelical Missions and Revolution Today."
    Missiology 1.1 (1973): 91-98.

_____. "Colour the Moratorium Grey." IRM 64.254 (1975):
    165-76.

_____. "Strategizing for World Evangelism." *World Evangeli-
    zation* (Oct. 1977): 3-4, 9.

Warren, M.A.C. "Eschatology and History." IRM 41.163
    (1952): 337-50.

Weber, Hans-Ruedi. "The Ecumenical Movement, the Laity and the
    Third Assembly." ER 13.2 (1961): 203-214.

_____. "The Bible in Today's Ecumenical Movement." ER 23.4
    (1971): 335-46.

Webster, Douglas. "Evangelicalism and the Ecumenical Move-
    ment." ER 6.4 (1954): 385-89.

_____. "Christian Mission in a Secular World." *Expository
    Times* 77.101 (1966): 292-96.

Wieser, Thomas. "The Experience of Salvation." IRM 60.239
    (1971): 382-94.

_____. "The Report on the Salvation Study." IRM 62.246
    (1973): 170-79.

Winter, Ralph D. "The Anatomy of the Christian Mission."
    EMQ 5.2 (1969): 74-89.

_____. "The New Missions and the Mission of the Church."
    IRM 60.237 (1971): 87-100.

_____. "Churches Need Missions because Modalities Need
    Sodalities." EMQ 7.4 (1971): 193-200.

_____. "Quantity or Quality?" EMQ 8.4 (1972): 232-42.

Winter, Ralph D. "The Two Structures of God's Redemptive Mission." *Missiology* 2.1 (1974): 121-39.

_____. "1980 and That Certain Elite." *Missiology* 4.2 (1976): 145-59.

_____. "Who are the Three Billion?" CGB 13.5 and 6 (1977): 123-26, 139-44.

Yoder, Bill. "European Congress on Evangelism." EMQ 8.2 (1972): 102-113.

Yoder, Howard W. "The Second Latin American Evangelical Conference." IRM 51.201 (1962): 75-78.

Index

About the Author

Rodger C. Bassham was born and educated in South Australia.
After training for the ministry at Wesley College and the University of Adelaide, he served as a circuit minister for five
years before studying for the Doctor of Philosophy degree at
Southern Methodist University in Dallas, Texas.

Rodger and Marlene Bassham, and their daughters Jane and Ann,
went to Papua New Guinea in 1978, where Mr. Bassham is Lecturer
in Theology at the Rarongo Theological College of the United
Church of Papua New Guinea and the Solomon Islands.

Books by the William Carey Library

General

American Missions in Bicentennial Perspective edited by R. Pierce Beaver, $9.95 paper, 448 pp.

The Birth of Misssions in America by Charles L. Chaney, $7.95 paper, 352 pp.

Education of Missionaries' Children: The Neglected Dimension of World Mission by D. Bruce Lockerbie, $1.95 paper, 76 pp.

Evangelicals Face the Future edited by Donald E. Hoke, $6.95 paper, 184 pp.

The Holdeman People: The Church in Christ, Mennonite, 1859-1969 by Clarence Hiebert, $17.95 cloth, 688 pp.

Manual for Accepted Missionary Candidates by Marjorie A. Collins, $4.45 paper, 144 pp.

Manual for Missionaries on Furlough by Marjorie A. Collins, $4.45, paper, 160 pp.

The Ministry of Development in Evangelical Perspective edited by Robert L. Hancock, $4.95 paper, 128 pp.

On the Move with the Master: A Daily Devotional Guide on World Mission by Duain W. Vierow, $4.95 paper, 176 pp.

The Radical Nature of Christianity: Church Growth Eyes Look at the Supernatural Mission of the Christian and the Church by Waldo J. Werning (Mandate Press), $5.85 paper, 224 pp.

Social Action Vs. Evangelism: An Essay on the Contemporary Crisis by William J. Richardson, $1.95x paper, 64 pp.

Strategy of Mission

Church Growth and Christian Mission edited by Donald McGavran, $4.95x paper, 256 pp.

Church Growth and Group Conversion by Donald McGavran et al., $3.95 paper, 128 pp.

Committed Communities: Fresh Streams for World Missions by Charles J. Mellis, $3.95 paper, 160 pp.

The Conciliar-Evangelical Debate: The Crucial Documents, 1964-1976 edited by Donald McGavran, $8.95 paper, 400 pp.

Crucial Dimensions in World Evangelization edited by Arthur F. Glasser et al., $7.95x paper, 512 pp.

Evangelical Missions Tomorrow edited by Wade T. Coggins and Edwin L. Frizen, Jr., $5.95 paper, 208 pp.

Everything You Need to Know to Grow a Messianic Synagogue by Phillip E. Goble, $3.95 paper, 176 pp.

The Indigenous Church and the Missionary by Melvin L. Hodges, $2.95 paper, 108 pp.

Literacy, Bible Reading, and Church Growth Through the Ages by
Morris G. Watkins, $5.95 paper, 240 pp.
A Manual for Church Growth Surveys by Ebbie C. Smith, $3.95
paper, 144 pp.
Mission: A Practical Approach to Church-Sponsored Mission Work
by Daniel C. Hardin, $4.95x paper, 264 pp.

Applied Anthropology

Becoming Bilingual: A Guide to Language Learning by Donald
Larson and William Smalley, $6.95x paper, 426 pp.
Christopaganism or Indigenous Christianity? edited by Tetsunao
Yamamori and Charles R. Taber, $5.95 paper, 242 pp.
*The Church and Cultures: Applied Anthropology for the Religious
Worker* by Louis J. Luzbetak, $6.95x paper, 448.
*Culture and Human Values: Christian Intervention in Anthropologi-
cal Perspective* (writings by Jacob Loewen) edited by William
A. Smalley, $5.95x paper, 466 pp.
Customs and Cultures: Anthropology for Christian Missions by
Eugene A. Nida, $3.95 paper, 322 pp.
Manual of Articulatory Phonetics by William A. Smalley, $7.95x
paper, 522 pp.
Religion Across Cultures by Eugene A. Nida, $3.95x paper, 128 pp.

Theological Education by Extention

*The Extension Movement in Theological Education: A Call to the
Renewal of the Ministry* by F. Ross Kinsler, $6.95 paper,
304 pp.
The World Directory of Theological Education by Extension by
Wayne C. Weld, $5.95x paper, 416 pp., *1976 Supplement only*,
$1.95x, 64 pp. booklet.

Popularizing Mission

Defeat of the Bird God by C. Peter Wagner, $5.95 paper, 256 pp.
The Night Cometh: Two Wealthy Evangelicals Face the Nation by
Rebecca J. Winter, $2.95 paper, 96 pp.
The Task Before Us (audiovisual) by the Navigators, $29.95, 137
slides.
The 25 Unbelievable Years: 1945-1969 by Ralph D. Winter, $3.95x
paper, 128 pp.
The Word-Carrying Giant: The Growth of the American Bible Society
by Creighton Lacy, $6.95 paper, 320 pp.
The Grounds for a New Thrust in World Mission by Ralph D. Winter,
$.75 booklet, 32 pp.
1980 and That Certain Elite by Ralph D. Winter, $.35x booklet,
16 pp.
The World Christian Movement: 1950-1975 by Ralph D. Winter,
$.75 booklet, 32 pp.

Area and Case Studies

Aspects of Pacific Ethnohistory by Alan R. Tippett, $5.95 paper, 216 pp.

Christian Mission to Muslims-The Record: Anglican and Reformed Approaches in India and the Near East, 1800-1938 by Lyle L. Vander Werff, $8.95 paper, 384 pp.

The Church in Africa, 1977 edited by Charles R. Taber, $6.95 paper, 224 pp.

Church Planting in Uganda: A Comparative Study by Gailyn Van Rheenen, $4.95 paper, 192 pp.

Ethnic Realities and the Church: Lessons from India by Donald McGavran, 8.95 paper, 272 pp.

The Growth Crisis in the American Church: A Presbyterian Case Study by Foster H. Shannon, $4.95x paper, 176 pp.

The How and Why of Third World Missions: An Asian Case Study by Marlin L. Nelson, $6.95 paper, 256 pp.

The Protestant Movement in Bolivia by C. Peter Wagner, $3.95 paper, 264 pp.

Toward Continuous Mission: Strategizing for the Evangelization of Bolivia by W. Douglas Smith, Jr., $4.95 paper, 208 pp.

Understanding Latin Americans by Eugene Nida, $3.95 paper, 176 pp.

The Unresponsive: Resistant or Neglected? by David C.E. Liao, $5.95 paper, 168 pp.

An Urban Strategy for Africa by Timothy Monsma, $6.95 paper, 192 pp.

Worldview and the Communication of the Gospel: A Nigerian Case Study by Marguerite G. Kraft, $7.95 paper, 240 pp.

Reference

An American Directory of Schools and Colleges Offering Missionary Courses edited by Glenn Schwartz, $5.95x paper, 266 pp.

Church Growth Bulletin, Second Consolidated Volume (Sept. 1969-July 1975) edited by Donald McGavran, $7.95x paper, 512 pp.

Evangelical Missions Quarterly, Vols. 7-9, $8.95x cloth, 830 pp.

Evangelical Missions Quarterly, Vols. 10-12, $15.95 cloth, 960 pp.

The Means of World Evangelization: Missiological Education at the Fuller School of World Mission edited by Alvin Martin, $9.95 paper, 544 pp.

Protestantism in Latin America: A Bibliographical Guide edited by John H. Sinclair, $8.95x paper, 448 pp.

Word Study Concordance and New Testament edited by Ralph and Roberta Winter, $29.95 cloth, 2-volume set.

HOW TO ORDER: Send orders to William Carey Library, 1705 N. Sierra Bonita Avenue, Pasadena, California 91104 (USA). Please allow four to six weeks for delivery in the United States.